D1560222

PRAYER AND PENITENCE

Also by Jeffrey M. Cohen

Understanding the Synagogue Service (1974)
A Samaritan Chronicle (1981)
Festival Adventure (1982)
Understanding the High Holyday Services (1983)
Horizons of Jewish Prayer (1986)
Moments of Insight (1984)
Blessed Are You (1993)

PRAYER AND PENITENCE

A Commentary on the High Holy Day *Machzor*

Jeffrey M. Cohen

JASON ARONSON, INC.
Northvale, New Jersey
London

This book was set in 10 pt. Palatino by Alpha Graphics of Pittsfield, New Hampshire, and printed by Haddon Craftsmen in Scranton, Pennsylvania.

10 9 8 7 6 5 4 3 2 1

Library of Congress Cataloging-in-Publication Data
Cohen, Jeffrey M.
Prayer and penitence : a commentary on the High Holy Day Machzor / Jeffrey M. Cohen : foreword by Immanuel Jakobovits : preface by Jonathan Sacks.
p. cm.
Rev. ed. of: Understanding the High Holyday services. 1983.
Includes bibliographical references and index.
ISBN 1-56821-046-9
1. Mahzor. High Holidays. 2. Judaism—Liturgy. 3. High Holidays—Liturgy. I. Cohen, Jeffrey M. Understanding the High Holyday services. II. Title.
BM675.H5Z72 1994
296.4'31—dc20 94-3077

Manufactured in the United States of America. Jason Aronson Inc. offers books and cassettes. For information and catalog write to Jason Aronson Inc., 230 Livingston Street, Northvale, New Jersey 07647.

To Gloria
with affection and gratitude

And to our children—
Harvey and Lorraine
Suzanne and Keith
Judith and Bobby
Lewis and our grandchildren,
Joel, Alexander, and Phil

Contents

Foreword

Prayer is to the spirit of the High Holy Days what *matzah* is to *Pesach* and the *sukkah* to the Festival of *Sukkot*. It is the basic essence of Rosh Hashanah and Yom Kippur, when once a year the Jew regenerates himself to reach his spiritual peak just as nature around him is in its most perfect state at this season. How does prayer achieve this?

Prayer in Jewish thought is primarily not intended to *express* man's emotions and needs. God knows our feelings and wants much better than we do, let alone than we can formulate them. Rather, prayer is meant to *impress* us, to stir our conscience, to uplift our spirit, to transport us from our mundane world around us to the inner world of our soul. Prayer is the bridge between Heaven and earth, between man and his Maker, instructing us on the difference between what we are and what we should be. Hence our prayers are fixed. For the truths and ideals they are to teach us do not change from one individual or from one age to another.

This applies to all our prayers throughout the year in their daily routine, but never more so than on Rosh Hashanah and Yom Kippur. "Seek God where He is to be found, call on Him when He is near" (Isaiah 55:6)—this, our Sages say, refers to the Ten Days of Penitence.

This "nearness of God" distinguishes the High Holy Days from the three pilgrimage festivals. The latter are so called because on these occasions, by biblical law, every Jew was expected *to go up* to the Temple of Jerusalem. The national and religious significance of these festivities could only be fully experienced by *coming to God* "in the place which He shall choose," in the words of the Torah. On Rosh Hashanah and Yom Kippur God *comes to us*. Through the intensity of our prayers we are to find His reality close by; He is "near," intimately at hand with and within us.

This special feature of the High Holy Day season is also illustrated by a striking halakhic rule. During the Ten Days of Penitence we insert a number of amendments into every *Amidah* prayer. If we miss any of these changes by mistake, the prayer is still valid and we can carry on—with one exception. In the third benediction, "the Holy God" is changed into "the Holy King," and if this change was omitted, we have to return to the beginning and repeat the *Amidah* all over again. Why is this so?

"God" is an abstract Being, remote, transcendent, and beyond human comprehension. We worship him as such all the year round. But during the penitential season, we are to relate to him as "King," a concrete Ruler, almost visible with crown and royal vestments, a Being whose presence is manifest, whom we can address and hear directly. And if at this season we merely perceive him as *God* and not as *King, a* distant abstraction rather than an immediate reality, then we have missed the whole meaning of these festivals and our principal prayer is invalid, requiring repetition in the correct form.

The *machzor,* with its superb liturgical compositions, is the key to this spiritual transformation. It is a kind of anthology, an imposing literary edifice constructed with building blocks collected from all layers of our sacred literature: from the biblical foundations of readings from the Torah and the Prophets together with numerous other scriptural passages, especially from the Psalms; from the major prayers composed during the talmudic era, including all benedictions; to the rich poetry of the *piyyutim* and *selichot* dating from the earliest to the late Middle Ages; right up to the Prayer for the State of Israel written only some forty years ago.

In this colorful mosaic every nuance of religious inspiration finds the most diverse expression. Some portray the awe of the Heavenly Judgment in a few bold strokes, deeply moving in their simplicity and grandeur, such as the *U-netaneh tokef* prayer. Others are highly intricate compositions, artistically pieced together with biblical and midrashic allusions that require careful study to be understood, contrasting Divine omnipotence with human frailty, or the efficacy of repentance with the doom of the unrepentant, or describing the ministrations of the High Priest in the Holy of Holies to secure atonement on Yom Kippur. Yet others are just hymns of glory, or pleas for compassion, sung to induce spiritual elevation as well as humility in the presence of God. The liturgy includes long confessional listings of our failings in alphabetical order, and serene reflections of the fleeting passage of life.

The impact of all these prayers is further enhanced by their antiquity and their universality. Whatever the relatively minor local variations between different rites, the basic texts unite the entire House of Israel both vertically and horizontally, across the ages and across the continents. Part of the extraordinary spell exercised by these prayers—still annually drawing far more Jews together than any other national Jewish cause or danger, any appeal or demonstration—lies in the very knowledge that these hallowed texts are recited in essentially identical terms by fellow Jews the world over, as they have been by our ancestors for centuries and millennia. Even the traditional tunes, likewise matured by age, have an exceptional power to pull tears and heartstrings otherwise scarcely touched by the passion of religion or the poetry of the spirit.

Yet much of this ornate splendor is often lost on the worshiper for sheer lack of comprehension. Unfamiliarity with the Hebrew language is of course itself a serious impediment. However well this can be overcome by a competent rendering into the vernacular, any translation remains but a pale reflection of the majesty radiating from the Hebrew original, and most of the allusions, alliterations and other literary devices are altogether lost in any foreign tongue. But even those perfectly conversant with the Hebrew language would find it hard fully to understand the plain meaning, let alone the deeper interpretation, of these liturgical compositions without the skilled guidance of a commentator, in much the same way as a display of supreme historic art or of some complex scientific exhibits cannot be appreciated by the uninitiated without the explanations of an informed guide. This volume seeks to provide such guidance.

Rabbi Dr. Jeffrey Cohen's painstaking work will convey to the worshiper a much wider understanding of our prayers, and, as an aid to the High Festivals *machzor,* it will be widely welcome for the light it sheds on some of the finest spiritual and literary creations of the Jewish genius.

May this commentary help to make the hours spent at prayer in our synagogues on the High Festivals ennoble and sanctify our lives throughout the year, thus making us worthy of the blessings for which we plead. For the real effect of our prayers is gauged not by how we feel when reciting them, but by what they have made of us long after the festivals are over—not by their momentary expression but by their lasting impression.

Lord Immanuel Jakobovits
Former Chief Rabbi, Great Britain

Preface

"Seek God where He is to be found, call on Him when He is near" (Isaiah 55:6). This, said the rabbis, refers to the Ten Days of Penitence, the most solemn period of the Jewish year beginning with Rosh Hashanah and culminating on Yom Kippur.

Often an apparently simple rabbinic commentary contains deep spiritual insight, and this is no exception. Clearly the rabbis were puzzled by Isaiah's words. The prophet tells us to seek God where He is to be found. But He is to be found everywhere. He tells us to call on God when He is near. But God is always near, as close as the human heart. What then did the prophet mean?

The chasidic master Rabbi Mendel of Kotzk once asked his disciples, "Where is God?" Bemused, they replied, "Is it not written that God fills the heavens and the earth? Surely God is everywhere." "No," replied the rabbi. "God is *where we let Him in.*"

The world is filled with the radiance of God. But to see it we must open our eyes. The universe sings the praise of its Creator. But to hear it we must learn to listen. God speaks, but in a still small voice. We must train our senses to see what lies beyond physical sight and hear what lies beyond the range of physical sound. That is the discipline of prayer. Prayer is letting God in.

It is not easy. Bombarded as we are by the rush and press of daily events, the noise of the media, and the ceaseless pressure of our ever-accelerating lives, we have little space left to pause, reflect, and wonder at the sheer splendor of existence. We can forget to pray. Or praying, we fail to open our hearts and minds to God. Prayer is a skill, an art, a discipline, and in our present culture of immediacy we often fail to give it time.

Yet even today Rosh Hashanah, Yom Kippur, and the days between have not lost their ancient power to move us with their majestic vision of God enthroned in glory as the moral force behind creation. From the first blast of the *shofar* on Rosh Hashanah to our final proclamation of God's kingship at the end of Yom Kippur, we are conscious of something altogether more vast than our daily concerns. Striving to make meaning of our lives, we sense—sometimes dimly, sometimes with dazzling clarity—that we are part of an immense history, spanning us, our parents, our children, and the people of which we are a part: Israel, the nation that staked its entire destiny on its covenant with God.

And we are moved. Whether by the poetry of the prayers or their music, whether by the synagogue or the feeling of congregation, whether by personal or collective memory, we feel brushed by the wings of eternity and in that reflective moment, we let God in.

That, I believe, is what the sages meant when they applied to these days the verse of Isaiah. God is to be found *where we seek Him*. He is near when *we come close to Him*. God does not change, but we change. And on the Ten Days of Penitence, coming close to God, we sense Him close to us.

In this book, Rabbi Dr. Jeffrey Cohen has performed an immense labor of scholarship, helping us to understand the history and spirituality of the prayers of these holy days. Always lucid and often thought provoking, his explanations guide us through the complex liturgy of Rosh Hashanah and Yom Kippur and help us to see it as the intricate and beautiful structure it is, the record of countless generations of Jews as they stood before God at this supreme time of self-examination.

Too few of us understand the background to the prayers we say. As a result, we may miss one of the most striking features of Jewish spirituality.

Jews did not build cathedrals. Jewish communities did not try to rival the splendor of the lost Temple in buildings that were merely "temples in miniature." To be sure, there were grand synagogues; the Talmud mentions one in ancient Alexandria and there have been others since. But by and large the genius of Judaism is not to be found in buildings.

If there is one architectural masterpiece in Judaism it is the prayer book itself, the cumulative creation of many hands and lands and ages. Here you will find passages from the Mosaic and prophetic books, sections from the book of Psalms, prayers from the "Men of the Great Assembly," meditations from the sages of the Mishnah and Talmud, and medieval poetry and mysticism, blended together and mellowed by age into an almost timeless harmony that makes the *siddur* a kind of palace built of words.

Tracing the history of the individual prayers is not unlike taking an archeological and architectural tour of the Old City of Jerusalem. The walls of Jerusalem have a most curious feature. Beneath the eight-hundred-year-old Ottoman battlements are stones from the periods of the Mamelukes, the Crusaders, the Romans, and the Hasmoneans. But each new builder of Jerusalem's walls used the materials left from earlier ages, so that stones from different ages lie next to one another, the new and old juxtaposed in an evocative mosaic of eras and cultures. That is what the *siddur* is like, too, and Dr. Cohen's commentary helps us see it.

This is particularly so of the liturgy of Rosh Hashanah and Yom Kippur. Around the central themes of God's sovereignty and judgment, Jewish tradition has built a vast structure of praises and supplications. On Rosh Hashanah the motifs are kingship, remembrances, and the *shofar*. On Yom Kippur they are confession, purification, and forgiveness. To these, each age has added its characteristic voice. We find ourselves at one moment in biblical times, remembering the binding of Isaac or the service of the High Priest in the Temple. Then we are transported to the Roman era in an elegy to the sages who died as martyrs. In the great *U-netaneh tokef* prayer we move to the persecutions of the Middle Ages. Time dissolves, and it is as if the entire Jewish people, scattered as no other, had come together in a chorus of voices, to which ours is joined. The full drama of Jewish history is here, as nowhere else. Here, in this architecture of language, this temple of words, is the most powerful collective expression of the nation that pledged itself to live as the people of God.

Something happens to us when we pray. Prayer is an act of self-exposure, in which listening is as important as speaking. We address God. But if we truly open our hearts we become aware that we are addressed, summoned to something greater than our daily, private concerns. A single challenge echoes throughout Jewish history, and if we listen, we too are touched by it. By joining ourselves to the words of our ancestors we become part of the people of eternity, the "kingdom of priests" and the "holy nation" whose chronicles of faithfulness inspire continuing astonishment and awe.

We are not isolated individuals. We are part of the most remarkable nation in history, the only one to have survived exile and dispersion through faith alone, and through that faith, in this century, to have returned to our ancient homeland and begun to speak again our ancient language, the language of the Bible. In prayer, the entire Jewish people speaks through us as we stand before God. In Isaiah's phrase, our heart "trembles and is enlarged."

Maimonides writes that the *shofar* of Rosh Hashanah contains a call: "Awake, O sleepers, from your sleep, and slumberers arouse yourselves from your slumber." That is what prayer on these holy days is like. It is a summons to wake to a wider vision of our lives and to the spiritual and moral challenge of Jewish existence.

True prayer is an awakening. Our ancestor Jacob once slept and dreamed of a ladder set on earth but reaching to heaven. The Torah then says, "Jacob awoke from his sleep and said, 'Surely God is in this place and I did not know it.'"

To wake and know that *God is in this place* is the true experience of prayer.

Chief Rabbi Dr. Jonathan Sacks

Introduction

What brings Jews to synagogue on Rosh Hashanah and Yom Kippur—so many of whom do not feel inspired to join us throughout the rest of the year—is truly a mystery. A mystery nevertheless to be savored; for at least the spell is still able to be cast, still the influence continues to be felt, still the Jewish heart continues to beat, albeit faster in some than in others.

A growing number of people, especially young, thinking people, are beginning to discover the need and the urgency of regular spiritual dialogue. More now are basking in the warmth and color of a vibrant religious way of life. More are appreciating the enrichment of family life that participation in the synagogue experience and the performance of home rituals offer. More are attending continuing education programs, having their eyes opened to the profundity and fascination of deeper study of Jewish sources. More are sending their children to *yeshivah* high schools, after which a period of learning in academies and seminaries in Israel has become the norm.

But there are still too many others who do not participate, for a variety of reasons ranging from a deficiency in their religious upbringing to an innate selfishness, indifference, or insensitivity to matters of the spirit. Yet even these people are reluctant to cut the umbilical cord with Judaism. No matter how far they have strayed from the path of Jewish practice, they still retain a deep sense of pride in being Jewish, and a wish to be numbered among the ranks of this timeless faith and this people, which is experiencing a weird and wonderful restoration of its fortunes after two thousand years of agony and oppression.

Chasidism has a profound tradition that exemplifies the varying shades of proximity to, and identification with, the core of Judaism's spiritual dynamic: When the Baal Shem Tov, the holy founder of Chasidism, had petitions to make, he would repair to a particular place in the forest, light a fire, and meditate in prayer. And his prayer was answered.

A generation later, when the famous Maggid, the preacher of Meseritch, had petitions to make, he would go to the same place in the forest, and would say: "Lord, alas, we can no longer light the fire, nor do we know the secret meditations that underpin the prayers; but we do know the precise place in this forest where it was once performed. And that must surely be sufficient!" And it was.

A generation later, Rabbi Israel of Rishiv was called upon to perform the same task. He sat down on his special throne in his dynastic center, and said: "We, alas, cannot light the fire; we cannot recite the meditations and prayers; we do not even know the precise place in the forest where it was, and should, all be performed. But we can tell the story of how it was done." And the story he told had the same effect as the actions of the other two!

There are many who assemble in our synagogues over this period who, like the Baal Shem Tov, are blessed with knowing how to light the fire—the fire of enthusiasm that spiritually warms and nourishes them and their children. They certainly know the place in the forest. In our modern-day idiom we would say that they can see the forest for the trees; they have the right Jewish priorities. They are also familiar with the prayers and meditations that well up naturally from their hearts and emotions to their lips.

There are others who, in the words of the Maggid of Meseritch, cannot light the fire or recite the prayers and meditations. These are they whose standards of Hebrew reading and comprehension make the *siddur* or *machzor* an abstruse and fairly insignificant book to them, but who, nevertheless, "know the place in the forest." They come to synagogue fairly regularly; they practice, or at least pay lip service to, the basic observances of Sabbath, the festivals and *kashrut*; and they give their children a better Jewish education than they themselves had.

But there are the majority—those who swell our ranks at this period—who find themselves unable to even locate the place in the forest, who are not even inclined to search for the place, who do not even know that there *is* a forest, inside of which there is a place of unique exaltedness. And yet, for all that, they *do* engage in Rabbi Israel of Rishiv's basic exercise. *They tell the story*! And they tell it by their presence. They affirm thereby that it is, after all, *their* story, and a glorious, multifaceted story, an ongoing story that is gathering momentum, spiritual power, and interest as it unfolds in our age. By their presence in synagogue, albeit sporadically, they ensure the continued existence of future generations of readers and hearers of that old–new story. And it may well be that among those initially uninterested hearers and readers some might well stumble upon the forest. Others might even locate the especially exalted spot. And a few—who knows?—might even succeed in lighting the fire!

So the presence of all Israel in synagogue at this time of the year is of the greatest significance. For we are all involved at some level in the telling of Israel's story.

Yet there are some who cannot even do that. We recall the tragic death of the Jewish hero Ilya Krichefsky, shot by a soldier as he jumped onto the back of an armored car in a desperate attempt to stop it moving toward the besieged Soviet Parliament during the abortive coup of August 1991. At his funeral, for the first time in Russian history, the Hebrew *Kaddish* echoed over a public address system in the center of Moscow, as part of a national ceremony. Asked how he felt when he heard the public *Kaddish* for his son, Ilya, Marat Krichefsky replied: "What is *Kaddish*? We are products of Russian culture, brought up without Jewish consciousness. But it was important for the nation to know that our son was a Jew who died for Russia."

Does this not say it all? That grieving, assimilated Jew has added a fourth character to our chasidic story, after Rabbi Israel of Rishiv. Marat Krichefsky is the man who cannot even tell the story of the prayers and the forest and the fire. And yet he knows that there is a great story, and he appreciates that the story must not be forgotten. And that must also be of some value to God! How many of us could have survived four generations of a Bolshevik and Soviet system, which snuffed out every vestige of Jewish identity, and yet still retain some residual sense of Jewishness, albeit sufficient only to recognize instinctively that the story must be told, if not by them then by someone who does still remember it?

The purpose of this book is to elucidate that story that Rabbi Israel of Rishiv was so keen to tell, the story that had the same effect as the potent spiritual ministrations of the great saints that went before him. It is the story of our yearnings and prayers at this period of the year, and of the great composers of those prayers down the ages, whose biographies form a multifaceted mosaic of Jewish religious and cultural expression in the many lands of our dispersal.

It is hoped that, with the background information provided in these pages, the prayers and services of Rosh Hashanah and Yom Kippur will take on extra dimensions of meaning, significance, and beauty, so that all who read it will be enabled to relive that story and to locate, nestling within its words, the forest, the place, the fire, and the authentic spirit of the prayers.

The idea of writing this commentary had been germinating in my mind for many years. Already during my student days at Jews' College, London, where I was given an understanding and love of Hebrew and rabbinic literature, and where I was introduced to the serious study of medieval Hebrew poetry, I had felt the need of such a commentary, both for myself as well as for the vast majority of worshipers on the High Holy Days for whom the *machzor* is a sealed book.

I waited in vain for such a commentary to appear, and finally, summoning courage from the advice of the Ethics of the Fathers, "Where there are no men, endeavor to be the man," I decided to undertake this formidable task. I did so in full awareness that the *chazan*'s admission of unworthiness applies most accurately to me: "Terror overwhelms me . . . since I am lacking in good judgment and knowledge."

The ultimate spur to embark upon this labor of love came from friends and congregants in the Kenton Synagogue, London, where I had the privilege of serving as spiritual leader from 1980 to 1986. After I had conducted a lengthy explanatory service one year, which was received enthusiastically, many expressed the desire to receive a copy of my talk in printed form. I immediately launched myself into the preparation of such a book. It was published in 1983, by Routledge and Kegan Paul, under the title *Understanding the High Holyday Services*. The present work is a much-expanded and updated version of that work.

The major problem confronting a commentator is how to decide on priorities in the light of the inevitably circumscribed length of his commissioned work. I have had to apply my own blue pencil to many interesting literary features and midrashic ideas in nearly every chapter, and I apologize in advance for any injudiciousness in omission, as well as for errors in commission. I have tried to present a blend of traditional interpretations and references together with my own insights and literary appreciation of the poetic creativity. The inspirational appeal of the former will, I feel sure, compensate for any shortcomings in the latter.

I would like to express my sincere appreciation to the Emeritus Chief Rabbi, Lord Immanuel Jakobovits, for having devoted many hours of his valuable time to reading the entire typescript of the original edition and for saving me from a number of pitfalls through his valuable criticisms and suggestions. I also thank him for graciously contributing the Foreword, as well as for his friendship and encouragement over many years. I also thank Chief Rabbi Dr. Jonathan Sacks for enhancing my book through the provision of his illuminating Preface. I acknowledge with thanks the permission granted by the editor of the London *Jewish Chronicle* to embody within this book several articles on the High Holy Days that first appeared in that newspaper.

My greatest thanks must go to my wife and children, without whose encouragement and sacrifice of the long hours that otherwise would have been devoted to them this work could never have been undertaken.

Jeffrey M. Cohen

Note on Transliteration

The following system of transliteration from the Hebrew has been employed:

Consonants		
	א	–
	בּ	– b
	ב	– v
	ג	– g
	ד	– d
	ה	– h
	ו	– v
	ז	– z
	ח	– ch
	ט	– t
	י	– y
	כּ	– k
	ך כ	– kh
	ל	– l
	ם מ	– m
	ן נ	– n
	ס	– s
	ע	–
	פּ	– p
	ף פ	– f
	ץ צ	– tz
	ק	– k
	ר	– r
	שׁ	– sh
	שׂ	– s
	תּ	– t
	ת	– t

Vowels		
	ַ	– a
	ָ	– a
short	ָ	– o
	ֶ	– e
	ִ	– i
	ִי	– iy
	ֵ	– ei
	ֵי	– ey
	ַי	– ay
	וּ ֻ	– u
	וֹ ֹ	– o
	ְ	– e

Part I

Rosh Hashanah

1

The Morning Service—First Day

The Term *Machzor*

The festival prayer book has long been designated by the term *machzor,* to distinguish it from the term *siddur,* as used for the daily and Sabbath prayer book. The distinction is not based upon any intrinsic difference of nuance in those two terms, for *machzor* derives from a postbiblical Hebrew root *chazar,* meaning "to do something again," "to come around," in the sense of "a cycle." Hence its application to the prayer manual for the annual festivals, which come around cyclically.

Siddur, on the other hand, or its cognate, *seder,* the noun by which the first major prayer book (the *Seder Rav Amram*) was known, means, simply, a manual arranged in the appropriate order (of daily prayers). The interchange of these two terms may be attested to by the fact that some medieval daily (nonfestival) prayer rites were popularly known by the term *machzor,* such as *Machzor Roma* (the Italian daily prayer book), *Machzor Vitri* (the Northern French rite of the school of Rashi) and *Machzor Rumania* (the prayer book of the Balkan communities).[1] All of this notwithstanding, in the modern period a clear distinction is made between the two terms.

A general term for the collection of prayers and hymns that are found in our *machzorim* is found in Sephardi circles, namely, *maamad* or *maamadot,*[2] a term derived from the context of the ancient Temple ritual. In Franco-

German communities the term *kerovetz* was especially popular, almost as a synonym for *machzor*. This was popularly (though quite erroneously!) explained as a *notarikon* (initial-letter acrostic) for the phrase *Kol rinah viyeshua Be-oholei tzaddikim* ("The sound of joy and salvation is in the tents of the righteous" [Psalms 118:15]).

An encounter with the *machzor* is what all Jews share in common when they attend the synagogue service. The majority of Jews in Western countries attend rather infrequently. The first century Alexandrian Jewish philosopher Philo records that many Jews in that city would only come to synagogue on three days in the year, and some only on Yom Kippur. Little has changed in 2000 years!

What has changed, however, and quite drastically, is the content of the synagogue service. And this was entirely due to the post-Temple need to provide an inspirational replacement for the sacrificial focus of Temple Judaism. As prayer, poetry, meditation, study, and exposition became the hallmark of the burgeoning talmudic academies of the early centuries C.E., each of these genres found its expression represented within the evolving liturgical output that changed the entire spirit and complexion of the synagogue experience.

The prayer book grew as a living organism, over many centuries and in many countries, although the earliest and greatest contribution to its formation and development was made in Palestine and Babylon during the talmudic period (first through fifth centuries), with inspired religious poets adding their distinctive embellishments during the succeeding five or six centuries. Later differences between Ashkenazi and Sephardi traditions, reflecting their respective poetic preferences as well as certain distinct halakhic principles, set in motion the trend toward the creation of other prayer rites in various countries of Jewish domicile.

Until the advent of printing in the fifteenth century, it was only the wealthy who could afford to purchase a written *machzor*, and they would present copies to their synagogues to mark special family occasions and anniversaries. Often only a single copy of such a volume might be available in a synagogue, and the *chazan* would be required to read aloud from it, with the congregation repeating the prayers after him, word for word. This was the origin of the repetition of the silent *Amidah*, namely, for the benefit of those who did not know the prayers by heart, and therefore relied upon repeating them word for word after the *chazan*. Even after the dissemination of printed prayer books, and the fairly universal degree of Hebrew literacy, the tradition of repeating the *Amidah* was regarded as sacrosanct, although its halakhic objective, of enabling the general congregation to fulfill its duty of prayer, was no longer required.

In the pre–fifteenth-century period of handwritten manuscripts, great efforts were made, and large sums expended, to create as beautiful and artistic a work as possible. The skilled artists and scribes who were commissioned to produce the illuminated *machzorim* were frequently accommodated, together with their families, at the home of the patron-donor, and their entire board and lodging constituted the essential element of their fee. If the donor was especially delighted with the finished product, he might add a farewell token of appreciation! Sometimes the tasks of writing the body of the text and the production of artistic embellishment were shared by two different persons. It was not unknown for a third person to be employed to insert the punctuation and vocalization of the text, *nikkud* (lit. "pointing") being regarded as a specialist skill, calling for a thorough knowledge of the rules of Hebrew grammar.

Many scribes would include a colophon at the end of their work—often in verse—providing precise details of the date and circumstances of its publication, including the name of the owner-commissioner, suitably embellished with fulsome praise of his generosity, wisdom, and greatness, and, of course, the name of the scribe himself.

Some of the leading rabbis, such as the famous fourteenth-century authority, R. Jacob ben Moses Moellin (*Maharil*), were averse to what they regarded as the esthetic excesses of some of the illuminated *machzorim*, believing that their beauty and fascination were a distraction to those attempting to concentrate on praying from them. *Maharil* would consequently never pray from such a *machzor*.

A criticism of the prayer book scribes, ventilated in the *Sefer Chasidim* of Rabbi Yehudah He-Chasid, leader of the twelfth-century German pietistic movement, the *Chasidei Ashkenaz*, was that they tampered with the text, adding or omitting words, in order to weave acrostic allusions to their own names into the body of specific prayers.[3] Another criticism—not uncommon also in relation to some modern editions—is that they frequently refer back to prayers that have already occurred, instead of writing them out in full, with the result that worshipers can get confused, or must interrupt what they are reciting in order to find the relevant prayer that should follow next.[4]

The earliest-dated *machzorim* we possess are products of the twelfth century, though fragments of such works, going back to the ninth century, were discovered in the Cairo *Genizah*.[5] With the advent of the age of printing, artistry vanished from the prayer books, with the exception of representations of the signs of the zodiac, some basic woodcut designs, and, occasionally, an ornate frontispiece. The first printed prayer book was the *Machzor Roma*, which appeared in Soncino in 1485, and within the next fifty years printed editions of all the main prayer rites made their appearance. The unique prayer rite called *Machzor Afam*, being essentially the old French rite as followed by the Italian communities of Asti, Fosano, and Muncalvo, resisted the march of technological progress, and was not produced in printed form, surviving only in manuscript editions.

Today, the two main rites are the Ashkenazi and the Sephardi, the former surviving in German, Polish, and Russian variants, and the latter comprising Eastern and Western (Spanish and Portuguese) versions. An Israeli version, originally confined to chasidic circles but now achieving much wider popularity, is the so-called *Nusach Sefarad* (Sephardi rite). This is, in reality, not a pure Sephardi prayer rite, but actually based upon a sixteenth-century synthesized version, produced by the kabbalist Isaac Luria, and combining the Polish rite of his day and the Sephardic rite current in Palestine at that period.

We have observed that all Jews, regular and irregular worshipers, share the periodic festival encounter with the *machzor*. The middle-aged among us will recall that, until fairly recent decades, the particular edition that people used was of little consequence, and was certainly not the talking point that it is today. There were only three or four editions with English rubrics and translation, and it was unthinkable for the English-speaking Jew to use a Hebrew-only edition! The more observant, *shtibl*-member would generally opt for the *Kol-bo* edition, published by the Hebrew Publishing Company, with its Yiddish translation, commentary, and numerous *techinot* (private devotional petitions), and its rubrics in Hebrew and Yiddish.

But there was also the element of nostalgia, coupled with a tincture of superstition. It was almost a demonstration of filial loyalty not to change one's *machzor*. It was not easy to do so anyway, since it was one's parents or synagogue that generally presented the set on the occasion of a *bar mitzvah* or wedding, endowed with a suitable inscription, whose nostalgic significance was enhanced with every passing year!

As most Jews of the mainstream variety did not use their festival *machzor* as a text to be studied, analyzed, and contemplated, but rather as the familiar accoutrement of their dutiful synagogue visit for that occasion, the relative appeal of any edition was not something that interested them or that they were competent to assess.

Over the past few decades this situation has, thankfully, changed, for a variety of reasons: the intensification of Jewish nationalism; widespread familiarity with the Hebrew language, making the language of prayer more intelligible and interesting; the great improvements in standards of Jewish education, effected particularly by the Jewish day schools; the thirst for Jewish knowledge that is being slaked by so many of our young people at *yeshivot* and seminaries in Israel; and last, but by no means least, the appearance of new editions—such as the *ArtScroll*—esthetically so superior to anything previously published and endowed with readable commentaries and relevant instructions and guidance through the labyrinth of rabbinic law and lore.

Conservative and Reform circles in America and Britain have also not been slow to exploit the *machzor* as a vehicle of religious relevance and inspiration. Their translations follow, with varying emphases, those of the traditional *machzor*, but set out to emphasize the contemporary relevance of some of the lofty ideas culled from the prayers, such as the brotherhood of man, creation and redemption, love, compassion, and charity. These editions are generally endowed with some very well chosen selections and quotations from classical and medieval sources, meditations from modern theologians and philosophers, and some most-inspired modern adaptations of the translation of traditional prayers.

English-speaking Jews should be grateful for such provisions, and for the added dimensions of meaning revealed through translations which are naturally not available to our Israeli brethren praying in the original Hebrew of the *machzor*. It is naive to imagine that even the most literate and observant Israeli does not need to be exposed to the new layers of meaning and inspiration that each successive generation is privileged to discover and reveal. It is a mistake to imagine that even the most committed and informed do not need to be regularly invigorated by inspired religious creativity and to be offered fresh water from the perennial reservoirs.

Nusach Ashkenaz

The Ashkenazi rite, for the adherents of which this book is primarily intended, was molded by the Jews of Germany, Poland, and Russia. The name *Ashkenaz* is first found in Genesis 10:3, as a descendant of Japhet, and again in Jeremiah 51:24, where it is mentioned in association with Ararat, a district in Eastern Armenia. In the Middle Ages this term was borrowed by Jews as a designation of Germany, and henceforth as a generic term (Ashkenazim) for the people under the religious and cultural influence of the area stretching from Northern France and Germany to Poland and Lithuania.

The differences between the Ashkenazi traditions and those of the Sephardim, who hail from Spanish and Portuguese provenance, are explained on the assumption that they go back to earlier, more pronounced, differences between the traditions of medieval Palestine and Babylon, respectively. The latter two communities had developed their own independent religious traditions, based on the principles evolved in their respective *talmudim,* and the decisions taken in those works and in the halakhic commentaries and codes produced under their influence.

Jews probably first came to the Rhineland area in the wake of the Roman conquests, and by the beginning of the Middle Ages they had flourishing communities in France and western Germany. Their spiritual life reached its apogee in the tenth to the twelfth centuries, when rabbinic luminaries of the caliber of *Rabbeinu Gershom,* Rabbi Meir of Rothenburg, Rashi and, from the twelfth through fourteenth centuries, the Tosafists guided their religious destiny. When new communities branched out in England and southern and central Germany, they remained "Ashkenazi," that is, within the religious and liturgical orbit of that tradition.

The tranquility and unity of Ashkenazi Jewry was violently disturbed with the Crusades, followed by the various accusations against the Talmud, culminating in thousands of volumes, contained in 24 wagons, being publicly burned in Paris in June 1242 by order of Pope Gregory IX. This was followed by the expulsion of the Jews from France in 1306 and the dire persecution that accompanied the Black Death (1347–1352), which all but obliterated the Jewries of the Rhineland and Western and Northern Europe. The leading scholars, fearful for the survival of authentic religious traditions, produced some of the most important halakhic and liturgical works, as well as some, such as *Machzor Vitri* and *Sefer Chasidim,* that encapsulated in more popular form the Ashkenazi heritage.

Many Jews who managed to escape the horrors sought refuge in lands where a greater measure of safety seemed to be offered. Some opted for the countries north of the Rhineland, but most chose to move eastward, and hence the development of large and influential Ashkenazi communities in Eastern Europe, all committed to the halakhic authority and the liturgical traditions of the original Franco-German rite.

In their new communities, a vibrant expansion of Jewish learning took place, under creative rabbinic leadership. This, combined with the importation and proliferation of variant customs and practices among the expatriot immigrants, ensured that their original halakhic and liturgical traditions did not become fossilized. Adaptation and modification became necessary, and men like the illustrious Vilna Gaon, as well as the great leaders of the various chasidic dynasties, all wove their own strands—some more boldly and extensively than others—into the basic fabric of the Ashkenazi mosaic. Thus, the liturgical texts and practices of many neighboring communities became characterized by slight, and occasionally not so slight, differences: on the matter of variant words or expressions employed and glosses inserted, in the precise order of a particular group of prayers they recited, on the question of whether a particular composition or psalm ought or ought not to be recited on a particular occasion or festival, on whether certain *piyyutim* (see below), should or should not be included, as well as in the matter of specific halakhic customs (*minhagim*) recommended and introduced by the religious leaders of individual communities. Differences in melodies also naturally developed as the respective *chazanim* and choir masters of those communities made their distinctive contributions.

Hence it was that numerous differences arose between the original German, or pure Ashkenazi, rite, and its modified Eastern versions, be they the *Nusach Polin*, the Polish rite, or the Lithuanian rites further to the East.

With succeeding upheavals in Europe, as well as the opening up of the New World, those Ashkenazi traditions were disseminated to countries far from their original matrix. Especially with the waves of emigration that accompanied the rise of Nazism, variant Ashkenazi rites—those of Frankfurt, of northern Germany, of the Vilna Gaon, of the various chasidic groups, of Poland and of Russia—all found new homes in the synagogues and *shtibls* of far-flung countries, from South Africa to Shanghai, from South America to Australia, and from England to the State of Israel.

Had it not been for the pioneering efforts of Wolf Heidenheim (1757–1832), who collected, analyzed, and compared a vast number of liturgical manuscripts and printed versions, as a prelude to his own nine-volume critical edition of the *machzor* (Roedelheim, 1800–1802), Ashkenazi communities to this day would have inherited a chaotic liturgical tradition. He made a unique contribution toward the standardization of the Ashkenazi *nusach*, and the unprecedented popularity of his editions, which were reprinted scores of times, and which soon became regarded as the authorized version, had the effect of swiftly displacing most of the localized differences that had hitherto existed.

It is especially in the modern State of Israel that that rich and variegated liturgical tapestry, brought there over the past four hundred years by successive waves of immigrants from many lands, with slightly varying traditions, has tended to become rather faded, as Ashkenazi Jews there have capitulated to a unified *nusach*, through the influence, primarily, of schools, religious youth clubs, the army, and local synagogues.

As regards the High Holy Day liturgy, Israelis tend to pay scant attention to the traditional *piyyutim* that are still so much loved in the Diaspora. Their omission of so many of these makes their services much shorter than those outside Israel. This lack of interest is either because the modern Israelis have their own, modern forms of secular Hebrew poetic expression, which are far more direct and intelligible than most of the complex medieval *piyyutim*, or because they tend to prefer a shorter and less formalized service.

The Morning Service on Rosh Hashanah commences much earlier than on a normal Sabbath, to ensure that the considerably extended order of service may be terminated at a reasonable hour in the early afternoon, to enable people to enjoy their festive lunch, as well as in order to comply with the law that prescribes that *Musaf* (the Additional Service) should be completed by about 1 P.M.

The Ark curtain, the mantles that enclose the scrolls of the Law and the cover of the Reader's desk are all in white on this occasion, a color that symbolizes purity.

All who serve as officiants during the services on the High Festivals are also obliged to wear a white linen robe called a *kittel*. It is worn by the synagogue Reader on three other occasions during the year: on Passover, when intoning a special prayer for the summer dew; on the seventh day of Tabernacles (*Hoshana Rabbah*), which has the special character of a day of judgment; and, finally, on the eighth day of Tabernacles when a special prayer is offered for winter rains to fall in the holy land.

The *kittel* calls to mind the white shrouds in which the dead are dressed before burial,[6] an association that should prompt man to reflect upon the brevity of life and the final account he will be called upon to render when he departs this world. Since without rain life cannot exist, the *kittel* was also prescribed for those two occasions on which we pray for rain. It is hoped that the sight of Israel's spiritual representatives, clad in shrouds, will melt the divine heart and wrest his precious blessing from him.

Another explanation of the *kittel*, taking into account its white color, connects it with the prophetic promise: "Though your sins are like scarlet, they shall be white as snow" (Isaiah 1:18). Accordingly, the *kittel* is worn to symbolize the pure state that is attained through repentance.

Some see in the *kittel* a reflection of the angels, who are said to be clothed in white garments.[7] The repentant souls, having received absolution, stand like the angels without sin.

The first part of the Morning Service follows the almost identical order of ordinary Sabbaths and holidays. The only difference lies in the insertion, very early on, of the *Shir Ha-Yichud* ("Hymn of Unity"). This is followed by the recitation of the *Shir Ha-Kavod* ("Hymn of Glory"), the "Psalm for the (particular) day of the week," and Psalm 27 (*Le-David Ha-Shem Oriy*), all of which are generally recited toward the end of the *Musaf* service.

It is conceivable that these were removed from the end to the beginning of the service on Rosh Hashanah in order that the congregation should leave the synagogue with the sound of the final notes of the *shofar* still ringing in their ears. This effect would be weakened if those regular concluding hymns had still to be recited. For the sake of consistency this arrangement was then preserved on Yom Kippur.

Praises before Petitions

The Morning Service is prefaced by two much-loved paeans of poetic praise. The first, *Adon Olam,* affirms the uniqueness of the Creator, and Israel's absolute reliance upon Him, morning and night and from the cradle to the grave. The second song of praise, *Yigdal,* is a far more sophisticated creedal outline of the cardinal Jewish beliefs. Although on weekdays throughout the year these hymns are not sung aloud by the congregation, perhaps out of considerations of time, and although, in order not to further draw out the already lengthy Morning Service on Sabbaths and festivals, only one is sung congregationally at each service, *Yigdal* at the Evening Service and *Adon Olam* at the Morning Service, yet on the High Holy Days no such considerations were allowed to weigh, and these two hymns are chanted aloud, by *chazan* and congregation, as a prelude to the service.

And this exalted position, even before we commence arranging our needs and petitions before God, is of more than passing significance. For Jewish religious thinkers are in fact divided on the issue of precisely what constitutes the essential kernel of Jewish prayer: Is it praise or is it petition? The answer to this may well hinge on the issue of the appropriate demeanor that the Jew should adopt when addressing his Maker in prayer. Should he adopt an existentialist posture, as a weak and sinful mortal, quaking in fear and angst at his abject unworthiness to even engage the attention of the Holy One, let alone to make personal demands of Him? Or, on the contrary, should he revel in the privilege of the intimate dialogue into which his tradition has initiated him, a tradition upon which he may wholeheartedly trust for confirmation of the propriety of a self-confident and assertive prayer-initiative? The approach one takes to this question will condition one's attitude to the issue of whether praise or petition is the foremost priority and basic motivation of Jewish prayer.

The twentieth-century Gaon, Rav Yosef Dov Soloveitchik of Boston, is a staunch exponent of the view that it is petition that is paramount, and that man's mood during prayer should be one of fear and unworthiness rather than joy and confidence. He asserts that "the arrangers of our prayers were long on supplication and short on praise."[8] He views both the essence and the requirement of biblical prayer as restricted to the realm of response to situations of crisis. Indeed, the early matriarchs and patriarchs are rarely depicted as having turned to God in prayer outside the contexts of crisis and need. Neither is prayer established in the Bible as a regular or mandatory spiritual requisite. When people were in dire straits they prayed and petitioned; without such a critical stimulus they were silent. Hence, for Soloveitchik, supplication is the backbone of the *service of the heart,* and when uttering the weekday Amidah, with its lengthy succession of petitional blessings, "if one uttered less than the nineteen prayers, he did not fulfill his duty, for he did not express properly (and fully) the *needs* of individual and community."[9]

In a particularly powerful passage, Soloveitchik describes the desperate need of the masses to utter *petition* in order to give expression to their manifold, basic, and deep-seated needs, and contrasts this with the more relaxed and voluntary genre of *praises*, favored by spiritually elite, antisocial mystical circles that are "rich in esthetic experience":

> Halakhah is concerned with human beings who "dwell in darkness and the shadow of death," and are driven to crime for a crust of bread. Such people inhabit a world of venal and ludicrous drives. Just such an ineloquent and confused lot the Halakhah taught to pray, placing in their mouths a clear formula. The common man is commanded to pray for the sick in his household, for his wine which soured and his crops which were ruined. . . . Halakhah cannot confine itself to lofty ascetics. Only supplication is capable of making prayer accessible to the masses.[10]

David Hartman sums up Soloveitchik's view of the most appropriate mood that the Jew should adopt in prayer, as that of "surrender, resignation, and total helplessness and dependency on God. For Soloveitchik, the inner spirit of the experience of reciting the *Amidah* is a sacrificial offering of one's whole being to God."[11] And something akin to the terror of such an experience should infuse the praying Jew, as he stands so unworthily before his Maker.

The chasidic masters, on the other hand, with profound psychological insight, helped immeasurably to lighten the crushing burden of the poverty of the masses by switching the focus and emphasis of prayer away from the expression of, and the consequent preoccupation with, needs, inadequacies, and failings, to the fraternal expression of spiritual joy, celebration, profound gratefulness, and praise for whatever gifts God bestows. By promoting singing and dancing in praise of God, and in general by fostering a mood of joyfulness and contentedness, Chasidism gave its adherents a religious confidence they could never otherwise have mustered, and helped to elevate praise high above petition in their order of priorities.

In the light of these two diametrically opposite approaches, we may view the introduction of the two hymns, *Yigdal* and *Adon Olam*, at the very outset of our prayers and before the enunciation of any needs and petitions, as playing a significant role in establishing what, for the liturgists who included these hymns at least, is the most appropriate mood for the praying Jew. They were clearly unhappy with the idea that we launch ourselves directly into "petitional blessing." For that is what the early blessings essentially are. They may appear to be merely praises of God; but to read them as such is to miss the point. For, when we bless God, in the *Asher yatzar* blessing, as the One "who wondrously heals all flesh," we would do a disservice to the framers of that blessing to imagine that they did not intend it also as an inferred plea to God to keep our bodies healthy, and to heal any of our physical defects. Similarly, when we praise God for making us the recipients of His Torah, it would be a hollow blessing if it was not infused by the hope and plea that He should continue to regard us as worthy to be its custodians. And so on, with all the subsequent fifteen *Birkot Ha-Shachar* blessings.

So, in order that we should not appear before God at the outset as selfish petitioners, obsessed with our own personal and national needs, these two hymns of praise were introduced into the prayer book. We put God before ourselves. We acknowledge His attributes. We submit ourselves as His subjects, and we sing joyful songs of praise to Him. Only then do we express our needs.

In the light of this we may also explain the collection of six disparate verses placed at the very outset of the Morning Service, among which is the *Mah tovu* verse composed by the heathen prophet, Bilaam—a verse not surprisingly objected to by several halakhists. An examination of all the verses will reveal, however, that they share a common spirit of joyfulness and gratitude to be part of "the throng" of Jewry, privileged to worship in the house of the Lord. Clearly this affirmation serves to send a clear signal to God that our first and paramount emotion is one of joyful praise for the good feeling that being His subjects induces. This mood is then reinforced by the two hymns that follow. Thus, together, they may be seen as serving to preempt the self-centered elements of the liturgy, namely the blessings that petition for our needs, by expressing, through both biblical verses and medieval poetry, a pure praise of, and joy in, the God of Israel.

אֲדוֹן עוֹלָם
Master of the Universe

Adon Olam is one of the first synagogue hymns learned by children, and remains one of the most popular throughout the life of the praying Jew. It speaks of God's attributes in a uniquely direct and personal manner, accompanied by the rhythmically flowing introductory demonstrative, *vehu* ("And it is He . . ."): *ve-hu hayah, ve-hu hoveh, ve-hu yihyeh, be-tifarah* ("And it is He that was, He that is, and He that shall remain, in splendor"); *ve-hu echad ve-ein sheiniy* ("And He is One—there being no second . . ."); *ve-hu eiliy* ("And He is my God . . ."); *ve-hu nisiy* ("And He is my banner . . .").

In our commentary to the *Yigdal* hymn we explain how Hebrew poetic meter is created (see below). Each line of *Adon Olam* conforms to an identical rhythm, effected by the repetition—in both the first and second halves of each line—of a subsidiary stress (*sheva* or composite *sheva,* mainly in the syllable *ve* or *be* at the beginning of each line) followed by *three* main stresses. Thus, the opening two lines:

Adon olam asher malakh
be-terem kol yetzir nivra,
Le-eit naasah ve-cheftzo kol
azai melekh shemo nikra

It also seeks to intensify the rhythm by the addition of a fairly basic kind of rhyme, effected by concluding each line with the syllable *ra.*

Unlike *Yigdal,* which deals with a variety of theological concepts and basic beliefs, *Adon Olam* is exclusively concerned with the nature of God (as expounded in the first six lines) and with Israel's total reliance upon Him in the face of life's unremitting crises, as well as in the hereafter when we have shed our mortal coil and awakened to a new and strange existence. It is, therefore, a most appropriate hymn to recite as the prelude to prayer. We have first to affirm with clarity the nature of the God we worship, and His paramount place in our lives and emotions, before we proceed to engage Him in prayer and petition. It may well have been composed originally, however, for recitation before retiring to sleep, as suggested by the penultimate line: "Into His hand I entrust my spirit during the period I shall be asleep and when I awaken." From that context—because of its popularity—it was probably taken up into the prayers of some of the statutory services.

In Morocco it was customary to recite *Adon Olam* at weddings, before the bride was brought under the *chupah.* Perhaps, notwithstanding the excitement of that particular moment of their life, brides may well have entertained understandable feelings of apprehension (particularly in an era of arranged marriages, when they may have had little acquaintance with their intended). The *Adon Olam,* with its clear and earnest expression of conviction that God is our Rock, refuge, and redeemer, may well have been employed in order to calm their nerves, and to assure them that heaven will protect them from any distress, and bless them with love and contentment.

Its authorship is uncertain. Some writers have attributed it to the tenth-century Babylonian Gaon, Sherirah, although it is more popularly attributed to the distinguished eleventh-century Spanish poet and philosopher, Solomon ibn Gabirol. The *Kitzur Shelah* quotes the early German pietist, Rabbi Yehudah He-Chasid as affirming that "whoever has the requisite intentions while reciting *Adon Olam*—that beautiful and praiseworthy hymn—I stand surety that his prayers will be heard, and no Satanic power will be enabled to neutralize them, particularly on Rosh Hashanah and Yom Kippur." The *Shelah* adds that this may explain why the custom developed to recite *Adon Olam* (at the beginning of our daily service) before the recitation of all our blessings and praises, as well as at the end of the service.[12]

The reference to this hymn as protecting against "Satanic powers" may provide the clearest rationale of its employment in the context of a *chupah*. It is well known that ancient, primitive, though fairly universal, belief had it that the bride was in danger of being seized by covetous demons, and that she was consequently in need of protection. If *Adon Olam* was believed to be as efficacious as Yehudah He-Chasid asserts, then its properties would have been particularly advantageous to the vulnerable bride.[13]

The variety of melodies that have been composed for this hymn attest to its position as one of the best-loved of our sacred compositions. It is a favorite of cantors, choirs and congregations, of the young and the old, and has even been set to a zippy tune to suit the annual chasidic Pop Festival in Jerusalem. It can certainly claim to have won the hearts of our people.

יִגְדַּל
Magnify the Living God

This most-loved hymn represents a poetic statement of Judaism's basic beliefs. We avoid use of the terms *creed* and *dogmas* in this context, because, although the great Maimonides (1135–1204) established a list of thirteen authoritative *Ikkarim*, or fundamental Jewish beliefs,[14] of which *Yigdal* is their poetic formulation, yet such a quintessential reduction of Judaism to its basic principles is not talmudically warranted.

Early rabbinic Judaism inclined rather toward the maxim, "Be as zealous of a light precept as of a weighty one, for you do not know the measure of each *mitzvah*'s reward."[15] The examples occasionally quoted, of early prophets[16] or teachers giving prominence to one or another of the Torah's teachings, such as Hillel who told a would-be convert that "'Do not unto your neighbor what you would not have him do to you,' represents the whole Torah, while the rest is commentary,"[17] were clearly intended polemically, as a sop to outsiders, rather than as a practical guide for the faithful. (Perhaps it was for that reason that Hillel quoted it as a negative formulation, rather than in the positive form in which it occurs in Leviticus 19:18, to avoid the charge that he was arbitrarily elevating one biblical principle above the others.)

Once Maimonides had established his list of principal laws, there were other outstanding Jewish philosophers, of the following century, men of the ilk of Hasdai Crescas, Simon ben Tzemach Duran, and Joseph Albo, who offered alternate lists of essential beliefs, thus underlining the hazardous and arbitrary nature of the exercise.[18]

Not surprisingly, therefore, there were several other leading authorities, such as Isaac Abarbanel and his younger contemporary, David ibn Abi Zimra (fifteenth to sixteenth centuries), who objected vehemently to the creation of any such lists of basic principles. In the words of the latter:

> I do not agree that it is right to make any part of the perfect Torah into a "principle," since the whole Torah is a "principle" from the mouth of the Almighty. Our Sages say that whoever states that the whole Torah is from heaven with the exception of one verse is a heretic. Consequently, each precept is a "principle" and a fundamental idea. Even a light precept has a secret reason which is beyond our understanding.[19]

The need to establish what are precisely *Jewish* beliefs may have arisen, as suggested above, out of polemical necessity, namely as a subtle method of emphasizing the erroneous beliefs of the other main religions. To attack their beliefs openly was naturally dangerous. Hence the method of polemic, whereby one highlights, and often overemphasizes, one's own true beliefs in order to imply that any alternate views, as espoused by the "others," are empty and false.

Viewed in this light, the verses of *Yigdal* may be seen to be aiming their missiles at both Christianity and Islam, as well as at early Sadducean doctrines, which the medieval Karaites—thorns in the flesh of the rabbinic authorities—reincarnated. Thus, the heavy reference to God as "One, with no unity like His unity" (1.2) is clearly meant to deny both the Persian dualistic belief as well as the Christian Trinity. The statement that "He has neither bodily similarity nor substance" (1.3) is a denial of Jesus and his pretensions to being God incarnate. The emphasis on prophecy being granted only to chosen initiates (1.6) and the incomparable status of Moses (1.7) represent a rejection of Mohammed's claim to being the one and only true prophet of God. The references to "the true Torah" (1.8) that "God will never alter or exchange" (1.9) are aimed at the Christian claim that the New Testament has superseded Israel's Torah. The references to reward and punishment (1.11) and to resurrection of the dead (1.13) come to reinforce both of these doctrines in the face of Sadducean and Karaite theology, which rejected any notion of the hereafter, since this is not explicitly enunciated in Scripture. Again, the emphatic statement that "God will send His Messiah *at the end of days*" is a categorical rejection of the Christian view that the Messiah has already come.

Another reason has been suggested as to why Maimonides saw fit to create this distillation of Jewish belief. His Thirteen Principles are formulated as a comment on the Mishnah, which promises that "All Israel has a share in the World to Come." Maimonides' concept of this—largely influenced by medieval Aristotelianism—was of a spiritual immortality. However, according to that doctrine, such an immortality was available only to those souls of requisite intellectual and philosophic attainment, who had achieved mastery of metaphysical truth. Thus, if "all Israel" was to be granted that reward, it was necessary that they should all be provided with the minimum knowledge of the truths of Judaism required for a Jew to qualify "intellectually and philosophically."[20]

We have referred already to *two* formulations of Maimonides' Thirteen Principles of Faith: his own formulation, which he published in his monumental Commentary to the Mishnah, as well as this poetic *Yigdal* version, which is attributed to one Daniel ben Yehudah, an Italian rabbi, who served as a *dayyan* (Judge of the Ecclesiastical Court) of Rome during the first half of the fourteenth century. *Yigdal* is all we possess of Daniel's poetic output. There is also a third version of the Thirteen Principles: the *Ani Maamin* ("I believe with perfect faith. . ."), which appears at the conclusion of the daily Morning Service, but regarding whose authorship there is no unanimous view.

It is the *Yigdal* version, however, that has achieved greatest popularity, most certainly on account of its rhythmic quality, which accounts for the many and varied melodies that have been composed for its recitation on Sabbaths and festivals. Thus, while the *Ani Maamin* prose version was relegated to the end of the Morning Service, as an *optional* private reading for the especially pious, it was the lively poetic version that captured the hearts of the masses of Jewry as one of their most dearly loved and well-known hymns within our communal worship.

Medieval Hebrew meter was derived from the Arabic system, which depends upon the regular repetition of lines containing the same number and pattern of stresses and half-stresses. Thus:

Yigdal Ĕlo / kim chai vĕ-yish / tabach
Nimtza vĕ-eyn / et el mĕtzi / uto

It will be seen that each of these half-lines contains three units, the first two of which comprise two main stresses (— —) leading into a subsidiary stress (*sheva* or composite *sheva*) linked to a main stress (˘ —).[21] These are rounded off with a short unit comprising just two main stresses. This pattern is sustained throughout the hymn. Thus, the final line:

Meitim yĕcha / yeh El bĕ-rov / chasdo
Barukh ădei / ad shem tĕhi / lato.

A fascinating aspect of *Yigdal*'s popularity is that it was translated by a London Wesleyan minister, Thomas Olivers, who then adapted his English version to the melody to which he had heard it rendered by Cantor Meyer Leone of the Duke's Place Synagogue. "Olivers' version, 'The God of Abraham Praise,' first published in 1770, became popular immediately, and is sung to this day in the Anglican service as a processional or general-purpose hymn."[22]

While throughout the year *Yigdal* is sung at the conclusion of the Friday and festival evening services, on Rosh Hashanah and Yom Kippur it serves also as the introduction to the Morning Service, and is sung together with *Adon Olam*, an equally popular, though more simplistic, hymn.

לְדָוִד ה׳ אוֹרִי וְיִשְׁעִי
The Lord Is My Light and My Salvation (Psalm 27)

Neither the significance nor the origins of many of our early liturgical compositions can be comprehended without recourse to rabbinic literature. Most of those compositions gained their place in the liturgy solely on account of a special interpretation given to each of them in rabbinic tradition. Without knowledge of that particular interpretation, the presence and purpose of many a psalm, prayer, or formula may frequently appear enigmatic.

Psalm 27 exemplifies this principle; for the text betrays not so much as a hint of why it was selected as the "Psalm for the New Year." Granted, it breathes a supreme confidence that God will protect the psalmist from his enemies. But this is a theme common to a large number of the psalms; and its particular relevance to the High Holy Days is tenuous!

Its adoration of the "house of the Lord," where the psalmist longs to spend his life, would also be more appropriate as a theme for *Pesach, Shavuot* and *Sukkot*, when the Jews made a pilgrimage to the Temple! So why was the psalm chosen for this festival?

For the answer we must turn to the opening words of the Midrash on this psalm.

> The Rabbis expound this psalm with reference to Rosh Hashanah and Yom Kippur: *The Lord is my light*—on Rosh Hashanah, the day of judgment, as it is written "He will make your righteousness shine clear *like a light*, and the justice of your cause like the noonday sun" (Psalm 37:6). *And my salvation*—on Yom Kippur, when He grants us *salvation* and pardons all our sins.

The Midrash proceeds to transform totally the import of the psalmist's references to his enemies, particularly "the evildoers who came upon me to devour my flesh." In the mystical imagination of the Rabbis, these are viewed as the guardian angels of the heathen nations of the world who assume the role of the accuser, attempting to have Israel condemned at judgment. They *stumble and fall*—because God does not allow them to open their mouths against Israel.

The Midrash develops this theme by pointing out that the Hebrew word for "the accuser" is *Ha-Satan,* whose numerical value (*gematria*) is three hundred and sixty-four. This indicates that there is just *one* special day in the (solar) year—the day of judgment—when the satanic spirit is absent and his demonic power neutralized. On that day, says the Midrash, God takes Satan on a tour of Jewry, making him witness their total preoccupation with fasting, prayers and atonement. At the height of Satan's confusion, God invites him to disclose what faults he has found in God's children. The accuser is forced to say, "They are, indeed, like the ministering angels; I cannot oppose them."

The recitation of Psalm 27, at the end of the daily morning and evening services, extends until after the seventh day of the festival of Tabernacles, *Hoshana Rabbah,* which also partakes of the nature of a "Day of Judgment." The reference to God hiding the psalmist "in his *sukkah*" also made its recitation appropriate for the duration of the Tabernacles festival.

There can be few psalms that breathe such faith and confidence in the guiding hand of God. It is an expanded counterpart of perhaps the most famous in that entire inspired collection, Psalm 23.

God's presence—felt so overwhelmingly by the psalmist—creates for him a sense of reassurance beyond the capability of even his parents to provide. The source of that confidence is twofold: the house of God and the ways of God.

First, the house of God:

> One thing I ask of the Lord, only this do I seek: to dwell in the *house of the Lord* all the days of my life, to gaze upon the beauty of the Lord and to worship in His temple.

The "house of the Lord" for King David was not the glorious physical reality into which his son, King Solomon, transformed it. Furthermore, as Samson Raphael Hirsch notes, not even the priests dwelt in the house of the Lord *all the days of their life.* So King David could only have been speaking figuratively, alluding to the life of holiness and of constant awareness of God's presence, which transformed everywhere he went into a veritable "house of God," in the spirit of the verse, "For the Lord thy God walks in the midst of thy camp" (Deuteronomy 23:15).

Second, the ways of God:

> Teach me Your ways, O Lord, and lead me on a level path, because of my insidious foes.

The psalmist views physical and spiritual salvation as inextricable. He wishes God to inspire him to holiness, because he recognizes that only then will he deserve to be "led on a level path" and to be granted relief from his enemies. This conviction is in fact encapsulated in the very opening words of the psalm: "The Lord is my light," that is, my spiritual kernel, "and my salvation," that is, my physical protector. With truth, holiness, faith, and justice on his side, the prophet senses his invincibility. And he concludes with a call to his people to share that confidence: "Hope in the Lord. Be strong and stout-hearted; and hope in the Lord!"

Throughout the period of the High Holy Days and Sukkot when this psalm is recited, although predominantly a period of repentance and remorse, it is the confident sentiments of this psalm that give us the temerity to face the bar of heavenly justice and to beg for health, happiness, and prosperity.

שִׁיר הַיִּחוּד
Hymn of Unity

The Hymn of Unity is so called because its predominant theme is a declaration of the absolute Unity of God, even though this particular concept, as well as the key word *yichud* ("Unity"), does not appear until the end of the section prescribed for the second day of the week: *Ve-hinnenu al yichudekha*—"Behold, we are the witnesses . . . to Your Unity."

The section for the first day of the week serves as a general introduction, describing the extent of our reliance upon God, as well as puny man's total inability to enter into any meaningful praise of, or dialogue with, the great and glorious Creator. Lines 5 to 17 of this section bear a strong association with ideas contained in the *Nishmat* prayer,[23] and, more particularly, in the *Akdamut* composition recited on *Shavuot*. A few lines from the latter poem will illustrate its influence:

> If all the heavens were parchment, and all their forests reeds,
> If all the swirling waters of the seas were ink,
> And all the earth's inhabitants were ready and skillful scribes,
> Who could yet declare in words the glory of the Universe?

The Hymn of Unity is attributed to Rabbi Samuel He-Chasid, one of the founders of the famous pietistic movement in twelfth-century Germany, whose members were known as the *Chasidei Ashkenaz*. His son, author of the popular *Shir Ha-Kavod* (Hymn of Glory), was the most distinguished leader of the sect, and this composition bears all the hallmarks of the philosophical and mystical propensities of that movement.[24]

I am of the opinion, however, that the poem, in the form in which we have it, has gone through a considerable editorial revision. It has the definite characteristics of a composite work, put together from a number of poetic compositions, some of which were alphabetical acrostics. This is obvious from a closer look at the section for the fourth day of the week, which is a complete alphabetical acrostic, though with no consistency in the frequency with which each letter is employed. Extracts of alphabetical acrostic material also appear in the sections of other days of the week; thus, in the concluding section of the second day, eight of the lines commence with the letter *alef*, a device that is carried over into the first three lines of the section for the third day of the week. Furthermore, in the latter section we find six lines commencing with the word *Kiy* and seven lines commencing with *Kol*. These are scattered throughout that particular section, but clearly originally belonged together as alternating couplets. Again, in the middle section for the fifth day, we find a cluster of lines commencing with the word *Eyn*, which must originally have been part of a separate poetic composition.

The *Shir Ha-Yichud* was originally recited in its entirety only at the *Kol Nidrei* night service, when the contemplative mood of the congregation was suited to its rather philosophical and mystical descriptions of the deity. Its introduction into the liturgy met with considerable opposition, however, particularly on the part of the distinguished sixteenth-century Polish authority, R. Solomon Luria (*Maharshal*). He prohibited it in the communities under his jurisdiction on account of its rather daring anthropomorphisms whose import could easily be misconstrued by those uninitiated into mystical speculation. These fears were not shared by his famous contemporary, R. Mordechai Jaffe, who allowed its recitation on Sabbaths and festivals. Although some communities wished to recite it daily, this was objected to by Jaffe and R. Jacob Emden on the grounds that such a practice would undermine the value of the composition, as people would have to rush its recitation in order to get to work. Perhaps by way of compromise, the lengthy poem was then divided up into seven sections, so that at least a part of it could be recited, with the requisite intention, on each day of the week.

Few Ashkenazi communities have retained its regular recitation, even on Sabbaths. On the High Holy Days, however, it is still customary to recite it at the beginning of the Morning Service.

הַמֶּלֶךְ
The King

The Reader commences here the main part of the *Shacharit* service. Whereas, on ordinary Sabbaths, he commences with the following sentence (*Shokhein ad*), on the High Holy Days, because the central theme of the liturgy is that of God sitting on the throne of justice, it was felt more appropriate to commence the service with the previous sentence (*Ha-melekh*) which encapsulates that key theme.

In some festival prayer books the reading is *Ha-melekh ha-yosheiv* ("The King *who* sits"), a version found in many early manuscripts. This reading, while contextually appropriate when it is linked to the previous verses (as it is on Sabbaths throughout the year), impairs the stylistic smoothness when it stands as part of an independent sentence, as on the High Holy Days. Its translation would then be, "The King who sits upon a high and exalted throne," without any related predicate. The reading found in most printed editions—*Ha-melekh yosheiv*—converts it into an independent statement: "The King sits upon a high and exalted throne."

שִׁיר הַמַּעֲלוֹת מִמַּעֲמַקִּים
A Pilgrim Song. Out of the Depths

Recent editions, such as Birnbaum and ArtScroll, have revived the custom of reciting Psalm 130, which was always optional. In chasidic synagogues it enjoys a respected status, and is recited aloud with great feeling by *chazan* and congregation.

Its recitation at this juncture is on account of its opening reference: "Out of the depths I call to you, O Lord." The Midrash on this verse observes: "A man should never pray on an elevated place, but rather on one that is on a low level, as it is written, 'Out of the depths I call . . . ,' since none are elevated in the presence of God."[25]

As this is the point at which the *chazan* of the congregation commences the main section of the service, this psalm, with its reference to the most appropriate position from which to utter prayer, was regarded as a fitting prelude. But the emotion that this psalm engenders, particularly through its opening words, "Out of the depths I have called you," does not stem merely from its serving as a proof-text for the correct position for the *chazan* to pray from, but rather from its petitionary force, suggestive of our truly calling *out of the depths*—of despair, of self-doubt, and of existential perplexity.

We have referred to the fact that the sentiments of this psalm did not originally constitute an essential part of this section of the prayers. Indeed, contemporary thinkers debate what the essential pathos, or desired mental and emotional posture, of the Jew should be when petitioning God in prayer. Rav Soloveitchik, for example, believes that we should be overwhelmed with feelings of unworthiness and discomfiture. He maintains that our ability to petition God at all derives merely from our covenantal relationship with our ancestors who stood at Sinai in the closest proximity to God, and who were privileged to have vouchsafed to them the divine revelation. That "merit of the fathers" has redeemed their children from an otherwise spiritually sterile and worthless life of perceived alienation from God that would have rendered prayer an impossibly audacious act.

It is from this conception that Rav Soloveitchik objects to the introduction of any contemporary liturgical compositions, or even the slightest change in the form of any prayer. We have to pray exactly as our ancestors prayed, since we are basically unworthy to stand in prayer before God. They have handed down to us the gift of prayer, and although we are permitted to utilize that gift and avail ourselves of our ancestral precedent and merit, we certainly cannot muster the confidence to augment it and to extend its parameters. Soloveitchik is particularly scathing, therefore, about the many modifications introduced in Reform worship. For Rav Soloveitchik, the sentiments of "Out of the depths I have called you" are most appropriate, therefore, to put us in the correct mood for prayer on this holy day, as well as to define our precise mental attitude toward the daring exercise of approaching and addressing God in prayer.

There are others, like Professor David Hartman, who cannot accept the necessity or appropriateness of that mood of abject helplessness, unworthiness, and insecurity:

> God said to Abraham: "I will establish My covenant between Me and you and your generations for an everlasting covenant" (Genesis 17:7). And again, as Moses said to the people: "I make this covenant, with its sanctions, not with you alone, but both with those who are standing here with us this day before the Lord our God and with those who are not with us here this day" (Deuteronomy 29:13–14). Creativity, adequacy, and boldness of spirit were not permitted by God only to those who participated in the founding covenantal moments; rather they define the on-going vitality of the eternal covenant between God and His human partners in every generation.[26]

For Hartman, the implications of those sentiments, "Out of the depths I have called you," would be quite different. They are not intended to induce existential terror, but simply to mirror the vulnerability that mortal man senses, and the need for divine mercy and help that he feels, as he struggles to contend with life's problems and anxieties.

In talmudic times it was the practice for the Reader to recite the *Amidah* from a position slightly lower than that occupied by the surrounding worshipers. This gave rise to the term *yoreid lifnei ha-teivah, "descending* to the Reader's desk." It has been suggested that the practice was abandoned as an anti-Samaritan gesture, since the latter made "prayer from the depths" a central feature of their worship.

The several references in the psalm to forgiveness of sin, making it most appropriate to Rosh Hashanah and Yom Kippur, resulted in the custom of many communities to include it only on these two festivals, though some prayer rites extend its recitation to all festivals.

יוֹצֵר אוֹר
Blessed Are You . . . Who Forms Light

This is the opening of the first of the *Shema* blessings whose theme is praise of the Creator for the gifts of light and darkness, day and night, the former in which to pursue ennobling work, the latter in which to enjoy bodily rest and refreshment. It is a quotation from Isaiah 45:7, with the one notable exception that the final phrase in Isaiah is not *u-vorei et ha-kol* ("and creates *all things*"), but *u-vorei ra* ("and creates *evil*").

The reason for the change was probably because retention of the authentic biblical version might have provided fuel for the adherents of the dualist Persian (Zoroastrian) religion. They believed that the world was created and preserved by two opposing forces, light and darkness, which manifest their will through good and evil, respectively. The reference to God as the creator of evil was accordingly altered.

אוֹר עוֹלָם
Yea, Eternal Light

This rather abstruse line can only be understood in the light of talmudic folklore, according to which the primordial light enjoyed by Adam was possessed of supernatural properties that enabled him to take in the whole panorama of creation with one glance. The Midrash states that God refused to bestow that gift upon the wicked generations of the flood and the builders of the Tower of Babel, so He stored it away for the exclusive enjoyment of the righteous in the hereafter.

This explains the first part of the line: "The light (*or*), by means of which the whole world (*olam*) could be surveyed, is stored away in the treasury of eternal life (*be-otzar chayyim*)."

Thus, according to this mystical idea, the light of the sun and moon (*orot*) that we enjoy is of a far inferior quality to that original unique source of illumination. Our light only merits its name when it is contrasted with darkness (*orot me-o-fel*). And it was our circumscribed light that God commanded (*amar*) and which came into being (*vayehi*).

Piyyutim

Not surprisingly, since the *Amidah* was, at first, the only prayer to be led by a *chazan*, the earliest *piyyutim*—poetic compositions—were designed for insertion into the *Amidah*. Because of their position in the "*Chazan*'s Prayer" they were even called *kerovot*,[27] after the name given to the *chazan* himself at that early period. He was known as the *karovah*, the one who "brings near" the prayers of Israel to the heavenly throne.

Until the introduction of *piyyut*[28] the prayers tended to be rather stiff and prosaic, with the exception, of course, of the book of Psalms, which was freely drawn upon as the main font of liturgical inspiration. But the Psalms were rather general in their themes, and, as the liturgy developed with an *Amidah* of eighteen (later nineteen) blessings, expressing a variety of different needs, theological concepts, national aspirations, and historical reminiscences, the need was felt for poetic compositions of an emotional and inspirational nature that amplified specifically each individual blessing of the *Amidah*. Hence the poetic expansion of the festival liturgy in this way, and its later extension into other parts of the services, particularly into the blessings preceding and following the *Shema* both in the Evening and Morning Services.

The *piyyutim* also came to fulfill a need for poetic and emotional compositions that were more relevant to the outlook of the age, more in the spirit of its needs and challenges, and more reflective of its particular social, political, and spiritual tensions. Where a Jewish community was the victim of persecution or discrimination, for example, or when it was granted a miraculous deliverance, it felt the need to express its feelings of anxiety, relief, and thanksgiving with an appropriate *piyyut*. As Hebrew literature developed, especially from the third to the seventh centuries C.E., with the rise of the Midrash, which gave the impetus to Hebrew poetry, men of spirit felt the spontaneous urge to be creative and artistic, and to compose beautiful poems in tribute to the Sabbath and the festivals.

The classical period of the *paytanim*[29] extended to the twelfth century. Those compositions that caught the imagination of the communities gained wider currency and became part-and-parcel of the synagogue prayer rites for those occasions. Some composers even succeeded in weaving a poetic web around the mundane ritual laws and customs of the sacred days.

To win the acclaim of the masses a *piyyut* had to have all the hallmarks of artistry. It had to observe the basic laws of rhythm and meter, it had to employ the choicest and most appropriate biblical phraseology, and it had to demonstrate the author's ability to mold the biblical vocabulary into new forms and expressions to suit the imagery being employed.

It was the *chazan* alone who recited the *piyyutim*. The congregation were unable to join in as handwritten *machzorim* were a rarity. Frequently a synagogue possessed but one *machzor* for the use of the *chazan*. It was only with the introduction of printing in the sixteenth century that this situation changed.

One of our earliest and most prolific liturgical poets (early seventh century) was Eleazar Kallir, a pupil of Yannai, the great pioneer of Hebrew poetry.[30] Unfortunately, very little is known of his life and activity, resulting in a web of legend being woven around him in the medieval period.

According to one tradition he was killed by his teacher Yannai in a fit of jealousy at Kallir's growing fame and influence.

Kallir devoted special attention to *yotzerot*, poetic insertions into the blessings before (and after) the *Shema*.[31] Some scholars are of the opinion that these were originally written as substitutes for the *Shema* at a time when the Persians, who occupied Palestine between 614 and 628 C.E., banned its public recitation. Such a central daily affirmation of the unity of God would have offended against the dualistic beliefs of the Persians. Hidden amid a profusion of poetry, however, it would be difficult to detect or anticipate its recitation.

Kallir—and his teacher Yannai—made significant contributions toward Hebrew philology and the development of the Hebrew language. Where a Hebrew word was not available in the classical literature to express a particular idea, they coined new words or word-formations. Their approach, which frequently involved sacrificing the rules of grammar and syntax, was severely criticized by the later medieval grammarians, particularly the great Bible commentator Abraham ibn Ezra[32] and the illustrious philosopher Moses Maimonides.[33]

The output of these early poets adorns our Ashkenazi festival and High Holy Day liturgies. The Sephardi communities, on the other hand, preferred to adopt the *piyyut* of their own Spanish poets, such as Ibn Gabirol, Judah Halevi, Abraham, and Moses ibn Ezra.

It has to be admitted that not all our great halakhic authorities were won over to the adornment of the basic liturgy by the inclusion of *piyyutim*, and Saadia Gaon (ninth to tenth century) and many other of the leaders of the famous Babylonian geonic seats of learning may be numbered among its most vociferous opponents. Although Saadia did turn his own hand to their composition, he nevertheless applied some very strict rules and criteria to what were appropriate forms of expression and what were inappropriate. He found many examples of the latter, and withheld his imprimatur to a large number of poems and expressions which, in his opinion, departed from or impaired the original structure of the prayer they were embellishing, or which injected ideas that were not directly related to the basic theme of the passage.

It was the great Maimonides who was perhaps the most outspoken of the critics of the freedom of expression that many *paytanim* chose to adopt, and he railed against those who employed exaggerated and inappropriate, if not offensive, praise of God:

> We cannot approve of what those foolish persons do . . . describing God in attributes that would be an offence if applied to a human being; for those people have no knowledge of these great and important principles, which

> are not appreciated by the average person. Treating the Creator as a familiar object, they describe Him and speak of Him in any expression they think proper, letting their eloquence run away with them, and imagining thereby that they can thus influence Him for their benefit. Such authors compose things that are either pure heresy or which contain such absurdities that prompt the reader both to laugh and also to grieve that anyone could have the temerity to apply such references to God. Were it not that I pitied the authors for their defects, and bore them no malice, I would have cited examples from their works to expose their errors. I declare that they are guilty not only of ordinary sin, but also of profanity and blasphemy! This applies also to the multitude that listens to the prayers of such a foolish person.[34]

Again, it should be stressed that, like Saadia, Maimonides was not against the institution of *piyyut*, per se, and he himself composed several poetic compositions, including one for *Neilah*. It was the impropriety of so many of the compositions of their contemporaries that aroused the ire of those two purists par excellence.

It may be assumed, therefore, that, due to the strictures of those distinguished authorities, a more critical appraisal was subsequently made of the work of any *chazan* offering his own religious poetry for general acceptance, with the result that few, if any, of the poetic compositions that won universal acceptance, and that were embodied into the standardized Ashkenazi and Sephardi *machzorim*, suffer from any of those denounced defects.

מֶלֶךְ אָזוּר גְבוּרָה
King with Might Begirded

This *yotzer*-poem is attributed to Eleazar Kallir. It contains twenty-five stanzas, each stanza comprising three short lines with no more than four words to a line. The first word of each stanza is *melekh* ("King"), and the succeeding initial letters of the second word in each stanza create an alphabetical acrostic.

The poem is a paean of praise, alluding to the midrashic idea that God donned a special robe of majesty on each of ten occasions when He went forth to achieve some great cosmic or historic purpose. The ten divine garments referred to here are *might* (see Psalm 65:7), *vengeance* (Isaiah 59:17), *majestic splendor* (Psalm 93:1), *radiance* (Daniel 2:22), *strength* (Psalm 93:1), *triumph* (Isaiah 59:17), *grandeur* (Isaiah 63:1), *crimson robes* (Isaiah 63:1), *a snow-white tallit* (Daniel 8:9), and *zeal* (Isaiah 59:17).

These different *robes* represent the varied attributes of the divine being and His presence as it is manifested in history. They may appear rather gross to the philosophical or sophisticated modern, whose concept of God is that of a pure spirituality; though religious soldiers, who sensed the active participation of God in the various struggles that led up to the establishment of the State of Israel and to the reunification of Jerusalem, frequently admitted to thinking militaristically in terms of a God of "might," "vengeance," and "triumph." Again, at times when we are filled with awe at the sight of a wonder of nature, do we not associate God with "grandeur"? And when we detect His presence among us as we stand in prayer on Rosh Hashanah and Yom Kippur, does he not also become, in a sense, enwrapped in "a snow-white *tallit*"?

Judaism in the medieval period struggled hard to defend these anthropomorphic references against their many detractors, and Maimonides, for example, vehemently denied any literal significance for such concrete references to the deity. He did recognize, however, the problem that it is well-nigh impossible for any ordinary intellect to know God, or for any ordinary emotion to be stimulated by contemplation of Him, except by means of such anthropomorphic similes.[35]

Devotional prayer itself would be well-nigh impossible without mentally sensing or invoking the proximity of a being who is, in fact, more than just "pure spirituality." The vocabulary of our prayers even promotes this through its many references to God's "name," "reign," "throne," "greatness," "holiness." Although these are one stage removed from any of the objected-to biblical references to parts of God's "body," they nevertheless still direct our emotions toward a conception of God that gives Him the trappings of monarchy, with the references to His "name" completing the image of personalized authority.

כְּבוֹדוֹ אִהֵל
Tentlike He Stretched Out the Sky

This prayer represents another *yotzer* composition from the pen of Eleazar Kallir. Poems of this genre, written for recitation before the section *Ve-ha-ofanim ve-chayyot ha-kodesh*, are accordingly called by the name *ofan*. It follows the alphabetical acrostic form, and opens with the word *kevodo* in order to provide a contextually smooth link with the last word of the prayer into which it has been inserted (even though this tends to obscure the fact that it is the following word, *iheil*, that opens the acrostic with its initial letter, *alef*).

The reference to God stretching out the sky "this day" is in conformity with the opinion of R. Eliezer in the Talmud[36] that the world was created on Rosh Hashanah. The word *be-rachamin* ("in mercy") emphasizes the rabbinic view that God's original intention was to create a universe ruled by the inflexible canons of strict justice. Man would have been regimented in the code of moral discipline and ethical behavior to which he would have had to conform. The noble challenge of free will would have had little place in such a system; but, on the other hand, sin would have been reduced to a minimum.

That God commenced Creation with this approach is inferred by our Rabbis from the exclusive use of the divine name *Elokim* (denoting "God of strict justice") in the first chapter of Genesis. God revised His scheme, however, and made the quality of mercy (*rachamim*) an equal partner, a fact that underlies the employment of the conjoint names *Adonai* (God of mercy) and *Elokim* in the second chapter of the creation story. Rosh Hashanah is, consequently, also the anniversary of the genesis of the quality of divine mercy, a fact that gives the author confidence that this will be extended to Israel on this day.

The phrase *mei-etmol kidamnukha* ("From yesterday began our petition to beseech you") refers to the ancient practice of fasting on the eve of Rosh Hashanah[37] during the *Selichot* period, and, generally, on as many days as possible during the month of *Elul*.[38]

The poet invokes the merit of the patriarchs in order to secure mercy for Israel. This is in line with the popular concept of *Zekhut Avot*, the origin of which is to be found in the Torah itself, where Moses invoked the merit of Abraham, Isaac, and Jacob in order to persuade God to have mercy on their sinful descendants after they worshiped the Golden Calf.[39] In this context, Kallir refers to Isaac, obliquely, as "the one for whom the King's valiant angels shed bitter tears" (*Lemar bakhu erelei melekh*). This is an allusion to the midrashic tradition[40] that, as Isaac lay bound on the altar, the heavenly angels shed tears at his impending doom. His impaired sight[41] is explained as having been caused by some of those heavenly tears that dropped onto Isaac's eyes.[42] (For further commentary on this composition, see Second Day, p. 109.)

וְהַחַיּוֹת יְשׁוֹרֵרוּ
The *Chayyot* Sing

This mystical passage names the five main sections of the heavenly angelic choir, depicted as lustily singing the praise of God. It was recited only in the Polish rite, and is a slightly expanded version of the formula recited on weekdays and Sabbaths that refers to only three angelic categories. These various categories are derived from Ezekiel's famous vision of the heavenly throne and divine chariot, supported by four bizarre beasts (*chayyot*) in human form, each with four faces and four wings.[43] The prophet also describes another weird creature that served as the wheels (*ofanim*) of the vehicular throne. As a counterpart to the cherubim (*keruvim*) that protected the Ark in the desert sanctuary and in Solomon's Temple, there are also heavenly cherubim that play such an active role that God is frequently referred to in the Bible as "He who sits enthroned upon the cherubim."[44]

Also referred to here are *serafim*, which figure in Isaiah's mystic vision of the heavenly court.[45] Rather than constituting the essence of the divine chariot, the *serafim* are probably its guardians.

The nature of the last category, the *arelim*, is even more obscure. The name occurs only once in the Bible, in Isaiah 33:7, where they are described as "angels of peace." From a talmudic passage[46] it would seem that they were regarded as the angels sent to seize the soul of man and transport it back to its source when the moment of death arrives. This idea might well have been inspired by Isaiah's reference to them, which was reinterpreted in the sense of "angels conferring *everlasting* peace."

Again, the modern mind might recoil at the inclusion of such fantastic elements of folklore in our sacred liturgy. It is apposite to point out, therefore, that such ideas do not owe their origin to mainstream rabbinism. Indeed, Judah Ha-Nasi, author of the Mishnah, ruthlessly excluded nearly all mystical material of this kind from his pioneering Code of Jewish law and religion.

Mystical speculation regarding the Creation (*Maaseh Bereishit*) and the heavenly Chariot (*Maaseh Merkavah*) was indulged in, especially in the Essene circles whose literature was discovered at Qumran, as well as among early Pharisaic circles in the last few centuries before the Common Era. While normative Judaism fought hard to ensure that angelology was never allowed to form the basis of a cult, it must be admitted that the existence of angels was widely believed in, by scholars and laymen alike, in talmudic times (first through sixth centuries C.E.). Their existence, it was considered, only served to enhance the sense of *mysterium tremendum*, the awful mystery, that surrounds God's majesty,[47] and it was with that objective in mind that mystical references and hymns were introduced into the liturgy. Rudolph Otto terms such hymns "numinous," by which he means irrational glorifications of God, whose sole purpose is to attempt to reproduce in words a formula that is calculated to induce emotionally an ecstatic state from which must automatically flow a keen sense of great *mysterium*[48] (see p. 204).

Such references—whether to God's robes or to this strange living Chariot—are not, therefore, to be read literally. They are but stimuli to a religious experience, without which prayer is a meaningless exercise.

The Repetition of the *Amidah* by the *Chazan*

The original, and main, role of the *chazan* was to lead the congregation in a verse by verse recitation of the *Shema*, as well as to repeat the *Amidah* aloud for the benefit of those members of the congregation who were illiterate or who could not memorize it. They would recite it, word for word, together with him, with the addition of the *Kedushah*. It seems that the rest of the service—apart from the Reading of the Torah—used to be chanted, word for word in unison, by the congregation from a seated position, with no one acting as a leader. (The Sephardim today chant the whole service in unison.) Apart from the leaders, elders, and sages of the community, who sat on benches or in special seats of honor, the rest of the congregation sat in rows, on rugs, on the floor behind the *bimah*. The *bimah* was used exclusively for the reading of the Torah, and the *chazan* recited the repetition of the *Amidah* from a stand behind the *bimah*.[49]

At a later period both the *chazan* and the congregation moved forward toward the front of the synagogue; and it was from there, before the Ark, that the *chazan* stood to repeat the *Amidah*. As synagogues grew larger, and it became impossible for those at the back to hear the *chazan*, it became the practice for him to pray from the *bimah*, and, with the development of liturgical compositions, to take a dominant role as leader of the whole service, not merely the repetition of the *Amidah*.

פְּתִיחָה
Opening of the Ark

In the practice of opening the Ark for particular compositions we again enter an area where considerable license was exercised throughout the centuries. Originally the Ark was opened during the course of a service only in order to take out the Torah scroll. This has remained the practice in all other rites except that of the Ashkenazim who, at a very early period, employed the practice of opening the Ark for particularly favored compositions, in order to stress their importance and to stimulate a greater degree of concentration during their recitation.

In Franco-Germany, in the thirteenth century, some communities adopted the custom of opening the Ark for the whole of the repetition of the *Shacharit* and *Musaf Amidahs*, closing it only for *Kedushah* and the Priestly Benediction. This did not win universal acceptance since many authorities preferred to open the Ark at intervals in order to highlight specific compositions. This had the added advantage of enabling the sacred honors to be distributed more widely among the members of the congregation. It was probably that consideration that accounted for the many compositions for which we, quite unaccountably, stand and honor with a *petichah*.

מִסּוֹד חֲכָמִים וּנְבוֹנִים
From the Counsel of the Wise and Understanding

One of the problems confronting the composers of *piyyut* was the fact that, from the halakhic point of view, some authorities were uneasy about introducing interruptions into the standard *Amidah*.[50] Because of this it became customary for the *chazan* to commence the repetition by seeking the permission of the congregation for such a poetic interruption. This is the purpose of this particular recurring composition, which is categorized as a *reshut* ("permission").

Its author is unknown. It is basically an assertion that whatever is being added by way of *piyyut* is strictly traditional, having been derived from "the company of wise men and sages" (*mi-sod chakhamim u-nevonim*), that is, from the authentic rabbinic tradition, not the author's independent ideas or interpretations. In an age when people were also most sensitive to the inroads of sectarianism, such as the Karaite heresy, it was probably also felt necessary to allay the fears of the community—especially where texts were unavailable for examination and control—and to assure them that any poetic innovations were strictly in line with Orthodox ideology.

יָרֵאתִי בִּפְצוֹתִי
Trembling, I Now Pour Forth My Prayer

Just as Aaron had first to seek atonement "for himself" before he could act as intercessor for "the whole assembly of Israel" (Exodus 16:17), so the Reader tremblingly (*yareitiy*) asks for divine mercy and indulgence as he presumes to embark upon this sacred responsibility, although keenly aware of his own spiritual shortcomings. This type of Reader's personal meditation is an essential part of the *reshut*.

The poet Yekutiel bar Mosheh of Speyer (eleventh century) skillfully conveys the *chazan*'s prevailing sense of awe by ending each phrase with the syllable *chil*, the common Hebrew word for "trembling." This was doubly appropriate, as this *reshut* was written to serve as an introduction to the following composition by Kallir, which opens with the phrase *At chil*.

Yareitiy is constructed as a name-acrostic: *Yekutiel bar Mosheh,* followed by the plea, *chazak ve-ematz yechiy* ("May he be strong and of good courage; may he live").

אָת חִיל
The Terrible Day of Visitation Is Come

In this alphabetical acrostic, Kallir alludes to a midrashic idea that it was Abraham, through his plea for mercy on behalf of the Sodomites ("Shall not the judge of the whole earth deal justly?"),[51] who convinced God that strict justice, untempered by mercy, could not possibly serve as a principle upon which to base the world—"If You want a world, then, Lord, there can be no absolute law; and if You insist upon absolute law, then there can be no world."[52]

The poet asserts that "this will be remembered at judgment," to Israel's credit, in recognition of that great patriarch. Kallir alludes to the midrashic idea that God wished to create Abraham even before Adam, on account of the former's unique spiritual attainment. His decision to send Abraham only after twenty generations was in order that he might repair the widespread moral damage inflicted upon the world by the wicked generations before him. Had they followed Abraham, no one could have achieved that.[53]

The birth of a child to Abraham and Sarah, which took place on Rosh Hashanah,[54] is regarded as a good omen for their offspring, so that this "day of visitation" will ever be propitious for divine mercy.

The final reference to the "ashes" of Isaac is based upon a very obscure midrashic tradition that Isaac was actually killed on the altar, and his ashes strewn across Mount Moriah. God then brought dew, commingled it with the ashes and brought Isaac back to life.

זָכְרֵנוּ לַחַיִּים
Remember Us unto Life

Remember us unto life, O King who delights in life, and inscribe us in the book of life, for Your own sake, O God of life.

This line is interpolated into the first blessing of every *Amidah* recited throughout the Ten Days of Penitence. The opening word, *Zokhreinu* ("Remember us"), was consciously employed in order to serve as a link with the similar phrase, found in the basic formula of the first blessing of the *Amidah: Ve-zokheir chasdei avot* ("And *remembers* the piety of the patriarchs"). The plea, therefore, is that, when "remembering" the merit of the fathers, God will, in appreciation, grant the blessing of life to their children.

The image of the "book of life" is found in the Talmud,[55] which depicts God as opening three records. One contains the names of the wholly righteous, the second those who are indubitably wicked, and the third book contains the names of the average person. The righteous are immediately inscribed for blessing and life; the wicked for punishment and death. The fate of Mr. Average, however, is held over from Rosh Hashanah until Yom Kippur, to give him a chance to tip the scale in his favor.

It has been asked why we are permitted to recite such a plea as "Remember us to life," when we know that it is in the nature of things that man must pass away, and the time must arrive when such a prayer simply cannot be responded to! We are not permitted to utter a *tefillat shav*, a vain prayer. Why, then, is this formulation permitted?

The answer must be that a prayer for life, even that uttered by a dying man with his last gasp, can never be considered a vain prayer. A *tefillat shav* is an *illogical* prayer, such as a prayer that something that has already occurred should be as if it had not occurred. The talmudic definition of this is the prayer of a man approaching the street where he lives, and, hearing the sound of a tumult (an ambulance or police siren), prays to God, "May the crisis not be in *my* home!"[56] The truth is that a crisis has already occurred and it cannot be reversed. If it is *not* in his home, he does not need to pray; if it *is* in his home, then his prayer cannot reverse a reality.

A vain prayer is also a petition for vain objectives, for material things that are transient and that will not enrich our lives by bringing lasting benefit. But *life* is quite different. It is God's greatest and most unique gift, offering unbounded potential and opportunity for personal spiritual development. God may well have determined to draw particular lives to a close during this coming year, but it cannot be in vain for us to seek to reverse that "evil decree." We do so rather boldly, by implying that it is in *God's* interest to grant us an extension of life. The *Zokhreinu la-chayyim* line ends with the assertion that it is *Lemaankha Elokim chayyim*—"for Thine own sake O Living God." In other words, we affirm that we promise to use that extension of life—if that is what it is in effect—for deepening our relationship with God and for propagating His will among our fellow men. A life of such quality is a life lived *lishmah*, "for God's sake." We are entitled to assume therefore—and pray—that He will not ignore such sincere and altruistic resolve. Indeed, as long as such a prayer is sincere, it must surely be appropriate, and well worth enunciating.

Another suggested answer is to point to the fact that the *Zokhreinu* prayer is couched in the plural, so that it goes beyond the issue of personal mortality and seeks heavenly guidance and inspiration for the continued life and vitality of the Jewish community in general, and for the particular congregations of which the petitioners are members. Viewed accordingly, it partakes of the genre of the *Mi sheberakh*, prayer for the congregation, that we recite each *Shabbat* after the *Yekum Porkan* compositions.

A different approach takes account of the fact that the Hebrew word for "life" is *chayyim*, a plural word. For the Jew, the totality of life is not the restricted period that we spend in this world, but must also encompass the other "life," the one that lasts for all eternity. Like an investment policy, to which we contribute for years in order eventually to realize a happy and secure future, so in the spiritual realm we likewise have to contribute and build up a substantial capital while on earth in order to secure the eternal benefits in the hereafter. Thus, the plea "Remember us *to life*" may also be construed as referring to the "life eternal" that our repentance secures for us. Viewed in this light, not only is our original problem removed, but indeed the *Zokhreinu* plea then becomes even more relevant during that fateful year when God terminates our existence on earth.

תַּאֲלַת זוּ
Desiring to Ease the Tribulations of the People

This composition by Kallir follows a reverse-acrostic structure, commencing with the last letter of the alphabet, *tav*, and ending with *alef*.

The poet departs from the general view regarding the origin of prayer, that it began as a spontaneous *cri de coeur* as mortal man sensed his desperate need for God's help in time of crisis. It is suggested in the opening line of this poem that the ability to pray, and the recognition of its power as well as its psychological benefit, was a definite gift conferred by God upon man.[57]

Reference is made to the nine blessings that constitute the *Musaf Amidah* on Rosh Hashanah and the idea[58] that this number corresponds to the nine invocations of the divine name in the prayer of Hannah (1 Samuel, chap. 2). This concept contains within it a veritable psychology of prayer. As we stand before God at this time we need to appreciate how desperately alone and vulnerable we are without God's guidance and blessings, and how nothing is irrevocable—not even Hannah's barrenness—if we pray sincerely enough. The urgency of Hannah's prayer, and the faith infusing her thanksgiving, are models to which we should aspire.

מִי כָמוֹךָ
Who Is Like You?

> Who is like You, O merciful father, who in mercy remembers Your creatures for life.

As in the case of the previous interpolation into the first blessing of the *Amidah*, so we have a similar sentiment prescribed for insertion into the second blessing of the *Amidah* throughout the Ten Days of Penitence.

Prayer has been described as "the expression of a primitive impulsion to a higher, richer, intenser life . . . a great longing for life, for a more potent, a purer, a more blessed life."[59] If, indeed, this is the prime motivation of prayer, then the High Holy Day liturgy is prayer in its most realistic and instinctive form. Not only the content but the whole spirit of the liturgy focuses the attention and concentration of the worshiper upon an evaluation of life in general and his own existential situation in particular.

These insertions into the first two (and, similarly, those of the last two) blessings of the *Amidah* express, most directly, our passionate longing for life, by which we mean not mere existence, but a life "for Your own sake,

O God of Life." Franz Kafka,[60] animated by a keen sensitivity toward the spirit of Judaism, made an apposite and penetrating observation, that "we are not sinful merely because we have eaten of the Tree of Knowledge, but primarily because we have *not* yet eaten of the Tree of Life." This is one of the fundamental teachings of the Jewish High Holy Day liturgy.

Again, the opening phrase, *miy khamokha*, is consciously employed in order to link it to the same phrase as contained in the basic formulation of the blessing: *miy khamokha baal gevurot*.

אַתָּה הוּא אֱלֹהֵינוּ
You Are Our God

An alphabetical acrostic devoted entirely to listing various divine attributes culled from the Bible, predominantly from the books of Isaiah and Psalms. Only two of the attributes are post-biblical: the description of God as *Chay Olamim* ("One who lives forever") is talmudic,[61] and the expression *Sitro yosher*, whose meaning is unclear, is not found elsewhere. Birnbaum avoids the problem by translating it merely as "He is invisible." Routledge has the rather enigmatic rendering, "His secret is rectitude," while De Sola has "His veil is rectitude." A more probable rendering is "His secrecy is justifiable," though D. Goldschmidt[62] believes that a textual error has occurred here, and that we should read *Sitro choshekh*, "His secret place is in obscurity," a phrase found in Psalm 18:12.

אַדֶּרֶת מַמְלָכָה
Your Glorious Kingdom

This prayer is another *piyyut* from the pen of Kallir, constructed out of the name-acrostic *Eleazar biribi Kilir*. It comprises five stanzas, each stanza containing three lines, with each line divided into three phrases, each of two (sometimes three) words. Each stanza concludes with the word *melukhah*, "kingdom."

The poem is introduced by, and signs off with, the refrain *tair ve-taria*, the first half of which is based upon Isaiah's spiritual war-cry: "The Lord goes forth like a warrior, he will rouse the frenzy of battle [*yair*]; he will shout [*yaria*] . . . and triumph over his foes."[63] This refrain encapsulates the theme of the whole composition in which the poet complains bitterly at the havoc wrought by the Roman conquerors in the holy land, and the fact that their haughty rule has extended for so long a period. He ends on a note of confidence that the one whose rule is exalted above that of any earthly monarch will presently restore independence to Israel.

אֵם אֲשֶׁר בְּצֶדֶק
Mother Who Has Grown Old in the Practice of Goodness

This composition is a poetic retelling of the story of the birth of Isaac, with special emphasis upon the biological miracle of a woman of ninety years being enabled to suckle her child.

The opening phrase, describing Sarah as "a mother who grew old in righteousness," is based upon the midrashic tradition that at the age of one hundred Sarah was as free of sin as she was at twenty.[64]

Sarah is supposed to have conceived on Rosh Hashanah, as did Rachel and Hannah.[65] Hence the reference in the final stanza to "the three barren women who were visited [with child] on this day." The poet, in his reference to Sarah's conception, emphasizes that it was "her Creator (*gochakh*) who visited her." This emphasis, based upon the actual biblical phrase, "And *the Lord* visited Sarah as he had said,"[66] seems, according to the Midrash, to be playing down the role of her husband in this happy enterprise! This inspired the comment of R. Judah b. Simon that "although Rav Huna has asserted that there is an angel specifically responsible for (generating) sexual passion, Sarah had no need of such things; for God in His glory visited Sarah."[67]

אַאֲפִּיד נֶזֶר אָיוֹם
To Him Who Is Feared, a Crown Will I Bring

This poem by Kallir follows a double alphabetical acrostic pattern, in that both the first and third words of each line commence with the same letter. It was composed as an introduction to the *Kedushah,* with which theme it is interconnected, and reference to which is made in both the opening and closing lines. There are also several references to categories of angels—*chayyot, serafim, peliim* ("nameless angels")[68]—which provides a further link with the *Kedushah,* which describes the praise of God uttered by the angelic choir. The structure of each phrase, with precisely *three* words, is similarly no coincidence, but is intended to highlight the threefold formula of sanctification: "Holy, Holy, Holy. . . ."

אֶתֵּן לְפוֹעֲלִי צֶדֶק
The Justice of My Creator I Will Praise

This poem was composed by Simeon bar Isaac (see pp. 107–108). The alphabetical acrostic pattern is followed by the name acrostic: *Shimon bar Yitzchak chazak*.

The poem is introduced by two lines (*yishpot teiveil . . . ve-hu ve-echad . . .*) that were intended to be employed, alternately, as refrains to each line. Because of the monotony of such unnecessary repetition, which in this instance does not enhance either the thematic or the metric quality, the refrains were omitted, with the first refrain (only) being repeated at the end of the poem to serve as a conclusion.

The poem opens with a phrase from Job 36:3. The biblical author of this title-verse is actually Elihu, one of Job's three friends, who attempts to justify the suffering God has brought upon Job ("The justice of my creator I will praise") by suggesting to him that suffering is a warning against sin, and that when the warning is taken to heart, the victims are always restored to well-being.

Most of the lines of this poem are direct borrowings of biblical verses, though the word order is frequently rearranged, with some words varied or omitted, in order to conform to the metric and acrostic structure.

The poet points out the unique synthesis of majesty and modesty that characterizes the divine attributes:

Supreme in strength, enthroned upon His height;
Yet mild is He, according to His might.

Although the Almighty controls the workings and destiny of the great cosmos, He attends, with equal concern, to the plight of the widow and orphan.

The poet refers to the talmudic idea that while God judges the whole world on this day yet He calls Israel before Him first. The reason for this is in order that He might be well disposed to the people of Israel while He is still in good humor, before His review of the wickedness of the nations provokes Him to anger.[69] Another reason is that the merit of Israel may also secure mercy for all mankind, in fulfillment of the universalistic promise to Abraham: "And in thee shall all the families of the earth be blessed."[70]

יְיָ מֶלֶךְ יְיָ מָלָךְ
The Lord Is King, the Lord Was King . . .

This composition was also written by Kallir in order to provide a poetic and mystic setting for the *Kedushah*. The *Kedushah* opens with the statement that "We [Israel] will sanctify God's name on earth just as they [the angels] sanctify it in the highest heavens." Kallir is inspired by this vision of Israel as an angelic counterpart; and in this composition he fuses together the attributes of both, making it difficult, at times, to ascertain whether he is referring to the angels or to Israel.

The poetic and metric links with the *Kedushah* are subtly contrived. The core of the *Kedushah* is the triple-evocation *kadosh kadosh kadosh.* Kallir keeps this threefold emphasis in the forefront. Hence his major refrain, *Adonai melekh, Adonai malakh, Adonai yimlokh le-olam va-ed,* is also a triple evocation, which Kallir has culled from three independent biblical phrases, and combined into one verse. (Kallir's composite verse is also employed in the *Yehiy khevod* prayer, recited each morning.)

The triple formulation, inspired by the *Kedushah,* also infiltrates the meter of this composition, providing three-lined stanzas with each line contributing (before the word *ve-kol*) a three-word phrase bearing three equal stresses. In addition, each line boasts a rhythmic alliteration established by a threefold alphabetical acrostic (*Ḡibborei ḡovah yaḡbiyru . . .*).

The different verbs employed in each line are ingeniously wrought synonyms, all conveying a particular nuance of the idea of "praising," "exalting." The word *ve-kol* ("with a loud voice"), which climaxes each phrase, is a further link with the *Kedushah,* which contains the phrase *az bekol;* and the opening word *addiyrei* also links up with another *Kedushah* phrase, *addir vechazak.* It will be noticed that Kallir was not concerned about replacing the letter *samech* with the like-sounding letter *sin.*

וּבְכֵן לְךָ הַכֹּל יַכְתִּירוּ
And Now Let All Acclaim Your Sovereignty

This composition is recited in the *Shacharit Amidah* on the first day, though its recitation is moved to *Musaf* on the second day. This practice might have arisen in order to do justice to both opinions in a talmudic dispute[71] as to the exact time of the day when God judges the world: whether early at *Shacharit* time, or a little later, at *Musaf.* By varying the time of its recitation we ensure that our minds are solemnly directed to the awesome process of judgment, and that we are in the appropriate mood, at the precise moment at which it is being enacted.

The introductory heading of the composition is omitted in a number of early manuscripts. Others have an alternative heading: *U-ve-khein dayyan emet attah* ("Indeed, you are a true judge").

The composition describes, in alphabetical acrostic form, the judicial qualities of God that prompt Him to allow His mercy to vanquish His wrath when sitting in judgment (*ba-din*) on the Day of Judgment (*be-yom din*).

וּבְכֵן תֵּן פַּחְדְּךָ
And Now Impose Your Awe

This composition preaches a universalistic message of the messianic era when fear of God will penetrate the hearts of all men and weld them into "a single band." This universal recognition of God will bring with it the acceptance, on the part of the other nations, of the primacy and uniqueness of Israel's spiritual heritage. The concomitant of this will be a heightened respect for Israel, as alluded to in the next paragraph: "And therefore, O Lord, give glory to Your people."

The origin of this prayer is disputed, as well as its specific purpose in the context of the third (*Kedushat Ha-Shem*) blessing of the *Amidah*. Its universalistic theme has suggested to some scholars that it was originally composed as an introduction to the *Malkhuyot* section of the *Musaf Amidah*, which treats of this specific theme.

Although our *Malkhuyot* section is introduced into the fourth blessing of the *Amidah* and the introduction we employ is the famous composition of Rav (later prescribed to be recited three times daily as the second paragraph of the *Aleinu*), the Mishnah[72] refers to the view of R. Jochanan ben Nuri that the *Malkhuyot* should be recited in the *third* blessing. The *U-ve-khein tein pachdekha* might well have been R. Jochanan's original introductory prayer that was retained in this blessing even though the verses of the *Malkhuyot*, which originally accompanied it, were later assigned to the following blessing.

It will be observed that this and the following two paragraphs are all introduced by the word *U-ve-khein*. A popular explanation relates this to the occurrence of this word in the book of Esther—*U-ve-khein avo el ha-melekh*—"and *then* (i.e., after my fasting and praying) I shall go to the king."[73] The analogy is clear: the way to win proximity to the divine King is to undertake the sincere approach, and the spiritual preparations of prayer and fasting, adopted by Queen Esther.

Notwithstanding this liturgical homily, a no less authoritative version, current throughout Franco-German communities, began the third paragraph not with the words *U-ve-khein tzaddikim* but with *Ve-az tzaddikim*. This suggests that our consistent version was, in fact, a later attempt at literary uniformity.

וּבְכֵן תֵּן כָּבוֹד
And So, O Lord, Grant Honor to Your People

The previous paragraph petitioned God to send "awe" (*pachdekha*) upon *all His creatures*. In this paragraph we move from the universal to the particular, and ask Him to send "honor" (*kavod*) to *His people, Israel*.

There seems to be a profound admission here that Israel is only destined to receive honor, or consideration, from the other nations in a situation where the latter are cowed into a posture of "awe" for Israel and for what she achieves through divine guidance, protection, and blessing.

The particular *kavod* that Israel has sought is not some vague token feelings of admiration for having been history's spiritual pioneers, but rather the very real, tangible and practical demonstration of *kavod*, by ensuring that we can enjoy *simchah le-artzekha ve-sason le-irekha*, "gladness in Your land and joy in Your [holy] city." Indeed, *kavod* in the Bible has the regular meaning of "material possessions," "abundance,"[74] in addition to its usual sense of "honor" and "glory." And that tangible *kavod* has certainly been won by our people, as a result of the countless and heroic sacrifices made in the cause of regaining and retaining our precious State of Israel.

And how accurate is the particular sequence here described. First comes *pachdekha*, the sending of "*Awe* upon all God's creatures"—the awe that attended the disclosures of the Holocaust and the extent of man's inhumanity to man, as well as the awe of a world war, with countless millions of young lives vainly sacrificed—followed, shortly afterward, by the attainment of the prized *kavod* of an independent state for the Jewish people!

But, for the authors of our *machzor*, the sequence of events does not end with the establishment of a homeland. Indeed, the inevitable challenge that flows from that is enunciated in the next paragraph, *U-ve-khein tzaddikim*. From here we learn that the type of society shaped by a Jewish state must be one wherein

> the righteous will see and be glad, the upright will exult, and the devout will shout for joy; iniquity's mouth will be shut and all wickedness will evaporate like smoke.

The denouement of such a spiritual consummation is the subject of the final two paragraphs of this blessing of the *Amidah*, namely (*Ve-timlokh attah Ha-Shem levadekha*), the situation wherein "You, God, rule alone over all Your works, on Mount Zion, Your glorious residence, and in Jerusalem, Your holy city," and where (*Kadosh attah*) the holiness of God and the reverence for His Name will be universally acclaimed under the potent and all-pervasive influence of Zion, the Torah that emanates from her, and the religion that is practiced within her.

But, however impressed, even overawed, we might be with the spirituality of Zion and Jerusalem, and the vast number of her institutions of learning, to which tens of thousands of students are drawn from all over the world, yet we would have to admit that that ultimate stage—referred to in the final two paragraphs—of God's sovereignty being acknowledged universally in Israel, is still a long way off. For Rabbi Barukh Halevi Epstein, however, the delay in achieving this is not unexpected. It is alluded to, in fact, in the phrase, quoted above, *simchah le-artzekha va-sason le-irekha* ("gladness in Your land and joy in Your [holy] city").

Rabbi Epstein comments on why the word *simchah* is used to describe the pleasure of enjoying the land of Israel, whereas *sason* is the term used to describe the spiritual joy of a full return to, and identification with, the holiness intrinsic in the city of Jerusalem. He tells us that the word *simchah* connotes the immediate satisfaction that is felt when one senses that one has commenced the initial stages of the attainment of a long-desired objective. *Sason*, on the other hand, is the far more intense and complete form of joy and fulfillment that comes with the knowledge that one has arrived at total attainment and completion of that objective.

This distinction is referred to in the Sabbath morning hymn, *El Adon*, where the phrase *semeichim be-tzeitam ve-sasim be-voam* occurs. This is a reference to the "satisfaction [*simchah*] when one sets out [to perform a religious or meritorious act] and the joyful fulfillment [*sason*] when one returns [from having fully completed it]."

Now, the gathering in of our exiles to the State of Israel is, in effect, only the first stage in the challenge of Jewish destiny. Hence the appropriate term of *simchah* ("initial satisfaction") is employed, in the context of *simchah le-artzekha*, the satisfaction of the *physical return* "to Your land." When looking forward, however, to the ultimate stage of *spiritual achievement*—the return to that state that is symbolized by the holiness of the city of Jerusalem—then it is the potency of *sason* that is highlighted, in the phrase *sason le-irekha*.[75]

For the while, let us bask in the *simchah*. The *sason* is assuredly on its way!

קָדוֹשׁ אַתָּה
You Are Holy

This paragraph, which leads into the closing benediction of the third blessing of the *Amidah*, was the original formula of this blessing (though probably without the accompanying biblical quotation, introduced by the phrase *kakkatuv*) according to the ancient Palestinian rite. In Babylon this was varied, with the opening words being transposed to read *Attah kadosh*. . . .

Throughout the Ten Days of Penitence the concluding formula of this blessing—*ha-El ha-kadosh*—is replaced by *ha-melekh ha-kadosh*, in order to emphasize the kingship of God.

The biblical basis for the concept of God as "holy" is the verse, *Kedoshim tiheyu kiy kadosh ani Ha-Shem Elokeikhem*, "You shall be holy, for I, the Lord your God, am holy" (Leviticus 19:2).

Not only is this summons to *imitatio dei* highly problematic—as if it were an easy thing for mortals to absorb the attributes of God!—but this designation of God as "holy" does not in essence add very much to, or clarify to any significant degree, any aspect of the nature of God. For, if the verse is suggesting that holiness is something we should strive after (and how else *can* it be achieved?), as a kind of self-purifying exercise that will help us along the route to proximity to God ("For I the Lord am holy"), then it cannot possibly represent the totality of the ideal (namely, God's holiness) toward which we are meant to be striving! So the biblical inference is clearly a non sequitur! Indeed, the logical inference from that line of reasoning would be that such an attribute of "holiness" is, in fact, wholly inappropriate when applied to God, since holiness, we have concluded, is merely and exclusively a *human* state or attribute of "preparedness" for proximity with the unknowable and indefinable deity. The latter, on the other hand, cannot possibly be endowed with an attribute that is merely "a stage toward," and consequently incomplete and imperfect in itself!

So, if we take this verse at its face value, then it is either telling us that (human) *striving after* holiness is tantamount to the totality of the divine attribute of holiness—which cannot possibly be the case!—or that the holiness of God is a highly restricted form of holiness, which leaves us totally in the dark once again as to precisely what the nature of divine holiness is. Either way, the instruction to emulate God's holiness is most problematic!

It was possibly this difficulty in defining the attribute of holiness when applied to God—and by the above verse-analogy to man—that prompted the talmudic sages to interpret *holiness* in its most basic, concrete, and literal sense, as derived from the core-meaning of the verb *kadash* in all the Semitic languages. Its primary meaning is "to be set apart, separate," and this may be either for a sinful purpose—hence the biblical words *kadesh* and *kedeishah* for a male and female prostitute—or for a life of *spiritual separateness,* and hence the other meaning of *kadosh,* "holy, consecrated." Hence the talmudic explanation of the phrase *Kedoshim tiheyu* as "*Be separate*—from immorality and other forms of sin."

This explanation helps to overcome, albeit partially, our original problem of how the biblical verse could possibly equate the holiness of God with that of Israel, by offering God's holiness as the rationale of the instruction to Israel to "be holy." The answer is that the verse is merely alluding to one basic facet of God's nature, namely His being totally "set apart" and unique. Israel is asked, therefore, to borrow that element of uniqueness and separateness on the moral, ethical, and religious plane, and to refrain from indulging in the heartless and gross practices of the surrounding nations.

Thus, the holiness of God and the holiness of Israel cannot be equated; but the talmudic interpretation of "holiness" does bring us a little closer to the creation of some conceptual bridge linking the two parts of that biblical verse.

Nachmanides (1194–1270) is unhappy with viewing the biblical verse as requiring a "holiness" that involves no more than *separateness* from sin. He prefers to view it as a far greater challenge, approximating more closely to the generally understood sense and usage of the term *kadosh* and *kedushah* (sanctity). He understands *Kedoshim tiheyu* as a biblical clarion call to Jews to inject a dimension of "sanctity"—which he understands as temperance, discipline, and moderation—into their normal and permitted physical and bodily appetites and activities. Thus, although the Torah permits one freely to have intercourse with one's wife, yet, for Nachmanides, "holiness" requires that one should not make unnaturally excessive sexual demands on her. Again, although Torah permits one to take many wives, yet *kedushah* would militate against this. Furthermore, while it is not against the letter of the Torah to eat like a glutton or to make oneself drunk, yet *kedushah*—as demanded by our biblical verse—urges one to eschew such behavior as being singularly inappropriate for a people seeking grace and favor in the eyes of God.[76]

So are we any nearer to understanding the implication of the opening phrase in our prayer, *Kadosh Attah*, "You are *holy*"? Probably not! But let us not forget that the greatest Jewish philosopher, Moses Maimonides (1135–1204), affirms the doctrine of "negative attributes," namely, that the only thing we can say about God is what He is *not*. We can refine our gross conceptions thereby, but we cannot get an iota closer to affirming anything positive about His real nature or state of being. This, of course, makes the biblical verse we have been struggling to clarify even more baffling; for how can it even attempt, in the realm of a recommendation toward positive action or holy status, to draw any possible analogy between man and God?

The problem remains. And what we all mean, or are meant to understand, by our particular praise, "You are holy," is unclear and mysterious. "You are infinitely different," "You are separate and detached," may well approximate what *kadosh attah* literally means. But we sense instinctively that that is the very opposite of the immanent relationship with his God that the man of faith believes himself to be part of. We know that the verse is recommending some form of human *imitatio* of the attributes and ways of God, in keeping with man's creation "in the image of God." It is when we seek to define those shared attributes that we come unstuck!

אַתָּה בְחַרְתָּנוּ
You Have Chosen Us

With the words *Attah vechartanu* we commence the middle blessing of the seven blessings of the *Amidah* recited on all festivals. This is referred to in the Talmud as *Kedushat Ha-Yom* ("Sanctification of the day"), as it contains references to the special quality of holiness with which the festival days are invested. The form of this blessing as it appears in the *Musaf Amidah* for Yom Kippur[77] is the most expansive because of the fact that the account of the ancient Temple service (*Avodah*) and the *selichot* were inserted into it.

The actual mention of the holiness of the particular (named) festival only comes in the following paragraph, *va-titein lanu* ("And you gave to us"). The purpose of *Attah vechartanu* is to serve as an introduction, by establishing from the outset why Israel merited to be the recipients of those precious holy days. It was a loving privilege conferred upon Israel because of her willingness to aspire toward spiritual "exaltedness above all tongues," in order to become a receptacle of holiness through the fulfillment of God's *mitzvot*.

The *Attah vechartanu* blessing is couched in the second person. The same blessing, though framed in the third person—*asher bachar banu mi-kol am* ("who has chosen us")—is employed as the evening *Kiddush* blessing for all festivals. A contracted version of it is also used as the blessing recited before the Reading of the Law (*asher bachar banu mi-kol ha-amim*).

This composition is reproduced almost verbatim in the *Attah yatzarta* prayer, recited on *Shabbat Rosh Chodesh* in the repetition of the *Musaf Amidah*.

Yaaleh Ve-Yavo

This is probably the most well known of the prayers for special occasions, being inserted into all the *Amidahs* (with the exception of *Musaf*) that are recited on all the major holy days, including *Rosh Chodesh*. It is also inserted into the Grace After Meals on those occasions.

It is a uniquely concise prayer, employing a succession of eight verbs to express the basic theme of "remembrance." It pleads for God to remember Israel, the merit of her forefathers, the promise of a redeemer in the form of the Messiah, son of David, and Jerusalem the holy city. The prayer seeks the assurance that all these precious symbols may be permitted to "rise, enter, reach (the divine presence), find sympathy, be graciously accepted, heard, visited, and remembered."

The "remembrance" is, naturally, a forerunner to national deliverance, and the composition actually employs the term no less than five times. Some commentators believe that this is based on the paradigm of Numbers 8:19, wherein the term *Israel* is repeated five times in order to signify the warmest degree of endearment. They adduce, by way of illustration, the analogy of a king who, in seeking information of the royal nanny regarding his only infant son, asks proudly, "Did *my son* sleep well? Did *my son* eat his food? Did *my son* go to school? and so on.

The relevance to the festivals of the *Yaaleh ve-yavo* prayer, and its motif of remembrance, is based upon the biblical verse, "And on the day of your gladness, and on your festivals, and in your new moons . . . they shall be for you as *an occasion for remembrance* before the Lord your God" (Numbers 10:10). On the High Holy Days, themselves specifically designated as *Yom Ha-Zikkaron*, "Day of Remembrance," this prayer is therefore particularly apt. Indeed, the eighth century Gaon, Paltoi, believed that *Yaaleh ve-yavo* was originally composed for the *Zikhronot*, the special "Remembrance" section, of the Rosh Hashanah *Musaf* service, which would naturally account then for the constant repetition of the word *zikhron* in this composition.

While no formula of this prayer is quoted in the Talmud, it does nevertheless point out that on the days when (in Temple times) there was an additional sacrificial offering (*korban Musaf*), the nature of the occasion should be highlighted in the *Avodah* blessing, that is the one beginning with *Retzeih*).[78] We actually omit *Yaaleh ve-yavo* when reciting the *Musaf Amidah*, since, inserted into the middle blessing (the *Kedushat Ha-Yom*, Prayer for the Sanctification of the Day), are extra compositions that adequately cover the sentiments of the *Yaaleh ve-yavo*. On the High Holy Days there is the prayer *U-mipnei Chata'einu* that refers to the harshness of our exile and banishment from our land, and our "inability to perform our duties in the House of thy choice." It calls directly upon God "to have compassion upon us and on thy sanctuary" and to "rebuild it" and to "reveal the glory of Thy kingdom speedily unto us." Thus, *Yaaleh ve-yavo* was clearly a mere duplication.

אֱלֹהֵינוּ... מְלוֹךְ עַל כָּל הָעוֹלָם
Our God . . . Reign Over the Whole Universe

We have referred to the infiltration into our High Holy Day liturgy of elements from the ancient Palestinian prayer book. Their presence is undoubtedly due to the fact that that source was the matrix from which so much of our festival *piyyut* is culled. These compositions were borrowed, therefore, together with their contextual material from the statutory Palestinian *Amidah*.

This factor explains the presence of the composition *Melokh al kol ha-olam*; for this prayer for the kingdom of God to be established was actually used in ancient Palestine not only on the High Holy Days but on all festivals.[79]

בָּרוּךְ... עוֹשֵׂה הַשָּׁלוֹם
Blessed . . . Author of Peace

The adoption of elements from the Palestinian liturgy into our festival prayer books also explains this special concluding formula of the final benediction of the *Amidah*, in place of the usual *ha-mevarekh et ammo yisrael ba-shalom*. The version *oseh ha-shalom* was, in fact, the common daily formula used in Palestine.

אֱלֹהַי נְצוֹר
Guard My Tongue from Evil

This prayer, recited at the conclusion of every *Amidah*, was originally composed and recited as a private meditation by Mar the son of Ravina, a fourth-century Babylonian talmudic sage. His disciples memorized their teacher's meditation and popularized it in their own synagogues and academies, to the extent that it soon became established as the official conclusion to the *Amidah*.

Unlike the blessings of the standard daily *Amidah*, all of which are couched in the plural, and most of whose thirteen central petitions are concerned with *collective* spiritual and nationalistic issues, punctuated with just a few personal needs—for divinely given wisdom (*Attah chonen*), heavenly pardon through confession (*Hashiveinu* and *Selach lanu*), bodily healing (*Refa'einu*), and agricultural blessing (*Barekh aleinu*)—the *Elokai netzor* is couched in the singular, and is suffused with an intense *personal* quality, dealing with the day-to-day impediments to the petitioner's happiness and peace of mind.

We can sense the author's anguish at having to contend with many bitter enemies, and his fear not only of the physical harm that they might do to him, but more, of the spiritual damage, dragging him down to their level, so that, in self-defense, he is drawn into adopting their unworthy tactics, responding in kind to their "evil tongue . . . guile and cursing."

One or two of Mar the son of Ravina's original references have been omitted in the standard version that we recite. His version included a petition that he might be "preserved from misfortune, from the evil inclination and from a bad woman."[80] The latter references may be explained as a result of the author's extreme piety and the life of austerity for which he was renowned in his generation.[81] Few details of his personal life have been preserved in the Talmud, though we may speculate from those two references to the dangers of feminine enticements as to what originally drove him into a life of saintly withdrawal.

It might seem strange that the climactic utterance of the *Amidah*, a prayer recited with such solemn, spiritual concentration, should be for preservation from such gross acts as evil speech and guile. Surely, after such a lengthy exercise in pure and holy expression, it is inconceivable that lips so used could be so easily abused! But Mar the son of Ravina clearly understood human nature, and appreciated how short-lived so many pious intentions and expressions often prove to be. Perhaps it was precisely in order to register this fact that he repeated this plea each and every day immediately after the central act of worship.

The recitation of daily prayers may help to discipline an individual and to make him conscious of spiritual ideals. It does not necessarily alter his nature, however, to the extent that it becomes impossible for him to surrender himself to unworthy thoughts and acts. Indeed, one of classical Chasidism's basic preoccupations was how to give guidance to its devotees in dealing with *machshavot zarot*, "unseemly thoughts" that invade the chasid's mind even while he stands in the midst of the recitation of the *Amidah*![82]

Why No Hallel?

Hallel is recited on all festivals that are biblically designated as *Mo'ed*, "appointed seasons," and on which work is prohibited. The exception is Rosh Hashanah and Yom Kippur, and the reason given in the Talmud is that "it is inconceivable, at a time when the books of life and death are open, and the king occupies the throne of strict justice, that Israel should sing such praises."[83]

Underlying this statement is a significant distinction between Rosh Hashanah and Yom Kippur, on the one hand, and all the other festivals, on the other. The latter are predominantly historical, and therefore commemorative. The spirit of such festivals is generated by means of the act of reliving and celebrating the history of our people at that early biblical stage of their national evolution. We look back with pride, and celebrate the redemptive process which brought us out of Egypt (on *Pesach*) to Sinai (on *Shavuot*) and on, through the desert (on *Sukkot*), to the Promised Land. We celebrate all that by reciting the joyous and vigorous Hallel psalms, which lyrically recall that glorious chapter in our history—*Be-tzeit Yisrael mi-Mitzrayim*—"When Israel came out of Egypt" (Psalm 114).

While those "*Hallel* festivals" look *backward*, Rosh Hashanah and Yom Kippur, on the other hand, are primarily concerned with looking *forward*, to our acceptance of a future set of values that will be spiritualized and refined through the soul-transforming experience that these occasions engender and the resolve that they inspire. But, realistically speaking, because our ability to achieve such a permanent self-transformation in the future must remain uncertain, it follows therefore that any such *Hallel* celebration is, at this time, premature and overconfident!

Hence, although Rosh Hashanah and Yom Kippur are certainly days for quiet confidence, yet, what Maimonides called *simchah yeteirah*, "extraordinary celebration,"[84] the likes of which *Hallel* symbolizes and expresses, is decidedly inappropriate.

אָבִינוּ מַלְכֵּנוּ
Our Father, Our King

On Rosh Hashanah we define God's relationship to us as "Our Father, our King," as well as our own relationship to Him (*im kevanim im kaavadim*) "as children, as servants."[85]

A child and a servant both have an obligation to obey implicitly whatever instruction is given to them by parent and master, respectively. There is, however, a significant difference. The child is in a special relationship to the parent that allows him to question the reasons behind the parental instruction and to indicate whether he is undertaking it with enthusiasm or with reluctance. The servant, on the other hand, has to suppress his own feelings and get on with the task.

In our dialogue with God both of these relationships coalesce. He is "Our Father." He must allow us the privilege of analyzing His will and examining His instructions. Indeed, this is the unique and most prominent characteristic of Judaism: the in-depth analysis of God's will, which constitutes our Oral Law that every Jew has the privilege and obligation to study. Our God is no tyrant; His instructions can all stand up to human inquiry, after which they will be shown, individually and collectively, to be an integrated mosaic of spiritual and moral refinement of the highest order. As "Our Father" we also believe that He is indulgent to us when our response to His call is less than enthusiastic. Without this belief the plea for atonement at this time would be a futile exercise.

Nevertheless, God is also "Our King," and even instructions that to our superficial glance may appear irrelevant must also be observed out of humility, love, and faith, and in the hope that the day will come when God will "open our eyes" to true enlightenment.

This coalescent relationship of "son" and "servant" is given clear expression by the prophet Malachi (3:17):

> They shall be mine, says the Lord of Hosts, My own possession . . . and I will spare them as a man spares *the son* [*beno*] who *serves* [*ha-oved*] him.

The *Avinu Malkeinu* prayer constitutes a lengthy catalogue of concise, direct petitions to God. There are, however, two dominant and recurring pleas: first, for the counsels of Israel's accusers to be destroyed and their malevolent intentions frustrated, and second, for the sick of our people—whether it be a physical or spiritual malady—to be healed, and for the whole nation to be inscribed for life and blessing. It concludes with a special appeal that God should grant this primarily through the merit of the saints and martyrs of our people in every generation.

The kernel of the *Avinu Malkeinu* goes back to talmudic times when the formula was first employed by Rabbi Akivah while officiating as *chazan* at a special service to intercede for rain during a period of drought.[86] The immediate heavenly response convinced the people that it was this particular mode of appeal that was the key to unlocking the gates of mercy. The inevitable result was that, while R. Akivah's *Avinu Malkeinu* contained but five lines, subsequent authorities and *chazanim* expanded the prayer to suit their particular needs and emotions. Hence, while the Sephardi version has twenty-nine lines, the Ashkenazi rite has thirty-eight and the Polish rite has forty-four lines. The great nineteenth-century liturgist, Seligman Isaac Baer, in his famous commentary on the Siddur, *Yakhin Lashon*,[87] testifies to having seen as many as fifty-three variants in the *siddurim* and manuscripts he consulted!

The *Avinu Malkeinu* prayer, because of its popularity and the efficacy attributed to it, was prescribed for recitation immediately following the *Amidah* on Rosh Hashanah, Yom Kippur and at morning and afternoon services throughout the Ten Days of Penitence and on fast days. It is not recited on *Shabbat*, however, because it is patterned on the weekday *Amidah*, with a direct correspondence of phraseology between the two. A few examples will suffice. The final line contains the phrase *choneinu va-aneinu* ("favor us"), which corresponds, in the *Amidah*, to the blessing *Attah chonein* ("you favor man"). The second line—*ein lanu melekh ellah attah* ("we have no King but you")—corresponds to the phrase in the first blessing of the *Amidah*, *melekh ozeir* (" A King who helps . . ."). The fourth line—*chadesh aleinu shanah tovah* ("renew unto us a good year")—corresponds to the phrase in the ninth blessing of the *Amidah*, *Barekh aleinu . . . et ha-shanah ha-zot . . . le-tovah* ("Bless *this year unto us* . . . for *good*"). The eleventh line—*Shelach refuah sheleimah* ("send perfect healing")—corresponds exactly to the phrase in the eighth blessing of the *Amidah*, *Ve-haaleh refuah sheleimah*.

This direct correspondence to the phraseology of the weekday *Amidah* explains why it is omitted on Sabbath,[88] and also why it is prescribed for recitation immediately after the *Amidah*.

Reading of the Law for the First Day

On Rosh Hashanah, as on other festivals, we call five people to the Reading of the Law. The Reading (*leining*) is chanted to a special melody, reserved especially for the High Holy Days. It is not as lively or wide-ranging a melody as for *Shabbat*, but is rather slower in tempo and more reserved and restricted in vocal range. This conforms to the mood of calm reflection and tranquil introspection that is the order of the day.

The *Miy She-Beirakh* prayers, recited for those called up, are also chanted to that same melody, and, if they are able to do so, they may even chant their blessings over the Torah employing the same High Holy Day melody.

Genesis, chapter 21, is read on the first day of Rosh Hashanah. This tells of the birth of Isaac, the problems posed by Ishmael's evil influence upon him, culminating in Ishmael's banishment from Abraham's home. It records the divine promise to Hagar of protection and prosperity for her offspring, and the peace treaty signed between Abraham and Abimelech.

Some writers have expressed surprise at the apparent heartlessness of Abraham in being a party to the banishment of his concubine, Hagar, and particularly of their child, Ishmael, exposing them to the dangers of a trek alone through the hostile desert.

It is difficult for us to put ourselves in the place of such a God-intoxicated person as Abraham, who lived not just with "faith in" God but with the absolute reality of His guiding presence. It was that same total reliance on the fulfillment, to the letter, of every promise made to him by his God that impelled Abraham to proceed, without a moment's hesitation, when he later received the command to take Isaac to the *Akeidah*. Just as the world was brought into being merely by the word of God, so, once that word had been uttered, it was tantamount to existing reality.

That "word" had been disclosed to Abraham not once, but countless times. His God had assured him, beyond a shadow of doubt, that He would "make him a great nation,"[89] "give this land *to your offspring*,"[90] a land stretching "from the River of Egypt to the great Euphrates River."[91] He had told him that He would make his offspring "as numerous as the dust of the earth,"[92] and "as the stars of the heavens."[93] On the matter of who would inherit Abraham, he had been assured that it would be "one who would emerge from your loins."[94] God had even given Abraham a clear picture of the fate of his children, who would be "strangers in a land that was not theirs."[95]

Particularly significant in this regard is the communication given to the pregnant Hagar on a previous occasion, after she had fled from the wrath of her mistress. She was given two disclosures: first, "I will greatly multiply your offspring, that it shall not be possible to number it for its multitude,"[96] and second, "his [Ishmael's] hand will be against everyone, and everyone's hand will be against him."[97]

It is inconceivable that Hagar, on her return to her master's home, would not have confided that exciting divine disclosure to Abraham, the father-to-be of that "multitude." For the headstrong concubine, who had already revealed her pretensions to superiority over her barren mistress—possibly even entertaining visions of supplanting her—this would have been a golden opportunity to consolidate her position, both in Abraham's affections as well as in the household.

Thirteen years later Abraham receives a divine call, assuring him once again that he would be greatly multiplied.[98] We must not forget that, at that stage, Abraham and Sarah had long since abandoned hope of there being any remote possibility of their producing a child. Thus, all those divine promises of fecundity would have been related, in Abraham's mind, exclusively to the offspring of Ishmael.

Even when God promises Abraham that Sarah would also have a child who would be a national progenitor, the distinction in the size of those respective nations is clearly enunciated. In the case of Isaac, Abraham is told that Sarah would be "the mother of nations," and that "kings of peoples would come from her."[99] We are not told of the particular *size* of her "nations," only about her capacity to produce offspring of regal quality. When Abraham immediately pleads that Ishmael should "live before You,"[100] that is, carry on the exclusive lineage, without complicating matters—Abraham clearly immediately grasped the potential for strife between the brothers and their respective national offspring—God tells him, "Regarding Ishmael, I have heard you; behold I have blessed him, and will make him fruitful, and will multiply him exceedingly; twelve princes shall he beget, and I will make him a great nation."[101]

Thus, the contents of the disclosure to Hagar, as well as the several personal disclosures, would have left Abraham in absolutely no doubt about two aspects of Ishmael's destiny: first, that God had determined that he would survive, to attain a degree of power and size that would vastly outstrip that of Isaac; and second, that Ishmael would lead a warlike and violent existence, pursuing, and being pursued by, others. In other words, that Ishmael was destined to be a fugitive all his life.

If Abraham was watching out for the first signs of the unfolding of God's purpose for Ishmael, it would have come as no surprise to him when Sarah communicated to him her desire to banish Ishmael, and set him on course thereby for the restless flight that he would forever experience.

Convinced that God had great, though awesome, plans for Ishmael,

Abraham was in no way callous, therefore, in sending the young Ishmael off into the desert with only his mother to protect him. As far as Abraham was concerned, his son had a far greater Protector than his mother to secure his safety!

"As He Is There"

The angel comforts Hagar, saying, "For God has heard the voice of the lad—*ba-asher hu sham* ("as he is there").[102] The precise meaning of the latter phrase is rather vague. The Aramaic Targum translates it "in the place where he is," an addition that would hardly have been necessary to state, for where else would God have heard Ishmael's voice?

Talmudic tradition took the phrase "as he is there" literally, understanding it as a comment on Ishmael's present state of moral innocence:

> *God has heard his voice*—In accordance with his deeds *there* (at this time) he is to be judged worthy of being saved, and not in accordance with the harm he would one day do. For the accusing angels chided God, saying, "To the one whose offspring is destined to destroy Your children You are providing life-saving water?" God answered: "At this moment is he righteous or wicked? I can only judge him in accordance with his present deeds—as he is *there*."[103]

This method of divine justice—as viewed through the rabbinic prism—seems, however, to be in conflict with the biblical approach to the "stubborn and rebellious son,"[104] the young delinquent who is totally beyond the control of his parents. The Torah prescribes that such a danger to society should be executed, and the Rabbis stress that such a person "is judged now (as a preventive measure) for his inevitable *future* conduct." Why, we may ask, do we not apply the same divine principle as was applied to Ishmael, and give that delinquent the benefit of the doubt?

There is no satisfactory answer to this problem, except to regard the situation of the "stubborn and rebellious son" as a unique case. A distinction may be made, however, between a heavenly approach to punishment and an earthly one. In the case of Ishmael, it was in the hands of God, who alone knows the future, to determine whether or not to interfere in the history and fate of mankind, and especially of His people, Israel, by removing a *future threat* to their safety. In the case of the earthly court, on the other hand, which is charged with removing a delinquent who constitutes a well-established *present threat*, and will deteriorate even more, in the estimation of both parents and fellow citizens, here the earthly court is given the authority and duty to rid society of a menace who strikes fear, now, and not only in the future, into every peace-loving citizen.

A judge, says the Talmud, must decide in accordance with what his eyes see. He cannot escape his responsibility, but must take immediate action to protect society. God also judges by that criterion; but as His eyes scan the future as well as the present, His judicial considerations are inevitably far more complex. Hence, no comparisons can really be made between the respective approaches of the Heavenly and earthly judge.

Some commentators maintain that the phrase "For God has heard the voice of the lad" is suggestive of the voice of submission, prayer, and repentance. This would provide a very simple answer to the problem we raised. Ishmael clearly deserved to be judged, therefore, as a sincere penitent, and reprieved, whereas the scenario of the "stubborn and rebellious son" is that wherein not a single demonstration of remorse or self-improvement has been made.

However, that generally applied, divine principle of "judging a person exclusively on the basis of his present actions" has a bearing on the issue of what we might call "recurrent *teshuvah.*" By this we refer to the individual who repents sincerely, and with earnest resolve not to repeat his misdemeanors, but nevertheless finds himself caught up in the web of his weaker nature and repeating the identical deeds. Do we say that his penitence, however sincere at the time of making it, is, nevertheless, patently a sham, and, as such, is a valueless charade that simply compounds the iniquity?

The answer would be that we do not adopt that attitude, but invoke the above principle of "judging the person on the basis of his present actions." A sincere remorse can totally efface any trace of the sin, and the act of effacing can be repeated if necessary. This may be difficult to justify, but the Maimonidean concept, shared by a number of other medieval philosophers, of sin as *a sickness*, may provide a rationale.

In his analysis of the Maimonidean view, Rav Soloveitchik observes: "Sin is an abnormal phenomenon. The healthy person, living a normal life, does not fall into the way of sin. Sin constitutes a sort of spiritual pathology."[105] He refers to the Book of Psalms for the origin of this analogy. There we find the parallelism of the two concepts: "Bless the Lord . . . Who forgives all thy *iniquities*, Who heals all thy *diseases*" (Psalm 103:3).

Viewing sin as an illness or disease helps explain how it is that, just as a person frequently suffers from the same recurring illness, so may he be susceptible to succumbing to a recurring sin. Its persuasive force, largely outside his emotional ability to control, necessitates that he be treated as a person who sins involuntarily, who fervently hopes that this time he will truly succeed in resisting it forever, and who requires—each time—the balm of forgiveness if he is ever to rid himself of his propensity toward it.

For the *Haftarah*, the story of Hannah[106] was selected. This describes her mental anguish at her unfulfilled desire for a child, her visit to the sanctuary at Shilo "to pour out her heart," and the response to her prayer, culminating, happily, in the birth of Samuel.

The relevance of these readings to the message of the festival is not difficult to discover. Rosh Hashanah is the time for expressing our firm conviction that "God is near to all who call upon Him in truth." It is the occasion when we affirm our belief and faith that if our cherished wishes are not fulfilled, it is no reflection on the justice of God. It might well be His inscrutable will that we must suffer years of frustrating waiting, as did both Sarah and Hannah before they were blessed with a child. Faith, prayer, righteous living, and patience ultimately wrest blessing from the divine grip. Despair and loss of faith put it even further from our reach.

Another message of the Torah reading is that of God's universal concern for all His creatures. Man may cast out his fellow—the same way that Ishmael was banished from his home—but God will never abandon His creatures. He may have selected Isaac as the repository of His spiritual message to mankind, but Ishmael is still an object of His loving concern. This message is reinforced in the story of Jonah, read on Yom Kippur, where God demonstrates to Jonah that *all* men are worthy of salvation, and that God hears the cries of *all* men when they issue forth from a truly contrite heart.

A rabbinic tradition[107] forges another link between the festival and the choice of Torah and *Haftarah* readings by asserting that both the conception of Isaac (described in the reading for the first day) and his binding (recounted on the second day) actually took place on Rosh Hashanah. Similarly, the birth of Samuel was chosen to be read on this day because he was also conceived on Rosh Hashanah. This coincidence is emphasized by the choice of the same Hebrew verb, *pakad*, "to visit (with child)" used in connection with both Sarah[108] and Hannah.[109] This verb has a particular association with Rosh Hashanah in that it also means "to remember," which is one of the major themes (*Zikhronot*—God remembering the merit of the Patriarchs) of our festival liturgy.

It is, however, amid the exalted prayer of Hannah, with which the *Haftarah* concludes, that we come closest to discovering the core message of Rosh Hashanah: that man's fate is totally in the hands of God and that we are all dependent upon His grace for every breath we take.

> The Lord ends life and preserves it;
> He brings down to the grave, and resurrects.
> He makes poor and invests with wealth.
> He brings low and elevates.
> He raises the poor out of the dust and the needy from the dunghill,
> To make them sit with princes and inherit a majestic throne.

Prayers for the Welfare of the Government

Jewish teaching lays great stress on *hakarat ha-tov*, expressing gratitude for kindnesses: whether to God, in the form of such blessings as the *Modim* (*Amidah* thanksgiving), or to man, in return for favors and services. A notable example of this principle is the Jewish tradition, stretching back nearly two and a half millennia, to offer up prayers for the welfare of the government and country that affords us asylum and protection. Such prayers were regarded as *de rigueur* even under the circumstances of a patently unsympathetic or even harsh host government. One is reminded of the humorous, though brilliantly perceptive, line in *Fiddler on the Roof*, when the rabbi is asked whether there is an appropriate blessing for the Tsar. His immediate answer is that there is, indeed, a blessing for the Tsar! He then proceeds to suggest the formula: "May God bless and keep the Tsar—far away from us!"[110]

When the Jews exiled in Babylon were granted their freedom (537 B.C.E.) by the Persian ruler Cyrus, the latter's famous "Declaration" stated that one of the reasons for granting permission for the Jews to rebuild their Temple was "so that they may offer sacrifices of sweet savor to the God of heaven, *and pray for the life of the king and his sons*" (Ezra 6:10). A mishnaic tract already recommended the importance of such prayers for a simple and pragmatic reason: "Pray for the welfare of the ruling power, for were it not for the fear of it, men would swallow each other alive."[111]

Such prayers were not, however, part of the statutory service, and no formulae are quoted or even referred to in the talmudic literature. The most plausible explanation of this is offered by S. D. Goitein, that "since the public prayer for the authorities, whether gentile or Jewish, possessed a practical aspect, namely demonstration of the community's allegiance, it had to be adapted to the circumstances and formulated accordingly."[112]

The extent to which Jews went—or, rather, had to go—in order to declare their allegiance is demonstrated by a prayer for the welfare of Muslims, recited in Arabic, that recently came to light in the Cairo *Genizah*:

> We also pray for all Muslims, males and females, who dwell in our country, their sons and daughters, male and female believers. May God hasten the healing of their sick, gather in their dispersed ones and let loose and liberate those who have been taken captive. May He spread over them the tabernacle of His peace. Amen.[113]

This prayer dates back to the twelfth century, and was customarily recited on *Simchat Torah*, when Muslim dignitaries were probably present.

We should not imagine, however, that it was only Jews who felt constrained, or who were obliged, to make such tokens of allegiance. Goitein reminds us that the medieval Muslims were regularly revolting against their leaders, as a consequence of which, at the Friday public services in the mosques, it was made obligatory to deliver a kind of sermon declaring the congregation's allegiance to the incumbent ruler and his family. If this was expected of "the faithful," it would appear quite natural that such a corresponding demand should have been made of the religious minorities.

There is no mention of any such specific prayer in the earliest Babylonian *siddurim* of Amram and Saadia (ninth to tenth centuries), nor in the eleventh century *Machzor Vitri,* written by Simchah ben Samuel, of Vitri in France, a disciple of Rashi. When precisely the first Prayer for the Government became popularized and accepted in a prayer rite is still shrouded in mystery.

Our *Ha-noten teshua* ("He who gives salvation") prayer, which made its first appearance in a printed prayer book in 1658, was probably introduced and standardized about a century before. This is based on the fact that, although "no examples of *Ha-noten teshua* are found among pre-expulsion (1492) Spanish *siddur* manuscripts," yet, "by the mid-1660s it is being recited throughout the Sephardic world, from England to Asia Minor."[114] It is conjectured that it was composed by a Sephardic émigré community early in the sixteenth century, which, insecure in its new environment and unsure as to its ultimate fate, felt it politic to express total allegiance and good will to its new host state, its government, and its citizenry. Since Franco-German Ashkenazi Jewry suffered from similar feelings of insecurity, this prayer was soon borrowed by them, and came to enjoy universal popularity. It is invested with special significance through its being recited by the rabbi rather than the *chazan,* and is generally listened to in perfect silence and with a quiet reverence that few other parts of the service can boast.

The Sounding of the Shofar

The Historic Role of the *Shofar*

Although we sound the *shofar* only on Rosh Hashanah, and once on Yom Kippur to mark the end of the fast, in biblical times its alarming call was heard very frequently.

Every morning in the Jerusalem Temple twenty-one blasts were sounded on the *shofar.* As the gates opened three notes rang out summoning the faithful to worship, and perhaps acting at the same time as an alarm clock for the slumbering priests. Accompanying the morning public sacrifices another nine notes were blown and a further nine accompanied the afternoon offering.

Each Friday eve the *shofar* announced the approach of the Sabbath. Six notes were blown. At the first sounding the laborers in the fields stopped work and made for home. At the second *shofar* blast the shops closed and city life came to a halt. The third blast was a signal to light the Sabbath lights. Then, after a brief pause, three further notes were sounded and the Sabbath began.

When Israel went into battle the *shofar* proclaimed the moment of attack. It was at the sound of the *shofar* that all the Israelites under the command of Joshua shouted aloud to bring down the walls of Jericho (Joshua 6:4). Gideon and a small band of three hundred men put to flight a vast army of Midianites by blowing on *shofars* and creating a mighty uproar, thus giving a mistaken impression of Israel's numerical superiority.[115]

The *shofar* was also employed at the inauguration of each Jubilee (fiftieth) year to announce the year of release, when all slaves were granted their freedom and all land was restored to its original tribal owners. The *shofar* figured so prominently at that inaugural ceremony that the name of the year of release was even called *yovel* (translit. "Jubilee"), which is the old Hebrew word for the ram's horn!

In medieval times the *shofar* was also used in the ceremony of excommunication, which imposed total isolation on any Jew who rebelled against the rulings of the court or who undermined the authority of the Torah. The threatening alarm of the *shofar* brought home to the one under ban the full reality of his estrangement from any social, religious, or commercial contact with any member of the Jewish community, while at the same time offering a public clarion warning of the penalty for associating with such a miscreant.

The *shofar* was also heard on fast days, attempting to rouse the people to repentance. It was heard each month to announce the appearance of the new moon, and at funerals its plaintive notes set the mood of the occasion.

One could add still further to this impressive list, which demonstrates the role of the *shofar* as herald at almost every major event and occasion in ancient times. Since Numbers 29:1 designates Rosh Hashanah as "a day of blowing," the *shofar* must have been particularly conspicuous on that day, and it has even been suggested that it was blown at regular intervals throughout the day.

The Notes of the *Shofar*

There are three types of sounds or notes made by the *shofar* in the course of the New Year liturgy. The most common one is the *tekiah*. This is a plain, unwavering note that is held for about five seconds before ending abruptly. The *tekiah* is always sounded at the beginning and end of each bar, and sandwiched between the two *tekiahs* is either the *shevarim* or the *teruah*.

The *shevarim* must be identical in length to the *tekiah* that precedes and follows it. It consists of three short blasts, each ending abruptly. The name *shevarim* means "broken," indicative of its structure as a *tekiah* "broken up" into three parts.

The *teruah* is likewise of equal length to the accompanying *tekiahs*. It comprises nine very brief notes, formed by the rapid insertion and withdrawal of the tongue into the mouthpiece of the *shofar*.

During the morning one hundred of these notes are sounded at key points in the service. Altogether sixty *tekiahs* are blown, twenty *shevarim*, and twenty *teruahs*. In order that the officiant who is blowing the *shofar* should not become confused he has an aide standing opposite him (the synagogue Reader being in the center) at the reading desk, who proclaims aloud the note about to be blown. Both are dressed in a white gown or *kittel*.

The first set of thirty *shofar* notes, that are sounded before the *Musaf Amidah*, are known as *tekiot dimyushav*, "the notes of the seated section," referring to that part of the service that one recites in a seated position, as opposed to the *tekiot dim'umad*, "the notes of the Standing Prayer," namely the (*Musaf*) *Amidah*.

The thirty notes of the *tekiot dimyushav* are divided into three groups: the first group, comprising twelve notes, followed by two groups, each of nine notes. After each group, most editions of the *machzor* print a short *Yehiy ratzon* petition, popular among the sixteenth-century mystics:

> May it be Your will, O Lord our God . . . that those angels that are evoked by the combinations of the shofar's *tekiah shevarim* and *teruah* notes should ascend before the throne of Your glory, and invoke goodness on our behalf, to pardon all our sins.

This version, from the *ArtScroll* edition, is actually a more "refined" version of the original form of this petition that is found, for example, in the *Machzor Kol-bo* (with Yiddish translation and commentary):

> May it be Your will . . . that the *tekiah shevarim teruah* that we sound this day should be woven into the heavenly veil by the appointed angel Tartiel . . . and Jeshua, Minister of the Presence, and Metatron, Prince of the Countenance.

It has been pointed out that we have no such reference anywhere else to any "Minister of the Presence" by the name of Jeshua, and that the only conclusion we can reach is that this is none other than a Christian reference to the name of their founder, *Jeshu*, that has infiltrated the *machzor* by some missionary in the employ of the printers![116]

The *Kitzur Shulchan Arukh* quotes an earlier authority who, not surprisingly, asserts that "one should be very careful not to utter with one's lips the personal names mentioned in (several versions of) this prayer. In many congregations they do not recite this *Yehiy ratzon* at all—and that is the best way."[117]

Some authorities objected to the recitation of the *Yehiy ratzon* petitions on the grounds that they constitute an interruption in the *mitzvah* of this section's *shofar* blowing, though such a view won few supporters and may well have been merely a cover for the more obvious objection to angelic references. Some rabbis were not opposed to references to angels per se, but objected to petitions that contained their often obscure names for fear that "they might become mixed up." The great kabbalist Isaac Luria consequently recommended that one should better recite a short confession between each section of the blowing.

The rabbi is given the honor of blowing the *shofar*, as he is presumed to be the most fitting person to sound the call to repentance. If he is unable to blow the *shofar*—which can happen—he will act as "proclaimer of the notes" or, to give it its Hebrew title, the *makriy*. The one who blows the *shofar* is designated *baal tokea* ("the master of the blowing"), and if his performance has been particularly faultless he can be sure that at the end of the service, when the last note has faded away, he will receive a loud token of appreciation from the congregation, which will shout the traditional formula of acclaim, *yishar kochakha* ("May your strength be increased").

Qualifications for a *Baal Tokea*

In large congregations there are often many volunteers to discharge the religious function and privilege of blowing the *shofar*. It is naturally an imperative that the person so chosen should be acceptable to the entire congregation. This calls for impeccable credentials as regards ethical and moral conduct, as well as long-standing, sincere, and comprehensive devotion to Jewish practice.

In many Orthodox circles, particularly in the *shtibls* (small, intimate prayer and study houses) and among the chasidic conventicles, such "basic" spiritual qualifications were taken for granted of all worshipers. The members of those select circles sought someone of unique piety who was truly worthy enough to sound the *shofar* to summon them to repentance.

Because inner religious sincerity, emotion, and devotion do not always measure up to external demonstration of piety, the following story, regarding the famous chasidic master Reb Levi Yitzchok of Berditchev is salutary.

It is related that one year the great master required the services of a *baal tokea*. As expected, he was inundated with applicants for that great honor of blowing for the illustrious rebbe. Reb Levi proceeded to interview every candidate, asking them to share with him the thoughts that generally passed through their minds while they were engaged in that holy exercise. Each candidate tried to outdo the next in disclosing to the master the particular *kavvanot* (mystical meditations) and *yichudim* (kabbalistic formulae to unite the disparate elements of divine emanation that are hanging unfettered in the cosmos) upon which his concentration was focused at that time. Surprisingly, with each succeeding candidate, Levi Yitzchok appeared more and more unimpressed.

Finally, he turned to one self-effacing disciple who, unlike the others, had not attempted to push himself forward to the head of the queue of those interviewed. When asked what his thoughts were when blowing the *shofar*, the man replied: "Rebbe, I am only a simple, unlearned Jew, with many daughters to marry off, and not a kopek to offer as a dowry. When the time for blowing arrives, I say to God in my heart, 'Master of the Universe, I have done *Your* will by blowing the *shofar* before You; now it is Your turn to attend to *my* needs by sending suitable partners for my daughters.'"

"Excellent," shouted Reb Levi Yitzchok, his eyes alight with pleasure. "You alone have expressed the most authentic of *kavvanot*! This is precisely the sort of *baal tokea* that I was looking for!"

The great rebbe was enunciating here a profound thought regarding the nature of our High Holy Day dialogue with God.

Throughout the year our Judaism involves us in a feverish cycle of hurriedly recited and stereotyped doctrinal formulae. We even manage to rush through some of the most inspirational and spiritually energizing psalmodic praises of God as if they were items of stock on a checklist. We become slaves to the words and concepts of others, though in truth we relate to them in a fairly superficial manner. Even those who find the time and motivation to immerse themselves in the Sea of the Talmud, absorbing its mind-blowing dialectic and plumbing its challenging philosophical, theological, and mystical depths, are frequently still indulging in an exercise that makes little impact upon their own psyche. They are activating their intellect, but the circuit does not stretch to link up to, and engage, their inner being.

On Rosh Hashanah we cannot afford that luxury. We have God's attention for a brief time. Throughout the rest of the year, we have to catch that attention. On this day—as we pass before Him—we have it, undivided, to speak, confess, plead, claim, and complain, in whatever manner we believe is most appropriate existentially.

God wants to hear our own, authentic words, not the old formulae and principles, not even the sacred *kavvanot* and *yichudim* of others, that He has heard too frequently before. He wants to recognize us, as individuals, beneath all the verbiage. He wants to hear our particular "still small voice," not merely "The Great *Shofar*" of collectivity.

Reb Levi Yitzchok's final candidate for the position merited it because his route to God was direct. It was a route that he himself had plotted, a route that emerged out of his own religious instinct, not from following the well-worn tracks on maps provided by others. The man who is so convinced that it is in God's hands alone to lighten life's burdens for him that he seizes the chance offered to him to articulate his dilemma, so boldly and clearly, at that special moment of the *shofar*'s summons to dialogue, that is the man who is most likely to win release and reprieve for the rest of his community, indeed for the remainder of his suffering brethren!

The Significance of the *Shofar*

The most popular explanation of the origin of the ritual of blowing the *shofar* on Rosh Hashanah relates it to the episode of the *Akeidah* ("binding of Isaac") in Genesis, chapter 22. The life of Isaac was saved, vicariously, by the offering of the ram "caught in the thickets *by its horns*." The *shofar* thus recalls Abraham's unquestioning and total obedience to the divine will that has represented, ever since, a model and ideal to which his offspring might aspire.

Other explanations have also been suggested, such as that the New Year, as the beginning of Creation, marked the moment when God became King of the Universe. Just as trumpets are sounded at the coronation of earthly monarchs, so is the *shofar* sounded to mark the enthronement of God.

Another explanation draws attention to the fact that at the revelation at Sinai "the sound of the *shofar* went stronger and stronger."[118] On Rosh Hashanah it is sounded, then, to summon us to renew that pledge made by our ancestors at Sinai.

Further explanations understand the *shofar* blowing as foreshadowing its role in the time to come, as herald to the day of judgment,[119] the ingathering of the exiles[120] and the resurrection.

Symbolism of the *Shofar*

If we consult any biblical concordance, which gives the basic meaning of the core three-letter roots underlying all Hebrew words, we will find that the precise root meaning of the noun *shofar* is unknown.[121] In Assyrian, the word *shappar*(*u*) is a wild goat, and, as this species may have been the favorite type of curved horn utilized in the ancient Near East, it may well have lent its name to all subsequent types of horn, whether obtained from a goat or any other animal.

Some homilists relate the word *shofar* to another, totally independent, Hebrew and Aramaic root, *shafar*, meaning "to be pleasant, beautiful, goodly."[122] By a little stretch of the imagination, they view this as the ultimate objective of the *shofar*'s summons, namely to make our actions more *pleasant, beautiful, goodly*—and Godly.

If we are already exploring the realm of the homilectical, then we may also allow ourselves a flight of symbolic fancy. The ram's horn cannot be used in its natural state. A great deal of preparation goes into its conversion into a *shofar*. And it is much the same with repentance. We cannot just appear in synagogue on Rosh Hashanah day and . . . repent. It requires considerable spiritual preparation for that to be authentically achieved. As with the raw ram's horn, *teshuvah* (repentance) is not man's natural condition. Nor is it an easily achieved emotional and spiritual state. Just like the horn has to have all its inner skin and sinews scraped away, and just as it has to be softened and bent into a required shape, with a mouthpiece chiseled out, so, symbolically, do we have to scrape away the dross of sin and lethargy that has clogged up our way to righteousness. So do we have to make our hearts softer and more sensitive to spiritual stimuli. So also do we have to "chisel out a mouthpiece," finding the appropriate personal expressions of remorse.

Repentance is not satisfied or effected merely by mouthing the traditional formulas. Like the *shofar*, *we have to create the sound*, the authentic response. For, "though the great trumpet may sound, it is the still, small voice that is heard."

לַמְנַצֵּחַ לִבְנֵי־קֹרַח
To the Chief Musician: A Psalm of the Sons of Korach

Quite apart from the thematic relevance of this psalm to the sounding of the *shofar*, there is a poignant and telling message underlying the selection at this time of a psalm composed by the sons of Korach.

Korach was the arch rebel against God and His anointed leaders.[123] He was swallowed up alive into the earth for his sin; yet his sons were untainted, having dissociated themselves from their father's wicked ways. It is most appropriate, therefore, that one of their psalms should have been honorably selected to serve as an introduction to the sounding of the *shofar* with its call to repentance.

The psalm is recited seven times, which some have explained on the basis of the fact that the divine name *Elokim* is repeated seven times. A more mystical explanation regards each recitation of the psalm as efficaciously bringing the divine presence down from the seventh and highest heaven to the throne of mercy at the closest proximity to man.

Psalm 47 is followed by a selection of verses, recited responsively, all but one of which (*Koliy shamata,* Lamentations 3:56) are from the psalms. Aside from the introductory verse (*min ha-meitzar*), which was included by some authorities in order to make up the significant number of *seven* verses, the initial letters of the last six verses form the acrostic *Kra Satan,* "tear in pieces the accuser." This imprecation was regarded as particularly significant by the sixteenth-century mystics of Safed who prescribed the recitation of these verses, and who, for the same reason, introduced into the liturgy the recitation of the *Anna be-khoach* prayer. The second line of that prayer—*k̄abbeil r̄innat āmkha; s̄agveinu t̄ahareinu n̄ora*—provides the same acrostic. For the sounding of the *shofar* the acrostic's sentiment is especially appropriate, as the Talmud[124] explains that the purpose of sounding the *shofar* was "in order to confuse Satan." According to *Tosafot*[125] his confusion arises from fear that this *shofar* might well be the messianic alarm that will herald Satan's own demise.

2

The *Musaf* Service

הִנְנִי
The Reader's Meditation

The *chazan* stands in fervent prayer reciting silently a most beautiful and strikingly personal plea to God to accept him as representative of his congregation, however unworthy he might be to assume such a sacred and exalted spiritual role. He asks God to overlook his particular shortcomings when receiving, through him, the prayers and supplications of the congregation.[1]

> Here am I, poor in deeds, quaking in dread of the One who sits as recipient of the praises of Israel. I have come to stand and make supplication before You on behalf of Your people, Israel, who have appointed me even though I am not worthy or deserving of that privilege.
>
> Therefore I do entreat you, O God of Abraham, God of Isaac, and God of Jacob, Lord, Lord, merciful and gracious God, bountiful One, awesome and revered One, make to succeed the task upon which I am setting out: to secure mercy for myself and for them that have appointed me.
>
> Please, let them not be held responsible for my particular sins, nor condemn them for my shortcomings; for I am, indeed, a transgressor. Let them not suffer for my faults. Let them not be embarrassed on my account, nor ashamed. Neither make me ashamed because of them.

> Accept my prayer as You would the prayer of a worthy sage, acclaimed for absolute integrity from his earliest youth.[2] Accept it as You would the prayer of one endowed with maturity and a sweet voice, the prayer of one enjoying the religious confidence of his fellows. Deprive Satan of his ability to accuse, and let our love become Your ensign, just as Your love banishes all traces of our transgression.
>
> Convert all Israel's fasts and periods of abstention into days of gladness and rejoicing, for life and peace. Oh how they crave after true peace![3] Let there be no impediment in my prayer. May it be Your will, Lord, God of Abraham, God of Isaac, and God of Jacob, the great, mighty and feared God, the Most High, called "I shall be what I shall be," that all the intermediaries that transmit the sound of prayers should carry my prayer before Your glorious throne, and present it effectively before you, on behalf of all the righteous people, the pious, the blameless and the upright, and to the glory of Your great, mighty, and revered name. For You do, indeed, hear mercifully the prayer of your people Israel. We bless You for hearing our prayer.

When we consider that in the medieval period the *chazan* was also the religious leader, this humble prayer, laying bare his spiritual inadequacies, is in marked contrast to the posture of spiritual perfection adopted by the ecclesiastical officials of some other faiths.

Half-*Kaddish*

The half-*Kaddish* is a kind of liturgical punctuation mark that serves to separate off certain parts of the service from other more important sections. Here it sets into sharper relief the *Amidah,* the most important prayer. Its call, that God's name should be "magnified and sanctified," suggests that its purpose is also to serve as an exhortation to the congregation to recite the next section with particular devotion and concentration.

Ashkenazi tradition doubles the word *le-eila* in every *Kaddish* recited during Rosh Hashanah and throughout the Ten Days of Penitence. The repetition of the word *le-eila* ("exalted") is to convey the idea that God is never more exalted than at this time of the year when the thoughts and prayers of all Israel are directed toward Him.

The number of words in a particular prayer was regarded as mystically significant and not to be altered. Thus, because an additional *le-eila* was being inserted at this time, authorities suggested that we should compensate by taking out one word. The most convenient way was to contract the two words *min kol* (*birkhata*) to *mikkol*—a regular contraction that does not affect the meaning.

This practice of doubling the word *le-eila* is a comparatively late innovation, there being no reference to it in any source before the fifteenth century, where it is referred to for the first time in the notes to the *Sefer Maharil* of R. Jacob ben Moses of Moellin.[4] There was, in fact, a considerable variety of practice in this matter in Ashkenazi communities. In Posen they only doubled the word in the first *Kaddish* that preceded the *Selichot* services. In Frankfurt the extra *le-eila* was only inserted on Rosh Hashanah and Yom Kippur—not during the rest of the Ten Days of Penitence—and only in the *Kaddish* recited by the *chazan*. Mourners did not include it.

Repetition of the *Amidah*

מִסּוֹד חֲכָמִים וּנְבוֹנִים
From the Counsel of the Wise and Understanding (see pp. 31–32)

אֻפַּד מֵאָז
From of Old This Is the Appointed Day

This is a poem by Eleazar Kallir, constructed as an alphabetical acrostic in rhyming, four-lined stanzas. The requirement of providing a concluding response for Reader and congregation gives the mistaken impression that the acrostic ends after the letter *reish* (*Rachum zekhor . . .*), support for which might be adduced from the fact that the next verse, recited by the congregation, commences with the letter *nun* (of the word *naaleh*).

It is probable, however, that Kallir's penultimate line originally did begin with the (letter *shin* of the) word *shofar*, but that subsequently the first two words of that line were transposed. The transposition was made in order to take account of five biblical quotations that were inserted immediately before that penultimate line, but which we have not retained in our *machzorim*. The final word of the last biblical quotation (Psalm 47:10) was *naalah*, and it was therefore felt preferable to juxtapose these two almost identical words,[5] even though it meant sacrificing the acrostic uniformity. When the biblical quotations were omitted, the original word order was not restored.

The poet alludes to the fact that it was on the first day of his creation—the anniversary of which Rosh Hashanah celebrates—that Adam sinned and was judged. Because God spared him the full measure of retribution, "that day was established from then on (*uppad me-az*) as a day of judgment" and divine indulgence.

The precise nature of Adam's punishment, and the degree to which he was granted remission, is a subject of discussion in the midrashic literature. God had originally warned him quite unequivocally of the consequence of eating from the forbidden tree: "For on the day you eat of it [*mot tamut*] *you will surely die*" (Genesis 2:17). A variant explanation of the phrase *mot tamut*, found in the *Targum Yonatan*, is "you will *deserve* death (*tehey chayav ketol*)," a rendering that allows for judicial discretion. This provides an explanation of why it was that God was not true to His word, and did not actually carry out the immediate sentence of death on Adam, but, instead, commuted it to banishment from the Garden of Eden and a livelihood secured only by sweat and toil.

Another rationale for this problem is to understand *mot tamut* not in the sense of peremptory execution, but rather as "you shall surely inherit the state of mortality." According to this explanation, Adam and his offspring were destined for immortality. His sin had the effect, however, of bringing the punishment of death into the world.

Several midrashim take up this theme of Adam's responsibility for the suffering and mortality of the human race. They depict Adam as visiting each person as he is about to die and questioning him as to why and in what spiritual state he is leaving the world. To every such inquiry, the same curt reply is hurled at poor Adam: "Woe is you. It is only because of you that I must leave the world!" The Midrash gives Adam the last word, however: "My child, I transgressed but one commandment, and was punished for that. See how many positive and negative laws of your Creator you have violated!"

The weakness of Adam's (midrashic) argument is, of course, patently obvious. For, while *quantitatively* he may have been correct, *qualitatively* the ramifications of that transgression, in terms of its effect on all his descendants, allow for no comparison between the respective offenses. Furthermore, Adam is really being disingenuous, for he was only bound to observe but one single command—and he failed to do so—whereas the Jewish people (and even the Noachites) have so many more to observe! There is a principle, however, of *Ein moshivin al ha-drash*, "One does not raise objections on midrashic traditions (in the way one is obliged to do for halakhic traditions)," so we should not really be pushing our critical analysis quite so strongly.

However, another midrash does in fact address the problem. It claims that Adam still exists, and twice a day he visits the patriarchs to confess his sin, sadly pointing out to them the place of the Garden of Eden where once he lived in heavenly grace. Perhaps this tradition was offered as a counterbalance to the first, to indicate that Adam does not, in fact, satisfy himself with the argument he adduces in defense of his single sin against the many transgressions of his descendants. On the contrary, he is to this day still plagued with guilt at what his sin has inflicted upon the human race.

Midrash is to be understood at various levels. The Adam described here is also the Adam in us all. We are all planted in a world that could so easily be transformed, by our moral effort, into a Garden of Eden, or that, on the other hand, could, as a result of our lethargy and hard-heartedness, become an untended jungle. The two midrashic traditions both stress, in essence, the nature of human responsibility and accountability, and how our actions impact upon our society, and conceivably upon the whole progress of the human race. If we weaken the moral foundation of that society, by acts of omission or commission, we make it that much easier for the whole structure to collapse. The midrashim teach us also that although, like Adam, we may think that we can excuse our moral inertia, as, for example, by comparing ourselves to others who are less concerned and responsible than ourselves, ultimately we shall be called to account for not listening to, or answering, the call of our conscience. We shall become worthless in our own eyes, just like Adam who felt the need to confess his sin to the patriarchs twice a day. This is the implied and timely message of the reference to Adam's forgiveness in this *piyyut*.

תֵּפֶן בְּמָכוֹן
When You Are Seated on Your Judgment Throne

This prayer is a beautiful and direct plea to God to leave His throne of judgment and occupy the throne of mercy.[6] It calls upon Him to take note of our sincere efforts to extricate ourselves from the constriction of our own passions. This seems to be the import of the phrase *mul even negef mitlachamim*, derived from Isaiah 8:14. "The attacking missile" (lit. "stone of attack") is one of the designations of the Evil Inclination according to the Talmud,[7] though some explain it as referring to the Accuser or Satan. The poet asks God to remember us compassionately, and particularly as the descendants of that patriarch, Isaac, who was so willing to surrender his life in the service of God.

The poem is constructed as a reverse alphabetical acrostic, perhaps symbolizing the retreat of God from His remotest throne of judgment (represented by the letter *taf*, the last letter of the alphabet) to the throne of mercy at the closest proximity to man (represented by the first letter, *alef*). There are four words to a line and four rhyming lines to each stanza.

The biblical and rabbinic allusions blend so naturally into their context in the poetry of Kallir, notwithstanding his masterly economy of words—the veritable hallmark of poetic expression. The second stanza is a prime example of this, wherein, in a mere eight words—*tzarat omer lo yadon, paamayim lo takum la-avaddon*—he expresses a lengthy and complex sentiment.

Lo yadon is an allusion to the curse *lo yadon ruchiy ba-adam* (Genesis 6:3)—"My spirit shall not abide in man"—uttered by God prior to bringing the flood. *Tzarat omer* here means "the threat of the utterance," and the second line of the stanza says "it shall not occur a second time for destruction." Thus, in a mere eight words the poet has called upon God not to repeat that terrible curse that He directed against the generation of the flood, but to ensure that His spirit remains eternally with us.

This device, of employing just two or three key words from a quotation, Kallir utilizes with great effect, leaving to his reader the task of mentally filling in the rest of the quotation in order to appreciate the full impact of the association. This is especially effective in the final line of the poem where the three words *eilleh divrei ha-brit* (Deuteronomy 28:69), which climax the *tokheichah,* the fearful retribution that is threatened if Israel rejects her Torah, are employed as a pregnant allusion to that lengthy catalogue of punishments. Again, the final three words, *be-zikhron shillush brit* ("remembering the threefold covenant"), employ the same device, as an allusion to the verse "And I will remember [*zakharti*] my covenant [*britiy*] with Jacob, and I will remember my covenant [*britiy*] with Isaac, and also my covenant [*britiy*] with Abraham" (Leviticus 26:42). Thus, again, in a mere eight words, Kallir succeeds in expressing the complex plea that, in recognition of God's promise to each of the patriarchs to grant rewards to their offspring, the fearful punishments detailed in the Torah must, of necessity, be neutralized.

Another important allusion is contained in the line *olam asher be-arbaah nadon* ("World which is judged at four times in the year"), based upon the mishnaic statement[8] that there are, in fact, four "New Years" when God's verdict on the world is given practical expression in terms of the richness or meagerness of the harvest bestowed. Passover is the "New Year" for grain, Pentecost for fruits, Rosh Hashanah for mankind, and Tabernacles for water.

The concluding plea of the Reader, asking for "a year of plenty, of dew, rains, and warmth," is based upon the prayer of the High Priest[9] that he uttered on leaving the Holy of Holies. It is quoted in full in the *Musaf Amidah* of Yom Kippur.[10]

אַף אוֹרַח מִשְׁפָּטֶיךָ
Though Your Path Is Judgment

This composition by Kallir employs the very complicated construction of a double alphabetical acrostic with *At-bash* formation, according to which the first line of each couplet follows the usual alphabetical order while the second line of the couplet creates a reverse alphabetical acrostic pattern.

The theme of the poem will be seen to be well suited to the alphabetical acrostic pattern, as it sketches in the history of repentance, demonstrating it to have been an active agent from the creation, through the patriarchal age, and throughout history, even until the longed-for messianic era. The alphabetical progression furthers the idea of this long history of repentance from the beginning to the end of time, and the reverse acrostic was perhaps intended to convey the vicissitudes of fortune—from periods of appeal and influence to others of *reversal* and rejection—suffered by the spirit of repentance as it strove for a permanent place in the hearts of men.

The third line makes reference to Israel having "sought thee *since yesterday*"—a statement that seems hardly appropriate for the *first* day of Rosh Hashanah! It appears again (*mei-etmol kidamnukha*) in the *Shacharit* composition, *kevodo iheil*, and is to be understood in the context of an ancient pietistic practice, of certain groups since the talmudic period, to fast on the day preceding Rosh Hashanah.[11] This was probably in compensation for an earlier custom of fasting on Rosh Hashanah itself, and during all the Ten Days of Penitence, including Sabbath. It was subsequently felt to be improper to impair the joy of holy days by fasting. Consequently, the four days on which fasting was suspended (two days *Yom Tov*, the intermediate Sabbath, and the day before Yom Kippur) were compensated for by observing them on the four days immediately preceding Rosh Hashanah. This explains why, if there are not four clear days for *selichot* in the week of Rosh Hashanah, we commence *selichot* from the preceding week.

Kallir, having referred in the previous composition to the missiles of the Evil Inclination, or human passion, is moved to include here a reference to Joseph, who valiantly resisted the charms of the wife of Potiphar. He is referred to allusively as *hasarat shekhem mi-sevel*, "the one whose shoulder was relieved of the fetters" (Psalm 81:7), in accordance with the talmudic opinion that Joseph was released from prison on Rosh Hashanah.[12] The poet pleads that the vindication, on this day, of Joseph's innocence of the sin of lust, should, vicariously, be credited to the merit of his children if ever they should fall prey to its temptation.

מֶלֶךְ עֶלְיוֹן
Highest Divinity[13]

A cursory glance at the alphabetical acrostic pattern of this composition immediately discloses the fact that it has been abridged from a longer composition in which all the letters of the alphabet were represented. The full version appears, in fact, in the Avignon *machzor* and in some fragments of the Cairo *Genizah* collection.

An editor has removed each alternate stanza, which commenced with the phrase *melekh evyon* ("The inconsequential king") and ended with the refrain *ad matay yimlokh* ("How long can he reign?"), and whose purpose in the composition was to serve as a foil by which to contrast "The Supreme King, who reigns forever and ever" (*la-adei ad yimlokh melekh elyon*) with the mortal, earthly monarch in whom people naively put their trust. It is conceivable that before each of the *melekh evyon* verses the Ark curtain was originally drawn, and that it was in order to avoid performing this distracting activity that those alternate verses were subsequently taken out. It might also have been removed as an act of internal censorship so as not to offend the monarchy of the host country, since the original version contains some rather strong expressions that, although motivated only by a pious attempt to enhance the total superiority of God, could nevertheless be construed as an attempt to demean the earthly monarch.

The first (*balah*) and last (*tenumah*) stanzas of the *melekh evyon* verses were subsequently readmitted before the final line (*tokpo la-ad*), although with the precondition that they were recited in an undertone, so as not to give offense.

וּנְתַנֶּה תֹּקֶף
We Will Celebrate the Mighty Holiness

This prayer is probably one of the most moving compositions in the whole of Jewish liturgy, despite the fact that it is unrhymed, not artistically constructed to include any poetic or acrostic devices, and the phraseology employed is not the rich biblical language that most of the *piyyutim* employ. Simplicity and directness are the hallmarks of this composition, with its message couched in short, clipped phrases of three or four words, suggestive of the brevity of man's life span and the sudden twists of fate. It opens with a glimpse into the heavenly Hall of Justice where the Almighty judge is engaged in reviewing the deeds of man. Unlike our administration of law, wherein a witness cannot act as a judge for fear of subjective impression or bias, God alone may act not only as "witness" to the crimes committed, but also as "judge, arbiter, and discerner."

וְתִפְתַּח סֵפֶר הַזִּכְרוֹנוֹת
And You Open the Book of Records

The phrase *Sefer Ha-Zikhronot* is found in the Book of Esther (6:1). It refers there to the royal chronicle of every significant event that occurred in the realm. It was while reading that record that Ahazuerus discovered the hitherto concealed fact that Mordechai had not been rewarded for his loyalty. God, similarly, has his royal "Book of Records," symbolic of the fact that nothing remains concealed from Him—"for You remember all that has been forgotten." Like Mordechai, if we have deserved reward, it will be forthcoming sooner or later, and if, God forbid, we deserve punishment, that fact is also indelibly recorded.

וְחוֹתָם יַד כָּל אָדָם בּוֹ
The Seal of Every Man's Hand Is Set Thereto

This idea is derived from a midrash that states that, at the time when we depart this world, God presents the sinners with a full record and reminder of their wrongdoing, and they sign it as a true record. The author of *U-netaneh tokef* has taken this idea and transferred it to the events of each Rosh Hashanah.

וְקוֹל דְּמָמָה דַקָּה יִשָּׁמַע
The Great *Shofar* Is Sounded, but the Still Small Voice Is Heard

The still small voice is a phrase derived from the aftermath of the famous episode of Elijah's defeat of the prophets of Baal on Mount Carmel. Elijah had to flee for his life from the wrath of the idolatrous Queen Jezebel, after he had exposed those false prophets and incited Israel to put them to the sword.

A tired and hungry fugitive, Elijah enters a cave, where God grants him a specially potent and personal revelation in order to lift his dejected spirit and to summon him to continue his zealous ministry:

> And behold the Lord passed by, and a great and strong wind rent the mountains, and broke in pieces the rocks before the Lord; but the Lord was not in the wind. And after the wind an earthquake; but the Lord was not in the earthquake. And after the earthquake a fire; but the Lord was not in the fire. And after the fire *a still small voice.* And when Elijah heard that, he wrapped his face in a mantle . . . and behold God's voice came unto him.[14]

The phrase *still small voice* (*kol demamah dakah*) has become such a popular idiom in the English language that few are aware of the inherent problem its translation presents. The Hebrew word *demamah* is from a root *dmm*, meaning "to be (struck) dumb," "to be silent." It is very difficult, therefore, to make sense of this concept, of a voice that is both "silent" and yet, at the same time, "small" (or "thin," which approximates closer to the usual meaning of the Hebrew *dakah*)!

It clearly can only refer, therefore, to an *inner* voice, the voice of the emotions, the silent call of the heavenly beloved that the God-intoxicated swear they can hear, so real is the proximity of the Presence.

God was demonstrating powerfully to Elijah that there was no place for fear, depression, or self-doubt, however bleak the circumstances of his plight. God could, of course, cause cataclysmic havoc—wind, earthquake, fire—to manifest Himself and to defend, protect, and guide His chosen prophet. But the most effective protection was the incomparable sense of security induced by the man of faith's own unswerving conviction that he possesses an inner guiding and directing voice, "a still small voice," that, though *still* and inaudible to those around, and though *small*, in the sense that the prophet himself may not always be totally certain that he hears and understands its import, it is indubitably a force within him, a manifestation of a higher will, in which the man of God should glory and in accordance with which he should continue fearlessly with his life's mission.

"The great *shofar* is sounded" on this holy day. But it is not that which will induce the ideal state of repentance. This can only be achieved by our listening out for what is within us—the still small voice. It is the internalization of our desperate desire for God's proximity that will create that potent inner voice. It is not the externally, and artificially, induced vibrations of even the greatest and loudest *shofar*. God may be sensed far more easily within our own soul—where He already resides—than by looking further afield for any evidence of His existence.

וּמַלְאָכִים יֵחָפֵזוּן
The Angels Are Dismayed

The reference to the heavenly angels "quaking with fear" is inspired by Job 4:18—"Behold, He puts no trust in his servants, and His angels He charges with folly." It is a philosophically perplexing notion. In the context of the book of Job it might be explained as referring specifically to the Satan—a free agent whose task is to exploit human weakness. The heavenly accusers also have cause for fear on the judgment day, "for they will not be vindicated in thy sight in law." God will, as it were, spring to the defense of His wayward children as they stand in the dock facing the onslaught of the accusing angels' condemnation.

וְכָל בָּאֵי עוֹלָם תַּעֲבִיר לְפָנֶיךָ
And All Who Enter the World You Cause to Pass before You

This key theme of the *U-netaneh tokef* composition might well surprise adherents of other faiths, who could be forgiven for regarding as an impertinence the confidence with which Jews associate the rest of mankind in their dialogical experience with the divine!

The truth is that we do *not* ask the Christians, Muslims, Hindus, or atheists whether or not they wish to be part of our New Year—and new world—celebration. We assume, gratuitously perhaps, that they will have no reason to object. In so doing, we follow that well-established talmudic principle *zakhin le-adam shelo be-fanav,* that one can take the initiative to act independently on behalf of another, if the end result will accrue to his benefit.

Thus, on Rosh Hashanah barriers of color, creed, and religions are conceptually removed. We perceive of ourselves as citizens of the world, rather than as a separate, "chosen" entity. In the context of human shortcomings we view ourselves as God would view us: as heirs to the same temptations and the same moral and ethical turpitude as those who adhere to other religious systems or to none.

In this sense Rosh Hashanah is truly the anniversary of Creation, and particularly the creation of (pre-Israelite) man. Unlike the other festivals, which celebrate the Israel–God encounter, mediated through history (as is the case with *Pesach,* by reliving the Exodus story), Revelation (*Shavuot*), and nature (through the agricultural aspects of *Pesach, Shavuot,* and *Sukkot*), the biblical source for Rosh Hashanah (Numbers 29:1ff.) gives no clue as to its precise significance. It invites us to think beyond ourselves, to transcend the parochial, to return not merely to our historical roots, but to the basic source of our humanity as children of Adam. Rosh Hashanah is the festival of "all who enter the world"; it is the festival of universalism, the celebration of authentic ecumenism.

None of the established religions can match the spiritual expansiveness of this festival. The major Christian festivals are all parochially tied to the historical and theological circumstances of the founder of the faith. The early Christians borrowed the Jewish *Pesach* (calling it by the Greek name *Pascha*), and converted it into a three-day festival celebrating the death and resurrection of Jesus. *Shavuot* was similarly assimilated into the narrow context of the ascension and the descent of the Holy Spirit upon the apostles. Christianity's other festivals celebrate the nativity, baptism, and passion of its founder. Significantly, Rosh Hashanah was totally ignored within this particularist scheme.

It is no different with Islam's two major festivals of *'id al-kabir* ("Great Festival"), closely related to the context of the pilgrimage (*haj*) to Mecca, and the fast of *Ramadan,* followed by the festival *'id al-fitr* ("Festival of Fast-Breaking").

No religion has at the core of one of its most important festivals such a sensitive concern for, and absolute identification with, "all who enter the world." We thereby translate into reality the challenge contained in the name of our spiritual ancestor, Abraham: "For the father (*Ab*) of a multitude of nations (*raham*) have I made you" (Genesis 17:5). It follows that, as sons of Abraham, we have to regard the multitude of nations as our brothers.

The hostility of those "brother nations" should not surprise us, nor deflect us from our universalistic mission. The aged patriarch, Jacob, was well aware of the strife that bedeviled the relationship between Joseph and his brothers. Yet in spite of—or more probably *because of*—that, he sent Joseph out alone on a potentially dangerous mission of reconciliation and peace. Joseph's *cri de coeur* to the stranger who set him on the right road, "My brethren I am seeking" (Genesis 37:16), has echoed hollowly and chillingly down the ages and pages of our history from ancient Shechem (v. 14) to the displaced persons' camps of postwar Europe and the Refusnik conventicles of the former Soviet Union.

Christian liturgy asks God to "forgive us our trespasses as we forgive those who trespass against us." It is a rather bold formulation that employs its own *alleged* readiness to forgive as a lever to secure a reciprocal divine compassion. In expressing it thus, it gets uncomfortably close to reversing the concept of *imitatio Dei* (imitating the ways of God), by asking God to follow the lead of man, and dispense a corresponding token of "Christian charity."

Judaism, on the other hand, begs for mercy to be dispensed on this day not as a reward for any inherent qualities of Jewish compassion, but as an undeserved expression of divine mercy:

> Our Father, our King, be Thou gracious unto us and answer us, for truly we are destitute of good deeds. Deal Thou with us in charity and lovingkindness and save us.

On Rosh Hashanah in particular we seek out our brethren of all faiths and involve them in our plea for divine mercy and forgiveness. We do it not for ulterior motives, but out of the sincere conviction that Israel's salvation and destiny is inextricably interwoven with that of the rest of mankind, that our mission cannot succeed if the way of divine compassion is barred to any human being, and that our inspirational light to the nations cannot burn brightly if any winds of divine displeasure threaten to extinguish it.

Hence, we involve "all who enter the world" in an act of repentance, prayer, and charity. We wind back the clock of time to the beginning of Creation, and we invoke all the biblical paragons, and especially the Patriarchs, in a supreme entreaty before the heavenly throne:

> Now therefore, O Lord our God, impose Thine awe upon all thy works, and Thy dread over all that Thou hast created, that all thy works may fear thee, and all creatures prostrate themselves before Thee, that they may all form one band to do Thy will with a perfect heart.

It is theologically fashionable to hail Christianity as enunciator of the doctrine of "love thine enemy." But no greater love has any religion than that it devotes the most sacred moments of its religious year to a plea for divine forgiveness to be extended to those who have made it victim to oppression, crusade, forced baptism, inquisition, blood libel, and anti-Semitism.

The anniversary of the Creation of the world is a most appropriate occasion for such universalistic sentiments, for it harks back to the period of prehistory and prereligion. It re-creates thereby the circumstances of an era devoid of political or theological turbulence and rivalry, an era of absolute unity and of inherent uniformity. It focuses on what once was, and what must once again be:

> And the Lord shall reign for ever and ever.
> In that day shall the Lord be One and His name One.

In one of the most profound comments contained in the Mishnah, we find a similar idea enunciated:

> Why was only one individual (Adam) created at the beginning of time? . . . So that no man should say to his fellow, "my ancestry is greater than yours." (*Mishnah Sanhedrin* 4:5)

Differences of class and rank, wealth and status, color and creed are accidental and superficial. They must never blur the essential unity and equal ity of all mankind. On Rosh Hashanah we affirm this unity; and this gives us the confidence to reach out across the abyss that has so often demarcated Jews from their neighbors, to pray fervently on behalf of "all who enter the world."

כִּבְנֵי מָרוֹן
As a Flock of Sheep

This expression, used by the author to describe the manner in which all creatures pass before God's throne, is borrowed from the Mishnah.[15] Even the later talmudic authorities were not too sure, however, of the precise meaning of the phrase. The universally accepted interpretation, adopted by all translations, is "like sheep," on the basis of the Aramaic noun *immra*, "a lamb." *Bnei maron* would therefore mean "young (lit. 'the offspring of') sheep."

The suggestion of the nineteenth-century scholar, N. Brüll,[16] that a textual error has occurred here, whereby a single word *ki-venumeron* has been erroneously split up into two words, has now received corroboration from the research of Professor N. Wieder into a number of medieval liturgical manuscripts.

The word *numeron* was a Greek word, the equivalent of the Latin *numerus*, meaning "a troop (lit. 'numbered formation') of soldiers." Thus, the Mishnah's intention was to depict Israel "as in (*ki-ve*) military formation," filing by the heavenly reviewing stand.

Following the Herd

The imagery of sheep, contained in this well-known quotation draws our attention to one prominent psychological characteristic of human behavior—that we tend to amble through life as aimlessly as sheep in their pen.

We are quite prepared to fritter away, at a very early age, that precious gift of moral self-assertion, of responsible decision-making over issues that affect the development of our character, our values, and our finely tuned consciences, surrendering instead to our herd instinct, preferring to follow, like sheep, those ahead of us in the line.

With little discretion, we create and follow morally flawed role models. We acclaim them for one or another aspect of their personality, appearance, or dress, or for some superficial achievements that came their way more by luck than by design.

Much of the malaise that erodes our present-day society can be reduced to that "herd" mentality that we—and especially our youth (following our example)—have developed.

Few people wish, or are allowed, to express themselves in their own unique way and to pursue a life-style best suited to their natural temperament, their deep personal needs, their spiritual inclinations.

Few have the guts to swim against the tide, to oppose their friends' values—if they consider them shallow and vain—for fear of being excluded from the circle and being regarded as an oddball.

Too many get caught up in a life-style that others determine for them. And, too frequently, the financial and moral strain of keeping up with the others is too great.

But the carousel is traveling too fast for them to get off; and they just cannot summon the moral courage to adopt that lonely alternative of opting out, of kissing good-bye to the prestige and hype of the glitzy social scene. And, after all—they reason—it is not fair to the children to deprive them of their full and equally glitzy social life.

How like sheep we truly are! How rigidly are our eyes transfixed upon our neighbors, to ensure that we are following them closely and cannot be suspected of lagging behind in fashion, in the attainment of worldly acquisitions, in doing the "in" thing, in the "in" place, and becoming a carbon copy of the "in" role model.

Were the rabbis who, centuries ago, employed this image of humans filing like sheep in front of the heavenly throne influenced by their assessment of the reality of human apathy and spiritual lethargy in their day? If so, then little has changed.

Our Rosh Hashanah challenge must be to convince ourselves, and our children, that individuality is the most precious gift a person can possess; that to follow like sheep, irrespective of where one is being led, is the most dangerous exercise imaginable, an abdication of the freedom, independence, and, above all, uniqueness given to us by the Creator.

When, on these High Holy Days, we pass under the Almighty's surveillance, we may indeed have to do so like sheep, docile, humble, and full of remorse. But as we pass along our pilgrimage through life, in the company of our fellow human beings, this is not a pose we should adopt.

Instead, we should be fearless and critical, determined to embrace abiding values and to spurn that which is clearly transient and superficial. We should be critical of our life-style and that of our children, subjecting their moral values, their behavior and their sense of decency, fairness, and compassion to close scrutiny.

We should never tire of reminding them that it is far more gratifying that others should follow them—especially in the direction of goodness, kindness, charity, and holiness—than that, like sheep, they should follow others.

בְּרֹאשׁ הַשָּׁנָה יִכָּתֵבוּן
On the First Day of the Year It Is Inscribed

". . . And on the Day of Atonement it is sealed." This extended period, before man's fate is finally sealed, applies, according to the Talmud,[17] only in the case of one particular category of offenders. The truly righteous do not require a deferment of final judgment—they are inscribed, and their fate sealed, immediately on Rosh Hashanah. The truly wicked likewise have their doom sealed on that day. It is for those who occupy a midway position, whose spiritual pendulum frequently vacillates between virtue and sinfulness, that a period of grace—the Ten Days of Penitence—is granted, for the exalted influence of Rosh Hashanah to inspire them to remorse and pious resolution.

וּמִי יָמוּת
And Who Shall Die

We all accept that death is inevitable. That is, unless it happens to be the death of someone close to us. In such circumstances the logic of death, and its role as providing that essential tension that gives urgency to human endeavor, and that serves in turn as a guarantor of creativity and progress, suddenly becomes incomprehensible. At such a time death becomes an implacable enemy rather than an inevitable stage through which all mortals have to pass.

Ben-Zion Bokser gave an inspired illustration that puts death into a helpful perspective. To someone who expressed a grudge against God for taking the life of his close friend, a truly righteous man who deserved to live forever, God appeared in a dream and demonstrated what life would be like if, indeed, all nature survived forever.

God placed him in an immortal world where not a flower faded nor a blossom withered. Summer came and went, but nothing changed one iota. The crowning glory of nature in full summer bloom, with its rich and varied hues and the majestic beauty and power of its intertwining stems, leaves and flowers, took on a fixed permanence. Perfection was preserved for all eternity; life was rendered permanently immune to the ravages of time.

For a while the dreamer placed into this situation was thrilled by it all, until the realization dawned that this static state meant that although nothing grew old, decayed, or died, nothing was born either! Though spared the sadness of witnessing decline and death, he could not look forward with eager expectation, nor observe with rewarding fascination, the birth of new life and its growth and development, and the marvels of the ever-changing face of God's earth and human society.

The dreamer soon tired of the sameness of everything: the same shapes, sizes, formations, and colors. He longed to witness, enjoy, and be inspired by the evolution of new plant, animal, and especially human, life. And when he awoke from his dream he was content to surrender the bittersweet gift of immortality, appreciating full well that the heady experience of even a limited life span—albeit with death as its sad though inevitable climax—was still far preferable to the boring immutability that was its alternative.[18]

By addressing itself to such core issues of human fate, *U-netaneh tokef* established for itself an unrivaled emotional appeal, notwithstanding the fact that the authorship of this most awesome composition is shrouded in mystery. Perhaps that is as it should be, for its sentiments are universal. Praise of God can be framed by numerous poets, each with his own individual style and emphases; but *U-netaneh tokef* identifies the singular mood, the deep-seated apprehension, that grips all alike at this period. Will we, and our dear ones, escape "the net which is spread for all creatures"? Will sickness, accident, violence, anxiety, and financial ruination stalk our lives this coming year? Will the angel of death knock on our door? We are *all* the authors of the *U-netaneh tokef* sentiments if the High Holy Day spirit has at all penetrated our hearts.

Its popularity is generally attributed to the efforts of Rabbi Kalonymos ben Meshullam, the celebrated eleventh-century liturgical poet of Mainz, Germany, though its attribution to the legendary Rabbi Amnon, who is supposed to have composed it as he lay dying in the agony of martyrdom, has become an inspirational axiom of Jewish folklore. Amnon is credited with having appeared to Rabbi Kalonymos in a dream, three days after his death, to teach him the prayer in order to popularize it in Israel.[19]

Reflections

U-netaneh tokef has never lost its emotional pull, neither has the relevance of its summons become dimmed even in our modern age. Indeed, in the light of the vagaries of highly competitive business enterprises, of the many casualties of our too-frequent economic recessions, of the rootlessness that characterizes our age, and the overwhelming tensions and problems that the fragmentation of family life has brought in its wake, some of the references in this composition do strike highly responsive chords. "Who shall go wandering . . . who shall be harassed . . . who shall be afflicted . . . who shall become poor . . . who shall be humbled" are all questions that, in an age of economic uncertainty, superficial relationships, and emotional turbulence, most of us will at some time be asking.

In the light of the typhoons and earthquakes that, in recent years alone, have caused such widespread devastation in countries and states quite close to home, the reference to our apprehension of the consequences of such natural disasters is also truly relevant. And with the worldwide scourge of AIDS, the reference to those who will die "by plague" takes on a telling immediacy.

It may be suggested, however, that this haunting prayer must lose some of its pathos when considered by so many of us from the coziness of our middle-class suburbia. After all, the very last thing we fear, as citizens of the most agriculturally and commercially highly developed countries of the world, is "death by hunger or thirst." If anything, most of us are waging a constant personal battle against the effects of too much food! Then again, apart from those who visit exotic safari parks, few of us are in danger of "perishing by wild beasts"! Furthermore, most of us try not to live in dangerous inner-city areas, cheek-by-jowl with violence and vice; indeed, we avoid like the plague any fraternization with gangsters and mafiosi. So what possible emotional or even cognitive chords can be struck by the references in this composition to our apprehension of "death by the sword . . . or by strangling or stoning"?

A brave and sensitive attempt to relate *all* these references to modern conditions of life has been made by Rabbis S. Rabinowitz, S. Kanter, and J. Riemer. It appears in the *Mahzor for Rosh Hashanah and Yom Kippur*, issued by the Rabbinical Assembly of New York, and is well worth quoting:

Reflections

When we really begin a new year it is decided,
And when we actually repent it is determined:

Who shall be truly alive and who shall merely exist;

Who shall be happy and who shall be miserable;

Who shall attain fulfillment in his days
And who shall not attain fulfillment in his days;

Who shall be tormented by the fire of ambition
And who shall be overcome by the waters of failure;

Who shall be pierced by the sharp sword of envy
And who shall be torn by the wild beast of resentment;

Who shall hunger for companionship
And who shall thirst for approval;

Who shall be shattered by the earthquake of social change
And who shall be plagued by the pressures of conformity;

Who shall be strangled by insecurity
And who shall be stoned into submission;

Who shall be content with his lot
And who shall wander in search of satisfaction;

Who shall be serene and who shall be distraught;

Who shall be at ease and who shall be afflicted with anxiety;

Who shall be poor in his own eyes
And who shall be rich in tranquillity;

Who shall be brought low with futility
And who shall be exalted through achievement.

But repentance, prayer and good deeds
have the power to change the character of our lives.

Let us resolve to repent, to pray and to do good deeds
so that we may begin a truly new year.[20]

אָדָם יְסוֹדוֹ מֵעָפָר
As for Man, His Origin Is from the Dust

The primary source of sin is pride and self-delusion, taking the psalmist's words "You have made him but a little lower than the angels" (Psalm 8:6) personally, as referring to ourselves. The relationship of man to the dust from which he was created is highlighted by the Midrash, which states that

> if man merits it, God says to him: "I created everything ready for your majestic arrival as the climactic event of creation, preparing nature for you like a laid table for an honored guest." However, if man behaves unworthily, God reminds him that both the gnat and the flea antedated his creation, leaving man almost as an afterthought.

This is reinforced philologically by the Hebrew word for man, *adam*, which may be related either to the word *demut* (the divine "image") or to *adamah* ("base earth").

The great Nobel prizewinner Shmuel Yosef Agnon demonstrated most admirably just how sensitive he was to the need of man to recognize his lowly origins at all times, especially at moments when a surrender to a little self-congratulation might have been excused. It is related that when the news broke that he had been awarded the Nobel prize for literature, all his friends and family, as well as scores of reporters and photographers crowded inside his home. One of the photographers asked him to pose at his study desk and pretend to be writing. Agnon obliged, and scribbled a few words on his writing pad while the cameras were clicking noisily away.

When most of the media people had left, someone went over and, out of curiosity, glanced at what the great man had scribbled down. There, staring up at him, were five words from our composition: *adam yesodo me-afar ve-sofo le-afar* ("As for man, his origin is of the dust, and his end is to dust!").

Not many people would be preoccupied with such humble and self-negating sentiments at that moment of supreme international achievement, attention, and acclaim!

וְכֹל מַאֲמִינִים
And All Believe

This prayer is another alphabetic acrostic. The authorship is not known for certain but it is now generally attributed to the earliest Palestinian Hebrew poet, Yannai (sixth to seventh centuries C.E.), who also composed the *piyyut*, *Az Rov Nissim,* in the Passover *Haggadah.*

Yannai's pioneering contribution to Hebrew poetry, his personality, and his numerous poetic compositions were only brought to light this century with the discovery of the Cairo *Genizah.* He was known hitherto only through some scattered references to him in early medieval sources. Through modern research many anonymous fragments of poetry have been discovered and attributed to Yannai's authorship, and this important literary figure has now been rescued from the oblivion of antiquity.

The poem proceeds in a stair-like progression of ideas. An idea of God is presented in the first stich (introduced by the definite article, *ha*), and the key word is then taken over to form the subject of the succeeding affirmation, introduced by the words *Ve-khol maaminim.* Thus:

> *HABOCHEIN u-vodeik ginzei nistarot. . . . Ve-khol maaminim shehu BOCHEIN kelayot.*

The popularity of this hymn ensured for it a place among the select group that are recited on both Rosh Hashanah and Yom Kippur.

The opening line of this twofold alphabetical acrostic poem describes God as "the One who takes firm hold of the scales of justice," a phrase derived from Deuteronomy 32:41. The Midrash[21] on that verse states that "in the same way that God does not influence the judicial process when reviewing the deeds of the other nations, so Israel must expect to be subjected to a comprehensive inquiry into her own actions." That the concept of the "Chosen People" does not confer upon Israel special immunity in the face of divine judgment, is the import of this poem.

The poem lays special emphasis on the divine quality of mercy that is extended to those who exhibit even a trace of remorse—"He opens the door to those who knock in repentance" (line 16). God is so long-suffering and indulgent that "He closes an eye to the rebellious" (line 15).

The phrase *ve-kholelam yachad* (line 10) has been misunderstood by all translations. The general rendering is "He is all-perfect" (Routledge), "all-embracing" (Birnbaum), "able to accomplish all things" (De Sola), "combines all together" (ArtScroll). None of these take account of the objective suffix (*am*) "them," attached to the verb. This relates back to the previous subject, namely, God's creatures whom he had "formed in the womb."

M. Zulay has shown that the verb *kalal* means "to complete an act of creation."[22] The whole stanza may, therefore, be loosely rendered, "And all believe that he fashioned them in the womb. He that is all-powerful *sees them safely born.*"

The following line—*ha-lan be-seiter be-tzeil shadday* ("He dwells in the secret place in the shadow of the Almighty")—is most perplexing. The subject—as in all the corresponding lines—can only be God. How, then, can we speak of *God* dwelling in the shadow of the Almighty?

This line is borrowed directly from Psalm 91:1—*yosheiv be-seiter elyon be-tzeil shadday yitlonan*. The classical commentators—Rashi, Ibn Ezra, and so on—all assume that the subject of the phrase is a righteous human being. They render accordingly, "He who dwells in the shelter of the Most High, who abides in the shadow of the Almighty . . . ," a rendering followed by most modern translations. From our poem, however, it is clear that early Jewish tradition took the subject of this phrase to be God Himself, a fact supported by the rendering of Targum, the official Aramaic translation of the Bible.[23] The doctrine is to be seen against the backcloth of the various manifestions—or extra concentrations[24]—of God's presence that are hypostatized in rabbinic literature, such as *Shekhinah* ("Indwelling") *Ruach Ha-Kodesh* ("Holy Spirit"), *Memra* ("created word"), *Kavod* ("glory").

וְיֶאֱתָיוּ
All the World Shall Come

In the preceding three paragraphs a vision of the future is presented when righteousness will be vindicated, the national restoration under the royal Davidic line effected, and all nations will be united in submission to the will of God.

The present composition, in blank verse, echoes this messianic hope, although emphasizing exclusively the universalistic theme and omitting any reference to the restoration of Israel's national fortunes.

The alphabetical acrostic pattern is not so easily discernible here. It makes its appearance as the initial root-letter of the verbs employed as the opening word of each phrase (viye*v*archu, veya*g*idu, veyi*d*reshu, viye*h*alelu, etc.). It will be noticed, however, that the letter *zayin* is represented twice, by the verbs *ve-yizbechu* and *ve-yiznechu*. What has occurred here is that these were originally separate, variant versions, one of which was probably inserted in the margin. A later copyist mistakenly embodied it into the main text, where it has remained!

The final word *melukhah* ("kingdom") enables the poem to blend into the context, as a link with the opening word of the next passage *ve-timlokh* ("And you shall be *King*"). It forms, therefore, an appropriate poetic climax to the third blessing of the *Amidah*, which concludes by blessing God as *ha-melekh ha-kadosh* ("The holy King").

וּמִפְּנֵי חֲטָאֵינוּ
But Because of Our Sins

This composition appears in the *Musaf Amidah* recited on all festivals. On *Pesach, Shavuot*, and *Sukkot* a phrase, *laalot ve-leiraot u-le-hishtachavot lefanekha* ("And we are unable to go up to appear and worship before you") is included in the opening lines, since on those festivals the pilgrimages to Jerusalem were made. This composition also inspired the *Attah yatzarta* prayer, recited on *Shabbat Rosh Chodesh* in the repetition of the *Musaf Amidah*.

This poignant plea to God, to restore the national independence of His people in their holy land, and to reintroduce the Temple service, is accompanied by an admission, in the opening sentence, that it was "on account of our sins that we were exiled from our country and banished far from our land." This may appear to some as a simplistic philosophy of Jewish history, one that would appear to be contradicted by the fact of our national restoration in the twentieth century, the very period of unprecedented assimilation! A popular response is to suggest that the gift of the land of Israel in our day is, indeed, totally undeserved, and is to be justified only as a token of divine love and mercy toward His reprobate children.[25]

The great thirteenth-century Bible commentator and halakhist Moses ben Nachman (*Ramban*) expands upon the basic principle enunciated in the opening line of this composition—that sin and exile are linked by cause and effect—by suggesting that the early stories in Genesis were included solely to promote this fundamental principle:

> God placed Adam in the Garden of Eden, which was the choicest place on earth and the residence of the divine spirit, until Adam's sin caused his banishment from there. The generation of the flood was removed from God's earth because of their sin, and only the righteous man (Noah) and his family escaped. Again, the sin of their descendants (who built the tower of Babel) caused them to be banished and scattered over the face of the earth. . . . God drove the wicked Canaanites from His holy land and settled there the people who performed His will. The history contained in Genesis would have served to teach Israel the lesson that by serving God they merited to inherit the land, and if they sinned against Him, the land "would vomit them out as it did the nation that came before them" (Leviticus 18:28).[26]

Nascent Reform Judaism, saturated by its idealistic vision of the Emancipation, found the very notion of the "exile" theologically unacceptable, and that it might be construed as a punishment for Israel's sin as absolutely anathema. Reform Judaism regarded Jewry's dispersion as a positive situation, enabling her to fulfill her prophetic mission of constituting "a light to the nations." Hence Reform's initial hostility to the theoretical principles and practical initiatives of the Zionist movement.

Rejection of the relationship between sin and exile meant that Reform Judaism could not possibly enunciate the opening sentiments of our *U-mipnei chata'einu* composition. Thus, in the 1866 edition of Joseph Aub's prayer book there is no reference to sin, merely the statement, "Our fathers were exiled from their land, and far removed from their soil."[27] The reason for this exile is made quite clear: "to sanctify Your Name in the world, from the rising of the sun unto the going down thereof." From the beginning of the twentieth century the doctrine of the ancestral exile was phased out entirely, as was, in due course, the entire paragraph.

However, for Reform Judaism, which claims to stand in direct succession to the teachings of the Hebrew prophets, such a "solution" raises more problems than it solves. For, as Jakob J. Petuchowski, one of its most distinguished theologians, explains:

> The doctrine that "we were exiled on account of our sins" is not a doctrine which was invented by Pharisaic or medieval Judaism. It is, in fact, a doctrine which is based on one of the more prominent teachings of the Hebrew Prophets. . . . To that extent, therefore, the traditional Jewish posture of reacting to persecution with penitence may be said to constitute an authentic element of Prophetic religion; and it remains one of the innumerable ironies of religious history that those who, more than all other Jews, claimed to represent the religion of the Prophets in the nineteenth century found it necessary to remove that element of Prophetic teaching which had always been a striking component of Jewish worship.[28]

For our younger generation—both those born and living in Israel as well as those of the Diaspora—who take our precious homeland so much for granted, there is a particular benefit in reminding ourselves that Judaism has always maintained that there is a moral and spiritual price to be paid for its possession, and that we must regard it as not only a haven against persecution, but more, as a unique stimulus to the most exalted values and principles of our religious heritage. Truly, that most potent message of "because of our sins we were exiled from our land" is most timely and significant.

Repentance and *returning* are covered by one and the same Hebrew word: *teshuvah*. Returning to our holy land must be viewed then, at the same time, as a summons to repentance, and as an opportunity to aspire to that state of moral and spiritual regeneration that will indeed cause the word *exile* to be expunged forever from the experiential vocabulary of our nation.

The plea for the rebuilding of the Temple and the restoration of the sacrificial system, contained in this composition as well as in the *Retzeih* blessing recited in every *Amidah*, has taken on a new significance in our day with the reunification of Jerusalem and Jewish possession of the Temple Mount.

The rebuilding of the Temple is universally accepted as an event linked to the advent of the messianic age. Rashi and Maimonides differ only in the method, not the period, of its restoration. Rashi,[29] inspired by the verse "The sanctuary which *Your hands* have established, O Lord" (Exodus 15:17),[30] maintains that the third Temple will appear miraculously as a fully built edifice provided by God. This view is clearly expressed in the *Nacheim* prayer, recited in the *Amidah* of the afternoon service on the Fast of *Av*: ". . . For with fire You did consume it, O Lord, and with fire You will, in future, restore it."[31] Maimonides, on the other hand, believed that the Temple would be built in the normal way, but by the Messiah, and that his ability to achieve its construction would serve to substantiate his messianic claims.[32]

The Talmud states that the future restoration will follow a particular sequence: First, Jerusalem will be restored, then the monarchy of the house of David will be reestablished, after which the Temple will be rebuilt to become a place of prayer for all nations. Finally, the sacrificial system will be reinstituted.[33] Our prayers for the restoration of these several spiritual institutions, none of which will function until the messianic era,[34] are, therefore, rather vague evocations of our desire to experience something akin to a national and spiritual state of vindication and fulfillment at the denouement of God's cosmic plan.

עָלֵינוּ
It Is Our Duty

Although in the second half of the Middle Ages this prayer became invested with such importance that it was introduced as the main conclusion to each of the three daily services throughout the year, it was originally reserved exclusively for the High Holy Day recitation, as an introduction to the *malkhuyot* verses (which acclaim the "Kingship" of God) of the *Musaf* Service on Rosh Hashanah.[35]

The popularity of the prayer grew because of its association with martyrdom. It was used, for example, as the dying prayer of the martyrs of Blois in southern France who were massacred in 1171. Its choice was probably determined by a particularly fierce reference that they applied to their merciless murderers: "For they worship vanity and slabber (*lehevel varik*) and pray to a god who cannot save." This phrase was subsequently expunged by the censor, but it is still widely recited, as, for example, in the popular ArtScroll and *Rinat Yisrael* editions. To foster a spirit of tolerance, *The Authorised Daily Prayer Book* (S. Singer's edition) of Anglo-Jewry has consistently omitted the reference.

Such bitter condemnation of their persecutors' faith by the victims of crusades and *autos da fé* is wholly pardonable. They must have been totally mystified as to how a religion of love could initiate, foster, and carry out such atrocities. (One is reminded of a comment by Elie Wiesel that the Holocaust is as much a problem for Christians as it is for Jews!)

Christian authorities in subsequent centuries were particularly incensed by the insulting reference to the founder of their religion, and were unimpressed by some Jewish efforts to demonstrate that the author never had Christianity or its founder in mind when he created his composition. To buttress this latter assertion a variety of theories were offered as to its period of authorship—ranging from Joshua (who had in mind the idolatrous Canaanite religion) to the Men of the Great Assembly (fifth century B.C.E.) who were attacking the Persian dualists.[36] What all these theories had in common was the crucial point that it was a pre-Christian prayer with no offense intended to the dominant religion.

It was through the testimony of converted Jews that medieval Christianity got wind of an unauthoritative and mischievous reinterpretation of the meaning of the prayer that was suggested by some through highlighting the fact that the numerical value (*gematria*) of the word *varik* ("slabber") added up to 316, equivalent to that of *Yeshu* (Jesus)!

Through the researches of Professor N. Wieder,[37] we now see that others even managed to include an additional oblique defamatory reference to the Muslim religion. This was achieved by insisting on a variant reading (*le-hevel*), *ve-larik*. With the additional letter, *lammed*, inserted into the second noun *varik*, the two words now added up to a numerical value of 413, the equivalent of *Yeshu Muchamet* (Jesus/Mohammed)!

Some congregations have a custom of reciting *Aleinu* aloud, word for word. This goes back to a decree of the Russian government in 1703, accompanied by the appointment of inspectors to visit synagogues in order to listen to its recitation so as to ensure that the offending phrase was omitted.

Because of the wide attention focused upon this prayer, Jewish internal censorship became particularly sensitive to any other expression that could be misinterpreted. This resulted in the practice of reciting in an undertone the verse *She-lo sam chelkeinu ka-hem ve-goraleinu ke-chol hamonam* ("He has not made our portion like theirs, nor our fate like their multitude"), which explains why we close the Ark while reciting that sentiment silently.

While all these medieval vicissitudes suffered by the *Aleinu* are of great interest, its reputed author, the great talmudist Abba Arikha[38] (third century C.E.), had only one purpose in mind: to highlight the sole kingship of God and to deride all idolators and the objects of their veneration. It breathes such an adoration of God that one medieval commentator, R. Eleazar of Worms (twelfth to thirteenth centuries), actually called the prayer "the Song of Songs of our liturgy."[39]

Aleinu is written in a style similar to that of the early *piyyut*, with short lines, of about four words to a line, and with a simplicity and clarity of expression. The reference to Israel "bowing and prostrating" is especially appropriate to the Temple practice of full prostration on the ground,[40] especially on Yom Kippur when these prostrations were increased in response to the extra invocations of the divine name. In recollection of this, it is still our common practice to make a full prostration on the ground during the *Musaf* recitation of *Aleinu* on the High Holy Days—this being the only time when Jews are permitted to perform prostrations on account of the significance it assumed in non-Jewish worship.[41]

לְתַקֵּן עוֹלָם בְּמַלְכוּת שַׁדַּי
To Perfect the World through the Almighty's Sovereignty

The above translation, followed by the ArtScroll edition, may be construed as a rather overidealistic sentiment. The Routledge translation has simply "when the world *shall be set under* the kingdom of the Almighty." The problem is the word *letakein*, which in the Bible has the much weaker nuance of "to straighten," as in the phrase *mi yukhal le-takein et asher ivto* ("Who can straighten what He has made crooked?") (Ecclesiastes 7:13). "Straightening out" or "correcting" the world, setting it on the right path, falls rather short of "perfecting" it.

That the prayer itself does not expect the state of perfection to be attained here on earth is indicated by the fact that it sets its sight at the outset on the modest achievement of a situation wherein "You will remove the abominations from the earth, and the idols shall be utterly cut off." (Indeed, such a reference lends support to the view that this is a very early, certainly pre-Christian, composition when idolatry was the great issue.)

That what is envisaged is not yet that of total perfection is indicated also by the reference to three categories of people who will coexist with the situation described as *tikkun olam*, a restored world. These are the *bnei basar* ("the children of flesh"), the *rishei aretz* ("the wicked of the earth"), and the *yoshvei teiveil* ("the inhabitants of the earth"). According to the *Zohar*,[42] the "children of flesh" are those who have only partially repented.

Thus, we have here a counterpart to the three general categories that the Sages refer to with regard to judgment on Rosh Hashanah: *tzaddikim* (the righteous), *beinonim* (those who stand at the crossroads between righteousness and wickedness), and *resha'im* (the wicked). Now, those who will achieve the desired state of *le-takein olam*, restoring the world, are clearly the *righteous*. The *bnei basar*, who have not completely repented, are the *beinonim*, and the *rishei aretz* are quite obviously the *resha'im*.

The restoration of the world that is hoped for in this prayer cannot be qualitatively superior to the state of the world at the beginning of human history. And the Torah makes no attempt to hide the imperfections of Adam and Eve, Cain and Abel. Indeed, they also fulfilled the terms of our prayer, they also "recognized and knew that to God every knee should bend and every tongue should swear." They did not worship idols and they accepted "the yoke of His kingship." But that did not mean that their world or their conduct was absolutely perfect. They were born human; and they had human imperfections. And so will we, even though the time will come when atheism will be a thing of the past, and "God will rule over us for ever and ever."

Our task, then, must be *le-takein olam*, in the spirit of Routledge's rendering: "when the world will be *set under* the kingdom of heaven." Such a world, of *submission* to heaven, our humanity can cope with. A world of *perfection*, on the other hand, makes men not "a little lower than the angels," but the very angels themselves!

The impossibility of achieving a state of perfection for the whole of mankind is illustrated by the story told of Reb Levi Yitzchok of Berditchev, "the poor man's rabbi," who, at the conclusion of Yom Kippur, once asked an illiterate tailor what he prayed to God for, since he knew that he could not have read the official prayers.

"I said to God," replied the tailor, "Dear God, I know You want me to repent of my sins. But I can tell You, they are so few, You wouldn't even notice them. Okay, on occasions, I admit, I failed to return to the customers the bits of leftover cloth. A technicality! Yes, there were even the odd occasions when I could not help it, and I did eat some food that was not Kosher! What's that I hear You say? A heinous crime? Well if it is, God, then forgive my impudence, but, with all due respect and deference, is *Your* slate so clean? What about the violence and tragedy You tolerate in Your world? The massacres of innocents, the slaughter of the pious, mothers robbed of their babes, young women bereaved of husbands, Starvation,

Pain, Sorrow. You must admit, God, that compared with my occasional misdemeanor You have far more to account for! I'll tell you what, Lord! Let's make a deal! You forgive me, and I'll forgive You!"

"Foolish man!" thundered Reb Levi Yitzchok. "You let God off too lightly! You had Him in the palm of your hand. You were in an excellent position to extract from Him the promise of redemption for the entire Jewish people!"

But Levi Yitzchok knew full well that the tailor had, in fact, struck the best bargain available to him. Redemption of the entire world is not so readily on offer. It is not an instrument we can operate. *Striving* for perfection, on the other hand, certainly *is* within our capacity. So is self-redemption, self-refinement, self-sacrifice, and self-renewal. And these are the challenges of this prayer—and of this period.

In the mystical tradition popularized by Isaac Luria, as opposed to the esoteric principles of the earlier Zoharic writings, the doctrine of *tikkun* becomes a cornerstone of the entire interactive mystical mosaic.[43] In mysticism it definitely does refer to the notion of perfecting the world. But it goes much beyond that, and embraces not only the idea of restoring the primeval harmony of the entire cosmos, but even the very daring notion of perfecting the harmony and unity of the divine being. The kabbalists believed that, at the very dawn of the creative process, the *Sefirot* (creative emanations, or self-extensions, from the essence of God) were too potent to be contained within their vessels, which were similarly made of spiritual light. What ensued was a cataclysmic *shevirat he-keilim*, "breaking of the vessels," which caused a spillage of primary divine substance to become diffused and strewn all over the cosmos.

This fissure in the divine composition—referred to as the separation of the Holy One and His *Shekhinah*—can only be repaired, and God made "whole," by the process of *tikkun*. This is achieved by man performing to the full his sacred task of redeeming all the evil in the world, through Torah, *mitzvot*, and prayer. Every manifestation of good and act of vanquishing evil sends back to the heavenly source some of those rays of spiritual light that were lost to God's Being. When the entire process will have been completed, in the messianic era, then, as our *Aleinu* prayer asserts, "God will be One and His name One."

As we have indicated above, this complex mystical idea of cosmic perfection and redemption is a much later development of the concepts and phraseology that appear in this prayer. At the time of its composition, *Aleinu* was no more than a plea for all mankind to mend its ways and to acknowledge the implications of the presence of God as a reality in the world.

הֱיֵה עִם פִּיפִיּוֹת
Inspire the Lips
אוֹחִילָה לָאֵל
I Will Hope in God

We have referred above to the diffidence with which the composers of liturgical hymns introduced them into the statutory services, and the need felt by them to preface their new compositions with a *reshut*,[44] which assured the congregation that their hymns were fully in line with Orthodox sentiment, and which, at the same time, expressed the sense of humility and inadequacy that burdened them as they assumed the role of representative of the congregation.

These two compositions were inserted here precisely to serve this purpose, as an introductory *reshut* to the major divisions of the *Musaf Amidah*: the *Malkhuyot*, *Zikhronot*, and *Shofarot*. These same two *reshut* compositions are utilized in the identical position (following *Aleinu*) in the *Musaf* service on Yom Kippur. Their purpose there is, likewise, to serve as an introduction to another major division of the *Amidah*, the *Avodah*, describing the order of the service of the High Priest in Temple times.[45]

It is clear then, that these *reshut* compositions were not originally written for the particular prayers to which they now serve as introductions. The *Ochilah la-El*, for example, is employed in Sephardi rites as the opening *reshut* for the repetition of the *Amidah*. That, indeed, seems to have been its original purpose, a fact that explains the presence of the verse *Adonai sefatai tiftach*, the prefatorial verse of the *Amidah*.

The composition *Heyeih im pifiyot* has clearly been adapted and expanded in order to make it contextually suited, particularly to the composition of *Al kein nekaveh* that follows. This is apparent from the fact that the version in the Sephardi rite is considerably shorter, comprising merely the opening requests for divine inspiration ("Our God . . . Teach them . . . and make known to them how they may glorify You"), followed by the plea that no impediment should be found in their speech ("Suffer them not to falter with their tongue . . . and guard their lips from uttering any word that is not according to Your will"). This, then, was the kernel of this *reshut*. It was expanded to include references to the sacred role of the *chazan* and the reliance of the congregation upon his ministrations, as well as to include an allusion to the following composition. This is achieved by means of the phrase *berekh lekha yikhre'un* ("They bend the knee unto You"), which corresponds to the verse *Kiy lekha tikhra kol berekh* in the *Al kein nekaveh* composition.

The second *reshut, Ochilah la-El*, is, similarly, an expanded version. Its kernel comprises one four-line stanza, with four words to each line, and the opening word of each line commencing with an *alef* to emphasize the personal nature of the plea. The added section contains three biblical verses (Psalms 16:1, 51:17, and 19:15), though the usual introductory formulae (*ka-katuv, ve-ne'emar*, etc.) have been omitted before each verse.

Attention is drawn by the Birnbaum footnote[46] to one phrase in the text—*bam she-onam*—that, it is claimed, "does not seem to make sense unless it is read as one word." There is no basis for this conjecture, especially in the light of the universal acceptance of the existing reading according to all rites and manuscripts. Had the text been suspect, alternative readings would have certainly presented themselves. Birnbaum, rather inconsistently, offers a textual emendation to solve the problem, while at the same time omitting the phrase entirely from his translation! The sense of the phrase that Birnbaum finds difficult, is, simply, "Let not *their great communities*[47] be let down *by them* (*bam*)," namely, by any unworthy spiritual leaders.

Malkhuyot

עַל כֵּן נְקַוֶּה
Therefore We Hope

This composition was certainly created in order to serve as an introduction to the *Malkhuyot* verses that give expression to the "Kingship" of God. It emphasizes the scope of this concept, which is not merely a graphic anthropomorphism but a real messianic expectation that, in the hereafter, wickedness will cease and all mankind will clearly and potently sense the nearness of God and be moved to give Him their total spiritual allegiance as monarch of the Universe.

The universalism of this composition is marveled at by one commentator in his comment on the phrase "when *the world* shall be subject to the Kingdom of the Almighty, and *all humanity* shall call upon Your name, and You will cause *all the wicked of the earth* to turn back to You." The *Iyyun Tefillah*[48] observes:

> How uniquely long-suffering Israel is may be inferred from these sentiments. For the Jew, who, throughout his history, has suffered anguish and oppression at the hands of the evil-doers, is, nevertheless, as concerned for the fate of his tormentors as he is for his own. So he stands, in solemn prayer, petitioning the Almighty to grant enlightenment to his enemies so that they may recognize God's sovereignty and share in the reward that is treasured up for the faithful.

כַּכָּתוּב בְּתוֹרָתֶךָ
As It Is Written in Your Law

This verse, which throughout the year we regard as an intrinsic part of the second paragraph of *Aleinu*, will be seen in the present context to display its true purpose, namely to serve as the first of the ten biblical verses employed here in the *Malkhuyot* as proof-texts to depict the Kingship of God. In our daily version of *Aleinu* we conclude by adducing merely the first and the penultimate of the ten verses.

Modern scholarship has proved that the *Malkhuyot* section was not introduced into the High Holy Day liturgy until the period of Rabbi Akivah and the Bar Kochba revolt against the Roman occupation of Palestine. Its introduction may have had a nationalistic motive to strengthen determination in order to prepare the nation for the forthcoming struggle to overthrow the foreign kingship and replace it with *the Kingdom of God*.[49]

That the *Malkhuyot* section was a later innovation may be inferred from the fact that, whereas the *Zikhronot* and *Shofarot* each have their own special concluding blessing, which makes a direct reference to the theme of the section, the *Malkhuyot* section does not. The latter had to be artificially provided with a blessing that was already an intrinsic element of the *Amidah* (*Barukh . . . mekaddesh yisrael ve-yom ha-zikkaron*).

Sounding of the *Shofar*

The list of notes sounded at this point to herald the *Malkhuyot*, as given in the Routledge and De Sola editions, is misleading. *Ten* notes are, in fact, sounded for each of the three sections (as correctly given in the Birnbaum edition), according to the following pattern:

Tekiah	*Shevarim-Teruah*	*Tekiah*	(four notes)
Tekiah	*Shevarim*	*Tekiah*	(three notes)
Tekiah	*Teruah*	*Tekiah*	(three notes)

At the end of the third (*Shofarot*) section a *Tekiah Gedolah* ("long drawn-out *tekiah*") is sounded. Again this has been omitted from those two editions.

הַיּוֹם הֲרַת עוֹלָם
This Day the World Was Called into Being

These verses reflect a fatalistic attitude toward human destiny. Just as man has no control over whether he is born "a son (of a household)" or "a servant," but, in either situation, can merely hope to be the recipient of as much favor as is consonantal with his particular position, so man has no control over the determination of his own status in the eyes of God. God assigns a position to man in accordance with the nature of the relationship with him that God desires. We must hope and pray for a filial relationship; but we must also accept that, inevitably, there will be epochs when we are undeserving, and are relegated to the subordinate status of servants.[50]

Within the context of the sounding of the *shofar*, which, in biblical times, heralded the manumission of all slaves in the Jubilee year, these particular verses may be regarded as a challenge to Israel to improve her relationship with God, and, if her status has hitherto been that of "servant," to regard the sounding of the *shofar* on Rosh Hashanah as heralding the end of that status and the opportunity for initiation into a new relationship with God as children of a loving Father.

Creation and Atonement

It may well be asked how this festival, commemorating the act of Creation, evolved into an occasion for introspection, remorse for sin, and atonement. A clue is provided by Maimonides:

> When a man contemplates the divine achievements analytically, he is immediately overwhelmed and over-awed by the knowledge of how restricted is his own knowledge by comparison with the Omniscient One. As King David said: "When I see Your heavens, the work of Your fingers—what is man that Thou art mindful of him or the son of man that Thou takest account of him?"[51]

This sense of awe before the majesty of Creation, with its attendant feelings of human worthlessness, finds expression in several of our High Holy Day liturgical compositions. We recall the *Maasei Elokeinu* poem, which contrasts "the work of our God" with "the work of man":

The work of our God.
In heaven beyond compare,
He maketh His dwelling the skies;
No angel His likeness share:
As grasshoppers men, in His eyes.

The work of Man.
By craft his devices are led,
'Mid guile his abode from his birth;
The place of the worm is his bed,
His grave is a cleft of the earth.[52]

Rosh Hashanah makes two clear points: that nature's power and glory are a mere manifestation—indeed, a pale reflection—of the unique omniscience and omnipotence of God, the Creator, that we celebrate and proclaim on this festival; and, equally important, that puny man must stand in awe and in awareness of his worthlessness, powerlessness, and sinfulness, as he confronts the genius and perfection that suffuse the universe.

It is less likely, however, these days, that that sense of awe before the grandeur of Creation will be sufficient to instill remorse for sin or fear of the consequences of defying the Being who is the embodiment of such creative power. The more modern man appears to have cracked the secret code of human existence—whether it be through the discovery of the basic DNA molecule of life or the mysteries of astrophysics—the more the glory of the Creator becomes overshadowed, if not eclipsed, by the power and genius of His creation.

While modern perceptions prefer to hail "science," or "the fruits of human progress," or "the wonders of nature," Rosh Hashanah comes to redress the balance and to restore the supremacy of the sacred Being who is the omniscient architect of all existence.

The ancient problem of the use of the plural formulation in the phrase "let *us* create man in *our* image after *our* likeness" (Genesis 1:26), falls away, we suggest, in the wake of the divine attribute of *Sof maaseh be-machshavah techilah,* that God's mere, initial thought instantaneously effects the final and complete fulfillment of that enterprise. Thus, simultaneously with the germination of the divine idea, "Let us create man," man came into existence. God was, therefore, in effect already addressing the newly created man when He said "Let us—*together*—create a mankind that will reflect our conjoint image and likeness." God was, at the very outset, inviting man to be copartner in the enterprise of generating a species that would reflect the divine glory.

God clearly needs man to be communicator of His word and spirit, exemplar of His ethical will, and reflector of His attributes of mercy, wisdom, and power within the world. It follows, therefore, that sin impairs the creative process, and slows down the planned rate of spiritual acceleration that is programmed to impel us toward the messianic fulfillment "in its proper time." Man cannot commemorate Creation without contemplating this role that has been allotted to him within it, and without lamenting the damage that his sin perpetrates upon the creative fabric and process. This, we suggest, is the logical association between the anniversary of the Creation of the world on Rosh Hashanah and the themes of sin, remorse, and forgiveness that are its predominant motifs.

Creation, sin, repentance—and forgiveness—all appeared together onto the stage of existence, according to the midrashic view of Creation.

Adam, on the very day of his creation, the sixth day, sinned by eating of the forbidden fruit. His remorse was so prompt and sincere that God immediately pardoned him, so that by the time the seventh day of Creation—*Shabbat*—dawned, Adam was able to utter a psalm for the Sabbath day, commencing with the words *Tov le-hodot La-Shem*, "It is good *to confess* to the Lord" (Psalm 92:1). All the major elements of Rosh Hashanah's celebration are inextricably interwoven, therefore, with its significance as commemorating the birth of the world.

Zikhronot

אַתָּה זוֹכֵר מַעֲשֵׂה עוֹלָם

You Remember What Was Wrought from Eternity

This composition, also attributed to *Rav*, serves as an introduction to the *Zikhronot*, the second major section of the *Amidah*, which emphasizes the infallibility of the divine memory, and the absolute comprehensiveness of God's surveillance of human actions: "There is no forgetting before the throne of Your glory; there is not a thing hidden from Your eyes."

Judaism's essential doctrine of reward and punishment is predicated upon this concept of the existence of a permanent record of all man's deeds, a record indelibly imprinted upon the divine memory. Herein may be the key to an explanation of the vagaries of divine proximity or distance from mankind—the latter situation enabling the spread of evil, oppression, and holocaust in a world supposedly filled with the spirit of God. For, just as in human relationships the degree of our emotional responsiveness toward our fellow is conditioned by the "memory," the cumulative stimuli and recollection of past dealings—and just as proximity flows from trust, loyalty, and shared experience, and distance is the corollary of distrust, neglect, and indifference—so the divine emotion is motivated by the stimulus of its "memory" of human dealings. Our evil drives God from an immanent relationship to a more distant, transcendent relationship with His world, wherein the intensity of His spirit is weakened and opposing forces are enabled to surface.

Just as God "remembers all the events of the Universe," and responds to good and evil accordingly, so Israel is, similarly, commanded never to forget both the kindnesses extended to her by her allies and friends, on the one hand, as well as the evil perpetrated against her by Amalek (Deuteronomy 25:17), on the other. *Imitatio dei* thus extends to the cultivation of a collective historical memory.

Whereas the usual procedure in quoting biblical proof-texts is to follow the order of *Torah*, *Neviim* (prophetic literature) and, finally, *Ketuvim*

Because the priests in the Temple had to perform ritual washing of their hands before commencing their sacred duties, our priests do likewise before ascending the Ark. Their hands are washed by Levites—members of their own ancestral tribe. A basis for this washing was found in the verse, "Lift up your hands in holiness [(i.e., in cleanliness) and bless the Lord]" (Psalm 134:2).

The priests are not permitted to wear shoes while blessing, and these are generally removed before washing. The hands of the priests are outstretched and their fingers parted in a specially prescribed manner, making a total of five "spaces" between the fingers of both hands. This is achieved by having the thumb of the right hand hovering above that of the left hand, and spacing out the middle of the four fingers of each hand. The mystics believed that these spaces were a kind of lattice window through which the divine Spirit "peeps" to see whether Israel deserves the blessing.

Because the priests have to concentrate intently upon their sacred duty, in order to ensure that they make no mistakes in the recitation of the exact formula, the *chazan* recites the blessing, word by word, before the priests. It is the duty of every priest over the age of thirteen years (*bar mitzvah*) to "*dukhan*." It should be realized that the priest is only the mouthpiece of God. He is not conferring his own private blessing, so the question of religious competence or degree of observance must not be considered—either by the congregation or the individual priest.

To induce extra concentration on the part of the priests, as well as to ensure that the attention of the recipients of the blessing does not become distracted by the priestly actions, the priests cover their faces and hands with their large *tallit*. The congregation should face the priests, but not fix their gaze upon them.

Before commencing their task the priests petition God to grant them fluency in their blessing, after which they recite in unison the benediction on the *mitzvah*: "Blessed are you . . . who has sanctified us with the sanctity of Aaron, and has commanded us to bless Your people Israel in love." At the conclusion of the priestly blessing the priests recite a private prayer, affirming that they have performed all that was prescribed for them, and that it now only rests with God to fulfill His side of the agreement, and to accord His blessing to Israel and to her land.

הַיּוֹם תְּאַמְּצֵנוּ
This Day You Will Strengthen Us

No more fitting a poem could have been chosen than this, with which we close the *Musaf* service. It is not a prayer, but rather a stirring evocation of optimistic faith—almost certainty—that God will, indeed, bless and forgive us because of our wholehearted prayers and confession. The Birnbaum translation has totally missed this sense of the Hebrew by rendering the verbs as imperatives ("strengthen us") rather than as imperfects ("You will, indeed, strengthen us").

Ha-yom te-amtzeinu is an alphabetical poem, each verb (*Amz, Barekh, Gadel*) commencing with a succeeding letter. The version we have is only a fragment of the complete alphabetical poem, which appears in full in the *machzor* of the Italian rite.

Interestingly, if we compare the main editions, we find that, after the fourth line, they differ from each other in one or more respects: the Routledge has one extra line (*Ha-yom tikhteveinu le-chayyim tovim*), making an eight-line poem; the last line in ArtScroll, Routledge, and De Sola is omitted in Birnbaum, and the line commencing *Ha-yom tishma* precedes *Ha-yom tekabbeil* in ArtScroll, Routledge, and De Sola, whereas in Birnbaum it follows it (in conformity with the correct alphabetical order!).

A detailed study of the *piyyutim* will demonstrate that a great deal of license was applied to them, and no reservation was felt by later religious authorities when it came to abbreviating, omitting, selecting, combining, and even altering compositions.

אֵין כֵּאלֹהֵינוּ
There Is None like Our God

This joyous hymn seems to have been based upon the verse in the *Kedushah,* beginning *Echad hu Eloheinu* ("Our God is One"). The recurring emphasis upon "*Our* God," "*Our* Lord," "*Our* King," and "*Our* Deliverer" is clearly intended to contrast our true God with the erroneous conception of Him espoused by the theologies of some other faiths.

A more logical order would have been to interchange the first two verses, in order to provide a question—"Who is like our God?"—followed by the answer: "There is none like our God." The reason for not doing so was clearly in order to maintain the acrostic *Amen ba* ("Amen has arrived"), a mystical kind of doxology with a messianic overtone.[59] Another, homiletical, explanation is that philosophical speculation on the subject of God ("Who is like our God?") can only yield constructive insights when it is undertaken from the starting-point of faith, by a mind already convinced that "There is none like our God."

עָלֵינוּ
It Is Our Duty (see pp. 88–92)

אֲדוֹן עוֹלָם
Master of the Universe (see pp. 11–15)

3

Tashlikh

תַּשְׁלִיךְ
Ceremony of Casting Away Sins

The ceremony of *Tashlikh* is beloved among observant Jews, although perhaps more for the enjoyment of its performance than for its inspirational appeal! How pleasant it is, on the first afternoon of Rosh Hashanah (or, if that day is a Sabbath, on the second afternoon), to take a stroll to a nearby park, there to meet one's friends and acquaintances and, together, to perform this brief, quaint ceremony of symbolically throwing away one's sins into a running stream. Some preserve an old custom of throwing pieces of bread into the water after reciting the prayers.

Although we find no clear reference to the *Tashlikh* ritual in rabbinic writings until the *Sefer Maharil*[1] of Jacob Moellin (fourteenth century), it is clear that by that time it had already undergone a long and checkered history dating back possibly over a thousand years to early talmudic times.

The origin of *Tashlikh* is obscure. According to Professor Jacob Z. Lauterbach[2] its genesis was as a superstitious act of intercession with the satanic demons of the sea. The throwing of crumbs was, accordingly, to serve as a propitiatory gift, to win the favor of those harmful forces, so that their accusations would be silenced and that they might even intercede on behalf of their benefactors on the judgment day. It has been suggested that the practice of throwing crumbs was curtailed in order to avoid fueling the malicious Gentile charge that the Jews were throwing poison into the wells! Lauterbach draws a parallel between *Tashlikh* and the Yom Kippur ceremony of sending away one of the goats into the desert—another place where demons were believed to lurk.

Many popular interpretations of the ceremony have been suggested, beginning with Jacob Moellin, who connected it with the midrashic idea that Satan transformed himself into a river to block the path of Abraham in order to frustrate his progress to the *Akeidah*. Another view associates the ceremony with the crowning of monarchs, which, in biblical times, always took place near a perennial stream[3] to symbolize the blessing of a long reign.[4] Rosh Hashanah, likewise, focuses upon God as King, and according to this interpretation the *Tashlikh* becomes a symbolic crowning of the heavenly Monarch.

The mystic school of Isaac Luria insisted that for *Tashlikh* one must go to a river in which there are fish. According to their interpretation of the symbolism, water was a merciful element (Moses, as a baby, had been saved by water), and the fish, which have no eyelids, are symbolic of God's ever open-eyed, sympathetic supervision of His people. The Lurianic practice was also to shake out the edges of their garments into the water. A writer of that school[5] states unashamedly that the purpose of this is to banish the evil spirits, created by our sins, which adhere to the hems of clothes.

The term *Tashlikh* is derived from Micah 7:19, "And you will cast [*vetashlikh*] all their sins into the depths of the sea," which verse forms the core of the formula to be recited at this ceremony. Other verses and psalms—notably Psalms 33 and 130—were added in the course of time.

Psalm 33 refers to the creation of the seas. Its introduction here might have been in order to refine the gross idea of the river as a residence of the demons—as suggested by this ceremony—and focus attention rather upon the role of the deep in the first act of Creation ("He gathers the waters of the sea as a heap; he lays up the deep in storehouses"), which, according to our tradition, took place on Rosh Hashanah.

Psalm 130 commences with the phrase "Out of the depths," which again links up with the verse from Micah, "And you will cast . . . *into the depths* of the sea," as if to suggest that, were it not for God's mercy, the sinner—rather than his sins—would have been deserving of a watery grave.

Different communities evolved their own special ways of performing *Tashlikh*. A most exotic way was that of the Jews of Kurdistan who physically jumped into the water to perform the ceremony. In some communities the entire congregation marches together to the river or stream, while in others it is a more private experience, offering another opportunity for a moment of introspection and reflective solitude.

In Israel, the Mediterranean Sea and Lake Tiberias are the popular sites for *Tashlikh*. It was not easy for the inaccessible villages of northern Galilee to find a perennial stream, so, from the eighteenth century onward, the inhabitants of those areas simply took themselves off to the highest vantage points, from which they would look toward either Lake Tiberias or the Dead Sea, and recite the appropriate verses.

In Jerusalem, the only natural spring is the Siloam pool, at the base of the Kidron valley. There, or at the Silwan tunnel through which the Gihon spring flows, Jews from all over the city excitedly assemble to perform the colorful ritual, to wish everyone in sight a *shanah tovah*, and to invoke for themselves and for the city of peace, a peaceful year to come.

Taking a Nap?

There is a widespread belief that it is forbidden to take a nap on the afternoon of Rosh Hashanah. Where this idea originated is unclear, but it infiltrated halakhic writings only in the sixteenth century, in the glosses of Rabbi Moses Isserles (*Remah*) to the *Shulchan Arukh*. He states: "There is also a custom not to sleep during the day of Rosh Hashanah (*Talmud Yerushalmi*); and it is an appropriate custom."[6]

The supercommentator, R. David ben Samuel Halevi (*Taz*), attempts to identify the particular statement in the *Yerushalmi* (Palestinian Talmud), quoting the maxim, "whoever rests (*man de-damikh*) on Rosh Hashanah, his good fortune will also rest (*damikh mazlei*)."

Rabbi Barukh Halevi Epstein notes that such a maxim does not in fact occur in any of our editions of the *Yerushalmi*. He is not unduly surprised by this, however, as

> there are numerous examples of subjects covered in the version of the *Yerushalmi* which was in the possession of the *Rishonim* [talmudic commentators and codifiers prior to the sixteenth century codification of Karo's *Shulchan Arukh*], and even complete tractates which they possessed, but which were lost to later generations, on account of our lengthy exile and harsh wanderings.

Epstein then proceeds to demonstrate that even if such a quotation is authoritative, it cannot be used to justify any prohibition against sleeping on Rosh Hashanah, since the word *damikh* means exclusively "to die" in the Aramaic dialect of the Palestinian Talmud. The maxim quoted by Taz can therefore only mean, "whoever *dies* on Rosh Hashanah, his good fortune has run its complete course (lit. 'died')." There is thus no talmudic basis for any prohibition of just taking a nap on this day![7]

The other main supercommentator on the *Shulchan Arukh*, Rabbi Avraham Abeli Gombiner (*Magen Avraham*), appositely observes that

> Rabbi Yehudah [He-Chasid] states that after midday it is permissible to sleep, since the angel [of mercy] has already been aroused on our behalf by means of the prayers and *shofar* sounds; and the *Bach* states that Rabbi Meir (of Rothenburg) used to take a nap on Rosh Hashanah. Indeed, he avers, sitting around idly is no different to sleeping!

While the above should set at rest the minds of those who are generally so exhausted after the spiritual exertions of the day that sleep simply takes over, it would be of interest, nevertheless, to try to discover precisely the reason why, somewhere in the distant past, some opposition to sleeping on this day built up. I offer the suggestion that it emerged from the superstitious, though widely held, belief that the forces of evil, in the guise of hostile demons, found their easiest targets among those who were asleep. This idea infiltrated mainstream Jewish belief, and was responsible for the introduction of Psalm 91 into the prayers on retiring to sleep each night. This psalm is referred to as the *Shir shel pega-im* (The hymn against evil mishap):

> Do not be afraid of terror by night . . . of the pestilence that stalks the darkness . . . no evil shall befall you, neither shall the scourge approach your tent; for He shall give His angels charge over you.

Such sentiments were most reassuring to the masses who earnestly believed, and dreaded, the powers of "the other side." Among those masses were also many of the most distinguished rabbinic authorities. We are told that "Rabbi Meir of Rothenburg and Rabbi Jacob Weil made it a point to speak these lines even before taking a nap during the day."[8]

It seems clear, then, that if one is vulnerable when asleep on ordinary days and nights to such attacks, how much more vulnerable is one on the day of judgment, when all our transgressions and weaknesses have been acknowledged, and it is only the grace of God that can redeem us. Satan and his cohorts of evil forces can have a field day venting their spleen on the defenseless and pathetic prisoners in the dock. It was accordingly felt advisable that we should keep our wits about us by not taking a nap, and handing them thereby an extra opportunity for picking us off.

As was always the case with such primitive superstitions, people were loath to discuss them or the measures adopted to combat them. Nevertheless, aided by rabbinic leaders sympathetic to their communities' deeper anxieties, a defense mechanism of customs, ritual practices, and prohibitions was activated in order to counter the effects of such beliefs. We suggest that the fear of sleeping on Rosh Hashanah belongs to this category.

4

The Morning Service—Second Day

מֶלֶךְ אָמוֹן מַאֲמָרְךָ
O King, Your Word Has Stood Steadfast

For the second day of Rosh Hashanah we cannot draw upon the inspirational poetry of Eleazar Kallir, as, at that early period in which Kallir lived, Palestinian Jewry still observed the original practice of keeping only one day of Rosh Hashanah. The Ashkenazi communities found here an opportunity to give honor to one of their own distinguished sons, Rabbi Simeon bar Isaac, Cantor of Mainz (b. 950) and one of the earliest composers of *piyyut* in Germany.

Besides being an inspired poet in his own right, Simeon bar Isaac was also an authority on the works of the famous poets of earlier generations. His own style is clearly influenced by them, and particularly by the poetry of Kallir. But it also possesses a tragic quality of its own, born out of the domestic tragedy into which he, personally, was plunged, combined with the bitter experiences of the Jewish communities of the Rhineland that are reflected in many of his compositions.

Legend has it that Simeon's brilliant young son, Elchanan, was kidnapped by a Christian maid and forcibly baptized. He was trained for the ministry, distinguished himself as a theologian and pastor, and ultimately rose to become Pope. The only heritage that remained with him of his early upbringing was the recollection of his initiation into the game of chess by his father, and, in particular, one unique opening gambit that he had been taught by him and that he had never seen any other player employ.

The legend relates how Rabbi Simeon once came to Rome to beg the Pope to rescind some anti-Jewish measures he had introduced. During his audience the Pope challenged the rabbi to a game of chess, and when the latter employed that particular gambit, the identity of his Jewish petitioner—and his own—was immediately discovered. At this point the legend divides into two versions. One claims that the son, Elchanan, abandoned his high position and his adopted faith to return secretly to the practice of Judaism in his home town. The second, more plausible, version has it that, after confessing his allegiance to Judaism before his father, he committed suicide. Support for the martyrdom version of the legend is forthcoming from this opening *piyyut* for the second day of Rosh Hashanah, which contains the acrostic "Elchanan my son, may he be granted eternal life, Amen."

The acrostic pattern is not as easily recognizable as, for example, in the poems of Kallir. The author signs his name, *Shimon bar Yitzchak*, by means of an acrostic pattern running through the initial letters of the *second* phrases of each three-phrase stanza. He repeats this in the fourth stanza, *S̄h̄omrei m̄itzvōt . . . n̄attleim*, the initial letters of the first five words of which make up the name *Shimon*. The usual continuation, giving the patronymic (*bar Yitzchak*), nestles amid the words of the eighth stanza (ending with the key word, *kadosh*): *b̄e-r̄achamim ȳakeir t̄z̄irei ha-tzon c̄h̄uk̄k̄am. . . .*

The reference to his son's name occurs in the twelfth stanza, in the opening two words *El chanan*. The first two letters of the fourth word (*b̄e-n̄oam*) of that line, and the initial letter of the sixth word (*ȳiddam*), make up the word *beniy*, "my son."

The prayer that he should be granted eternal life begins with the sixteenth stanza (*ȳēra'eh . . . C̄h̄aȳyot*), making up the word *yechiy* ("may he live"), and continues in the twentieth line, which actually commences with the words *Le-chayei olam* ("for eternal life"). The twenty-fourth stanza, *Īm̄rey n̄ichumekha*, adds the formula *Amen*.

The poem is closely related to the three central themes of the *Musaf Amidah*: the *Malkhuyot*, *Zikhronot*, and *Shofarot*.[1] Hence the words *melekh*, *zekhor*, and *shofar*, successively employed three times as the initial word of each stanza.

The opening reference, to God's "word" (*maamar*) being steadfast, is probably intended here as *synecdoche*, representing the ten occasions (*asarah maamarot*)[2] in the Genesis account of Creation when the term *Va-yomer Ha-*

Shem ("And God said") is employed. On this anniversary of the creation of the world the poet marvels at the fact that God has allowed His precious handiwork to remain the possession of sinful mankind. That privilege, he avers, is not by reason of the merit of Adam's descendants, but merely because God has determined to judge man mercifully.

כְּבוֹדוֹ אִהֵל
Tentlike He Stretched Out the Sky

This composition, constructed according to the alphabetical acrostic pattern, is attributed to Eleazar Kallir, though, as we have observed above, he would have written it for the first day of Rosh Hashanah at a period when only one day was observed in Palestine.

The idea that God stretched out the heaven "like a tent" is derived from Isaiah 40:22:

> God sits throned above the circle of the earth,[3] whose inhabitants are like grasshoppers. He spreads out the skies like a fine curtain, He stretches them out *like a tent* to live in.

It is a moot point whether or not this verse may be interpreted as a directive to man to contain his explorations and restrict his activities to the planet earth.[4] What is clear, however, is that the prophet conceives of the earth and heavens, in a mystical sense, as supporting the divine spirit like a throne. Isaiah expresses this concept with even greater clarity in the last of his utterances, "These are the words of the Lord: The heaven is my throne and the earth my footstool" (Isaiah 66:1).

Each line ends with the word *melekh* ("King"), and the poem is a plea to the divine King to shower upon Israel the full measure of His mercy when reviewing all our actions. In the fourth stanza the poet describes his people as "Sons of the King" (*bnei melekh*), an idea expressed in Deuteronomy 14:1 and amplified in *Avot* 3:17. The Talmud[5] draws attention to the fact that Israel retains the title of "sons" even in the context of denunciation: "foolish *sons*" (Jeremiah 4:22), "faithless *sons*" (Deuteronomy 32:20), "corrupt *sons*" (Isaiah 1:4).

In the fifth stanza the poet asks for God to show "kindness" (*chesed*) to Abraham,[6] who is referred to as "the one to whom the three mighty messengers of the King were sent," an allusion to the visit of the three angels as described in Genesis, chapter 18. The "kindness" is that the prayers and petitions of his offspring should be accepted. He then proceeds to invoke the merit of Isaac, "for whom the angels shed bitter tears,"[7] and Jacob, who spent the night on the place where the angels ascended and descended.

אֲתִיתִי לְחַנְּנָךְ
I Come to Supplicate You

This is another poem by the illustrious German poet, Simeon bar Isaac.[8] As he himself acted as a cantor in Mainz, it is probable that he would have composed this as a purely personal meditation, or *reshut*,[9] prior to leading the congregation in the recitation of the *Amidah.*

It follows an alphabetical acrostic pattern, ending with the author's name *Shimon* interwoven into an acrostic formed by the initial letters of each word of the concluding lines: *S̄helach m̄e-ittekha ēizer ū-terufah n̄aamekha.*

It expresses the usual sentiments of the *reshut*: the abject lowliness and unworthiness of the cantor to represent his congregation, his profound dread and awe at the task imposed upon him, his lack of both knowledge and merit, and his confidence that God will, notwithstanding, send mercy and deliverance to His people.

The poet likens the cantor, standing before God begging for mercy, to "a poor man begging at the door." The reference is borrowed from the midrashic statement that "when a poor man stands at your door, God stands at his right hand (—as it says, 'For He stands at the right of the needy' [Psalm 109:31]). If you give to him, remember that He who stands by him will reward you; but if you refuse, He will punish you."[10] The poet gives this idea an ironic twist by employing it as a lever with which to wrest mercy from God. We stand at God's door begging for mercy. God, as it were, has a religious obligation to accede to our petition!

The poet has no qualms about referring to himself as of absolutely no consequence: "What am I and what is my life? I am a worm and a maggot."

Such sentiments flow as a natural concomitant of true fear of God, as defined by Maimonides.[11] And this doctrine has been responsible for generating a genre of prayer characterized by an almost Kierkegaardian intensity of self-conscious restlessness and despairing self-deprecation.[12] One such gem, recited every morning, clearly reflects this attitude:

> Sovereign of all the worlds. . . . What are we? What is our life? What is our piety? What is our righteousness? What our success? What our strength? What our might? What shall we say before Thee, O Lord our God and God of our fathers? Are not all the mighty men as nought before Thee, the men of fame as though they had never existed, the wise as if without knowledge, and men of understanding as if devoid of discernment? For most of their achievement is inconsequential before Thee, and the pre-eminence of man over the beast is an illusion, for all is vanity.[13]

The cantor's *reshut* was composed in this same spirit, though the despair is never quite so profound as to deflect him from his purpose or make him believe that divine mercy is unattainable. As an individual he is acutely aware of his particular unworthiness, although he never imputes this to the holy congregation which he represents. A congregation may be comprised entirely of sinful individuals, but collectively the spirit of God descends upon them all. As *Knesset Yisrael*—the congregation of Israel—they become transformed and elevated into a spiritual entity with the mystic power to storm the very gates of heaven.

אִמְרָתְךָ צְרוּפָה
Your Word Is Pure

This is another poem from the pen of Simeon bar Isaac, following the alphabetical acrostic pattern. The concluding lines form a name acrostic followed by the appeal, *yechiy*, "may he live," thus: *Bo s̄h̄uannu m̄e-ōlam va-yaaneinu n̄oraot, b̄e-r̄iȳtz̄uy c̄h̄inuneinu k̄abbel . . . ȳec̄h̄altzeinu . . . mitachalueȳ.*

This composition was created to follow on from the foregoing poem, and it opens with the concluding phrase of the latter, "All your words, O God, are pure and tested" (Proverbs 30:5).

In the second line the author calls upon God not to probe too deeply (*al tedakdek*) when reviewing Israel. The verb *ledakdek* occurs in the oft-repeated rabbinic axiom that "God probes the righteous (*medakdek im ha-tzaddikim*) as finely as a hair's breadth." God is reminded that He, Himself, employed the quality of mercy when creating the world,[14] and that His biblical attribute of being *rav chesed* ("abundant in mercy")[15] means that when judging the average person—whose sins and good deeds are in counterpoise—God is believed to nudge the scale of merit so that it comes down in favor of acquittal.[16]

At the beginning of the fifth stanza Abraham is alluded to as *Ezrachiy*, "the one who came from the east." This is based upon the rabbinical identification of *Eitan ha-ezrachiy* (mentioned in the heading to Psalm 89 as its author) with Abraham.[17] The poet asks that Abraham's merit, as the prince of mercy who entreated God to spare the wicked inhabitants of Sodom and Gomorrah, should stand to the everlasting credit of his offspring, so that "the accuser would be silenced."

Abraham, in our tradition, is the paramount exemplar of the quality of *chesed* ("mercy"). The third verse of this Psalm 89—as ascribed to Abraham—states "the world must be established by *chesed*," and the prophet Micah ends his prophecies with the words "ascribe truth to Jacob, *chesed* to Abraham" (Micah 7:20).

תָּמִים פָּעָלְךָ
Your Work Is Perfect

Writing under the influence of the works of Kallir and his imitators, Simeon bar Isaac introduces here a variety of the ordinary alphabetical acrostic.

This poem employs the reverse alphabetical acrostic (*Tashrak*), whereby the first line commences with *tav*, the final letter of the alphabet, and subsequent lines continue working backward to the letter *alef*.

As with the composition *Atitiy le-chanenakh*,[18] the poet, on reaching the letter *alef*, signs off with a line (in this case, two lines), the initial letters of each word of which make up his own name. While this is easily discernible in the final stanza (*S̄efateinu m̄edovevot ōz u-vetzidkato n̄ichyeh*), it is not so easy to discover in the penultimate stanza. It is, in fact, compressed into the three words, *S̄hem̄eynu āl . . . ven̄iyv*.

In the second stanza the poet petitions God to accept the prayers offered on this holy day as substitutes for the sin-offerings that would have been brought in Temple times. This is in accordance with the prophecy of Hosea who already foresaw the time when "our lips will make payment for bulls" (Hosea 14:3).

The next stanza contains an interesting midrashic allusion. The poet states that if Israel has indeed strayed from the true paths, "let there be remembered the ordered altar (of Abraham) together with the *ritual slaughter knife* (*maakhelet ha-maakhilah*) which was provided from then onwards."

The term *maakhelet ha-maakhilah* means, literally, "the knife that enables us to eat," and the Midrash explains this to mean that "any meat that Israel enjoys in this world is only through the merit of Abraham when he took the slaughter knife with him to the *Akeidah*."[19] This concept underlies the familiar rabbinic idea of the table as an altar and one's food as representing an act of sacrifice. Abraham's readiness to perform the supreme sacrifice was rewarded by God by transforming his knife into a ritual slaughtering knife for the future satisfaction of his offspring. In the context of the vegetarian ideal—which represented God's original plan for man—this midrash suggests that the slaughter and consumption of meat is merely a concession to Israel, won through the merit of the *Akeidah*.

שֻׁלַּחְתִּי בְּמַלְאָכוּת
I Am Sent on the Mission

This is another poem from the pen of Simeon bar Isaac who strongly favors this four-line stanza construction, technically referred to as *meruba* ("quatrain"). Each line contains four words, the rhyme being provided by the last syllable of each line. The four lines of each stanza all commence with the same letter, and as the stanzas form an acrostic of the author's name, this becomes converted, in fact, into a fourfold name-acrostic!

The charge of conceit is frequently leveled at those *paytanim* who employed this device of the name-acrostic. In fairness to them, however, one must appreciate that they were offering the public the fruits of their talent in an age when there were no regulations to restrict plagiarism. They were also writing before the age of printing, at a period when the name of the author was too easily separated from his work. The name-acrostic was, therefore, one of the only methods of ensuring the author's recognition.

The first stanza is detached from the rest of the poem, and assigned for recitation by the Reader. In the Birnbaum and ArtScroll editions, the Ark is opened especially for this stanza, while in the De Sola edition the rubric has the Ark opened before the end of the previous blessing, *mechayyeh ha-meitim*. The special attention given to the first stanza is clearly on account of its purpose, which is to serve as a brief *reshut*, the Reader's personal petition for God to accept his prayers on behalf of the "select community" that he represents.

The third stanza (*Eirekh tekiateinu*) asks God to enable the objective of our particular system of *shofar* blowing—which is "to confuse the accuser" (*arbeiv katteigor*)[20]—to be realized. It is the Talmud that suggests that the system of *shofar* blowing we employ is "to confuse the accuser," or, more accurately, "to confuse Satan."[21] The specific aspect of the system that aroused the talmudic curiosity was the splitting up of the blowing into two separate groups of notes: one group blown before the *Musaf Amidah*[22] and the rest blown during its repetition.[23]

The way in which this particular system of blowing helps to confuse Satan, and to deflect him from his intention to condemn, is not too clear. *Tosafot*[24] explains that Satan is aware that the great *shofar* will herald the final day of judgment when "God will make death to vanish forever."[25] Thus, when he hears the first group of notes "Satan becomes quite agitated," believing that the final moment might well be at hand when his own powers are to be curtailed. Just as he is recovering from that shock, realizing that he must have been mistaken, Israel embarks upon her main crescendo of blowing. This totally overwhelms Satan, who is put to flight long enough for Israel to conclude all her prayers and to receive divine mercy.

This must be regarded, however, as a quaint homiletical justification of a custom whose origin was uncertain to the talmudists. A tradition, elaborated in the Palestinian Talmud, attributes the bipartite blowing to a period of religious persecution when the Romans prohibited the sounding of the *shofar* out of fear that it might be used as a signal for an insurrection. They used to send inspectors to the synagogues to ensure that the Jews complied with the edict. As the original custom was to blow during *Shacharit* the inspectors left satisfied at the end of that service. Because of these extenuating circumstances, the rabbinic authorities permitted the communities to delay the blowing until *Musaf*. When the persecution was over a compromise was effected between those who wanted to retain the status quo and the purists who wished to return to the original practice. Thus the *shofar* is blown both in the *Musaf Amidah* as well as—not *in*, but immediately after—the *Shacharit* service.

שְׁמוֹ מְפָאֲרִים
They Glorify His Name

The poem "*Shemo mefo'arim*," by Simeon bar Isaac, was chosen for recitation on the second day of Rosh Hashanah. For the first day we recite Kallir's *Ta'iyr ve-taria*.[26] Because the latter contains a reference to "the *shofar*'s blast," it was regarded as inappropriate for the Sabbath day when such blowing is suspended. For this reason, if the first day falls on a Sabbath we interchange the two compositions, reciting "*Shemo mefo'arim*" on the Sabbath and *Ta'iyr ve-taria* on the Sunday. The former composition is especially appropriate for the Sabbath as it makes specific reference to that day and to the fact that we have to content ourselves then with *zikhron teruah*—"a [mere] *mention* of the command of blowing."

This composition extends for four or five pages in most editions. It commences with seven stanzas, all of which are subsequently used, successively, as the refrains for the rest of the poem. Each stanza is comprised of three rhyming lines.

Each of the first six stanzas of the introductory section employs the name acrostic, *Shimon*, in a form that, as we have seen in some of his other poems,[27] is not so readily apparent. The letter *nun*, with which the second lines of each stanza commence, forms the ending of his name. Another point to notice is that the themes of these introductory stanzas follow successively the order of *Malkhuyot*, *Zikhronot*, and *Shofarot*, ending, at the seventh stanza, with another *Malkhuyot* line.

In the remainder of the poem—commencing with the line *Eder va-hod*—the opening lines of each stanza follow the ordinary alphabetical acrostic pattern, the middle lines of each stanza form the acrostic *Shimon bar Yitzchak chazak ve-ematz* ("Simeon bar Isaac, be strong and of good courage"), and the third lines of each stanza are all biblical quotations. As with the introductory verses, the latter follow through the themes of *Malkhuyot*, *Zikhronot*, and *Shofarot*, with three successive stanzas being devoted to each theme.

The poet describes God's greatness as too intense to be contained within the world. He challenges all God's creatures to deepen their awareness and knowledge of God's ways. He recalls the *Akeidah* sacrifice—which was responsible for the introduction of the ritual of blowing the ram's horn—in order to keep alive the spirit of that unique demonstration of faith. He calls upon God to "bare His arm to save us from our foes," though, as usual, Simeon bar Isaac does not specify which particular enemies he has in mind.

The poet fervently prays for God to destroy the chains of bondage and to gather His dispersed people to the promised land, there to restore the Temple, its courts, altars, and sacred vessels.

Reading of the Law—Second Day

The reading for the second day of Rosh Hashanah is the account of the *Akeidah*, the binding of Isaac,[28] surely one of the most inspiring and challenging monuments to the power of faith and its ability to instill absolute confidence into the hearts of the devoted, even when they, or those most dear to them, are "walking in the valley of the shadow of death." No wonder then that the *Akeidah*, as a unique symbol of martyrdom, became a favorite theme in wider religious thought, art, and literature.

The essential character of the Rosh Hashanah festival could be said to have been molded by the *Akeidah* account, for the blowing of the *shofar* is explained[29] as a reminder of the ram sacrificed by Abraham at the *Akeidah*, a substitution forced upon him as he prepared to make the supreme sacrifice in absolute and loving obedience to the divine command.

"And God Tested Abraham"

One of the perennial problems associated with this entire episode is the question of why it was that the omniscient God required putting Abraham to any such test. He assuredly knew the nature, quality, and degree of his faith, and his preparedness to respond at all times with the cry of *hineini*, "here I am, Lord, waiting to fulfill Your will." Naturally, the scope of the present work allows for but a passing reference to the approach of some of our classical commentators.

Moses Nachmanides observes that we should not approach the concept of "testing" from the perspective of God. It only applies to man, since his free will enables him to respond to his higher instincts or to reject them. So God's instruction to Abraham was not in the nature of a God-administered "test," but rather a request that, from *Abraham*'s perspective, tested his constancy and loyalty.

So, if God was not testing Abraham, to discover his ability and willingness to respond to God's will, what precisely was the point of the exercise? Nachmanides's answer is that it was in order to provide His beloved and pious subject, Abraham, with the opportunity for demonstrating to the world the piety and self-sacrifice *that God knew him to possess.* This opportunity was not for self-aggrandizement—which Abraham would have rejected—but rather in order to earn greater merit for him and, indirectly therefore, for his offspring. Nachmanides tells us that, in the divine scheme of things, one cannot compare the reward for *potential* (that is, *un*demonstrated) *piety* to that for piety that has been publicly tested on the anvil of adversity.

We might call it divine accountability. If God is going to confer eternal reward on a person or a nation, such a decision has to be justified publicly before the bar of history, so that the nations of the world can have no quibble with that decision. God enabled Abraham to respond to a challenge that, for Abraham (alone), was a test, so that, in the passing thereof, God would be enabled to confer upon him and his posterity the blessings He longed to share.

Isaac Abarbanel explains, in similar vein, that although the usual sense of the verb *nisah* is "to test," yet it may also be understood as a denominative of the noun *nes*, which means "a banner," "an ensign," "a mast," from the semantic idea of "loftiness." Thus, the phrase *Ve-Ha-Shem nisah et Avraham* may also mean that, by means of that opportunity afforded to him to demonstrate his perfect trust and faith, "God exalted (lit. "raised aloft") Abraham," in the eyes of all mankind.

Furthermore, in the *Zikhronot* ("Remembrance") prayers of the Rosh Hashanah *Musaf*, the merit of Abraham's faith at the *Akeidah* is asked to be accounted to the eternal credit of his offspring:

> Consider then the binding with which he bound his son upon the altar, suppressing his compassion in order to perform Your will with a perfect heart. So may Your compassion conquer Your anger against us, and in Your great goodness may Your great wrath turn aside from Your people, Your city, and Your inheritance.

The reading of this episode on Rosh Hashanah serves to provide us with a glimpse into the way a unique man of faith responded to the divine call. We cannot be expected to match those standards of self-sacrifice. We are expected, however, to provide some reflection of them in our own lives. This idea has been most forcefully expressed by Rav Joseph Soloveitchik:

> Does not the story of the Akeidah tell us about a great, awesome drama of man giving himself away to God? Of course Judaism is vehemently opposed to human sacrifice; physical human sacrifice was declared abominable. Yet the idea that man belongs to God, without qualification, and that God, from time to time, makes a demand upon man to return what is God's to God is an important principle in Judaism. . . . God claimed Isaac, and Abraham gave Isaac away. . . . The call "Take your son, your only son, whom you love so much, and bring him as a burnt offering" is (symbolically) addressed to all men.[30]

The *Haftarah*, from the prophecies of Jeremiah,[31] expresses the reciprocal divine response to all that faith, loyalty, and sacrifice displayed by

Israel. Its message exudes encouragement and love, promising Israel that the dark night of exile and suffering will ultimately give way to a dawn of national restoration.

The link with Rosh Hashanah appears in several passages of the *Haftarah*, most notably in the two images employed to describe God's relationship with Israel: "I am *a father* to Israel and Ephraim is my first born,"[32] and, "He that scattered Israel will gather him, and watch over him *as a shepherd watches his flock*."[33] Both of these images figure prominently in our Rosh Hashanah liturgy.

A further link with Rosh Hashanah is forged by the reference in the *Haftarah* to the matriarch Rachel, who is depicted as lamenting and weeping for her children in exile.[34] This echoes the references, in the Torah and *Haftarah* readings for the First Day, to the longings for maternity expressed by Sarah and Hannah. Whereas they both longed for the personal fulfillment that motherhood confers, Rachel longs for the national fulfillment that can only be secured by the rebirth of her children and their restoration to the ancestral homeland.

The *Haftarah* ends with one of the most poignant pleas for God's mercy, while at the same time expressing the conviction that, because the penitence was sincere, it must be accepted:

> Turn to me, and let me return; for You are the Lord my God. For after I repented I was filled with remorse, and after I realized my errors I beat my thigh in agitation. I was ashamed and confounded.[35]

Why No *Yizkor*?

At this point in the service, on the last day of every other major festival, we recite *Yizkor*, the memorial prayers for the departed.[36] Several reasons have been suggested as to why it is omitted on this festival.

Since *Yizkor* was introduced as a prayer for recitation on Yom Kippur alone,[37] and since the Ten Days of Penitence were considered as one penitential unit, Yom Kippur, being the climactic point of that unified period, was therefore considered the appropriate occasion for reciting *Yizkor*.

Another suggested reason is that since we have to proceed without delay to the blowing of the *shofar* immediately after the Reading of the Torah, *Yizkor*, rather than be moved to a position of minor importance after the *Musaf Amidah*, was saved for recitation on Yom Kippur.

Some have suggested that its omission is because it was felt that there would be something rather incongruous about praying for the dead on this festival when we are so totally preoccupied with life and the living. It is my view that this explanation is close to the truth, but that it misses the essential rationale. I suggest that it was due rather to there being a tincture of superstition involved in calling attention to the dead at this time.

The simple and superstitious masses took very seriously the talmudic advice, *al tiftach peh le-Satan* ("One should not open one's mouth to Satan").[38] This meant, in essence, that one should avoid saying anything that might give Satan an open invitation to seize upon it in order to put it to the test.

Countless examples are quoted in the medieval literature of hapless individuals who had visited upon them the identical fate of the one to whose fate they had merely alluded. *Sefer Chasidim* tells of a student who, after studying a portion of Jeremiah that prophesied the most grievous illnesses and sufferings, suddenly fell ill and died. Hence also the great reticence of anyone to be called up to the reading of the *tokheichah*, the Torah portion that prophesies the bitter condemnation and the catalogue of illnesses and plagues that will befall a sinful Israel.[39] For a similar reason, if people referred to any blessing they possessed, such as a certain number of children, they were most careful to append to any such reference the preventive plea, *beli ayin Ha-Ra* ("May no evil eye [attach itself]").

Therefore, we may understand why it was regarded as dangerous to make such a vigorous and direct reference to the dead members of our family on the occasion of Rosh Hashanah, when our own lives hang so precariously in the balance, and Satan is so well poised to tip us over into oblivion. By Yom Kippur, of course, we should have completed our tokens of penitence and secured a divine favor that no satanic forces could reverse. Hence, the *Yizkor* was deferred until then.

5

The Jewish Doctrine of Repentance

What constitutes repentance? Is it sufficient to feel remorse and to resolve in one's heart not to repeat any unworthy act, or does Judaism demand some practical expression of regret in the form of a *penance*? In biblical times there was a prescribed ritual whereby an individual or community manifested its contrition. This consisted of rending one's garments, praying, fasting, putting on sackcloth, and sitting in the ashes. The penance of the people of Nineveh, as described in the book of Jonah,[1] was so demonstrative that even their beasts were made to share in its expression. Like their owners, they also were draped in sackcloth and deprived of food or drink.

In the sacrificial system there was a specific sin-offering—the *chattat*—prescribed for individual sins. It goes without saying that the mechanical act of sacrifice was never intended to effect atonement of its own accord. A code that called upon its adherents to love God with all their "heart, soul, and might"[2] would never have been so inconsistent as to require nothing more than a mere formalistic act in order to heal the strained relationship between God and man caused by the intrusion of sin. The sacrifice was meant to be without any doubt only the climax of a very strenuous act of invocation and petition along the lines enumerated above.

A fundamental part of the sacrificial cult was the laying of the hands on the head of the beast and the public acknowledgment of guilt by specifying the particular sin committed.[3] Human pride being what it is, it is difficult to imagine that anyone emerged from such an ordeal with anything other than a deflated ego and a very real sense of humility. The sacrifice was secondary in importance to the cry of confession; and it may be said to have existed only in order to evoke such an emotional response. When David was severely censured by the Prophet Nathan for his sin with Bathsheba, his first words were "I have sinned."[4] There is no mention of any subsequent sacrifice brought by David. His spontaneous confession sufficed to obtain forgiveness.

For the Rabbis of the Talmud, repentance was entirely a state of mind. The Temple having been destroyed, prayer and study replaced the sacrificial cult as a means of communication with the deity. It was natural, therefore, that they should have redefined repentance as a psychological state and played down any external forms of penance other than private fasting, which was often employed as a means of atonement.[5]

The classic rabbinic definition of true repentance takes account of the overriding passion in man, which is ultimately responsible for leading him into sin. R. Judah said "the truly penitent man is one who is able to resist when the same opportunity for sin recurs for a second time with the same woman, at the same season, in the same place."[6] In other words, true repentance can only be gauged by the strength of resolve that the individual has built up within him and which, if the repentance had been sufficiently sincere, would give him ample resistance even to repeated, alluring, and sensuous enticements. The repentant sinner, who has resisted the urge to sin a second and a third time, is, according to some rabbis, more beloved of God than the purely righteous man who was never exposed to such a temptation and who consequently has had no opportunity to vanquish his baser instincts.[7]

When it came to offenses against one's fellow man, an inner remorse was not regarded as sufficient. "The Day of Atonement," declares the Mishnah, "only effects atonement for transgressions between man and God; but for transgressions against one's fellow man one must first appease one's fellow."[8]

In their practical concern to protect the rights of every citizen, the Rabbis denied the possibility of pardon to the man who had defrauded his fellow man until he had made full restitution. In the case of tax and customs collectors who, in talmudic times, were notorious for their indiscriminate fraudulence, it was well nigh impossible for them to locate and recompense every individual whom they had robbed. The Rabbis[9] instructed them—and others who had defrauded the public—to reimburse those individuals whom they definitely knew to have been defrauded by them, and to devote the balance to the communal funds. One who had assaulted, insulted, or stolen from another was not entitled to assume that, merely on payment of a monetary recompense, he had fulfilled his penance. It was equally necessary for him to offer a humble request that his victim should forgive him his offense. So important was it for a man to obtain a verbal pardon from the one he had wronged that Jewish law specified the steps that might be taken if the victim is cruel enough to withhold forgiveness from a true penitent.

> The penitent should bring three of his acquaintances, and, before them, he should again entreat his victim's forgiveness. If he still withholds it, the penitent should repeat the encounter with two further groups of people. If forgiveness is still not granted he need do nothing further, but rather is the sin transferred to the one who will not forgive.[10]

There is a special procedure to be followed if the victim had died before the penitent had had a chance of obtaining his pardon.

> He should assemble ten men at the grave of the man he had wronged and he should confess before them his sin and his sincere repentance. If he had extorted money he should return it to the heirs. If he did not know their whereabouts, he should deposit the money with the court of law.[11]

Although the Talmud, as we have seen, considers repentance as an attitude of mind calling for few outward manifestations, there were pietists in the Middle Ages who firmly believed that in order to be cleansed of sin one had to submit oneself to bodily mortification. The chief exponents of this doctrine were the so-called *Chasidei Ashkenaz,* the German pietists who flourished in the Rhineland during the twelfth and thirteenth centuries.[12] They found a scriptural basis for their concept of a mortifying penance in the account of the Prophet Isaiah's "call":

> And one of the Serafim flew to me, having in his hand a burning coal which he had taken with tongs from the altar. And he touched my mouth and said: "Behold, this has touched your lips, your guilt is taken away and your sin forgiven."[13]

These teachers distinguished four types of penance, all prerequisites for the total eradication of the taint of sin. The first is "the repentance of opportunity." This is the mildest form of penitence, corresponding to the established talmudic definition: the opportunity to repeat a sin presents itself but the penitent does not succumb. The second type is "the preventive form of penitence." Within this category the penitent must hold aloof from any experience or situation that might present him with the temptation to repeat his sin. Third in order of severity is "the penance of correspondence," wherein the penitent is expected to endure that intensity of physical pain that corresponded to the amount of pleasure he derived from committing the sin. Finally comes "the biblically prescribed repentance," whereby the truly penitent has to inflict upon himself tortures corresponding to the pain that would have accompanied the imposition of the penalties prescribed by the Bible for his particular sin. Where the Pentateuch prescribed flogging the penitent must submit to the forty lashes, and where the biblical penalty was death he was expected to undergo "tortures as bitter as death." Penitents were known to lie in the snow for hours in the winter and to expose their bodies to ants and bees in the summer in order to fulfill this last category of repentance.

While the masses of Jews could never have been expected to aspire to the standards of those pietists, the existence of such pockets of extreme piety acted as a vital counterweight to the opposing forces of indifference and assimilation. The sight of such a pietist performing his rigorous penance would not have left the heart of the everyday Jew unmoved. His thoughts must inevitably have turned to the matter of his own sins and the means he might employ to achieve his own spiritual regeneration. A religion enriched by the literary legacy of such movements, and spurred on by the lofty ideals of such saints, acquires an extra spiritual dimension.

What is the divine response to human sin and atonement? Does the God of justice administer judgment according to the strict letter of the law or does the "quality of mercy drop as the gentle rain from heaven"?

The whole basis of the prophetic ministry rested firmly on the assumption that the God of Israel was a forgiving and merciful father. "Have I any pleasure in the death of the wicked, says the Lord God, and not that he should turn from his evil way and live?" Ezekiel[14] here expresses a conviction shared by all the prophets. It was, in fact, more than a conviction; it was their whole raison d'être. The prophet could never accept—nor was he intended to accept—the role of passive "foreteller" of the nation's fate. He saw himself rather as a "forthteller." His message of doom was always conditional upon the nation's refusal to accept his call to repentance. The inevitability of doom was alien to his whole thinking. The announcement of doom is, in reality, merely the pronouncement of the penalty that is compatible with the nation's crimes.

The prophet's duty is to shake them out of their complacency, to prosecute, to condemn, to cry "guilty" until the nation trembles, and to threaten them with the punishment they truly deserve. But the prophet's moment of supreme fulfillment comes when his threats are negated, and his promises invalidated, by the nation's repentance and the divine decree of forgiveness. The role of the prophet is thus unenviable. His victory as a prophet lies in his defeat as an individual. He can never claim the affection of men, for even in the moment of their salvation his threat of doom must appear to have been misguided. If the prophet is the counsel for the prosecution, God is the counsel for the defense.

This dilemma of the prophet represents the theme of the book of Jonah, the reading of which is prescribed for the afternoon service on the Day of Atonement. Jonah could not rationalize that paradox of prophetic pronouncement and divine indulgence. Summoned by God to go to Nineveh, capital of Assyria, and there to pronounce her imminent downfall, his whole belief in the reliability and infallibility of God's word is shaken to its foundation when the people repented, and God revoked His decree.

Jonah had been more concerned to witness the accurate fulfillment of his prophecy than with the fate of "the great city in which there are more than a hundred and twenty thousand people who do not know their right hand from their left." Jonah wished to be a foreteller rather than a forth-teller. Compassion had no place in Jonah's conception of divine judgment. If God had proclaimed doom, then surely He had foreseen the ultimate repentance, and rejected it. Otherwise, why compromise his elected prophet by putting into his mouth a false prediction? Jonah's chief concern was to find a solution to this problem.

The lesson Jonah—and mankind—had to learn was that the ways of God and His method of dealing with His world are indeed inscrutable. They do not conform to our own preconceived notions of logic, neither do they show deference to the reputation of a prophet, priest, or saint. If any consistency may be found at all, it is in the divine sensitivity to sincere atonement. God will not disclose the fact or time of the repentance of an individual or a nation even to His prophets—and certainly not to a Jonah. The moment of repentance is sacred and intimate. For God to have granted foreknowledge of it to a third party would have been an act of betrayal. The true prophet should rejoice with God that His mercy has been given the opportunity to vanquish His anger.

The talmudic Rabbis further developed the doctrine of the divine eagerness to grant forgiveness. Man is helped by God along the path of repentance. He has only to exhibit the early flutterings of a remorseful heart for God to implant within him additional strength of purpose. Rabbi Issi said that God says to the Israelites, "My children, open to me the gate of repentance as minutely as the eye of a needle, and I will open for you gates wide enough for carriages and wagons to enter through them."[15]

The Rabbis were aware that the existence of such a belief could lead to abuse, whereby people might salve their consciences by deluding themselves into thinking that divine mercy is inexhaustible and extends even where only a token gesture of penitence is offered, unaccompanied by sincere resolve. They therefore took pains to disabuse the naive of such a contention:

He who says: "I will sin and then make repentance; I will sin again and make repentance," no opportunity for true repentance will ever be granted to him. He who says, "I will sin and the Day of Atonement will grant absolution," the Day of Atonement will not, in such a case, confer absolution.[16]

The motive for repentance does have a bearing upon the divine reaction to it. The Talmud distinguishes three motivations: one who repents out of conviction based upon *love of God;* one who repents out of simple *fear of the consequences of sin;* and, the lowest category of repentance, that which is prompted by *suffering and affliction*.[17] The Rabbis were cautious in their statements about the comparative effect of these three motives for repentance. According to one view,[18] repentance occasioned by love of God has the effect of totally effacing any trace of the individual's sin, whereas repentance out of fear prompts the Almighty merely to disregard the record of that particular sin. Penitents in both of these categories are regarded as "sons" of God, whereas those whose penitence was only brought about as a result of suffering are relegated to a servant–master relationship with Him.[19]

Repentance cannot be confined to the nonrepetition of a particular sin. The consciousness of sin, and the positive desire to remove its taint, impose upon the penitent a duty of striving for a total regeneration, whereby his whole way of life becomes reconsecrated. An oft-repeated phrase in rabbinic literature is "Repentance and good deeds."[20] Good deeds are considered as the logical corollary of the act of repentance. The implication is that it is inconceivable for a true penitent to regret and desist from one act of sin while perpetuating another. Repentance must be unconditional and unrestricted to qualify for acceptance.

Rabbi E. Dessler (1891–1954) warns us, however, against attempting an overambitious and unrealistic level of repentance and resolve:

We have been taught that only the most dramatic arousal of our soul from its slumber will be effective for repentance. Nevertheless, when the penitent makes his resolution for the future, he must ensure that it is appropriate to the spiritual level he has attained. For if he attempts to overreach himself, he will fail, God forbid, and his repentance will be nullified. Thus, although his desire for repentance and his remorse has to be at the most intensive level, yet, if it is to be sustained, he must restrain his temptation to take upon himself too much at the outset, and realize that even such (spiritual) longings have to be controlled.[21]

This profound psychological insight may be related to the etymology of the word for "penitence," which comes from the Latin *poena*, "pain, punishment." This is suggestive of the very type of self-mortification that

Rabbi Dessler warns us against. Judaism's way to penitence, on the other hand, is through *teshuvah*, a sincere and straightforward "returning"—a retracing of one's steps from the byway of iniquity to the highway of righteousness. Such an act of remorse should not involve any such sensation as *pain*, neither should it focus the mind on *punishment*. Quite the contrary, it should fill one with relief and joy in anticipation of divine pity, forgiveness, love, and grace.

It is for this reason that Yom Kippur is a day of fasting, but not a day of mourning. Hence, Sephardim actually refer to it as "the white fast," as opposed to *Tishah B'Av*, the commemoration of the destruction of the Temple, which is called "the black fast." Hence the plea that climaxes each section of the *Al Cheit* confession, *Ve-al kulam Elohah Selichot* ("And for all of those sins, O God of forgiveness, forgive us, pardon us, grant us atonement"), is sung, rather than uttered in whispered awe, and why so many of its melodies are positively suffused with cheerful and optimistic vitality. There is absolutely no *poena* on this day. It is a pure festival, a day of hope and reconciliation.

Is divine forgiveness ever withheld? The rabbinic concept of divine mercy allowed for even the most inveterate sinner to obtain immediate mercy. The Rabbis took their lead from the case of Manasseh, King of Judah (696–641 B.C.E.), whose reign stands out as one of the darkest periods in the religious history of Israel. Idolatry, apostasy, murder, and immorality are all included in the list of charges made against him. Yet, according to the testimony of 2 Chronicles 33:12–13,

> When he was in distress, he entreated the favor of the Lord his God and humbled himself greatly before the God of his fathers. He prayed to Him, and God received his entreaty and heard his supplication. . . . Then Manasseh knew that the Lord was God.

However, for one grave sin—leading a multitude into sin—divine forgiveness is withheld. Such a sinner, declare the Rabbis, is not even given the opportunity to repent. For profanation of God's name there can be no forgiveness during the lifetime of the offender, but the combined efforts of his penitence, the Days of Atonement, his suffering, and, ultimately, his death will succeed in securing for him eventual redemption.[22] Within the definition of profanation of God's name the Rabbis particularize the case of a religious leader who by his conduct brings religion into disrepute.[23]

Allowing for a few notable exceptions, it can be said in general that Judaism believes that salvation is within the easy reach of man. The paths to it are not tortuous or strewn with pitfalls and trials. Man has but to face in the right direction, and God will lead him to his destination.

Bein Keseh Le'asor—The Intervening Period

The term *Ten Days of Penitence* suggests that the entire period of the High Holy Days should be used for soul-searching and repentance. It is too easy to regard this exercise as adequately and exhaustively achieved once Rosh Hashanah is over, so that Yom Kippur becomes relegated to a sort of postscript.

It is the early morning *Selichot* services during the days between Rosh Hashanah and Yom Kippur that especially attune the emotions of the small proportion who attend such midweek services to the spiritual objectives of the period. The *selichah* compositions offer an urgent and inspirational summons to us to participate in the process of spiritual cleansing and renewal that is a prerequisite to making peace with God and to cementing as full a relationship as it is within man's capacity to achieve.

It is *Shabbat Shuvah,* the intervening "Sabbath of Repentance," that especially serves this purpose for the general community of Sabbath morning attenders. The name derives from the opening words of the *Haftarah,* the specially prescribed reading from the prophetical book of Hoseah (14:2): "Return, O Israel [*Shuvah Yisrael*] to the Lord thy God." This is one of the two Sabbaths in the year (the other one being *Shabbat Ha-Gadol,* the Sabbath preceding Passover) when it is the prerogative of the rabbi to recite the *Haftarah,* in order to lend a greater urgency to its message. The sermon on this occasion will naturally be especially rousing, and the message particularly directed to any disturbing trends or patterns of behavior within the Jewish community.

Every Sabbath afternoon, during the intervening half an hour or so between the Afternoon Service (*Minchah*) and the Evening Service (*Maariv*), recited at the termination of Sabbath, the rabbi leads a *shiur,* or study circle. On *Shabbat Shuvah,* however, it takes the form of *drashah,* or public discourse, attended by many more congregants than usual. In the State of Israel it is common to see street posters announcing the theme of the *drashah* and the distinguished rabbinic authority who will be appearing as a guest speaker. In England and America, the Jewish press will also carry such advertisements.

The nature of the *Shabbat Shuvah drashah* varies with the type of congregation. While Jews lived in the ghettoes of Eastern Europe, and their education was largely restricted to *cheder* and *yeshivah,* that is an exclusively Jewish, and talmudic, diet, the *drashah* on this special Sabbath took the form of a deep, analytical tour de force ranging over all the sources and codifications of Jewish law relating to any aspect of the High Holy Days. It was an occasion for the rabbi to display his talmudic expertise; and the greater the scholar, the sooner he left his congregation behind him in the labyrinthine byways of rabbinic dialectic. It mattered little. Quite the contrary—it was expected! For the members of the audience, the art was to give the impression to their neighbors that they were following every subtle deductive and inductive nuance. This was achieved by occasionally nodding or finishing off the rabbi's recurring terms. The astute could sense when the rabbi's voice was rising excitedly, indicative of the fact that he was making a novel and subtle distinction, of which he was especially proud. That would be a most appropriate moment to display a smile or allow a chuckle to escape, just sufficiently audibly to impress three or four of one's immediate neighbors!

I vividly recall this situation in some large Orthodox synagogues in the 1950s, when the problem was compacted by the rabbi having been expected to deliver his address in Yiddish to provide a heightened sense of nostalgia for the elderly congregants who hailed from *der heim*. Today, this situation has all changed in the larger English-speaking and non-chasidic communities. The *drashah* is naturally in English, for, notwithstanding the brave attempt to revive the Yiddish language and literature at several universities, it has hardly become even a third language for the vast majority of Jews. Indeed, one rarely meets a Yiddish speaker these days—even among the largely Israel-trained and Hebrew-speaking rabbinate. The contemporary rabbi is expected to be a fluent communicator in the English language. He is also expected to bear in mind the professional nature and intellectual and cultural preoccupations of his community. Inevitably, the contemporary *drashah* will approximate more in form a lecture, and will concern itself with areas of Jewish learning that are more relevant to contemporary moral and spiritual concerns.

Visiting *Kever Avot*

Sometime during the High Holy Day period, tradition requires that children make a visit to *kever avot*, the graves of their parents. Observance of the fifth commandment, requiring respect to be shown to parents, does not cease at their death, and a token of loving remembrance is expected at least once a year. A private prayer is offered for the repose of their soul, and a few minutes are spent in silent and awed recollection of all their love and sacrifice, and the debt that is owed to them. Where parents lived by high principles and religious standards, that is an appropriate moment to reaffirm one's commitment to those values that they cherished, and to bring, in the words of the mystics, an *illuy* ("elevation") to their souls, by continuing and augmenting their sacred effort. A memorial candle is also kept burning *throughout* Yom Kippur in tribute to their memory.

Kapparot

Unique is the ancient religion that can claim to be devoid of some elements of superstition. In Judaism these were not native to its teachings. Quite the contrary, the Bible warns us in many places against divining, sorcery, or witchcraft. But, in the popular imagination, reflecting the deepest levels of irrational human fears, fueled by early primitive animistic notions, especially those of evil spirits populating the world and directing their baneful influences against vulnerable humanity, such ideas appeared plausible. In spite of vehement rabbinic opposition to such "Amorite practices," they succeeded in infiltrating and transforming the complexion of certain rituals, especially those concerned with human rites of passage (birth, circumcision, marriage, and death), as well as those of this period of the year when human fate was, in any case, held to be in the balance.

The ceremony of *kapparot* ("expiation"), performed before Yom Kippur, or by some before Rosh Hashanah, has just such a basis. It is not mentioned in the Talmud, and is not referred to in rabbinic sources until the ninth century, where it is commented upon by the Babylonian *Geonim*. The ceremony consists of taking a cock (for a male) or a hen (for a female), swinging it around the head three times, after which the following formula of vicarious substitution is recited:

> This shall be my substitute, this my exchange, this my atonement. This rooster will meet its death, while I shall enter and proceed to a good and lengthy life, and to peace.

The rooster is then slaughtered, and either it or its cash value is given to the poor. Many religious authorities were most concerned, however, for the ambivalent feelings of the poor at receiving such a "sin-laden gift." This aspect of the ritual compounded the general unease that many felt regarding its superstitious basis, a situation that prompted the recommendation that, instead of a rooster, money should be used for the ceremony. This had sound biblical warrant, since the half shekel, contributed by the Israelites in the desert, is referred to as "a ransom for one's life" (Exodus 30:12). This made *kapparot* a far more acceptable ritual for many, and has enabled it to survive in this form until the present day.

Some of the leading representatives of the school of kabbalistic study that flourished in Safed in the sixteenth century, notably Rabbi Isaac Luria, invested the ritual with special mystical significance. This gave it a much-needed impetus that assured its continuation, at least within the chasidic tradition, which leaned very heavily on mystic doctrines, especially those endorsed and developed by Luria. The opponents of the ceremony received unexpected support from perhaps the most illustrious of the Safed mystics, Joseph Karo, who, in his great code of Jewish law, the *Shulchan Arukh,* takes issue with his colleagues, and states that "the custom should be stopped."[24] Sephardi Jewry, which defers to Karo in matters of law and ritual, consequently abandoned the ritual, whereas Ashkenazim, for whom the variant decisions of Rabbi Moses Isserles are more authoritative, felt constrained to preserve the practice. In his gloss to Karo's statement, Isserles states: "There are Geonim who have recommended this custom, as have many later authorities. It is also practiced in all our [Ashkenazi] communities; and this may not, therefore, be changed, for it is hallowed by tradition."[25]

A present-day authority, Rabbi Chaim David Halevi, offers two reasons for abandoning *kapparot.* The first reason takes account of the real danger that, with vast crowds of people queuing up to have their roosters slaughtered by the *shochet* (ritual slaughterer) on the eve of Yom Kippur (a very short day), the pressure on the slaughterer is enormous. He has to dispatch the fowl so quickly, and is frequently so exhausted with the burden of work, that there is every reason to fear that he will not be able to give close attention to all the detailed regulations involved, and might easily unwittingly render the fowl *treifa* (unacceptable to be eaten).

His second objection is based upon the biblical prohibition of cruelty to animals. While, as a concession to human appetite, the Torah gave us permission to take an animal's life, nevertheless unnecessary slaughter, when not directly required for food, cannot be condoned. Rabbi Halevi condemns the practice in the strongest of terms: "Why should we, of all times on the eve of this holy day, display unnecessary cruelty to animals by slaughtering them without mercy at the very time when we come to seek life for ourselves from 'the living God.'"[26]

Eve of the Festival Procedures

Two special meals are prescribed for the eve of Yom Kippur. A full festive meal should be eaten in the early afternoon, and a light snack, called *Seudah ha-mafseket* ("meal of cessation"), which is taken on returning from the short afternoon service at synagogue (at which the full *Al Cheit* confessional is recited).

As many people cannot take off work for the whole afternoon before the fast, there is generally only time to eat the full festive meal, and the custom of eating the *Seudah ha-mafseket* is no longer so widespread. The main meal now commences around 4:30 P.M., to enable it to be finished, the dishes to be washed and put away, and the family to get to synagogue in time for the evening service, which commences at around 6:30 P.M.

At the *Seudah ha-mafseket*, the bread is dipped into honey as on Rosh Hashanah. Only easily digestible, nonspicy food and nonintoxicating drink should be consumed at this meal, so that one enters into prayer without feeling uncomfortably full or with one's senses dulled by liquor.

Before leaving for synagogue some have a custom to bless their children with a special and most beautiful blessing. This is added to the customary formula of blessing recited each Friday evening at the Sabbath table. The father places his hands upon the head of his offspring, and offers up a fervent prayer:

> May it be the will of our Father in heaven to instill into your heart love and reverence for Him. May the fear of God be with you all your days, so that you may not sin. May your craving be for the Torah and the commandments. May your eyes search for truth; may your mouth speak wisdom; may your emotions be controlled; may your hands engage in good deeds and your feet run to do the will of your Father in heaven. May He grant you righteous sons and daughters who engage in Torah and the fulfillment of the commandments all their days. May He grant that you earn a comfortable and good livelihood, through His generosity and not through the support of flesh and blood, a livelihood that will give you the freedom to serve the Lord. And may you be inscribed and sealed for a good, long life, among all the righteous of Israel. Amen.

The officiants, who lead the services on the High Holy Days, all wear the white *kittel*,[27] and it is also worn by many other religious Jews, whether or not they are officiating. Custom also recommends that women wear white dresses, as a symbol of purity, and that they refrain from wearing any jewelry.

Part II

Yom Kippur

6

The Evening Service

The Spirit of the Day

Gentiles often refer to Yom Kippur as the "black fast." It is not a term that any Jew would think of using, and is akin to the Christian attribution of *Old* Testament to our immortal Hebrew Bible. Black is synonymous with depression and mourning. Yom Kippur, on the other hand, is suffused with faith, optimism, and life.

The feelings of the Jew on this day may be compared with those of a bright student who has worked conscientiously and has mastered his work. He appears for the examination with confident expectation, and yet with more than a modicum of tenseness. Similarly, the Jew is confident that he will be received with compassion and mercy—and it is this that gives the day the character of a festival—yet he cannot totally banish from his thoughts the reality of being subjected to a rigorous scrutiny. The seemingly paradoxical plea of the Psalmist, "rejoice with trembling," well sums up the emotional mix.

Peaks and Troughs

The Yom Kippur service, like life itself, has peaks and troughs. For *Kol Nidrei* everyone is present. Who would have the temerity to move from his seat, to disturb his neighbor's concentration, to frustrate his ascent to the summit of the mountain of the Lord? Unthinkable.

Yet not so unthinkable to arrive next morning quite a few hours late, by which time most of *Shacharit* has been recited! This is a pity, because, with so few people in synagogue, *Shacharit* is truly a most spiritually uplifting experience. The synagogue is airy and decorum is excellent, with the nearest worshiper several rows away, almost out of earshot! One can raise one's voice in prayer, and sing, however tone-deaf one might be. At such a time no close neighbor will look disapprovingly. One can think, ponder, search one's conscience, express remorse, do proper *teshuvah*.

Shacharit, like *Kol Nidrei*, is a peak. And physically we are also at our peak, refreshed from a long sleep, which is every bit as nourishing as food. There is, after all, no excuse for going to bed late on *Kol Nidrei* night—unless of course one follows the practice of an ancient pietistic guild who would stay up all of that night reciting psalms!

Many admit to waking up particularly invigorated on Yom Kippur morning. They feel whole, at one with themselves, unified. Body and soul, inclination and conscience, form one accord. Tensions and dichotomies are banished. *Mens sana in corpore sano*. Physical and mental faculties collude to abandon their respective daily preoccupations—the body's insatiable passion for food, drink, pleasure, and nourishment, and the mind's restless creation of ideas, and the incessant juggling act it performs with thoughts, knowledge, information, emotions, ambitions.

One warms to the alliance they have suddenly and unexpectedly made. One senses that it is in response to a command from on high. *Haneshamah lakh ve-ha-guf she-lakh* ("The soul is thine and the body is thine"). On this day our lease on the latter is truly suspended, our bodies are truly "thine."

To return to our peaks and troughs, the peak is maintained until after *Yizkor*. For many, this Memorial Service for the Departed seems to be the very centerpiece of the day—a compacted overture and finale. Some synagogues even offer a shift facility of *Yizkor* services throughout the afternoon. Out of nowhere people appear, pay their respects to the departed—and depart!

Then comes the trough, as, once *Yizkor* is over, the *shul* rapidly empties and people wend their way home for a few hours of rest, offering a parting salute to their neighbor—"See you at *Neilah*!" It goes without saying that this is not what the rabbis envisaged when they preached about the essential partnership between *shul* and home!

Neilah is undoubtedly a peak. And, like mountaineers making the final, painfully slow, yet exhilarating, ascent to the summit, we move inexorably toward the climax of this unique day at a measured and deliberate pace. Our legs ache as if we had truly scaled a peak. The *shul* is stuffy, but its lack of oxygen only serves to heighten the sense of high altitude spiritual exertion. The muscles of our throats—relaxed and docile during the rest of the year—now feel somewhat strained and rebellious at the end of an unexpected twenty-four-hour marathon of singing and shouting.

Yom Kippur, with its peaks and troughs, certainly epitomizes life itself—except that, with life, we are not so eager to reach the climactic stage of the "closing of the gates." Indeed, we comfort ourselves with the thought that the gates will remain open forever.

Judaism's message is that *Neilah* comes to us all, and that perhaps it is not a bad thing as we go through life to keep looking at our watch in order to remind ourselves that the hour is late, that "the day is short and the work is great, the laborers are sluggish and the reward is much, and the Master of the house is urgent" (*Avot* 2:20).

A Day Like Purim

Yom Kippur is an occasion that evokes within people varying attitudes and responses. Many dread it; some don't mind it. A small minority even confess to enjoying its uplifting effect upon them. All three categories would agree, however, that Yom Kippur is definitely not a day of pleasure and excitement.

What prompted the medieval kabbalists, therefore, to make a play on the full (biblical) name of that festival—*Yom* (*Ha-*)*Kippurim*—and dub it *Yom Ke-Purim*, "a day like Purim"? Was it some tasteless joke, to compare our most solemn day with the boisterous carnival spirit of Purim? Hardly. Those God-intoxicated mystics did not make jokes about religion. We are entitled to inquire, therefore, into their motive behind such a strange analogy.

A closer analysis will reveal that it is not so farfetched, and that some significant points of contact between these two festivals can be located.

In our preoccupation with celebrating and reenacting the victory celebration of the Purim struggle, we make only a passing reference to the fact that it was only at the eleventh hour that the Jews of Persia escaped their doom. Only after three days of fasting, prayer, and petition, only after tense and dangerous maneuvering and negotiation on the part of Queen Esther with her husband, the king of the Medes and Persians, "whose laws cannot be revoked," only after great national introspection and apprehension, was the hangman's noose finally prized off the Jewish neck. Thus, the historical Purim was, for those who lived through it, a paradigm of Yom Kippur. They also experienced "days of awe," of uncertainty as to their fate, pangs of self-doubt, and the deep and desperate need for faith and reliance upon the mercy and grace of God.

This was certainly in the minds of those kabbalists when they explained the name *Yom Kippurim* (Day of Atonement) as *Yom Ke-Purim* (a day like Purim). They were suggesting thereby, that on that most sacred day we should also feel a sense of spiritual anxiety, as if the forces of sin were poised to surround us, and to destroy us personally, culturally, spiritually, and nationally—as was the situation for the Jews of ancient Persia in the Purim saga.

In order not to impair our joyous annual celebration of the ultimate victory, it is on the day before Purim that we recall the agonies that preceded the ecstasy of victory. It is then that we observe the fast day—*Taanit Esther*—with petitionary prayer and confession, *Selichot* and *Avinu Malkeinu*. It is then that we relive and commemorate the other, more fearful face of the historical Purim.

Yom Kippur again lives up to the analogy, because this festival also joins a fast day to a feast day, for our rabbis tell us that it is a mitzvah to eat a celebratory meal and to drink on the day before Yom Kippur. Thus, in the case of both Purim and Yom Kippur, we have the juxtaposition of two contrasting moods: fear and fasting one day, joy and indulgence the next. The only difference is that on Purim the celebration follows the fast, whereas on Yom Kippur it precedes it.

But there is also another characteristic shared by these two festivals. In both situations the drawing of lots figures prominently. The very name *Purim* means "lots," recalling the method employed by Haman to determine the most propitious day for his attack on the Jewish community. Similarly, in biblical times, one of the highlights of the Yom Kippur celebration was the *Seir Ha-Mishtale'ach*, the scapegoat ritual. The Torah states that two goats had to be selected at the outset. One was to be offered as a communal atonement sacrifice to God; the other was designated as "the banished goat" (*Azazel*), and sent out to roam the desert, symbolically laden with Israel's sin. The two goats were identical, and the choice as to which goat was to be used for which purpose was determined by lots.

The theme of lots is highlighted again in the Yom Kippur ritual in the context of the story of Jonah, which is read during the Afternoon Service. "And the mariners said to each other: 'Come and let us cast lots, that we may know on whose account this evil is upon us.' So they cast lots, and the lot fell upon Jonah."

So here, again, we have the double link between these two festivals, which prompted those sages to declare Yom Kippur as *Yom Ke-Purim*, a day like Purim.

But what is the significance of these lots? What message do they convey of such importance that they should be highlighted as factors linking the two festivals? The message seems to be that life is a game of chance, a lottery, and that there are twists of fortune and irrational, unexpected, occurrences for which one cannot plan and against which one cannot insure or protect oneself. The dangers lurk where one least expects them, and the good fortune announces itself frequently without any notice.

Life is capricious. There is no logic behind the blind hatred of a Haman. Anti-Semitism is a Purim. It is as if lots are drawn to determine, arbitrarily, who will be our ally and who our enemy. Chance factors, fickle whims of statesmen and monarchs, subjective or slanted assessments, conjecture and intrigue—all conspire, with mind-baffling capriciousness, to determine whether the lot will be kind to us or otherwise.

Similarly with the lot drawn for the goats at the Yom Kippur ceremony. Their message is that there is no logic, no consistent criterion, for determining who is for God and who for *Azazel*—who will remain within the orbit of religious life and who will go outside into the desert, defecting from the ranks and abandoning our sacred traditions.

Again, the unexpected factors come into play, influencing our decisions in either direction. Distractions, pressures, beguiling attractions, moments of weakness or carelessness, loneliness, despair, chance meetings, brainwashing, new acquaintances, moments of passion—all these can send us off, like *Azazel*, into the desert. And, conversely, sudden insights and flashes of intuition, unexpected deliverance from danger, experiences of religious emotion and exultation, the joy of fulfilling a mitzvah, the comfort of having God to guide one (especially at a moment of trial or indecision), the religious companionship, the fraternity of synagogue social and spiritual life—any of these factors can suddenly, without previous motivation, send one scuttling in a new and more positive direction. It is all a game of chance. Life plays tricks, casting lots with our fate. And this is the burden of our defense before the heavenly throne at this sacred period.

We are telling God, in effect, that, in a society as complex as ours, with all its tensions and pressures, all its beguiling and dangerous ideologies, all its competitiveness, its sham, its tasteless seductions, we, poor mortals, cannot really be held solely responsible for all our actions. We are victims of complex circumstances, actions, interactions, and reactions.

The law-abiding or religious may only be so because of a conducive environment that molded them that way, even against their own natural inclinations. Perhaps the criminal, the agnostic, or the atheist would never have been so had they been given the saints' opportunities, heredity, or environment.

So we are not completely responsible for our sins. Life is, after all, a lottery, and some of us draw winning tickets while others draw blanks. It is a *Yom Ke-Purim*, a day like Purim.

The Prohibition against Wearing Shoes

The Rabbis explained the biblical injunction of "afflicting one's soul"[1] on this day as referring to five specific "afflictions" or abstentions (*innuyim*)—from eating, drinking, perfuming the body, cohabitation, and the wearing of shoes.[2] While the first four are normally conducted in the privacy of one's home, it is the abstention from wearing shoes (*neilat ha-Sandal*) that is the one most obvious to the eye of the observer at synagogue on Yom Kippur.[3]

Today we hardly identify the wearing of shoes as one of life's basic pleasures, although in biblical and talmudic times shoes attracted much attention as a status symbol. When the psalmist said, "Against Edom I cast off my shoe,"[4] he was symbolizing the low estate to which that country was about to fall. It was to become a vassal state, and the prophet accordingly performed the same symbolic act—removing the shoes—that served in later talmudic times as a symbolic token of acquisition when transferring possession of a slave to a new owner.[5]

Wearing shoes was the prerogative of the upper classes. In the Song of Songs the king pays this tribute to his beloved: "How comely are thy steps *in shoes*, O high-born daughter."[6] Because shoes were regarded as an important adornment they were proscribed on those occasions when it was appropriate to convey a spirit of humility and dejection, as in the cases of a mourner, or on the Fast of *Av*, when lamenting the loss of the Temple, and on Yom Kippur, when standing in the dock of the heavenly court.

In the course of time a distinction was made between leather shoes and those made of other materials, such as cloth or wood, with the result that only leather shoes are now regarded as affording "pleasurable" comfort, and are therefore forbidden to be worn. Slippers or plimsoles are permitted, as are shoes made of synthetic materials, although most of those who observe this abstention would not wear the latter in order to avoid contravening the principle of *marit ha-ayin*, not giving a mistaken impression (that one is breaking a religious law). White plimsoles—to match the white *kittel*—are the most popular choice.

Wearing a *Tallit*

Kol Nidrei is the only occasion in the year when the congregation wear a *tallit* for the evening service. This practice is peculiar to the Ashkenazim, and became widespread through the influence of the famous authority, Rabbi Meir of Rothenburg (d. 1293), who officiated as Reader on the High Holy Days wearing the *tallit*. His congregation felt compelled to do likewise, and from there the practice spread.

As the duty of wearing *tzitzit* only applies to daytime,[7] the *tallit* has to be donned while it is still daylight, and the *Kol Nidrei* service is commenced, accordingly, in the early evening.

Rabbi Meir's innovation was based upon the circumstances attending the original divine disclosure to Moses of God's thirteen attributes. Rabbinic tradition has it that "God enwrapped himself in a *tallit*, like a *chazan*, and disclosed these attributes to Moses."[8] Since the attributes are recounted in the *Kol Nidrei* service, Rabbi Meir felt that it was appropriate, therefore, for the *chazan* to be wearing the *tallit*.

בִּישִׁיבָה שֶׁל מַעְלָה
By Authority of the Heavenly Court

The footnote in the Birnbaum edition asserts that this formula was introduced by the famous thirteenth-century authority, Rabbi Meir of Rothenburg, in order to encourage Jewish transgressors to return to synagogue and pray with the community on this holiest night of the year. It had the dual purpose of serving as an invitation to those defectors, as well as a plea to the regular worshipers to accept them in their midst and to welcome them back. Birnbaum refers to the talmudic statement that "any fast wherein Jewish transgressors do not participate is no fast" (*Keritot* 6b).

Birnbaum follows here the popular theory of the great nineteenth-century liturgical authority, Leopold Zunz. However, Zunz's attribution of the *Bi-yeshivah shel maalah* formula to Rabbi Meir of Rothenburg has now been shown to have been erroneous, since there is a clear reference to such a declaration in the writings of Rabbi Eliezer bar Yoel Halevi (*Raviah*) of Bonn, the teacher of Rabbi Meir of Rothenburg. He already refers to it as "an established practice to enter synagogue and declare the absolution of the vow, in order to enable the congregation to pray together with any person who has transgressed by disobeying any decree *of the community*."[9]

It is now clear that this formula was a solemn declaration, lifting any *local* decree of excommunication that had been imposed upon a reprobate member of the community. Among the terms of such a ban were that he could not be given a Jewish burial, his child was not to be circumcised, and *the community was not to allow him to attend a service in synagogue*. On *Kol Nidrei* night this last condition was relaxed, but, since the ban had been solemnly imposed with a formula invoking "the authority of the heavenly court and the authority of the earthly court; with the consent of the Omnipresent One and with the consent of this congregation," the very same formula had to be employed in order to suspend the ban on this occasion.

Although this formula originated, as we have seen, in Ashkenazi circles, it was soon adopted also by the Sephardi communities. Having established itself, some rationale for its continued recitation had to be offered for those situations—the majority—wherein there were no excommunicants present in synagogue. The popular rationale was to quote the talmudic tradition that "any fast in which there are no transgressors participating is no fast."[10] The weakness of such a rationale is clearly apparent, in that the talmudic statement was hardly intended to be taken strictly literally. Furthermore, it would have been most uncharacteristic to create a prayer or formula—postulating the presence of transgressors and granting authority for them to be included in the congregation—merely in order to substantiate a rather abstruse talmudic maxim!

כָּל נִדְרֵי
All Vows

The theory that has gained the widest popularity in the past is that of Joseph S. Bloch who suggested in 1917 that the origins of *Kol Nidrei* go back to the Visigoth persecution of the Jews of Spain—and their forced conversion to Christianity—in the seventh century C.E.[11] Their conversion vows were made under the most fearful oaths and adjurations. They had solemnly to profess their belief in the new faith, and they had to renounce Jewish practices under penalty of death. They remained secretly faithful, however, to their ancestral beliefs, and on the holiest night of the year these *Marranos* made an effort to celebrate it with their fellow Jews by sneaking into synagogue.

They were sorely troubled, however, about the fact that, in so doing, they were breaking solemn oaths and vows, even though they had been taken under duress. Bloch asserted that the *Kol Nidrei* was introduced for their benefit, to enable them first to crave absolution.

This theory is linked to an explanation of the term *avaryanim*, in the preceding formula, which regards it as a transliteration of the term *Iberians*—that is Spanish Jews, residents of the Iberian peninsula. It also explains the presence of the succeeding biblical verse, *ve-nislach le-chol adat* (Numbers 15:26), which occurs in the context of idolatry.

The standard melody for *Kol Nidrei* is also stylistically most appropriate to either of the above theories. "The motifs alternate between solemn syllabic 'proclamations,' as in the opening, intensely devotional wave-like phrases, and virtuoso vocal runs."[12] The slow, deliberate, almost mournful notations would have the effect of impressing upon the Jewish defectors the seriousness of their actions and their urgent need of divine forgiveness.[13]

This theory of a Spanish origin, however plausible, is, nevertheless, historically unsubstantiated. The first references to this prayer in our literature come from eighth-century Babylonia, the main center of Jewish life and culture. Spain was not yet on the Jewish map, and, in any case, the Babylonian authorities in a Muslim country would hardly have adopted, on the holiest night of the year, a composition recited for Spanish converts to Christianity and related exclusively to their personal dilemma!

Another theory, suggested by Samuel Krauss, is that the Rabbis of the eighth century introduced the *Kol Nidrei* declaration of absolution of vows for polemical reasons, in order to refute the Karaite denunciation of that practice as being totally without basis in Jewish tradition.

The Bible[14] restricts the privilege of granting absolution to a husband and a father, who may absolve their wives and unmarried daughters, respectively, of any vows they express, providing they are canceled on the day they are uttered. Oral tradition extended the scope of this privilege, granting a *Bet Din* (ecclesiastical court) the right to annul the vows of any Jew, under clearly established conditions. This innovation was hotly contested by the Karaites who accepted no institution without a clear biblical foundation. The Rabbis themselves were forced to concede that "the absolution of vows hovers in the air and has no basis upon which to lean for support,"[15] and Karaite writers, especially Daniel al-Qumisi, their vigorous ninth-century spokesman, poured scorn on the Rabbis "who break vows even on the eve of the Day of Atonement."[16]

There were two, diametrically opposite, Jewish reactions. Some Babylonian *Geonim*[17] wilted under the criticism, and actually abolished this entire judicial procedure. Even the talmudic tractate *Nedarim*, which is devoted to the subject, was withdrawn, by the *Geonim* Yehudai (eighth century C.E.) and Natronai (ninth century), from the curriculum of their academies.

An entirely different, and most courageous, response was emphatically to insist upon the validity of the institution of absolution. This resulted in an exaggerated overemphasis, culminating in the creation of a special formulation—*Kol Nidrei*—to be recited at the most solemn moment of the year, when the entire community was assembled. It was considered by the protagonists of this approach that the whole integrity and authority of the Oral Law was at stake here, and that such a dramatic gesture of confidence was both required and fully justified at such an impressionable hour.

Even this theory of the origin of *Kol Nidrei* has been subjected to sound criticism on the grounds that it would appear that the composition actually antedates the period of the Karaites, since the *Gaon* Yehudai (circa 750 C.E.) refers to it as being an already firmly established custom!

Clearly, the true circumstances surrounding its origin have still to be demonstrated beyond any shadow of doubt.

The Ashkenazi and Sephardi versions of *Kol Nidrei* are written in Aramaic. However, the Italian tradition and the Babylonian liturgical manual, *Seder Rav Amram*, have a pure Hebrew version.

Various categories of oaths, vows and promises are enumerated:

1. *Nidrei*: "Religious obligations." The *neder* is a comprehensive term for any kind of religious obligation that a person takes upon himself, such as a vow to bring a sacrifice or to become a Nazarite. It should be stressed that absolution for any of the categories listed in *Kol Nidrei* can be secured only for obligations unpaid to God. No prayer can excuse or absolve a Jew from any firm promise or commitment to his fellow man unless released by the latter.

2. *Esarei*: "Obligations." The term *issar* is found in Numbers 30:3 as a cognate accusative of the verb *Lessor*, "to impose upon oneself a restriction." The basic meaning of the verb is actually "to tie," and it is used widely in rabbinic terminology to denote "that which is forbidden," *asur*. While the *neder* denotes a recognized and standard religious obligation, the *issar* suggests a personal obligation to which the donor wished to bind himself.[18]

3. *Charamei*: "Pledges." The *cherem* is used in the Bible to denote an object devoted to God or for a sacred purpose, such as for use in the sanctuary. It is also used to denote spoils of war that escaped destruction (from the verb *charam*, meaning, basically, "to destroy").

4. *Konamei*: "Promises." This is in the same category as the preceding, except that it refers to pledges made by employing the dedicatory formula *konam* ("consecrated!").[19]

5. *Kinnuyei*: "Substitute terms." This is an allusion to the mishnaic principle that "any terms used by people as substitutes for the official formulae for uttering vows are as binding as the officially accepted terms."[20]

6 *Kinnusei*: "Variant terms." This term is also enumerated in the Mishnah as a formula that must be regarded as binding. Such terms as *konam* and *konas* (sing. of *kinnusei*) were actually Gentile mispronunciations of the Hebrew term *korban* ("I sacrifice, devote"). Maimonides blames the Ethiopians and the French for having popularized such inaccurate variants, which were even adopted later by Jews.[21]

7. *Shevuot*: "Oaths." The terms *shevuah* and *neder* are the most common. The term *shevuah* also occurs in the biblical passage dealing

with a father and husband's right of annulling the vows of their family.[22] The term is used when taking a vow to deny oneself any benefit from a particular object.

מִיּוֹם כִּפּוּרִים זֶה
From This Day of Atonement until the Next One

A fundamental difference exists between the Ashkenazi and Sephardi versions of the above formula. The Ashkenazi formula is "prospective," declaring that any unfulfilled vows uttered during the coming year should be null and void. The Sephardim, on the other hand, have a "retrospective" formula, annulling any vows made "from the last Day of Atonement until this Day of Atonement."

The latter version is undoubtedly the original one, as evidenced by all the geonic sources from the period of Yehudai *Gaon* (circa 750).

The change to the prospective version was made in the eleventh century by Rabbi Meir ben Samuel, son-in-law of Rashi and father of the great *Rabbeinu Tam*. The latter supported his father's objections to the retrospective formula on the grounds that (1) annulment of past vows has to be performed by an experienced *dayyan* (judge) or by three laymen acting as a court of law, whereas, according to the prevailing custom, the Reader alone recites the declaration of annulment; (2) according to Jewish law, the actual vow has to be specified; (3) a prerequisite for annulment is the expression of regret (*charatah*) at having made the vow, whereas our congregations merely sing along with the *Kol Nidrei*; (4) there is no one to annul the vows of the Reader!

To overcome these objections, the retrospective formula was changed to the current Ashkenazi prospective version, which is not so much a ritual of annulment as a plea that God should preserve us from making unfulfilled vows, and, in the event of their being made, that He should regard them as nonbinding commitments.

However, the discarding of a time-honored version met with considerable resistance, which resulted in many communities rejecting its recitation altogether. The Sephardim opted to retain the original version, the Ashkenazim generally accepted the innovation, and some communities compromised and recited both versions!

Our adjusted version has been left, however, with an anomaly; for, while the key sentence now refers to the future ("from this Day of Atonement until the Day of Atonement to come"), the verbs have been left in the past tense: "All vows . . . which we *have vowed* [*dindarna*] and *have sworn* [*u-de-ishtevana*]"!

Kol Nidrei is recited slowly three times, with the Reader raising his voice a little at each recitation. Surprisingly, the repetition was not introduced for any mystical or halakhic reasons, but merely to prolong the service for the sake of latecomers and enable them to catch up with the congregation and finish praying *Maariv* at the same time as the rest. This was especially important as synagogues were generally only permitted to be built outside the towns, and it was dangerous for people to make the return journey home on their own in the darkness.

בָּרוּךְ אַתָּה... שֶׁהֶחֱיָנוּ
Blessed Are You . . . Who Has Kept Us in Life . . .

This blessing over the festival (*Birkat ha-zeman*) is recited on other festivals together with the *kiddush*. Since on a fast day no *kiddush* can be made, the blessing was transferred to an honored position just before *borkhu*. In the *siddur* of the great Babylonian Gaon Saadia (882–942), however, it is prescribed for insertion in its usual position after the *Amidah*.[23]

אֱלֹהַי, עַד שֶׁלֹּא נוֹצַרְתִּי אֵינִי כְדַאי
My God, Before I Was Formed I Was Unworthy

This short piece is tailor-made to serve as a climactic plea by the private worshiper, expressive of his feelings of abject unworthiness and his acknowledgment of the utter vacuity of his life. To spare the *chazan*'s feelings, he is not called upon to utter publicly such sentiments in his repetition of the *Amidah* (perhaps for fear that some ungracious wit might shout out "here, here!" to the confession that his life serves no useful purpose!).

The phrase, "Behold, I am like a vessel filled with shame and humiliation before You," is quite an extreme affirmation. Shame is not, however, necessarily an unworthy attribute. Mark Twain noted that man is the only animal that blushes. He then added, characteristically, "or needs to!" It was Friedrich Nietzsche who called man "the beast with the red cheeks," testimony to the frequency with which man had such occasion to blush.

God could hardly have imposed upon man responsibility for his moral and ethical lapses without making him ill-at-ease for them. The external or internal blush is the divinely implanted mechanism of human self-accountability—the prerequisite to accountability before God. Before Adam and Eve committed their first sin, we are told that "they were naked, the two of them, man and his wife—*ve-lo yitboshashu—but were not ashamed*" (Genesis 2:25). Not only were they not ashamed before each other—which, as man and wife, was perhaps understandable—but they were actually unable to feel shame of any kind. (This we suggest is the full import of the reflexive form of the verb, in its *Hitpa'el* conjugation.)

They did not yet possess the mechanism for the *self-activated* feelings of shame and remorse that come with awareness of sin. It was only when they engaged in sin that they automatically experienced the pangs of conscience that were meant to accompany it. Then, and only then, did they become aware of the dimensions of sinful potentiality inherent in every other aspect of human endeavor. That dawning of the realization of the unbounded nature of human desire marked the onset of their emotional and sexual self-awareness. From then on, they realized just how naked and vulnerable they were. And their donning of fig-leaf clothing was but a natural and instinctive reaction to those feelings of shame and vulnerability.

But that self-same shame is also man's saving grace, for, at the moment when he is in the greatest danger of succumbing to any moral onslaught upon his weaker nature, and of losing control of himself and his free will in the process, then shame—in greater or lesser measure, depending on aspects of one's nature and nurture—signals its presence, offering man some opportunity, however slight, of backtracking and taking stock of the ramifications of his impending action.

It has to be realized also that shame and trust relate to each other in an essential manner. Where there is total trust between two people that their confidences will never be divulged, there also the element of shame will largely vanish, to the extent that the most intimate confidences may be mutually exchanged. Shame is generated to the degree that fear of disclosure is entertained. And this may account for the mutual shame that Adam and Eve felt as a consequence of their sin. Trust had gone out of their relationship. There was a third party playing off one against the other. Eve had colluded with the serpent to frustrate the wishes of her husband. Shame came in to fill the vacuum left by the absence of trust.

The author of this plea refers to the human being as "a vessel filled with shame and humiliation." This legacy of shame, inherited from Adam and Eve, can only be banished by trust. Trust in God will banish any sense of shame or embarrassment that we may have in relating to Him, in addressing Him directly rather than hiding behind the words of the prayers, and in involving Him as a direct and active source of guidance for all the considerations and decisions of our everyday lives. All the rebbes and role models, gurus and guides, are no substitute for that sense of perfect trust in Almighty God that can banish our shame and our crushing sense of worthlessness, as enunciated so passionately by the author of this piece, in his desperate and pessimistic assertion that "before I was formed I was unworthy, and now that I have been formed, it is as if I had not been formed." It is to be hoped that by the time Yom Kippur is over, we can all frame a far more optimistic philosophy of human existence.

יַעֲלֶה
O Let Our Prayer Ascend from Eventime

The unique appeal of this poem is grounded in its simplicity. The basic structure of the corresponding lines of each three-line stanza is identical. Only the middle word of each line changes from stanza to stanza, and the added words follow a reverse acrostic design. The three verbs, employed consecutively in each stanza, are culled from the prayer *Yaaleh ve-yavo ... ve-yeira'eh*, recited on all festivals and *Rosh Chodesh*. The poet employs these three verbs consistently in the masculine form of the third person, even though several of the subject nouns are feminine. Grammar was clearly secondary in his mind to the maintenance of a simple and uniform setting.

The poem serves as an introductory petition to all the prayers recited on *Kol Nidrei* night and throughout the following Day of Atonement, expressing the fervent hope that they will all ascend (*yaaleh*) to the heavenly throne and be efficacious.

The final word of the first line—*mei-erev*—and the last phrase of the third line of each stanza—*ad arev*—together form the biblical phrase, "from evening unto evening,"[24] which specifies the duration of this great fast day.

All the subject nouns listed in this poem—*tachanuneinu, shavateinu*, and so on—are both appropriate and readily comprehensible. The one exception occurs in the first line of the fourth stanza—"O let our *menuseinu* ascend at sunset." Routledge renders the noun freely as "hope," Birnbaum as "trusting faith." The meaning of the noun *manos*—"flight," "escape"—is, however, beyond question, which gives little sense in this context. Some manuscript versions of the poem substitute the noun *milluleinu* ("our words"), others *mechilateinu* ("our pardon"). D. Goldschmidt tortuously justifies the present reading by explaining that "if our prayers are accepted, then that will be the instrument of our 'escape' from the evil decree."[25] ArtScroll has "Our [plea for] refuge."

The identity of the author of this poem is not established with certainty, though it is thought to have been written by Yose ben Yose, a very early Palestinian poet (circa fifth century C.E.). Yose is the author of the composition *Omnam ashameinu*, recited later, and of various compositions on the theme of the Day of Atonement ritual in Temple times (*Avodah*). Although the latter were not incorporated into the Ashkenazi tradition, they have been preserved in the *siddur* of Saadia Gaon who was a particular admirer of Yose's poetry. Yose's poetry is characterized by a simple style, an uncomplicated technique, and a fervent piety.[26]

שֹׁמֵעַ תְּפִלָּה
O You Who Hear Prayer

This composition comprises a medley of biblical verses, culled mainly from the Psalms but including one verse from Deuteronomy, two from Jeremiah, two from Isaiah, and one each from Job and 1 Chronicles. The verses pay tribute to the majestic holiness of God, His mighty acts at Creation, His omnipotence and omniscience, and, in consequence, our paramount duty of praising and worshiping Him. The climax of the passage is a simple, direct appeal for clemency, arguing that "the soul is Thine, and the body is Thy work: have pity on thy labor." What more effective and guileless argument could be adduced? Which artist would want to destroy the masterpiece into which he had invested all his skill and his unique spirit? Thus, it is "for Thy name's sake" that God must pardon our iniquity, "however great it is."

These verses were not randomly chosen merely because they reflect the central themes. A close examination will reveal that a literary device is employed here governing the particular choice of verses. There is a stair-like progression—as used effectively in the parallelism of some of the psalms—whereby either the basic or a subsidiary idea in one line, or a key word in the line, is carried over as a link with the following line. The ideas thus progress smoothly and impressively toward the climactic plea for mercy.

Many will be surprised by the quotation from Psalm 74:

> Thou didst crush the heads of Leviathan,
> Leaving him a prey to beasts of the desert . . .
> By thy power thou didst divide the sea,
> Crushing the dragon's heads upon the waters.

Such mythological references to God having had to struggle with primeval creatures before being enabled to create the world are clearly in blatant conflict with our pure notion of the unity and omnipotence of the Creator!

Professor Yehezkiel Kaufmann[27] suggests that the later biblical writers were actually unaware of the status of these references as pagan concepts, particularly in the light of the fact that paganism is nowhere even hinted at in the biblical account of Creation. The author of these psalm-verses would have regarded such references as native to Israel's legendary tradition.

Kaufmann believes that these motifs were actually inherited not from Babylonian mythology—wherein *before Creation* God had to struggle for supremacy over *contending gods*—but from pre-Israelite, native, Canaanite tradition (known to us from Ugarit).[28] In our biblical version of these myths God has to deal exclusively with His own rebellious *subject-creatures*. Furthermore, this is always *after creation*, once God's rule was already clearly established.

In our own, recast version of the myths, Leviathan, the serpent,[29] the great sea monsters,[30] Rahab and the fleeing serpent,[31] and so on, are all portrayed merely as demonic creatures of God. Their rebelliousness—like man's—becomes a source of real or potential evil and a danger to the stability and survival of the world. In that sense, God is constantly in a relationship of contention with them, as reflected in these rather gross anthropomorphic references.

The literary form of this composition reflects one of the earliest stages of formalized liturgy. Before our great sages of the talmudic period made so bold as to express publicly their own devotional sentiments, which paved the way for the development of sacred poetry, prayer was restricted to the recitation of biblical verses. These were probably chanted antiphonally, by leader and congregation.

דַּרְכְּךָ אֱלֹהֵינוּ... לְמַעַנְךָ אֱלֹהֵינוּ
Our God, It Is Your Way . . . For Your Sake, O Our God
אָמְנָם אֲשָׁמֵינוּ עָצְמוּ מִסַּפֵּר
Truly Our Transgressions Are More Than Can Be Numbered

The composition *Omnam ashameinu* is introduced by the two verses that serve, alternately, as the refrains to each stanza. Most editions of the *machzor* fail to appreciate this function of the opening verses, and do not insert, therefore, the usual initial word reference to them in the appropriate places at the end of each stanza.

The author of this composition was the great pioneer of Hebrew liturgical poetry in Palestine, Yose ben Yose.[32] His first refrain-verse reminds God that one of His essential attributes is that of "being long-suffering towards both the righteous and the wicked." Yose had in mind here the talmudic explanation of the dual form (*erekh*) *apayim* ("[slow to] anger")—instead of (*erekh*) *af*—in the list of divine attributes.[33] The dual form is to indicate that God's tolerance is extended, in equal measure, to both.[34]

The second refrain-verse, "Act for Your own sake, not ours," reflects a similar sentiment to that of the concluding verses of the preceding composition. We are God's handiwork, over which He has labored. It is for His sake and in His interest, therefore, for His plan to end in success, and for man's destiny to lie in salvation rather than destruction.

The poem *Omnam ashameinu*—considerably abbreviated in our *machzor*—follows an alphabetical acrostic pattern. A separate, four-line stanza is devoted to each letter of the alphabet, each line of which commences with that particular letter. This provides a lengthy poem of eighty-eight lines, which, when allowances are made for a refrain after each stanza, makes a total of one hundred and ten lines! It is no wonder that the poem has suffered much abbreviation at the hands of editors. The Routledge and De Sola editions end the poem after the letter *yod*. Birnbaum and ArtScroll, following a fairly widespread Ashkenazi practice, omit the poem entirely, while somewhat incongruously maintaining the introductory refrain-verses followed by the very last stanza of the poem, *Taaleh arukhah*.

Another reason for the abbreviation of Yose's poem is the fact that its despairing and nationally self-deprecatory sentiments, coupled with its chronicle of woes, transform it almost into a dirge, which is not in keeping with the spirit of the *Yom Tov* of Yom Kippur.

אֵל מֶלֶךְ יוֹשֵׁב
Almighty King Who Sits on the Throne of Mercy

Routledge consistently omits this introductory section to the thirteen divine attributes, as well as the attributes themselves. While other editions of the *machzor* repeat these sections four times, as accompaniments to the various *selichot* ("Penitential hymns"), Routledge includes it only once in its version of the Evening Service (p. 40).

God is addressed as "King who sits upon the throne of mercy," in accordance with the rabbinic belief that although God begins by occupying the throne of justice, yet, at the sound of the *shofar* on Rosh Hashanah, He abandons it for the throne of mercy.[35]

The phrase *mitnaheig ba-chasidut* ("you govern with piety") is unclear. Some commentators connect it with the biblical phrase "with the pious (*chasid*) you show yourself as pious (*titchassad*),"[36] which the *Targum* relates to the three patriarchs, each of whom received the full measure of reward for their piety. This does not explain, however, the particular nuance of the term *chasidut*, which suggests a reward in excess of what was deserved.

Gersonides[37] comes closest to a satisfactory explanation. He relates the expression to the experiences of King David who composed the verse. David was reflecting here on the fact that, whereas his own heinous sin with Bathsheba was, nevertheless, instantly pardoned,[38] his predecessor, King Saul, lost his kingdom for a comparatively minor offense![39] David's rationale of this is expressed here. Because he strove to be a pious man (*chasid*) throughout his life, and only once was vanquished by the onslaught of his passion for Bathsheba, God, in return, also displayed *chasidut*, a unique degree of loving indulgence. Saul, on the other hand, who showed indifference to God all his life, was punished with a commensurate absence of such divine *chasidut*. In this introduction to the Thirteen Divine Attributes, the author asserts that the quality of *chasidut* governs God's relationship with His people.

מַעֲבִיר רִאשׁוֹן רִאשׁוֹן
You Make Them [the Sins] Pass Away One by One

Rashi explains this rather vague talmudic statement[40] to mean that, rather than placing all the good and evil deeds in the scales together, and risk having to condemn man, God places them in in small clusters. If, in the first cluster, they are equal in number, or if the good deeds outweigh the bad, God then "removes the sins" from that cluster, and pardons them, leaving only the good deeds in the scale, to augment the good deeds of the subsequent clusters.

אֵל הוֹרֵיתָ לָנוּ לוֹמַר
God, Who Did Instruct Us to Recite the Thirteen Divine Attributes

This is based upon the well-known talmudic statement that,[41] when disclosing to Moses His attributes,[42] "God enwrapped Himself in a *tallit* like a Reader and indicated to Moses that when Israel sins, if they recite these attributes in prayer, God would pardon them."

וְנַקֵּה
And Acquitting

According to our *Selichot* version of the Thirteen Attributes, the single word *ve-nakeh* ("And He acquits") represents the final divine attribute. However, if we compare this with the actual biblical source,[43] we find, rather surprisingly, that we have curtailed the full version of this attribute, which, in the original, conveys the very opposite sense! The biblical text has *ve-nakeh lo yenakeh*—"And He does *not* acquit [the guilty]."

The reason we have abbreviated the attribute is in order to convert it into a positive formulation, to conform with the other attributes. According to our version we must understand the word *ve-nakeh* in the sense of "He acquits *the righteous*."

Abbreviating a biblical verse in this way does, however, run counter to a talmudical principle that "we may not stop in the middle of a verse (in order to create a separate verse) at a place where Moses did not stop."[44] This prohibition was understood, however, to apply only when reading from the Torah. To employ a half-verse in the context of prayer and petition was regarded as outside the scope of the prohibition.[45]

אֱלֹהֵינוּ... סְלַח נָא אֲשָׁמוֹת
Our God . . . Forgive the Errors

This *selichah* composition follows on from a miscellany of biblical verses, all of which deal with the theme of forgiveness. One of the verses commences with the phrase *selach na la-avon* ("Forgive, I beseech thee, the iniquity of this people"), and this is employed here by the author to provide the initial words for each line of his rhyming couplets. The succeeding word of each line provides an alphabetical acrostic pattern.

This poem is attributed to the pen of the distinguished thirteenth-century talmudist and leader of German Jewry, Rabbi Meir of Rothenburg. He is best known for his elegy *Shaaliy serufah ba-esh,* composed after witnessing the public burning of cartloads of Torah scrolls in Paris in 1242. This is recited by Ashkenazim among the *Kinnot* for the ninth of *Av.*

The poet calls upon God to forgive His people notwithstanding their degeneracy and rebelliousness. He offers no defense; he proffers no extenuating circumstances. Although he employs some very strong terms when particularizing His people's acts of treachery, sinful Israel still remains in the closest proximity to God. Hence his description of Israel as "Thy people," "Thy children," "Thy faithful," "Thy chosen," "Thy worshipers," "Thy flock," "Thy loved ones."

Suspicion has been cast on the authenticity of the opening word of the fifth line *ha-kol modim*—"Forgive . . . *all those* who confess their sins." All the other object-clauses refer to Israel's several misdemeanors, whereas this solitary line would stand as a complimentary designation. It has been suggested that the original version was *hevel modim* ("the *insincerity* of those who confess").

It has also been suggested that a word has dropped out of the line commencing with the letter *pey*. This line alone has no direct object: "Forgive I beseech thee, lest they be punished from thy heaven." D. Goldschmidt[46] conjectures that a word like *piggulam* ("their detestable behavior"), might have been originally in the text. He was probably influenced by the expression *ve-gam paggel* in the second stanza of the next composition.

אֱלֹהֵינוּ... אָמְנָם כֵּן
Our God . . . Yes, It Is True

This *selichah* hymn is believed to have come from the pen of Rabbi Yom Tov ben Isaac of Joigny, who perished in the York massacre of 1190. In 1978, when a memorial tablet to the Jewish victims was unveiled at Clifford's Tower, this composition was appropriately chosen to be intoned.

Our editions have omitted the opening stanza wherein the initial words of a two-lined introductory couple form the author's name acrostic "Yom Tov." Our version starts at the beginning of the alphabetic acrostic, *omnam*.

There might also be an intended allusion to the king, Richard I, whose absence on a crusade enabled the massacre to take place. His soubriquet was *coeur-de-lion* ("The Lion-Hearted"), and the fourth line employs the verb *sho'eig*, "to roar," with the specific nuance of "a lion's roar."[47]

The meter of the poem, following the medieval system that was inspired by Arabic meter, achieves its effect by having each line conform to a regular pattern of stresses. Throughout the poem a pattern of 3-3-2 stresses is maintained, as may be observed in this example of the scansion of the first stanza:

Ómnám kéin / yétzér sokhéin / bánú
Bákh le-hátzdéik / ráv tzédék / va-anéinú

The opening words *Omnam kein* are supercharged with biblical allusive significance. They were first uttered by Job: "Truly, I know, it is so" (*Omnam yadati kiy khein*),[48] as an admission of the truth of the assertion made by his friend, Eliphaz, that mere man can never be justified or found to be pure in the eyes of his Maker.[49] The implication was clearly that all Job's troubles must have been justified, and attributable directly to his sinfulness.

In employing these words, the poet is making a similar assertion that Israel must indeed have sinned, but that she was an unwilling party to a sinfulness that was engendered by the *yetzer sokhein*, the "evil impulse that holds total sway."[50]

In the second stanza, Satan, the accuser, is described as *meraggeil*, "a spy," the same term used to describe the spies sent by Joshua in order to discover the weaknesses and the most vulnerable areas in the defenses of the holy land.[51] Satan, likewise, attempts to penetrate our people's moral and spiritual defenses. He is, therefore, also to be regarded by God as "a fabricator," whose book (of charges against Israel) must be rejected as a forgery. He is a *katteigor* ("prosecuting counsel") who must be silenced forthwith. Indeed, in the opening two chapters of the Book of Job, Satan is cast in that identical role.

The merit of Abraham, the *ezrach* ("easterner")[52] is invoked in the fourth stanza to ensure that "the lily flourishes." This phrase is an allusion to Hosea 14:6, wherein the prophet summons Israel to repent, promising them that, as a reward for faithfulness, they would blossom and "flourish like the lily."

The low estate of preexpulsion Jewry, who "by the Crown were regarded as domestic animals to be milked and utilized, and by the common people and the Baronage . . . were regarded as wolves to be extirpated,"[53] is forcefully reflected in the final three stanzas, wherein the poet alludes to the plight of his people and asks God to account their insults, tears, and humiliation as representing a total retribution for all their sins.

כִּי הִנֵּה כַּחוֹמֶר
As Clay in the Hand of the Potter

This composition, by an unknown author who lived probably during the eleventh or twelfth century, is based upon Jeremiah's famous parable of the potter:

> These are the words which came to Jeremiah from the Lord: Go down at once to the potter's house, and there I will tell you what I have to say. So I went down to the potter's house and found him working at the wheel. Now and then a vessel he was making out of the clay would be spoilt in his hands, and then he would start again and mold it into another vessel to his liking. Then the word of the Lord came to me: Can I not deal with you, Israel, says the Lord, *as the potter deals with his clay*?

The Hebrew of the last phrase—*hinnei ka-chomer be-yad ha-yotzeir*—provided the theme and inspiration for this composition, wherein the poet expands upon Jeremiah's imagery to include a variety of craftsmen—stone masons, blacksmiths, seamen, glaziers, drapers, and silversmiths—all of whom mold, select, and reject their raw material at will. Israel is God's raw material, and the plea is that we will always be regarded as the choicest material with which God will choose to carry out His purpose.

The recurring final line of each stanza—*la-brit ha-beit ve-al teifen la-yeitzer* ("consider the covenant and disregard the evil inclination")—links the composition to the context of the Thirteen Divine Attributes of mercy. "The Covenant" actually stands as a synonym for those attributes, in an allusion to the talmudic statement that "a covenant (*brit*) was signed with the Thirteen Attributes that (whenever they are invoked in prayer by Israel) they will never be disregarded."[54] The attributes are a kind of mystical key to unlock the treasury of mercy.

God is also asked to "disregard the *yeitzer*." This is a plea for Him to overlook His own value judgment that "the inclination [*yeitzer*] of man's heart is evil from his youth upwards."[55]

While modern Hebrew has popularized the word *hegeh* (found here at the beginning of the fourth stanza) in the meaning of "a steering wheel," the precise sense in which our medieval author understood it is not too clear. It has, consequently, been rendered variously as "an anchor" (ArtScroll and Routledge, based on Heidenheim), "helm" (Birnbaum), "rudder" (De Sola), and "oar."

The third words of each stanza follow an alternating alphabetical progression (*ēven, ḡarzen, h̄egeh, z̄ekhukhit, ȳeriah, k̄esef*), which suggests that we have represented here a mere remnant of an originally complete, alphabetical acrostic poem.

זְכֹר רַחֲמֶיךָ
Remember Your Mercies

The remainder of the *selichot*, from this point onward, follow, almost identically, the liturgy of the *Selichot* services for the week preceding Rosh Hashanah, the Ten Days of Penitence and for fast days.[56]

The present composition comprises biblical verses from the books of Psalms, Exodus, and Deuteronomy, all of which have as their key word *zekhor* ("remember"). God is implored to remember that His relationship with His people has always been grounded in mercy and love. He is called upon to remember that He chose Zion to be the residence of His divine presence, and that God, therefore, has a close interest in securing its immediate restoration. He is also asked to remember the age-old covenant with the patriarchs, and the promise that their offspring would inherit the holy land, not only in those far-off days, but *le-olam*, "forever."

כִּי אָנוּ עַמֶּךָ
For We Are Your People

This popular composition is generally sung to a cheerful and optimistic melody, in the spirit of its sentiments, which emphasize the inextricable bonds uniting God and Israel. These bonds connote a multifaceted relationship: we are His people, His children, His servants, His congregation, His inheritance, His flock, His vineyard, His product, His beloved, His treasure. And God is no less possessive of this relationship than is Israel to be its beneficiaries.

The inspiration for this artless outpouring of mutual dependence was derived from the midrashic comment on the verse "My beloved is for me and I am for my beloved" (Song of Songs 6:3). The whole book of the Song of Songs was viewed by our sages as an allegory on the love between God and Israel, and the above verse led the Rabbis to exemplify the many metaphors used in the Bible in order to define this reciprocal love-relationship. Our poet has excerpted these from that midrashic exposition.[57]

In the last few stanzas, prescribed for recitation by the Reader, there is an unexpected change of mood and sentiment. Having highlighted all that which unites God and Israel, attention is suddenly focused upon that which divides: "We are brazen-faced, but Thou art merciful and compassionate; we are full of sin, but Thou art full of mercy."

The objective of this transition is, undoubtedly, to pave the way for the confession of sins that follows. It would have been a presumptuous contradiction to sing of our total and righteous immersion in God and then immediately to have proceeded to a lengthy confession of sin. However, since the transitional, self-condemnatory sentiments are themselves in sharp conflict with the happy and confident tenor of the main composition, they were prescribed for recitation by the Reader alone.

וִידּוּי
Confession of Sin

The *Vidduy*-confessional follows shortly after the recitation of the "Thirteen Divine Attributes" because of the tradition, referred to above, that God promised Israel that the recitation of that formula, which emphasizes God's qualities of mercy, would never fall on deaf ears, but that forgiveness would immediately be forthcoming.

In Temple times the High Priest invoked the *Tetragrammaton*, the personal name of God, ten times while making confession. Hence the Talmud[58] prescribed that, in our liturgy, we recite the *Vidduy*-confessional a corresponding number of times: in the silent version of the *Amidah* of the five statutory services of Yom Kippur, and again during their repetition.

Confession was *the* predominant feature of the Day of Atonement liturgy in Temple times, following the biblical prescription, "And he (Aaron) shall make confession over it (the goat) for all the sins of the children of Israel" (Leviticus 16:21). Three full confessions were made by the High Priest: one for himself and his family, one for his Levitical tribe, and the final confession, a general one for all Israel.

After the destruction of the Temple, and with the passing of time and other pressing preoccupations for the religious leaders, a degree of uncertainty set in regarding the precise formulae that had been employed on some special occasions in the Temple. We must not forget that there was a reticence—which later became a full-blown prohibition—against committing to writing any blessings, prayers, or orally transmitted religious traditions, in order to avoid sectarian tampering and infiltration.

The version recorded in the Mishnah is as follows:

> *Anah Ha-Shem aviytiy pashatiy chatatiy le-fanekha ani u-veitiy . . . Anah Ha-Shem kapper-na la-avonot ve-la-peshaim ve-lachataot she-avitiy ve-she-pashati ve-she-chatatiy le-fanekha.*
>
> I beg of You, Lord, I have committed iniquity. I have transgressed, I have sinned against Thee, I and my household . . . I beg of You, Lord, forgive now the iniquities and the transgressions and the sins, for I have truly been a perpetrator of iniquity, transgression, and sin.[59]

A comparison with the form of this confession as quoted and recited in our *Avodah* prayer will reveal that the three categories of sin referred to appear in a different order, namely *chatatiy avitiy pashatiy*. The reason for this is that the version in the Mishnah follows the tradition recorded by the (second century C.E.) teacher Rabbi Meir, who had a formative influence on the creation of mishnaic traditions. However, Rabbi Meir was born several decades after the destruction of the Temple, so he had no first-hand knowledge of Temple traditions and formulae.

The majority of his colleagues could not accept that the order of sins in his version could have been authentic, for the simple reason that, although the categories appear to be merely synonymous terms, they do in fact have their own respective and specific connotations. *Chataot* are defined as sins committed in error, *avonot* are sins committed as a result of a reluctant succumbing to one's overwhelming desires, and *pesha'im* are calculated and determined acts of rebellion against God and His Torah.

For this reason the majority view regarded the latter order of categories as the most logical, leading from the least to the most serious violations. They expressed their objection to Rabbi Meir's version by observing that once the High Priest had sought—and, it is hoped, obtained—forgiveness for the *avonot* (as in the phrase *she-avitiy*) and for the *pesha'im* (as in the phrase *ve-she-pashatiy*), that is, for the two most heinous crimes out of the three, it seems illogical to then proceed to a seeking of repentance for the *chataot*, the sins committed in error. Surely, if God is prepared to forgive the most heinous of offenses, He will be indulgent about those committed in error.[60] For the Sages, the most effective approach to God, from a psychological point of view, was to soften Him by first wresting absolution for those committed in error, moving from there to an appeal for God to take account of man's passions and weaker nature, with which the Creator Himself had endowed man, before, finally, with God already in a forgiving mood, coming in with the ultimate plea for indulgence for man at his most rebellious and sinful level.

Rabbi Meir stood his ground, however, for the simple, and single, reason that his version actually followed the order that the Torah itself employs, in Leviticus 16:21. Go argue with the Torah!

In talmudic times there was no uniformity of opinion as to the precise formula of confession to be recited; neither could the talmudists agree on the central issue of whether it was necessary to specify the individual sin or whether a blanket confession would suffice.[61] It was only in the third century that Rav and Shemuel—who had a formative influence on the development of the liturgy—popularized appropriate confessionals. Rav's composition, *Attah yodea razei olam* ("You know the mysteries of the Universe"),[62] which is quoted in full in the Talmud,[63] won its way into all prayer rites.

The Talmud quotes the opening words of various confessionals composed by a number of sages, though only a few of these have been identified with existing passages in our liturgy. Rabbi Jochanan's prayer, *Ribbon ha-olamim,* is mentioned, as well as Shemuel's *Mah anu meh chayyeinu* ("What are we? What is our life?"). The latter is recited in the *Vidduy* of every service during Yom Kippur. As a measure of their popularity, these two compositions were combined into one that is recited near the beginning of the daily morning service throughout the year.[64]

Another prayer quoted in full by the Talmud is the composition of Rav Hamnuna, *Elohai ad she-lo notzartiy* ("My God, before I was formed I was of no worth . . ."). Because this confession of human worthlessness was couched in the first person singular, it was felt to be more appropriate for recitation by the individual worshiper in the silent *Amidah.* Perhaps its sentiments were also regarded as a little too embarrassing for a Reader to recite publicly. In recognition of its popularity it was prescribed as the closing confessional for every service.

אָשַׁמְנוּ
We Have Trespassed

The *Vidduy* section of the *Amidah,* which commences with the alphabetical confessional *Ashamnu* ("we have trespassed"), is introduced by a short, humble preamble, *tavo le-fanekha tefillateinu* ("Let our prayer come before thee"), acknowledging our full awareness of the need for confession. The closing words, *aval anachnu chatanu* ("Truly we have sinned"), represent, in the view of Shemuel,[65] the basic formula of confession.

Although this confessional is generally attributed to the *Geonim* of Babylon (ninth to twelfth centuries), it has been demonstrated by A. Marmorstein[66] that during that period the basic confessional consisted of a mere four words: *chatanu ashamnu he'eviynu ve-hirshanu.* This was expanded into our alphabetical version during the thirteenth century, and only won its position as a generally accepted version during the following century.

The *Ashamnu* confessional was dubbed *Vidduy Zuta,* "the short confessional," as opposed to the *Al Cheit,* which is called *Vidduy Rabbah,* "the long confessional." The catalogue of sins listed in the *Ashamnu* betrays repetitiveness occasioned by the need to fill up all the letters of the alphabet. Hence we have two identical verbs used twice: *he'eviynu* and *aviynu,* as well as *hirshanu* and *rashanu.* It should also be observed that in the confessional of the High Priest he employed only three verbs: *chatu, avu,* and *pashu* ("They have sinned, committed iniquity and transgressed"), proving that we have in our *Ashamnu* an artificially expanded composition. Its popularity and appeal are in no way impaired, however, by this consideration.

It is significant that our formulae of confession are all couched in the plural, as if to suggest that it is society that fosters the climate and conditions wherein sin is engendered in the heart of the individual. An unfeeling society will nurture despair on the part of the disadvantaged. From despair flow crime and sin. An irresponsible society will, similarly, breed delinquency, violence, and sin. The plural formulation indicates that, although the individual commits the act, society at large must bear the responsibility.

It will be noted that, throughout the confessional, there is not one reference to sins of neglect or omission in the performance of specific ritual practices. The catalogue of sins is restricted to the domain of ethics and morals, as if to emphasize that no Jew who strives after piety may ignore his responsibilities to his fellow man.

This was not the case, however, in the prayer book used by preexpulsion Jewry in England, as preserved in the *Etz Chayyim* of Jacob ben Yehudah, *chazan* of London.[67] There, the short confessional—which was recited each day at the beginning of the morning service[68]—was considerably expanded to include enumeration of ritual offenses, such as "I have desecrated the Sabbath" . . . "I have eaten forbidden foods" . . . "I have eaten without reciting the prescribed blessings." So wide-ranging is that version of the short confessional that it includes confession for sins as serious as "neglect of Torah study" and "profaning your holy name," on the one hand, and as innocuous as "calling a friend by a nickname," on the other!

עַל חֵטְא
"For the Sin Wherein We Have Sinned . . ."

Just as our short confessional is an expanded version, so the *Al Cheit*—the long confessional—is a considerably expanded version of an original composition containing a mere six lines confessing sins committed (i) *be-ones* (forcibly), (ii) *be-ratzon* (willingly), (iii) *bi-shgagah* (in error), (iv) *be-zadon* (brazenly), (v) *ba-seiter* (in secret), and (vi) *ba-galuy* (openly).

It was probably composed by the very first known liturgical poet, Yosi ben Yosi, whose period of activity is debated by scholars as being anywhere between the third and tenth centuries![69] The current view is that he must have lived around the end of the third and the beginning of the fourth centuries.

His simple version, employing six very general categories of sin, without particularization, may be explained against the background of the talmudic dispute alluded to above:

> It is necessary to specify (within a confession) the precise sin for which atonement is being sought. This is based upon the verse, "Oh, this people have sinned a great sin, *and have made for themselves a god of gold*" (Exodus 32:31)—this is the view of Rabbi Judah ben Bava. Rabbi Akivah objected, quoting the verse, "Happy is he whose transgression is forgiven, whose sin is *covered*" (Psalm 32:1).[70]

Thus, Rabbi Judah found a proof-text wherein the specific sin is publicized, namely the making of the Golden Calf, whereas Rabbi Akivah, although, admittedly, on the less-authoritative basis of a psalm verse, finds that the biblical ideal is the situation where (the precise nature of) a sin is "covered" or "*concealed*" from public awareness. For Akivah, the post-Temple period, wherein there is no possibility of securing atonement by the bringing of a sacrifice, has rendered the confession of sin a private and intimate exercise between man and God.

If the talmudic dispute was left at that, all would have been clear-cut, with Rabbi Akivah prohibiting the specification of any sins. This would at the same time account for the fact that Yose ben Yose's original version is couched in such concise and general terms, and also why the versions of Amram Gaon, Saadia, Maimonides, as well as the present-day Sephardi prayer book do not specify particular sins. However, this would create serious problems for our version of the *Al Cheit*, which does in fact specify all the numerous and varied sins that we (may) have committed. It would also beg the question of how we could come to disregard the ruling of Rabbi Akivah!

However, in the *Tosefta* collection, the view of Rabbi Akivah is quoted with the prefatorial statement: "Rabbi Akivah says it is *not necessary* to specify the sins, since it states, 'Happy is he whose sin is covered. . . .'" Indeed, this is the proper reading in the Talmud, according to the main early codifiers, *Rabbeinu Hananel, Alfasi,* and *Rosh.* This means that our *Al Cheit* composition does not therefore infringe propriety, and is condoned by Rabbi Akivah, even though his view is that the exercise of such a detailed confession is not strictly required.

We can now understand why Yose's original version was formulated in such general categories.

Maimonides and many other prayer rites present a single alphabetical version of twenty-four lines, whereas the Ashkenazim expanded this into a double acrostic composition of forty-four lines. It is conceivable that the Ashkenazi version is actually a conflation of two totally independent alphabetical confessional compositions. This would explain the several examples of tautology, such as confessions for "the utterance of the lips," "the words of the mouth," and "the expressions of our lips."

If we examine the list of confessions in *Al Cheit,* we find repeated references to parts of the body: *immutz ha-leiv* (hardening of the heart), *bittuy sefatayim* (utterance of the lips), *dibbur peh* (words of the mouth), *chozek yad* (violence of the hand), *lashon ha-ra* (evil tongue), *einayim ramot* (haughty eyes), *azzut metzach* (an obdurate brow), *kallut rosh* (light-headed levity), *kashyut oref* (being stiff-necked), and *ritzat raglayim le-hara* (allowing one's legs to run to do evil).

As we stand, on Yom Kippur, denying ourselves every bodily pleasure to enable our souls to soar upward, unfettered, in order to plead our cause, this confessional's emphasis upon crimes committed by the body assumes a special significance.

It offers, in effect, a plea of extenuating circumstances by placing the blame upon the several parts of our bodily frame, and their propensity toward sin. The real "self," it is inferred, is our indestructible soul, whose purity we acknowledge each morning in the *Elohai neshamah*: "My God, the soul which You have placed within me is pure. You have created it; You have formed it and breathed it into me. You preserve it within me; You will take it from me and restore it to me in the hereafter."

Thus, we assert that our nucleus is pure, for it is exclusively the physical frame that the soul inhabits that is its source of contamination. And in our confessional we leave God in no doubt as to the many organs of the body at whose door we lay the guilt. We ask, however, that the merit of the soul should secure forgiveness at the same time for its corporeal partner.[71]

וְעַל חֲטָאִים
And for the Sins

In this short list forgiveness is petitioned for any act that in Temple times would have necessitated the bringing of any of the specific categories of sacrifice enumerated or that would have attracted one or more of the biblical or rabbinic penalties listed. Though the Temple and sacrificial system has long since vanished, the ancient ritual is referred to here in order "to impress upon us the nature of the tribute which it would be our duty to offer by way of atonement, and which, today, can be adequately replaced only by means of prayer and sincere repentance."[72]

Imagine the expense and the effort for a penitent in making the journey to the Temple at Jerusalem, selecting and purchasing his sacrifice, queuing up to have it ritually slaughtered and offered, as well as the expenses of accommodation and the loss of income during the stay if he came from the provinces. Though this is impossible to quantify, it does give us some idea of the equivalent effort we are expected to put into our self-scrutiny, our expression of remorse and resolution, our prayers and meditations, in order to remove the evil decree.

וְעַל כֻּלָּם אֱלוֹהַּ סְלִיחוֹת
And for All These, O God of Forgiveness

This line is repeated, as a refrain, at the end of each of the four divisions of the *Al Cheit* confessional. The specific designation of God as *Elo'ah selichot*, "God of forgiveness," was inspired by Numbers 14:20 where God announced His decision to reverse His sentence and pardon Israel with the words *salachtiy kidvarekha*, "I have forgiven, as you petitioned." This reprieve was granted to the Israelites on the tenth day of *Tishri*, and henceforth Jews believed that this date, on which Yom Kippur occurs, is a blessed day when atonement is annually granted.

The Psychology of Confession

To many, the notion of an annual period of confession, remorse, and breast-beating is quite absurd. For, viewed from the perspective of Almighty God, what can He think of people who repeat the identical sins and do not appear to be spiritually more sensitive with the passing of each and every year? What sort of charade is that general *Ashamnu* confession we never tire of uttering—and with such fervor, to boot? And what sort of lengthy and specific *Al Cheit* catalogue of sins is it that we gabble through as if it were some stockroom checklist?

It seems clear that true remorse does not come very easily to us. We seem to have a built-in mechanism of self-justification. This was well understood by the Rabbis when they felt constrained to prescribe a fixed formula of confession for us; for they knew so well that most of us would find it well-nigh impossible to actually pinpoint our faults and shortcomings, let alone our blatant sins of commission and omission.

They were also careful to couch those two confessionals in the plural, knowing that we would all wish to comfort ourselves with the thought that it is *others*, not ourselves, that need to make such a confession. And they were particular to make the list of sins and offenses so lengthy and comprehensive that most of us will come away feeling quite smug that so few of the entries on that list apparently apply to us! It is a truism that our ego will justify anything, and will convince us at all times that we are as pure as driven snow, and that it is other people who bear all the faults and shortcomings, and are so shortsighted that they cannot see things as we do!

If that were the end of the matter, it would not be so problematic for man. He could bask in his self-confidence and luxuriate in his self-righteousness. But there is, in fact, another side to man's nature that gives him no mental tranquillity even when he is able to rationalize his actions and justify his behavior to himself. Mark Twain was referring to it when he observed that man is the only animal that blushes—or needs to!

That blush is the greatest spiritual boon. It betrays the fact that there is, in essence, a deep-seated core of guilt-awareness that is so endemic to the nature of man that, no matter how much he may rationalize and justify his actions—to himself and to others—there is, nevertheless, an instinctive awareness of a Third Party who cannot be hoodwinked, but who knows our inner thoughts and perceives all our actions. And that blush, that guilty, or unpleasant, or perhaps merely uneasy feeling that comes over us when we are engaged in an undignified, immoral, or unethical act, is the most profound and powerful acknowledgment of His presence in the world. If it is true that only humans blush, then perhaps that is what it means that we are created "in the image of God." It means that we are naturally disposed to be good, that we feel at our best when we are engaged in the performance of good deeds, righteous conduct, kindliness and generosity. And it is that blush that sounds the inner emotional alarm. It triggers off the awareness that our divine image is being tarnished, and that we are blurring the unique distinction between man and beast. And most of us are programmed to find that unacceptable, for our overwhelming urge is, if anything, to be more than man, not less, by seeking to transcend our animal instincts and control our base urges. Indeed, had it not been for that motivation, man would have destroyed himself long ago.

And this tension between two natural yet contrary human responses—self-righteousness and self-justification, on the one hand, and a deep-seated awareness of our terrible shortcomings compared with what heights of spirituality we are truly capable of attaining, on the other—is the tension that lies at the heart of what Rosh Hashanah and Yom Kippur set out to achieve.

If we sense that tension—even if we cannot resolve it—it is half the battle. If we succeed in resolving it—and how many can?—victory is ours!

Selichot

אֵל רַחוּם שְׁמֶךָ
Your Name Is Merciful God
עֲנֵנוּ יְיָ עֲנֵנוּ
Answer Us, O Lord, Answer Us
מִי שֶׁעָנָה לְאַבְרָהָם
He Who Answered Our Father Abraham

While we have applied the nomenclature *Vidduy* (confession) to the *Ashamnu* and *Al Cheit* compositions, they actually belong to the genre of *selichot*, "prayers for forgiveness." Indeed, they and their preceding section, *Zekhor lanu berit*,[73] together with these three compositions, appear as one unit that serves as the concluding section of the daily *selichot* prayers recited during the week preceding Rosh Hashanah, as well as during the Ten Days of Penitence and on fast days.

These *selichot* are also somewhat similar to those recited on the festival of *Sukkot*, which we popularly call *hoshanot*. Indeed, the alphabetical list in the first of our three compositions—commencing *Asei lemaan amitakh*—is identical with that contained in the *hoshana* for the first day of *Sukkot, Lemaan amitakh*. Again in our first composition, following on after the end of the alphabetical acrostic, there is an appeal to God for forgiveness on account of the merit of all our biblical ancestors (this is also the subject of the third composition, *Miy she-anah le-Avraham*), our holy places, and our saints and martyrs. This is paralleled very closely by the composition for the second day of *Sukkot, Even shetiyyah*.

The common origin of all these compositions lies in a very old Temple ceremony enacted as a special petition for rain. These *selichot* originated as a liturgy for the regular fast days introduced in Temple times because of a lack of rain. From that context they were borrowed for recitation on the historical fast days also, as well as during the High Holy Day period. Their recitation on the festival of *Sukkot* is clearly because of the association of that festival with petition for rain.

These very old *selichot* and *hoshanot* represent one of the earliest forms of post-biblical poetry known to us. Professor Joseph Heinemann, who made a special study of their origin and literary form,[74] has enumerated their main characteristics: (1) they are made up of a large number of short, stereotyped lines; (2) each line consists of but two or three words; (3) the alphabetical acrostic is generally employed; (4) there is a primitive type of rhyme achieved by the employment of a recurring pronominal suffix at the end of each line (amit*ekha*. . . . berit*ekha*. . . . tifart*ekha*. . .); (5) they have none of the features of style characteristic of the *piyyut* in general, nor do they possess any internal structure whatsoever.[75]

The first two of our compositions certainly betray these features, and Heinemann tells us that they belong, like the *hoshanot*, to the category of *litanies* originally chanted during processions or circuits around the altar. Such processions were a common feature of the service for fast days in Temple times, and to this day the procession is the central feature of the *Sukkot* services.

The third *selichah* composition—*Miy she-anah le-Avraham* ("He who answered our father Abraham on Mount Moriah, he shall answer us")—is based upon the formulae, preserved in the Mishnah,[76] of the expanded blessings of the *Amidah*, which were recited on special fast days instituted during periods of drought in Temple times. In seven of the *Amidah* blessings they would insert a plea to God to "answer" and deliver them from famine, just as He had delivered (1) Abraham (from Nimrod's fiery furnace), (2) our ancestors at the Red Sea, (3) Joshua at Gilgal (Gilgal was his base at the time of the miracle of the walls of Jericho), (4) Samuel at Mitzpah (when he won a decisive battle against the Philistines), (5) Elijah at Mount Carmel, (6) Jonah (from the belly of the fish), and (7) David[77] and Solomon[78] in Jerusalem (when they were confronted with famine).

The Ashkenazi version of this *selichah* is considerably expanded by the addition of other biblical examples of righteous people who were miraculously delivered, and the list is subject to much variation in other prayer rites. The Ashkenazi version has departed but slightly from the formula of the Mishnah that has *Miy she-anah . . . hu yaaneh etkhem* (instead of *yaaneinu*).[79] In the French, Italian, and Yemenite rites the formula appears as *Kesheanita . . . kein aneinu*, "just as you answered . . . , so answer us." This is an interesting version, as it provides a link, for this composition also, with the structure of the *hoshana* composition, *Kehoshata eilim belud . . . kein hoshana*, recited each day of *Sukkot*. (For some more general remarks on the nature of the *selichot*, see pp. 225–229).

אָבִינוּ מַלְכֵּנוּ

Our Father, Our King (see pp. 49–50)

עָלֵינוּ

It Is Our Duty (see pp. 88–92)

לְדָוִד ה׳ אוֹרִי וְיִשְׁעִי

The Lord Is My Light and My Salvation (see pp. 18–20)

אֲדוֹן עוֹלָם

Master of the Universe (see pp. 11–15)

יִגְדַּל

Magnify the Living God (see pp. 15–18)

7

The Morning Service

(For commentary to first part of Morning Service, see pp. 10–24)

סְלַח לְגוֹי קָדוֹשׁ
Forgive a Holy Nation

This self-designation as a "holy nation" is not to be considered as presumptuous, for God Himself so describes Israel: "For you shall be unto me a kingdom of priests *and a holy nation*" (Exodus 19:6). Psychologically, to regard oneself as holy is, in itself, a great stimulus to holiness. Israel is encouraged, therefore, to think of itself as a holy entity. It is for this reason that synagogues preface their names with the letters ק"ק, an abbreviation of *kehillah kedoshah*, "holy congregation."

To impugn this holy state was regarded almost as an act of blasphemy. Thus, according to the Talmud[1] the prophet Isaiah died a violent death at the hands of the wicked king Manasseh as a punishment for having impugned the holiness of his people by saying, "I dwell among a people of unclean lips" (Isaiah 6:5).

The composition of *Az be-Yom Kippur*, to which the line *Selach le-goy kadosh* forms a refrain, as well as the composition *Kadosh addiyr ba-aliyyato*, which follows, are designated *yotzerot*,[2] as they were composed for insertion into the first of the two blessings preceding the *Shema*: *yotzeyr ha-me'orot*.

That blessing of the *Shema* pays tribute to God as "Creator of the luminaries" (sun and moon), and this particular theme is emphasized in the *yotzerot*. In the present composition it is linked to the theme of repentance, particularly in the last line of the second stanza (line 8): *dofkey bi-teshuvah le-yotzeir or*, "knocking repentant at the door of *the Creator of light*." An examination of the composition will reveal a further twelve references to "light," as the poet extends the imagery from the literal context of heavenly luminaries to a general metaphor for enlightenment. His license for this was inferred from the last verse of the actual *Shema* blessing itself—*Or chadash* ("O cause a new light to shine upon Zion")—which was a later messianic sentiment introduced into a blessing that refers exclusively to the light of the planetary luminaries.[3]

The composition opens with the line, "On Yom Kippur *You taught* pardon." This is based upon the rabbinic tradition that it was on the 10th of *Tishri*—Yom Kippur—that Moses descended from Mount Sinai, carrying the second set of tablets of stone. That day of reconciliation between God and Israel was established forever as the most spiritually propitious time when "You will pardon our iniquity and our sins, and You will take us as your own possession" (Exodus 34:9).

The poem is full of allusions to rabbinic interpretations, which would necessitate a far longer and more detailed commentary than the present one in order to elucidate fully. We may draw attention to just two, as an example of the poet's approach. The opening line of the second stanza (line 5)—*gavru chata'im ba-aniy yesheinah* ("Sins swell mightily when I am asleep")—gives little sense when read literally, for it is hardly possible to sin while asleep! The poet is clearly writing in the spirit of the midrashic interpretation of this verse:

> *I am asleep but my heart is awake* (Song of Songs 5:2)—The assembly of Israel says this to the Holy One, blessed be He: *I am asleep* [i.e., I may well be indolent] when it comes to fulfilling all the commandments, *but my heart is awake* [i.e., sensitive] to the fulfillment of acts of kindness.[4]

Our poet was thus employing the verse *Aniy yesheinah* ("I am asleep") in the midrashic sense of "indolence," which gives good sense to his assertion that indolence is the cause of "sins swelling mightily."

There is another midrashic allusion in the opening line of the tenth stanza (line 37)—*korveinu le-yeshakha be-or sheney ofarim* ("Draw us near to Your salvation by the grace of the two fawns"). The last phrase is an allusion to Song of Songs 4:5—"Your two breasts are like two fawns, twin fawns of a gazelle." The whole of this book, with all its passionate, almost erotic, poetry, was regarded by our Rabbis as an allegory on the relationship between God and Israel. Thus, "your two breasts" is explained by the Midrash as a metaphoric allusion to Moses and Aaron, "for just as the breasts are the beauty and glory of woman, so Moses and Aaron are the pride of Israel; and just as the breasts nourish the babe with milk, so Moses and Aaron nourished Israel with Torah."[5] The Midrash continues to explain the metaphor of "twins," as applied to Moses and Aaron, in the sense of their having been identical in piety, even though Moses was superior in prophetic attainment.

The poem follows a double alphabetical acrostic pattern, with the last syllable of each alphabetical line rhyming with its partner in the couplet. The two refrains that preface the poem—*Selach le-goy kadosh* and *Chatanu tzureinu*—were intended to be used, alternately, after each stanza. As frequently occurs with lengthy poems, the refrains are omitted in order to avoid impairing the effect of the poem itself.

בָּרוּךְ שֵׁם כְּבוֹד מַלְכוּתוֹ
Blessed Be the Name of the One Whose Glorious Kingdom . . .
מַלְכוּתוֹ בִּקְהַל עֲדָתִי
His Kingdom Is within My Assembled People

These verses, which serve to introduce the composition *Kadosh addiyr ba-aliyato*, were intended to serve as refrains throughout the composition—the former after every line, the latter after every couplet. This poem belongs to the genre of *piyyut* known as *ofan*, which was composed for insertion into the first blessing before the *Shema*, immediately prior to the section commencing *Ve-ha-ofanim ve-chayyot ha-kodesh*. (In the Polish rite this is actually replaced, on the High Holy Days, by the formula *Ve-ha-chayyot yeshoreiru*.)

The first refrain anticipates the rallying cry that was inserted by the early synagogue into the *Shema Yisrael*, after the first verse, notwithstanding the fact that it constituted an interruption of a biblical passage. Throughout the year, the formula *Barukh sheim kevod malkhuto le-olam va-ed* is recited in an undertone, but on Yom Kippur the congregation recites it loudly and confidently.

In early talmudic times the word *malkhut* (kingdom) had a polemical significance, as it was the official term used by Jews to denote the rule of the Roman conquerors. When Jews recited the formula "blessed be the name of the one whose glorious *kingdom* [*malkhuto*] is forever and ever" they were implying that only God's *malkhut* would be enduring, but Rome's would be short-lived. Roman inspectors were aware of the implication of this verse, and, for that reason, Jews had to recite it in an undertone for fear of retribution. On Yom Kippur, however, the requirement of emphasizing God's sole sovereignty gave them the courage to recite it aloud.

The second refrain takes up this theme of God's *malkhut*, and asserts that, although the promised national restoration—as a prelude to the establishment of God's kingdom on earth—has not yet occurred, the seeds of the latter are nevertheless germinating within the national spirit of the Jewish people.

The alphabetical acrostic composition, *Kadosh addiyr ba-aliyyato*—each line beginning with the word *Kadosh*—was written as an amplification of the Sanctification formula—*Kadosh kadosh kadosh*—that precedes it.

וְהַחַיּוֹת יְשׁוֹרֵרוּ
The *Chayyot* Sing (see pp. 29–30)

The Repetition of the *Amidah* by the *Chazan* (see pp. 30–32)

אֵימֶיךָ נָשָׂאתִי
I Suffer Your Terrors

The author of this meditation is Meshullam ben Kalonymos, a tenth- to eleventh-century scholar and founding father of one of the most distinguished families of medieval Germany for a period of some four hundred years. The Kalonymos family, which hailed originally from Italy, produced numerous rabbis, theologians, poets, and communal leaders for the communities of the Rhineland. They had a penchant for poetry, and at least twelve members of that family contributed toward producing a vast number of elegies chronicling the sufferings of German Jewry during the tragic period of the Crusades. Meshullam himself was held in high regard by Rashi as a distinguished talmudical scholar and author of responsa, and he helped to lay the groundwork for the development of rabbinic learning, as well as a poetic tradition, in Franco-Germany.

This meditation is another example of the *reshut*[6] genre, wherein the Reader makes an urgent plea for divine guidance and indulgence as he assumes the role of intercessor for his congregation. The opening words sum up his feelings of inadequacy at the awesome responsibility that he must assume.

The composition is constructed according to an alphabetical acrostic pattern of four-line stanzas, with four words to each line. To preserve the metric uniformity of only four stresses to each line, the poet was constrained to employ contracted forms of nouns. Hence, *zaak* ("a cry") for the regular biblical noun *ze'akah,*[7] *erekh* ("healing") for *arukhah,*[8] *chesher* ("rain") for *chashrah,*[9] *keshel* ("stumbling") for *kishalon,*[10] *cheyshel* ("weariness") for *chulshah,*[11] *peletz* ("quaking") for *pallatzut.*[12]

אִמַּצְתָּ עָשׂוֹר
You Adopted the Tenth Day

This alphabetical poem is also by Meshullam ben Kalonymos. It was composed to follow on from the preceding *reshut,* and opens with the concluding word of that composition. Not surprisingly, we find the same employment of contracted forms of nouns. Hence, such forms as *li-techiy* ("for life") for *li-techiyah; miteika* ("from the *shofar* blast")[13] for *mi-tekiyah,* and *at* ("the One who came") for *attah.*[14]

Having focused, in the *reshut,* upon his own difficult situation as Reader and intercessor, he now turns his attention to the subject of the congregation he represents. He attempts to wrest divine compassion by alluding to their humble and dejected state and the burden of the fast: "Their young and old are fasting today; they are hungry and tired. Look at them all standing barefoot, robed in white."

זָכְרֵנוּ לַחַיִּים
Remember Us Unto Life (see pp. 33–34)

תַּאֲוַת נֶפֶשׁ
The Longing of Our Soul

This poem follows the reverse acrostic—*Tashrak*—pattern, together with the popular metric form of four-line stanzas, with four words to a line. Again we have the appearance of contracted nouns, so favored of Meshullam ben Kalonymos. Thus, *ahav*[15] ("love") for *ahavah, eiked* "binding") for *akeidah,* and *enek* ("cry") for *anakah.*[16]

The poet reminds God of the abiding love that His people have for Him, a love as deep and trusting as that of a tender infant for its father. God cannot avoid the consequences of this relationship and cast off His errant children, for He has entered into an irreversible covenant with them when He established the bond of circumcision with their father Abraham. The phrase *beritekha chok bi-she'eiram* ("Your covenant is sealed in their flesh") is derived from the blessing recited at the circumcision ceremony.

In the penultimate stanza the poet asks that Abraham, "the righteous intercessor (on behalf of the Sodomites)," should teach us how to make an effective intercession on our own behalf, so that "we would gain the protection of a thousand shields." This is an allusion to the verse, "Your neck is like the tower of David . . . whereon hang a thousand shields" (Song of Songs 4:4). The Midrash on this verse depicts Abraham as complaining to God that, whereas God had promised him "I shall be a shield *to you*" (Genesis 15:1), this promise did not appear to contain any such commitment to his offspring. The verse in the Song of Songs is represented as God's answer to this, namely, that while God served as one shield to Abraham, His protection of Abraham's offspring would be a thousandfold.[17]

עַד יוֹם מוֹתוֹ
Until the Day of Man's Death

As usual, the refrain appears as the heading of the poem. This is borrowed from the almost identical verse that occurs toward the end of the *U-netaneh tokef* composition. The idea that God waits patiently, until man's last moment of life, in the hope that the evil decision may be reversed, is based upon the verse, "Say to them, As I live, says the Lord God, I have no pleasure in the death of the wicked, but that the wicked turn from his way and live" (Ezekiel 33:11).

This unrhymed composition, also from the pen of Meshullam ben Kalonymos, follows an alphabetical acrostic pattern. It belongs to the genre of *tokheichah* (literally "reproof"), didactic poems that offer guidance as to right conduct and the development of an appropriate moral philosophy of life. They are written in the spirit of the Wisdom literature, and have a particular affinity with many passages in the Books of Job and Proverbs.

The poem opens with a quotation based upon Job 15:14, "What is man that he can be clean, or he that is born of a woman that he can be righteous?" The second line offers a moralistic maxim to reinforce this assertion of the total vanity of the human estate: "If the fire can consume fresh trees, how much more easily will it devour dry grass?" The "fresh trees" stand, metaphorically, for the righteous, the "dry grass" for the wicked.

In the lines commencing with the letters *zayin* and *chet*, Meshullam skillfully employs the natural alliteration offered by the flexibility of Hebrew roots, which, by a slight change of vowel, convey a variety of related ideas. Thus: "Let every creature (*yetziyr*) consider this, and no impulse (*yeitzer*) will lead him astray to sin against the Creator (*yotzeir*). The womb (*be-eiro*) is his origin, the grave (*boro*) his destiny, and his Maker (*bor'o*) will examine man's account."

This is continued in the following line: "Impurity (*tamei*) flows from his flesh; he defiles himself (*mittammei*) after his death."

Having asserted that man is of little consequence, and in no position to think that he can delude his Maker, the poet reminds us that only by accumulating good deeds, acquiring knowledge and leaving behind a good name can we defy death, by bequeathing to posterity a heritage of inspiration and constructive endeavor. If we succeed in achieving that, then indeed, "the day of death is better than the day of birth." For on that day we can look forward, with eager anticipation, to having God, at our side, pointing out for us exactly where we succeeded in making our finest and most enduring contribution to life.

The idea of God waiting for and being prepared to receive the penitent, even if his remorse is delayed until the very last day of his life, is a difficult one to accept. At least so it was for an associate of the grandfather of the best-selling author Herman Wouk.

In his popular book *This Is My God,* Wouk refers frequently to his saintly grandfather and teacher, Reb Mendel Leib Levine, who was clearly the inspiration of Wouk's religious life. He relates that Reb Mendel had a religiously zealous lodger in his Bronx apartment who could not possibly come to terms with the fact that an atheistic pork eater, leading a totally dissolute life, could nevertheless repent on his dying day, and by that one act could enter guiltless into divine grace, while he, the lodger, spends a lifetime of obedience and sacrifice trying to please God, only to end up with an equal reward!

Reb Mendel's explanation for such a paradox was that "cancelling the past does not turn it into a record of achievement. It leaves it blank, a waste of spilled years. A man had better return," he said, "while time remains to write a life worth scanning. And since no man knows his death day, the time to get a grip on his life is the first hour when the impulse strikes him."[18]

Reb Mendel was, of course, absolutely correct. Judaism's developed concept of reward and punishment would be totally frustrated, apart from being patently unfair, if there was but one level of reward and one level of punishment. A righteous system—and what other can we envisage?—must give credit for levels of attainment. It must take account of the volume of pious deeds performed, just as it must distinguish between a single, uncharacteristic act of sin, on the one hand, and a way of life wherein "sin crouches [regularly] at the door." The man who repents on the last day of his life may well be regarded as a penitent, and spared punishment as a sinner. He cannot, however, expect to enjoy the rich rewards promised for those who have stored up a treasury of merit.

יוֹם הַמִּיתָה מִיּוֹם לֵידָה הוּטָב
The Day of Death Is Better than the Day of Birth

The Midrash[19] illustrates this notion by referring to two ships seen sailing near land. One of them was leaving the harbor on its outward voyage, the other was coming into the harbor. Everyone was cheering the outgoing ship, giving it a hearty send-off. The incoming ship, on the other hand, was hardly noticed.

A wise man, looking at this situation, observed that this was paradoxical, for surely rejoicing was quite premature for a ship only just setting out on its voyage, given the many hazards that ships encounter while on the high seas: pirates, storms, collisions, and so on. Rather should the rejoicing be reserved for the ship that is actually arriving at its destination, having safely negotiated the hazards and safely delivered its passengers and cargo.

So it is with life. When a human being is born, everyone rejoices, but when he dies everyone laments. It should, however, be the reverse, for no one knows whether that child will be able to survive the many troubles and obstacles with which his path to manhood will be strewn. It is when a man has lived blamelessly, and died in peace and with a good name, that rejoicing is in order. From that perspective it may be said that "the day of death is better—that is, a more appropriate occasion for celebrating—than the day of birth."

אִחַדְתָּ יוֹם זֶה בַּשָּׁנָה
You Have Chosen This One Day in the Year

In this poem Meshullam employs a complex double pattern of alphabetical acrostics. The first line of each couplet follows the ordinary alphabetical acrostic sequence, whereas the second lines follow a reverse alphabetic acrostic (*Tashrak*, etc.).

The opening line reminds God that He has established this day as "a healing balm for the lily (*shoshanah*)." This is a popular metaphor for Israel, as first used in the Song of Songs (2:2): "As a lily among brambles, so is my beloved among the maidens."

In the second stanza attention is drawn to the therapeutic value of prayer and songs of praise, which, after the destruction of the Temple, provided emotional and spiritual solace to the dispersed nations, while vicariously compensating for the inability to offer sacrifices.

The poet invokes the merit of the patriarch Jacob, described in the Torah as "the perfect man who dwelt in the tent"[20] (*yosheiv ohalim*), and he refers to the tradition that the image of that patriarch is engraved upon the divine throne.[21]

This tradition is based upon a midrashic rendering of the tribute given to Jacob by his angelic adversary when he changed Jacob's name to Israel: "For you strove with God (*sarita im Elohim*) and prevailed."[22] The Midrash explains this as "you became a heavenly authority (*sar*), *residing* with God."

The union of God and Israel is symbolized, according to the poet, by the fact that "God has joined his name to theirs," a reference to the name

"Israel," whose final syllable represents the name of God. This merging of identity suggests a marriage relationship, which leads the poet to refer to the beautiful imagery of Jeremiah: "I remember the devotion of your youth, your love as a bride (*ahavat kelulotayikh*)." For the sake of the rhyme, Meshullam inverts the latter phrase to *kelulat ahavim*.

אַתָּה הוּא אֱלֹהֵינוּ
You Are Our God (see p. 36)

מוֹרֶה חַטָּאִים
You Teach Sinners

In this poem, we have the double name acrostic, *Meshulam biyribiy Kalonymos chazak* (Meshullam son of Kalonymos, be strong!), formed by the initial letters of the first lines of each stanza, and, again, by the initial letters of the second lines. The third lines of the stanzas are taken from the first half of each succeeding line of *Ashrei* (Psalm 145), and with consummate skill the poet manages to fit all of this complex structure into a fine rhythmic and rhyming mold.

The poet emphasizes the efficacy of regular worship, and he hails the fervor and love with which Israel addresses its praise to God. He highlights the four services of the Day of Atonement (excluding the *Kol Nidrei* service of the previous evening) and the seven "praises." This is an allusion to the verse "Seven times a day I praise thee" (Psalm 119:164), which the Talmud[23] understands as referring to the blessings before and after the *Shema*. In the morning we recite two blessings before the *Shema* and one after; in the evening, two before and two after, making a total of seven "praises."

In the ninth stanza God is described as *kofer eshkol* ("a cluster of henna blossoms"), imagery derived from the allegorical interpretation of Song of Songs 1:14. It is employed by our poet in the sense in which the Talmud explains the phrase *eshkol ha-kofer* (which our poet has transposed), namely, "the One to whom everything belongs (*she-ha-kol shelo*) will grant me atonement (*mekhaper*)."[24]

The poet looks forward to the restoration of Zion and the Temple service, but asks that, in the meantime, the prayers and confessions of his people should be as acceptable as the offerings of the ancient sanctuary.

אַדֶּר יְקַר אֵלִי
I Will Declare the Glorious Majesty of My God

This poem is introduced by two verses, intended by the poet to serve, alternately, as refrains to each couplet of rhyming lines. As we have observed, these are invariably omitted in our editions from the body of the poem in order to avoid monotony. In this instance, the poet uses the refrains in order to construct a name acrostic. Thus, *m̄elekh s̄h̄okhein . . . l̄evadekha m̄elokh*, in the first line, and *m̄aazin s̄h̄avah . . . l̄e-ammo m̄eichish* in the second, convey the name *Meshullam*.

The first and second lines of each stanza are both constructed according to an alphabetical acrostic pattern, and there are but three words to a line. Unlike Meshullam's previous compositions, which are written from the standpoint of the human petitioner and his efforts to secure atonement at this time, this poem is theocentric, focusing, almost exclusively, upon the general attributes of God. It contains no specific allusion to Yom Kippur—other than the reference to "them that afflict themselves"—and the references to God's indulgent and forgiving nature appear almost *en passant*.

This description of God's attributes leans toward the mystical, even though most of the references are drawn from biblical phraseology. Meshullam introduces the themes of the celestial court, God's "tent," the *Seraphim* who surround Him, and, most significantly, *Chashmal*, a category of angel whose name is derived from the famous vision of Ezekiel[25] and that is referred to by the Talmud as having figured in the early system of *Merkavah* mysticism, which was based upon Ezekiel's vision. What is of particular interest here is that the Kalonymos family, to which our poet belonged, was the principal vehicle for transmitting mysticism—and particularly *Merkavah* literature—to Germany, and it was this family that provided the leading lights of the pietistic movement of *Chasidei Ashkenaz*, which produced a whole literature of esoteric material.[26] Thus we may detect in this composition some early indications of the mystical propensities of a founding father of that distinguished tradition.

The Talmud[27] explains the term *Chashmal* as a contraction of three words: *c̄h̄ayyot eis̄h̄ m̄emal̄elot*, "creatures who speak words of fire." A second etymological interpretation is also offered by the Talmud: *chash*, "they are silent (only when God speaks; otherwise)," *mal*, "they speak incessantly."[28]

אָנָּא אֱלֹהִים חַיִּים
Living God, Inscribe for Life

This poem is constructed according to a complicated alphabetical acrostic scheme, which is known as *At-bash*, wherein the first lines of each three-line stanza follow the ordinary, forward alphabetical acrostic pattern, but the initial letters of the second lines follow a reverse acrostic. According to this scheme only eleven stanzas are required to provide acrostically for every letter of the alphabet.

It is believed that one of the primary reasons for building an alphabetical acrostic into a poem was to facilitate the learning of the poem by heart, as well as to prevent additions or deletions. Where the alphabetical arrangement is as prominent as in the *At-bash* scheme, all of these objectives would stand the best chance of being realized.

The poem is a simple and direct plea to God to have compassion on Israel, to accept her fervent prayers as if they had been sacrifices offered on the Temple altar, and to cleanse us of all our iniquity.

The poet describes Israel as *deveikekha,* "those who cleave to you," an image borrowed from Deuteronomy 4:4—"And you who cleave (*ha-deveikim*) to the Lord your God are alive (*chayyim*) this day." Because the Torah promises life (*chayyim*) as the reward for "cleaving" to God, the poet climaxes each line of the opening stanza with the word *chayyim.*

In the second stanza the poet asks that the reward of life be granted "at a time of grace" (*eit ratzon*), by which he means immediately, while we are engaged in our Yom Kippur prayers. He is clearly thinking of the verse from Psalm 69:14, "O God, let my prayer unto you be a moment of grace (*eit ratzon*)."

Having already petitioned for our prayers to be regarded as if we had offered sacrifices in the Temple of old, the poet makes a further oblique allusion to this in the fifth stanza, simply by employing the word *ha-tzefufim,* "we who are *crowded together* to worship you." This verb is borrowed from the well-known passage in the Mishnah that lists, as one of the miraculous occurrences in the ancient Temple, the fact that, although the people stood crushed together (*tzefufim*), they were yet able to prostrate themselves fully on the ground.[29] Thus, by applying this verb—charged with Temple association—to his own community, the poet reinforces his earlier plea.

In the ninth stanza God is described as *mikveh yisrael,* "the hope of Israel," an image drawn from Jeremiah 17:13. The Rabbis gave a homiletical slant to this phrase, based upon the other sense of the word *mikveh,* namely, "a ritual bath": "Just as the *mikveh* purifies those who are unclean, so the Holy One, blessed be he, purifies Israel."[30]

הַיּוֹם יִכָּתֵב
This Day It Shall Be Inscribed

Although this composition appears as an introduction, and is repeated as a conclusion, to the following composition, *Ayumah bachar,* it does not, in fact, have any poetic or thematic association with it. It is simply an exhortation uttered by the Reader in order to rouse his congregation to pray with greater devotion and concentration, and to consider fully the implications of this awesome day when "life and death are recorded in the book of memorial."

It is tempting to suggest that in some communities the Readers would proclaim this formula aloud to their congregants whenever the attention of the latter seemed to be on the wane, or decorum impaired, during the lengthy services of this day. Its recitation would certainly have been more decorous than the usual call for silence. Our theory gains support from the fact that the exhortation calls upon the congregation three times to be upstanding while no such instruction is, in fact, observed while reciting the following composition!

אֲיֻמָּה בְּחַר
His Chosen Sons of Might

This composition, omitted from the Birnbaum edition, is attributed by Zunz[31] to Joseph ben Isaac ibn Abitur, one of the earliest Spanish poets and scholars (900–970 C.E.), who laid the foundation for the golden age of Spanish scholarship, particularly in the field of talmudic learning.[32] A tradition has it that he translated the whole Talmud into Arabic for the benefit of the Caliph al-Ḥakam II.

Joseph found himself at the center of a bitter controversy over his candidacy for the post of Rabbi of Cordova. This position became vacant on the death of the famous Rabbi Moses ben Chanokh (d. 965), whose leadership and erudition had enabled Spain to establish its own rabbinic authority independent of that of the Babylonian *Geonim*. The community was split over the appointment into those supporting Joseph and those in favor of Chanokh, son of the previous incumbent. The Caliph supported the latter, and Joseph was constrained to leave Spain after having been excommunicated by the opposing faction, emboldened by the Caliph's support. The ban followed him wherever he wandered, and he suffered miseries. He was eventually befriended by a wealthy silk merchant called Jacob ibn Jau who was a friend of the Caliph and who persuaded the latter to bring Joseph back to assume a specially created post of Patriarch of Spanish Jewry.[33]

Joseph devoted himself particularly to the creation of *piyyutim*. He composed many poems for Sabbath and festivals, and he was the first Spanish poet to describe the order of the ancient Temple service (*Avodah*) in poetry.

The present poem follows the alphabetical acrostic pattern, ending with the poet's first name, *Yosef*. Until the letter *yod* the alphabetical pattern is easily discernible as the initial letter of the first lines of each three-line stanza. From the letter *kaf* the acrostic appears more frequently, at the beginning of the first and second lines of each stanza, and from the letter *samekh* to the end of the poem it is represented in the first two letters of these lines.

This poem was clearly composed to be inserted into the morning *Amidah*. Every third line highlights the fact that it is at this particular service that mercy is sought, and the plea is intensified by the repetition, throughout the poem, of the three final lines—*bi-tefillat ha-shachar* ("in the morning prayer"), *be-eit temid ha-boker* ("at the time of the morning sacrifice"), and *be-zot tefillat yotzeir* ("during this early service").

אַךְ אָתִים בְּחִין לְפָנֶיךָ
They Come Pleading before You

Another poem from the pen of Rabbi Meshullam ben Kalonymos. After the introductory word to each line—*Akh* ("truly")—the poet constructs his alphabetical acrostic. Although in previous poems early editors have omitted the refrain where its frequent occurrence tended to mar the rhythm or to inject monotony, for some reason it was retained here.

The poet describes Israel's total confidence in God's mercy, and he begs that this will be speedily displayed so that there will be an end to the nation's unbearable persecution ("Deliver them from the dire destruction").

In his account of the nation at prayer on this sacred day he describes them as "washed in purity" (*tevulim*), a reference to the practice of attending the *mikveh* ("ritual bath") on the eve of Yom Kippur.

וּבְכֵן אִמְרוּ לֵאלֹהִים
So, Say to God

This alphabetical poem by Meshullam ben Kalonymos is a passionate outpouring of reverence and love for God. It calls upon Israel to praise the wonders of the Creator—"So say to God, how wondrous are Your works" (Psalm 66:3)—and it provides a catalogue of those wonders and attributes that are to be praised.

Most of the descriptions are taken directly from biblical phrases whose meaning is quite clear. Having already noted Meshullam's inclination toward mysticism,[34] it is not surprising, therefore, that he should have borrowed mystical references from the visions of Daniel and Ezekiel.

In the seventh stanza he describes God's throne as "a blaze of flames," His servants as fiery beings, and a river of fire as encompassing them all. This description is derived from Daniel 7:9–10: "As I looked thrones were placed, and One that was ancient of days took His seat . . . His throne was fiery flames, its wheels were burning fire. A stream of fire issued and came forth from before Him."

The image of God as a "consuming fire" appears in the Pentateuch itself, though various attempts were made by ancient and medieval exegetes to soften the concept. Thus, the *Targum* on the verse "For the Lord your God is a consuming fire"[35] renders, "for the *memra* (manifested will) of the Lord your God is a consuming fire," and Nachmanides (thirteenth century)[36] explains it as merely a metaphor for the divine anger and retribution that is visited upon idolators.

One cannot escape the fact, however, that fire plays a part in many biblical accounts of the manifestation of the deity to man, such as in the episodes of the divine appearance to Abraham at the "Covenant between the pieces,"[37] to Moses at the burning bush,[38] in the pillar of fire that went before the Israelites by night[39] and at the revelation on Mount Sinai.[40]

The ninth stanza continues the mystical theme in its reference to "those who bear his chariot" as being "full of eyes all around." This is taken from the well-known description of the celestial court given in Ezekiel 1:18.

In the thirteenth stanza Meshullam includes a reference to the doctrine of divine predetermination. The phrase *ha-kol tzafuy*, "All is foreseen," is taken from the maxim of Rabbi Akivah, "All [man's fate] is foreseen, yet permission [to act freely] is granted."[41]

וּבְכֵן גְּדוֹלִים מַעֲשֵׂי אֱלֹהֵינוּ
And Thus, Great Are the Works of Our God

This is also an alphabetical acrostic, though much tighter in plan, with each phrase, rather than each stanza, commencing with a succeeding letter. It will be appreciated how much more difficult it is to carry through such a literary device.

The poem sings of the unique power of God, who, notwithstanding His transcendence ("He has made His habitation in heaven so high"), is, at the same time, capable of manifesting Himself immanently and personally ("He hastens to heed the humble prayers of His people").

There is one stanza, however, which appears, at first glance, to have been misplaced, since it stands in stark contrast to the rest of the poem, by castigating man and his worthlessness, rather than praising God and His greatness. This is the penultimate stanza, commencing *Maasei enosh* ("The works of man"). It will be immediately apparent that this stanza actually interrupts the alphabetical progression of the poem, intruding between the stanzas commencing with the letters *reysh* (*Rachum limratzav*) and *shiyn* (*Shomei'a shevaot*). Furthermore, its structure differs from that of the rest of the poem, in that it conforms to a *reverse* alphabetical acrostic pattern, following the *Tashrak* sequence.

However, although this stanza does give the appearance of having been misplaced, it is, in fact, in the position originally assigned to it by its author, and it is only as a result of subsequent, and incomplete, editorial surgery that it has been left in its place with no fellow stanzas of the same ilk to indicate its original force and purpose.

In fact, in the original version of this poem, each stanza describing God's greatness was followed by a contrasting stanza dealing with man's guile, worthlessness, and mortality. The first of the two stanzas was introduced by the words *Maasei Eloheinu* ("The works of our God"), and the contrasting stanzas were all introduced by *Maasei enosh* ("The works of man"). The change of alphabetical structure was also significant. When describing God's works the acrostic worked forward to convey the idea of constructiveness and creativity; when describing man, however, a reverse acrostic was employed to denote his backsliding and contrariness.

At a later time some authorities secured the removal of all the *Maasei enosh* stanzas from their position, presumably because they felt that to make a comparison of God with man was a highly unsatisfactory and irreverent method of highlighting God's attributes, which are absolute and infinite. They therefore placed all those stanzas together *at the end of the poem*, and for some time the *Maasei enosh* collection of stanzas was recited as a separate poem.

Once the reputation of the *Maasei enosh* stanzas had been impugned, it was not long before other weaknesses were discovered. It was realized that making it into a separate poem created more problems than it solved, since it now expressed a most forceful and uncompromising denunciation of man's estate, and thus played into the hand of the accuser on this very day when man's fate hung by a thread.

The difficulty was provisionally overcome by reciting those stanzas in an undertone. This, in effect, doomed their survival in the context of a repetition of the *Amidah*, which was prescribed to be recited aloud.

A later copyist, having deleted the *Maasei enosh* poem because no one was bothering to recite it silently, decided to allow just the first stanza to remain, at the end of the *Maasei Eloheinu* poem, as a relic of its original presence. Later editors, ignorant of all this editorial development, and assuming that the *Maasei enosh* stanza stood as a single independent piece, moved it to its present position as the penultimate stanza. They did this for stylistic reasons, because, contextually, it fitted in best there, qualifying the preceding phrase which made reference to God's human creatures (*kol maasav*).[42] The inserted stanza constituted, therefore, an apt definition of the true nature of those creatures.

However, all the difficulties were still not resolved, for it was then realized that the introductory key phrase *Maasei Eloheinu* ("The work of our Lord") could hardly follow on immediately after that chronicle of man's shortcomings, as it might be construed as a criticism of God for creating a weak humanity! A later editor wisely solved this problem by adding the word *Aval* ("but") at the beginning of the phrase. The sense is now clarified: man's actions are, indeed, base and unworthy, "but the work of our Lord"—in sublime and total contrast—is unique and exalted.

Our recitation of the *Maasei enosh* stanza in an undertone thus goes back to one of the early stages of this editorial saga, when the whole collection of the original *Maasei enosh* stanzas were all recited silently.

הָאַדֶּרֶת וְהָאֱמוּנָה
Majesty and Faithfulness Are His

This alphabetical litany originated in a genre of early esoteric literature—the *Heikhalot*—which has been attributed to the talmudic schools of Rabbis Akivah and Ishmael (first to second century C.E.). They were composed in order to induce a state of ecstasy on the part of members of the select mystical fraternity as they embarked upon their spiritual exercises in order to receive revelations of the heavenly *merkavah* ("chariot"). This particular hymn is taken from the work *Heikhalot Rabbati*, which contains some of the earliest extant *piyyutim*.

Tradition has it that Rabbi Akivah heard the angels singing these songs as he approached the divine chariot, and that he was taught there the full import of its mystical connotation. Rabbi Ishmael asserted that God is more enthralled when these hymns are sung by Israel than by the angels, and it was on the strength of these assertions that a selection of these hymns has been included in our liturgy. Rudolph Otto[43] has designated these as "numinous hymns," that is hymns that seek to express in words the atmosphere of mysterious awe—the *mysterium tremendum*—that God's presence generates.

Gershom G. Scholem, in his celebrated book *Major Trends in Jewish Mysticism*, observes that

> almost all the hymns . . . reveal a mechanism comparable to the motion of an enormous fly-wheel . . . and within them the adjurations of God follow in a crescendo of glittering and majestic attributes, each stressing and reinforcing the sonorous power of the world. The monotony of their rhythm—almost all consist of verses of four words—and the progressively sonorous incantations induce in those who are praying a state of mind bordering on ecstasy.[44]

This last point is of particular importance; for a mere reading of the translation of this hymn, with no sense for the rhythm to which these lines conform in the original, or knowledge of the mystical exercises to which they originally provided a stimulus, might otherwise leave one mystified as to the strange poetic judgment that accorded this repetitive composition a place in our liturgy.

וּבְכֵן... וּבְכֵן
And Thus . . . And Thus . . .

The succeeding collection of seven hymns, six of which commence with the word *U-ve-khein*, all belong to the same genre of "numinous poems" as *Ha-adderet ve-ha-emunah*. Their insertion at this stage of the *Amidah*—leading up to the recitation of the *Kedushah* ("Sanctification")—is on account of the fact that the dominant characteristic of this genre is its preoccupation with the concept of God's holiness (*kedushah*) that these hymns attempt to represent and capture in words. Indeed, the kernel of the *Kedushah*—the triple affirmation of God's holiness (*kadosh kadosh kadosh . . .*)[45]—may be considered the climax of the mystic's ecstatic experience.

These hymns, and the mystical spirit they generated, even left their imprint upon the Sephardi version of the *Kedushah* composition itself:

> A crown will Your myriad angels on high present to You, O Lord our God, together with Your people Israel in their earthly assemblies. Together they will recite Your triple sanctification.

The scene of the *Kedushah* is set in the heavenly court where the angels are addressing their praises. These "numinous poems" set the mood for the *Kedushah* by offering a mystical description of the nature of those various categories of angels and their particular modes of praise, as well as by utilizing the phraseology of the *Kedushah* for their key words. Thus the hymn *U-ve-khein to'oratz ve-tukdash* ("And thus You are revered and sanctified") is constructed out of the opening words of the *Kedushah*: *Naaritzkha ve-nakdishkha* ("we will revere You and sanctify You"). The following hymn, *le-yosheiv tehillot* ("Unto the One who is enthroned amid praises") is similarly inspired by the statement in the opening verse of the *Kedushah* that Israel employs "the very same mystic utterance as the holy *Seraphim*" (*sod siyach sarfei kodesh*). That hymn attempts, therefore, to give expression to that unity of direction and activity that exists between the heavenly and earthly choristers. They truly share the praise of God; the Angels say *kadosh* and Israel responds with *barukh*.

The succeeding hymn, *U-ve-khein serafim omdim lo* ("And thus *Seraphim* stood by him"), opens with a phrase—*Zeh el zeh sho'alim*—borrowed directly from the *Kedushah*: *meshortav sho'alim zeh la-zeh*. It also takes up another of the *Kedushah* themes, that of the angels themselves being unable to determine the precise locus of God's glory: *ayyeih Eil eilim* ("Where is the supreme God?"). The reason for this is their failure to comprehend the panentheistic concept, that "the Universe is not where God is located, but he is the location of the Universe."[46]

The refrains of this hymn, *serafim omdim . . . sheish kenafayim*, and so on, from Isaiah 6:2, and *vekara zeh el zeh . . . kadosh kadosh kadosh*, and so on, from 6:3, provide an appropriate lead-in to the *Kedushah*.

וּבְכֵן לְךָ הַכֹּל יַכְתִּירוּ
And Now Let All Acclaim Your Sovereignty (see p. 39)

The *Kedushah*

We have referred above to the themes from the *Kedushah* that have infused the previous collection of hymns. In order finally to seal this link, the key word of each of those hymns—*U-ve-khein*—is employed again as an introduction to the *Kedushah* itself: *U-ve-khein u-lekha taaleh kedushah*.

For fuller treatment of the *Kedushah* prayer, the reader should consult the standard commentaries on the daily prayer book.[47] We shall confine ourselves to but two aspects—one literary, the other historical.

Within the *Kedushah* we have a literary device that has been defined as "*a chain technique*, which always links the last words of the *chazan* with the first words of the congregational responses." Thus, the last word of the congregational response, *melo khol ha-aretz KEVODO*, becomes the first word of the next statement by the reader: *KEVODO malei olam*. The penultimate word of the same sentence, *barukh*, is also taken up as the opening word of the next phrase. Similarly, the final word of congregational response, *mimkomo*, becomes the opening word of the next line recited by the Reader, and the same chain technique continues with the subsequent sentences ending with the words *shema* (*omrim*), *echad*, and *le-dor va-dor*. Eric Werner, who describes this chain technique as "a kind of climactic parallelism," states that it is a most ancient form of Semitic praying.[48]

The insertion into the *Kedushah* of the opening verse of the first paragraph of the *Shema*, as well as the last line of its third paragraph (*Ani adonai elokeikhem*), calls for some explanation. Its origin has been associated with the persecution of the Jews of Babylon by the Persian King, Jezdegaard II (circa 455 C.E.). Among his attempts to curb even private religious practices was the banning of the *Shema*, since its emphasis on God's absolute unity was construed by the dominant Zoroastrian religion as a denial of their belief in a dual deity, of good and evil.

The Rabbis of the day were forced to accede to the removal of the *Shema* prayer from its usual position in the liturgy. However, in order to keep alive its recitation, they smuggled a reference to it into the *Kedushah*, by reciting just its first and last lines. Presumably these were recited rapidly and in an undertone so as to be inaudible to the ear of any Persian inspectors.

During the period of the persecution the *Shema* would have been indicated in this way during every *Kedushah*, on weekdays and Sabbaths. Once the political climate improved, and the decree outlawing its recitation was relaxed, the custom of including these two verses from the *Shema* was abandoned in the case of every *Kedushah*, except that of *Musaf*. It was retained in this service in order to preserve a record of the deliverance from that particular persecution. The choice of *Musaf* was because the *Shema* is not prescribed for that service, and thus no unnecessary repetition was involved in its recitation.[49]

וּבְכֵן תֵּן פַּחְדְּךָ
And Now Impose Your Awe (see p. 39)

קָדוֹשׁ אַתָּה
You Are Holy (see p. 42)

סְלִיחוֹת
Penitential Prayers (see pp. 149–165; 225–226)

אָבִינוּ מַלְכֵּנוּ
Our Father, Our King (see pp. 49–50)

Reading of the Law

The Torah reading (Leviticus, chapter 16) provides a full description of the atonement rituals for Yom Kippur that Aaron is charged with initiating at the desert *mishkan* (sanctuary), and that are to remain operative as an "everlasting statute" (v. 34). And hence, in both Temples, until the destruction in the year 70 C.E. brought about the cessation of the sacrificial system, the basic biblical rituals remained in place.

Moses is charged with warning Aaron that entry into the Holy of Holies is to be restricted to but once a year, on this day. This warning came immediately after Aaron's two sons, Nadav and Avihu, lost their lives because they brought "strange fire which God had not commanded them to bring" (Leviticus 10:1). While there is much debate as to the precise meaning of that phrase, it is clear that in some way they were remiss in not adhering strictly to the regulations governing the sanctuary, and did not treat it with the awe and respect that their privileged proximity to it demanded. Having lost his children so tragically, Aaron was probably fearful for his own safety, and eager therefore to have every detail of the required procedures and regulations spelled out for him.

As regards the particular sacrifices to be brought as sin-offerings on this day, he is instructed to atone first for himself and his family before making atonement for the whole nation. He is told to immerse himself in water before donning simple vestments of white linen (foreshadowing the simple white *kittel* worn in synagogue by the officiants and some laymen). These represented quite a contrast to the golden vestments he wore on all other occasions, "for splendor and distinction" (Exodus 28:2), and reinforced the sense of humility, self-negation and contrition that was appropriate to the day.[50]

He is told further to take two he-goats and place them at the entrance of the Tent of Meeting. He is then to cast lots in order to determine which of the goats shall be offered as a sacrifice to God and which is to be sent out "to *Azazel*" (16:8) in the desert, symbolically laden with the iniquity of Israel. That the choice between the two goats was made on such an arbitrary basis as the drawing of lots is perhaps indicative of how one chance circumstance, experience, or association can so easily affect the entire course of our lives, for good or otherwise, and how carefully, therefore, we have to tread through life's minefields of capriciousness, with an attitude of vigilance, objectivity, fairness, and maturity.

Once the respective goats had been designated, Aaron slaughters a bullock as a personal and family atonement offering, and then makes his preparations to enter the Holy of Holies. The precise order of two of these preparations was the subject of a bitter dispute between the Pharisees and the Sadducees during the period of the second Temple.

The Torah states as follows:

> And he shall take a censer full of coals of fire from off the altar before the Lord, and his hands full of sweet incense beaten small, and bring it within the veil (partitioning off the Holy of Holies from the rest of the Sanctuary). And he shall put the incense upon the fire before the Lord, that the cloud of incense may cover the Ark-cover that is upon the testimony, that he die not. [Leviticus 16:12–13]

The Sadducees, who believed that within the Holy of Holies there actually existed a physical manifestation of God, maintained that the purpose of this biblical prescription, to put incense upon a fire pan, was in order to create a savory smoke screen. This was necessary in order to obscure the inside of the divine abode so that the High Priest would not catch sight of the divine Presence, and suffer the penalty of death. Hence their interpretation that the above verses required the High Priest to place the incense on the fire, and raise the cloud, *before* he actually entered inside.

The Pharisees, on the other hand, believed any suggestion that God was physically manifest to be nothing short of blasphemous. They were vehement in wishing to disabuse anyone of following the view of the Sadducees,[51] and they confidently interpreted the verses to require that Aaron first enters the Holy of Holies, and, after glimpsing its inside, that he adds the incense to the fire pan to create the aromatic vapors. Indeed, a straightforward chronological reading of the verses would suggest that the Pharisaic view is more plausible, since the end of verse 12 clearly states that he is to bring them (the burning coals and also the incense) within the veil, and only then (v. 13) to put the incense onto the coals.

The Torah portion continues with the instruction given to Aaron to sprinkle the blood of his sin-offering on and in front of the Ark cover as an expiation rite, and to repeat this with the blood of the goat that was designated "for the Lord." He then petitions God for forgiveness for the transgressions of the nation, and the Torah makes it quite clear that "there shall be no man in the Tent of Meeting when he goes in to make atonement in the holy place" (v. 17). Not even the priests were allowed to remain there at that moment, perhaps for fear of distracting the High Priest or inhibiting him in his spontaneous and intimate petition.

On emerging from the Holy of Holies in Temple times the High Priest would utter a short prayer for a year of plenty and prosperity (see our commentary to this, pp. 220–225). After this he had to perform a further act of sprinkling of the blood, this time around *karnot ha-mizbe'ach*, "the horns of the [inner, gold-plate] altar,"[52] located within the area in front of the Holy of Holies. Each of the four corners of the two altars in the Sanctuary (the other being the bronze or burnt-offering altar located in the courtyard of the Sanctuary) was endowed with "horns" or protruding cubes, and any refugee seeking asylum was safe once he had reached and seized hold of the horns of the bronze altar.

The Torah prescribes that in order to purify the altar, the blood of the *chattat*, "sin offering," had to be sprinkled around the horns. Horned altars have been discovered at Megiddo and elsewhere in Israel, though the origin and precise significance of the horns is still unknown. We might conjecture that they served a simple and practical purpose of forming a barrier around the top of the altar, so that the blood that was sprinkled or drained off there would congregate, and remain an entity at least for the duration of the purification rituals, rather than spill over the sides of the altar at the outset.

Sprinkling of the Blood

The symbolic basis of blood as a purifying agent, and the prohibition of its consumption, is explained by Maimonides[53] in a highly original manner. Since the consumption of blood was an essential element in many ancient idolatrous cults, particularly those of the Sabeans, Maimonides believes that the Torah's attitude was clearly motivated by the wish to wean Israel away from such practices.

Those idolatrous cults believed that blood was the food of the spirits. By consuming blood, therefore, the idolators imagined that they were sharing with the spirits and entering into a fellowship with them. Those otherwise malevolent beings would become transformed thereby into friendly allies.

Since many people recoiled instinctively, however, from consuming blood, they adopted a substitute method of achieving that proximity to the spirit world. They killed and roasted an animal, having first collected its blood in a vessel. They then sat *around the blood* and ate of the roasted flesh. They believed that, in this situation, the spirits would come to partake of the blood, and, by dining in such close proximity, that same objective of closeness and fraternity would be established.

Maimonides points out that an identical phrase, which occurs nowhere else, is employed by the Torah in the context of the prohibition of idolatry (Leviticus 20:5), on the one hand, and the consumption of blood (Leviticus 17:10), on the other. This phrase—"I will set My face against"—proves that the two prohibitions serve the same objective: the eradication of idolatry.

In a most radical departure from the talmudic interpretations of the verse, Maimonides offers his own explanation of the statement, *lo tokhlu al ha-dam* ("You shall not eat anything with the blood)." He renders it, "You shall not eat anything *around* the blood" (Leviticus 19:26), and believes that this is a clear allusion to the idolatrous practice we have referred to of partaking of the meat of a sacrifice while seated around its vessel of blood. This verse actually continues with the warning: "neither shall ye practice divination or soothsaying," which would indeed seem to substantiate the idolatrous reference that Maimonides detects.

Maimonides tells us that "the Israelites were inclined to continue their rebellious conduct and follow the doctrines in which they had been brought up [in Egypt],"[54] and it is for this reason that the prohibitions of consuming blood or even eating sacrificial meat "around it" were instituted. To ensure that the people did not slip back into that idolatrous practice, the Torah required that the blood of sacrificial animals had to be collected and sprinkled over the altar, while the blood of any beast or bird killed for ordinary consumption had to be covered up with earth (*kissuy ha-dam*, Leviticus 17:13).

The Torah went to the other extreme in its designation of blood as a purifying agent. While the ancient idolators regarded blood as impure (even though they consumed it), by reason of it being the food of the spirits, the Torah declared it to be the very source, force, and nourishment of life. No greater affirmation could there be, therefore, of the belief that God would grant mercy and life to the sinner, than the presentation of the blood of life to Him, and no more appealing gesture could be made than for the suppliant to symbolically offer his very life as an admission of the severity of his sin and the acknowledgment of his readiness to forfeit that life if the Almighty required it.

The *Azazel* Ritual

Once that sprinkling had been completed, it was time to perform the ritual of the sending away of the second goat to *Azazel*. Aaron was instructed to place both hands upon its head, to make a confession of the sins of Israel, and to transfer thereby the iniquity of the nation.

The precise meaning of the term *Azazel* is unclear, since it is found nowhere else in the Bible. The modern Israeli slang imprecation, *lekh la-azazel* ("go to the devil") is suggestive of the sense in which it was traditionally understood. Although this view, that the reference was to some desert demon, as part of the notion of a "scapegoat," was espoused by such notable commentators as Ibn Ezra and Nachmanides, Dr. J. H. Hertz, in his popular Soncino edition of the Pentateuch, rejects such an explanation out of hand. His argument is that "the offering of sacrifices to 'satyrs' [or spirits] is spoken of as a heinous crime in the very next chapter [17:7]; homage to a demon in the wilderness cannot, therefore, be associated with the holiest of the Temple rites in the chapter immediately preceding."[55] Hertz prefers to explain the term *Azazel* as a contraction of the words *eiz azal*, "the goat that is dismissed, entirely removed." Indeed, that was the nuance underlying the popular mishnaic term, *Seir Ha-Mishtale'ach*, "the banished goat."[56]

Another explanation views the word as a name-place, an uninhabited area of precipices and jagged rocks, from which the he-goat would be sure never to return. This interpretation is supported by the biblical reference to "sending it off to *Azazel*, to the wilderness" (16:10). This would make it synonymous with the term *eretz gezerah*, "an inaccessible region" (v. 22).

The symbolism of the laying on of hands (*semikhah*) is clearly the same as the laying of hands upon the head of one's student by a rabbinic scholar conferring ordination. In the latter situation, it implied that the ordinand possessed the authority upon which people might rely (*samakh*), since responsibility for decisions on questions of right and wrong, propriety and impropriety, had been devolved to him. Similarly, the laying of the hands (*ve-samakh yado*) upon the head of the sacrificial animal betokened the belief that part of the responsibility for the sins of the nation had been laid upon it.[57]

A special courier was at hand to receive the *Azazel* goat and to lead it into the desert (16:20). Although anyone was eligible for such a task, in practice it was generally kept as the preserve of the priesthood.[58] Because the courier was a key actor in the dramatic ritual of removal of sin from Israel, he was shown the greatest deference while discharging his duty:

> Some of the most prominent men of Jerusalem would accompany him to the first (of the ten booths situated along the route). At each booth they would offer him food and water, and accompany him to the next booth.[59]

Since the journey was a most arduous one, walking along hilly and rough terrain under the hot desert sun, the courier could easily become dehydrated and collapse. Hence the offer of refreshment, even though it was a solemn fast day. There was a distance of 2,000 cubits separating each of the ten booths. (This is the maximum distance permitted for a person to walk from his home on Sabbath or Yom Kippur. Hence the necessity to establish new "abodes" for those accompanying him along the route.) The courier's final walk, from the tenth station to *Azazel*, was 4,000 cubits, and he had to walk alone, since only he had the concession to walk beyond the permitted limit. They did not establish an eleventh booth, however, to enable them to accompany the courier on his last stretch, since the Torah prescribes that the goat's final destination be *eretz gezerah*, "a desolate region," from which such company is obviously precluded. The total distance he covered, of some 24,000 cubits, is equivalent to approximately 15 kilometers.

Although the Torah does not prescribe it, the Mishnah teaches that during the period of the second Temple the courier would guide the goat over a precipice, to ensure that the sins of Israel died with it. Perhaps this act was also inspired by the vague term *eretz gezerah*, which might also mean "the region of tearing in pieces." Such a violent end to the goat would fulfill that nuance of the term, if that was, indeed, the authentic requirement. Again according to mishnaic tradition, the courier would tie a strip of red wool to the horns of the goat before hurling it over the precipice. This wool would provide a miraculous and happy augury of divine forgiveness by turning white.[60]

On his return from the desert he had to undergo a form of purification—as did Aaron himself—since both had become contaminated by contact with the animal to which the sins and impurities of Israel had been transferred. This involved taking a bath and washing the clothes they had worn for the ceremony.

The Five "Afflictions"

The Torah reading then moves from the arena of the dramatic public ritual of the High Priest to the personal and intimate observances of each individual: "In the seventh month, on the tenth day of the month, you shall afflict your souls, and shall do no manner of work. . . . It is a Sabbath of solemn rest unto you and you shall afflict your souls" (Leviticus 16:29,31).

"Afflicting the soul" is a very vague notion, and clearly some concrete definition of its parameters was required. This is provided by the Mishnah,[61] which enumerates the five *innuyim* (afflictions) that tradition prescribed. These are abstentions from eating and drinking, bathing one's body, perfuming, wearing leather shoes, and marital intercourse. The last four only are required of a mourner, who is expected to forgo bodily pleasure, but not to "afflict" himself. He is already emotionally afflicted, and the nature of his loss will automatically create a mood of solemn introspection. On Yom Kippur, however, such a mood has to be induced; and the abstention from eating and drinking serves this objective most effectively.

Eating produces a state of satisfaction, as the Torah itself asserts in the verse "And you shall eat *and be satisfied*, and bless the Lord your God" (Deuteronomy 8:10). Indeed, it may be said that "being satisfied" is biblically mandated, to the extent that one is not halakhically obliged to "bless the Lord," by reciting Grace, unless one has eaten sufficient to induce that feeling of satisfaction (*kedey seviah*).

So the Torah is most concerned that we should enjoy God's blessings to the full, since only if we are in a contented frame of mind can we bless God with sincerity.[62] Judaism does not believe in celibacy or in depriving oneself of the good things of life. Quite the contrary, as the psalmist puts it: "Serve God amid joy; come before Him with exultation" (Psalm 100:2). The Talmud actually asserts that when our days are over and we come before the heavenly throne, we shall be called to account for any legitimate, God-given pleasures that we abstained from.[63] Through joy we express appreciation to God for all He has bestowed upon us. By consciously rejecting those blessings, we display ungratefulness and a lack of appreciation for the generosity of the One who "opens His hands and satisfies the desire of every living thing" (Psalm 145:16).

It is against this background that our abstention from food and drink on this day should be viewed. We symbolically assert that we are unworthy to receive all God's bounty, that we are in no way entitled to the satisfaction that eating and drinking induces within us, and to the good feeling that the other four pleasures afford.

Regarding the latter four abstentions, they may be explained in the context of the nonsociability that we are expected to display on Yom Kippur. We are very much "on our own," standing without support or defense counsel before the bar of the heavenly court. We pass truly "like lambs," in single file. Thus, anything that demonstrates social and joyful interaction is forbidden. We bathe and apply cosmetics or after-shave in order to appear fresh and appealing to others. In earlier times, leather shoes were a luxury that only the wealthy could afford, and would wear at important social gatherings. If one lived alone on a desert island, one would hardly bother with any of these—certainly not with the frequency that we social beings generally do. And marital relations are, of course, the most potent, intimate, and pleasurable demonstration of a mutual interaction and need.

Perhaps A. J. Heschel's remarks about human *needs* are also relevant to the rationale underlying these five abstentions:

> Needs are looked upon today as if they were holy, as if they contained the quintessence of eternity. Needs are our gods, and we toil and spare no effort to gratify them. Suppression of a desire is considered a sacrilege that must inevitably avenge itself in the form of some mental disorder. We worship not one but a whole pantheon of needs, and have come to look upon moral and spiritual norms as nothing but personal desires in disguise.
>
> It is, indeed, grotesque that while in science the *anthropocentric* view of the earth as the center of the universe and of man as the purpose of all being has long been discarded, in actual living an *egocentric* view of man and his needs as the measure of all values, with nothing to determine his way of living except his own needs, continues to be cherished. If satisfaction of human desires were taken as the measure of all things, then the world, which never squares with our needs, would have to be considered an abysmal failure. Human nature is insatiable, and achievements never keep pace with evolving needs.[64]

On Yom Kippur we put our needs into a proper perspective. We affirm that we have really only one ultimate need, and that is for God's grace. If we have that, everything else will follow. We will then have satisfaction from all that we do and from everything that we possess. Because then, all our eating and drinking, and all the satisfaction of our various physical appetites, will be all the sweeter, in our confidence that they come to us as a gesture of divine love and grace. Without that grace, we have nothing, and we are nothing. And on this day we set aside, therefore, all else, and pursue, with humble single-mindedness, the forgiveness and mercy of the source of all blessing.

Six *Aliyot*

On Yom Kippur we call six people to the Reading of the Law. The number of people we call on each occasion is determined by its importance and holiness. On Mondays and Thursdays, on minor fast days, and on *Chanukah* and *Purim* (as well as on *Shabbat* afternoons, when the Torah reading was only introduced as a compensatory measure for those unable to hear it read during the week) we call up *three*. On *Rosh Chodesh* (new moon days) and *Chol Ha-Moed* (intermediate days of *Pesach* and *Sukkot*) we call up *four*. On festivals, *five*; on Yom Kippur morning, *six*; and on *Shabbat* morning we call up *seven*.

Although Yom Kippur is described as "the Sabbath of Sabbaths," and although in the popular consciousness it is spiritually incomparable, we still call up the highest number of people on an ordinary Sabbath, since the seriousness of the punishment for willfully violating Sabbath is greater than that for Yom Kippur. Violating the Sabbath brings with it the capital punishment of death by stoning, whereas for violating Yom Kippur there is no humanly administered death penalty. It is left to God to exercise His divine punishment of *karet*.

Another reason for the preeminence of Sabbath over Yom Kippur is that Sabbath is designated as *Shabbat Lashem*, "a day [devoted] to the Lord" (Exodus 20:10), whereas Yom Kippur is described as *Shabbat Shabbaton hiy la-khem*, "A Sabbath of Sabbaths *unto you*." Sabbath is a testimony to God as Creator; Yom Kippur serves Israel exclusively, to enable her to obtain forgiveness.[65]

The *Haftarah*

The passage chosen as *Haftarah* (Isaiah 57:14–58:14) encapsulates some of the most sublime and timely insights into the authentic message of Yom Kippur. Isaiah has much to say to a community that, particularly on Yom Kippur, is so preoccupied with scaling the heavenly gates that it overlooks the fact that the keys to those gates are kept here on earth. And the keys are constructed not only out of prayer and ritual, but also out of integrity in one's dealings, charity, and concern for the welfare of one's fellow and one's society.

It has been pointed out that the "notable men of Jerusalem," who would have reveled in the spirituality and purity generated by the uninterrupted rituals that were being performed in the Temple, and in the special atmosphere created by their proximity to the priests and others assembled in the Temple court to witness this once-a-year spectacle, and to worship in the beauty of holiness, nevertheless chose to leave the Temple and to miss the spectacle in order to accompany the sole courier taking the *Azazel* goat out of Jerusalem, relieving his loneliness and making his journey more tolerable. What a wonderful expression of sensitivity and kindness, and what a practical demonstration of the true priorities of Jewish spirituality![66]

It is precisely this point that Isaiah is eager to make. And he does so with consummate skill in the second verse, by exaggerating the transcendence of "the God who is high and lofty, that inhabits eternity, whose name is Holy . . . who dwells in the high and holy place *with him that is of a contrite and humble spirit.*" God is most particular with His companions, unlike man who is dazzled by rank and ostentation.

The well-known maxim "there is no peace for the wicked" is taken from the last verse of Chapter 57. The wicked are assured that they will not enjoy any inner peace or satisfaction from their wrongdoing or their ill-gotten gain. This is in sharp contrast to the assurance Isaiah gives, a few verses earlier, that to the penitents there will be a double measure of peace: "Peace, yea peace, to him that is far off and to him that is near." *Rashi,* following the rendering of *Targum,* explains the "far off" in the sense of those who have been reared from their distant childhood to a life of religious observance, and the "near" as those who have only recently abandoned their evil ways and accepted the yoke of the law.

Conceivably, the reference to a separate peace for each of the above categories might suggest that they each experience a different type and quality of spiritual peace. The peace enjoyed by the "far off" partakes of a tranquillity born of long familiarity with the fruits of a religious life. The peace enjoyed by the *baalei teshuvah,* the born-again Jews, on the other hand, is of necessity less comprehensive. They can still be expected to endure a certain degree of emotional turbulence and confusion as they struggle to find their own religious level amid the multilayered foundations that underpin the collective Jewish experience.

Chapter 58 opens with an ironic denunciation of those whose religiosity is mere sham. The prophet wants his criticisms to be trumpeted ("like a shofar raise your voice"). "Tell my people their transgressions and the house of Jacob their sin." According to *Rashi,* "my people" refers to the scholars of the Torah, whose sins, even the inadvertent ones, are construed as an act of rebellion. Isaiah mocks the naïveté of those so-called pietists, who observe the letter of the law but believe that mechanical observance is a substitute for inner charitable feelings:

> Yet they seek Me out daily, and delight to know My ways, [parading] as a nation that did righteousness and forsook not the just laws of their God. They ask Me for righteous laws, and say they delight in approaching God.

Such externalism prompts its exponents to ask in naïve amazement how it can be that "we fast but You do not see it; we mortify ourselves but You pay no heed?" A smug belief that God is bound by the forces of action and corresponding reaction, particularly when the "action" is so superficial, is most unworthy—particularly of scholars of the Torah. If that is the depth of our Yom Kippur fasting—Isaiah asserts—then it is not only valueless, but also sacrilegious:

> On such a day you are keeping no fast that will carry your cry to heaven. Is it a fast like this that I require, a day of mortification such as this, that a man should bow his head like a bulrush and make his bed on sackcloth and ashes?

It is clear from this passage that in the period Isaiah was referring to, after the return from the Babylonian captivity (circa 520 B.C.E.), religious exhibitionism went beyond the boundary of the acceptable, reflecting the awakening of nationalistic rather than religious emotion. It was concentrated *on* the Temple and its ritual, but not *in* them.

If such religious exhibitionism is detected in our own age—also a period of "return" to our homeland and religious self-determination—then we have a precedent for it in Isaiah's day as a natural concomitant of the unreal circumstances of an age of redemption. That, however, does not excuse it. It has to be corrected, and exchanged for true religious values:

> Is not this what I require of you as a fast; to loose the fetters of injustice . . . to snap every yoke and set free those who have been crushed? Is it not sharing your food with the hungry, taking the homeless poor into your house, clothing the naked when you meet them and never evading a duty to your kinsfolk? . . . Then, if you call, the Lord will answer; if you cry to Him, He will say, "Here I am."

The prophet then proceeds to castigate those who call upon God only in times of personal crisis or who identify religiously only on occasions (such as the High Holy Days) when they are shamed into doing so by the fact that everyone else is making that symbolic token of identification. It is the regular communion with God every Sabbath, not the occasional visit, that God seeks:

> If you cease to tread the Sabbath underfoot, and keep My holy day free from your own affairs, if you call the Sabbath a day of joy and the Lord's holy day a day to be honored, if you honor it by not plying your trade, not seeking your own interest or attending to your own affairs, then you shall find joy in the Lord, and I will set you riding on the heights of the earth, and your father Jacob's patrimony will be yours to enjoy.

8

Memorial of the Departed

הַזְכָּרַת נְשָׁמוֹת
Memorial of the Departed

At this moment, those who have lost near relatives stand in silent and nostalgic contemplation, entering into the serious spirit of *Yizkor*. *Yizkor* means "remembering." But do we ever forget those precious people whose absence has left such a void in our lives? So is this special memorial service really necessary?

The truth is that nature cushions us from morose preoccupation with thoughts about the dead, however precious they were to us. Thus, although visions of our loved ones, and recollections of their actions and words, do periodically flit through our minds, generally these thoughts have to jostle with competing impressions and experiences while we are being distracted with other activities or conversations. Not so during *Yizkor*. At this moment the departed are given our complete attention—a consecrated attention—as befits their immortal spirit.

Then again, how infinitely more meaningful and symbolic it is to remember the departed in synagogue, on a *Yom Tov*, in the context of a sacred prayer, making mention of their personal Hebrew names. And all this in an atmosphere of whispered reverence.

We do believe that there is a world beyond the grave, that death is, indeed, a starlit strip between the companionship of yesterday and the reunions of tomorrow, and that, just as we sometimes breathe a sigh of relief when awakening out of a nightmare, so it will be the moment after death.

Colonel David Marcus, who created the Army of modern Israel, had this to say about death:

> I am standing upon the seashore. A ship at my side spreads her white sails to the morning breeze and starts for the blue ocean. She is an object of beauty and strength, and I stand and watch her until at length she is only a ribbon of white cloud just where the sea and sky come to mingle with each other.
>
> Then someone at my side says, "There, she's gone!" Gone where? Gone from my sight—that is all. She is just as large in mast and hull and spar as she was when she left my side, and just as able to bear her load of living freight to the place of destination. Her diminished size is in me, not in her!
>
> And just at the moment when someone at my side says, "There, she's gone!" there are other voices ready to take up the glad shout, "Here, she comes!" And that is dying!

"The dead cannot praise God" (Psalm 115:17). However overwhelming is the volume of our grief, especially if our bereavement has been fairly recent, we must still praise God—on behalf of the dead. By so doing, we acknowledge that death is a fact of life; that it is a law, not a punishment; that it is as necessary to the constitution as sleep; and that we shall, assuredly, rise refreshed in the morning.

The memorial prayers are also recited on the last day of Passover, the second day of Pentecost, and the eighth day of Tabernacles (*Sheminiy Atzeret*). It might seem inappropriate to detract from the joy of these festivals by reciting a prayer that inevitably promotes sadness and tears. The Rabbis, however, looked more deeply at the psychological effect of their institutions, a fact that explains, for example, the permission to observe a private fast on a Sabbath, which they granted to those who had experienced bad dreams. The rationale was that the fast actually restored peace of mind and promoted happiness (*oneg*) by eradicating the deep-seated fears that were responsible for the bad dreams. It therefore actually aided the troubled person to enjoy the pleasure of the Sabbath.[1] Similarly were our sages aware that to shed a silent tear, and recall one's dear ones through *Yizkor*, actually had a beneficial and therapeutic effect, and that, by releasing the emotions, one's residual grief was definitely dispelled. For this reason—totally in consonance with modern views on the psychology of bereavement—they did not see any conflict between the recitation of *Yizkor* and the joyous experience of a festival day.

It was in the context of the liturgical ritual of Yom Kippur that the very practice of reciting a memorial prayer for the departed[2] first arose. The *Shulchan Arukh* merely states that "it was a custom to contribute charity on Yom Kippur on behalf of the departed."[3] Moses Isserles, quoting the *Mordechai* (thirteenth-century German halakhic authority), adds the comment, "And we make mention of the names of the departed souls, since they also obtain forgiveness on the Day of Atonement." This idea inspired another German authority, Rabbi Jacob Weil (fifteenth century), to explain the plural form *Yom Kippurim* (lit. "Day of Atonements"), in that it atoned for both the living and the dead.

The *Yizkor* service was clearly popularized in Ashkenazi circles, who extended its recitation to the three other festivals. The honored place it subsequently came to occupy was probably the result of the tragic history of the Franco-German communities, from the period of the Crusades to the end of the Middle Ages. The endless lists of martyrs were carefully recorded and preserved in the *Memorbuch* or *Yizkor-buch* of the various communities, and read out at *Yizkor* time. In the course of time the lists were expanded to include not only the martyred but all departed members, and this enabled our custom, of reciting *Yizkor* for individual relatives, to evolve. The *El malei rachamim* memorial prayer for martyrs of the Holocaust and for the heroes of the State of Israel's defense forces is, therefore, more in line with the original function of this memorial service.

9

The *Musaf* Service

הִנְנִי

The Reader's Meditation (see pp. 65–66)

חֲזָרַת הַתְּפִלָּה

The Repetition of the *Amidah* by the *Chazan* (see pp. 30–31)

מִסּוֹד חֲכָמִים וּנְבוֹנִים

From the Counsel of the Wise and Understanding (see pp. 32–33)

שׁוֹשַׁן עֵמֶק

Lily of the Valley

יוֹם מִיָּמִים הוּחָס

The Day Preeminent Above All Others

צְפֵה בְּבַת תְּמוּתָה

Look Upon Those Appointed to Death

אֶשָּׂא דֵּעִי לְמֵרָחוֹק
I Will Fetch My Knowledge from Afar

These four compositions, all from the pen of Eleazar Kallir, form one poetic unit, as is clear from their metric and acrostic structure. The first composition forms the acrostic *Shabbat Shabbaton* ("Sabbath of Sabbaths"), which is the biblical description of Yom Kippur (Leviticus 16:31). The second composition is created out of the acrostic Yom Kippurim, and the third forms the acrostic *Tzom He-Asor* ("Fast of the tenth day"). The employment of this type of subject acrostic, drawing attention to aspects of the festival, is a departure from the usual pattern, wherein the poet constructs the acrostic poem either out of his name or out of the letters of the alphabet.

Kallir utilizes these three acrostics to form the refrains of the fourth, and final, composition of this group, *Esa Dei'i Le-mei-rachok*. The three acrostics are first set out together as an introduction to this composition, each introduced by the word *ve-nakdishakh*, before being employed, individually, as a refrain at the end of every third line.

Since *Esa Dei'i* constitutes the climax of this cluster of four compositions, the poet signs off, as it were, by employing the name-acrostic *Eleazar biribbi Kallir*. Purely in order to facilitate the employment of his refrains at least twice in the course of the poem, and not having enough letters in his name to cover the number of lines he required, he was constrained to repeat some of the letters of his name. For the sake of uniformity, he chose to repeat those letters that formed the first line of each of his three-line stanzas. Thus, the first and second lines of each stanza commence with the same letter.

Although our Ashkenazi rite has these compositions for recitation during *Musaf*, the old Italian and Balkan traditions—as reflected in their respective *machzorim*—prescribed their recitation during the *Shacharit Amidah*. The metric link between these four compositions is also apparent from the uniform length of each line-phrase, comprising a mere three words.

אֱנוֹשׁ אֵיךְ יִצְדַּק
Can Man Be Proved Righteous?

The above four-poem cluster is interrupted in the Polish rite by the insertion of another composition, *Enosh Eikh Yitzdak*, constructed from an alphabetical acrostic, with five words to each line. This is a *tokheichah*, a moral exhortation, drawing attention to man's worthlessness as he stands before the supreme judge. The opening sentiment, "How can mortal man be proved innocent in the presence of his Maker?" derived from Job 9:2, is in line with the existentialist outlook of, say, Kierkegaard (1813–1855), who viewed the human situation as one of homelessness and estrangement, and his prevailing mood one of despair and angst, as, facing the yawning abyss of the world, he contemplated his own worthlessness and insignificance, his limited intellect combined with his moral lethargy, all of which inhibit his grasp of true reality.

The poet parts company from Kierkegaard—as does the whole spirit of Judaism—in one major respect: whereas that distinguished Danish theologian and philosopher believed that man's only hope is to take a gamble, in fear and trembling and by a leap of faith, that on the other side of that leap he will find God,[1] the poet here assures the Jew that reality, peace, and salvation are to be found on earth, by submitting to the Torah's way of life, "in love, fear and purity." The Torah alone can bridge that yawning abyss; it alone can "resolve the dissonance of this troubled earth."[2]

אִמְרוּ לֵאלֹהִים
Thus Say unto God

This popular composition calls upon Israel to praise the wonders of the Creator: "So say to God, how wondrous are Your works," a verse taken from Psalm 66:3. It is infused with happy confidence, affirming God as the one who "hastens the redemption of his people . . . speeds forgiveness to His community and fulfills for us all his promises."

Nearly all the phrases and allusions are borrowed from the Bible—principally from the Psalms and Isaiah—and their meaning is clear. One phrase, however, has occasioned difficulty: *soleyach l'am zu ba-zo* (fourth stanza), literally, "forgiving this people with this." The phrase *am zu* occurs in the Song of the Red Sea (*am zu gaalta*, "This people whom you have redeemed," Exodus 15:16), and in Isaiah 43:21 (*am zu yatzartiy liy*, "This people whom you have created"). But what sense can be made of *ba-zo* ("with this")? Various suggestions have been offered. Some interpret it as referring to the Torah, namely, God forgives Israel ("with this"), i.e., on account of Israel's merit gained through observing the Torah. The Torah is frequently referred to as *zo*, "this," as in the liturgical affirmation *Ve-zot ha-torah*, "And *this* is the law."

Others explain it as referring to the merit of circumcision, which was also accompanied by the demonstrative *zo* ("this") at the time it was promulgated to Abraham: *zot beritiy* ("*This* is my covenant," Genesis 16:10).

The phrase could be explained far more simply, however, in the sense of "forgiving this people *at this hour*." The word *ba-zo* would then be elliptical for *ba-zo ha-shaah* ("at this time"). Finally, it could also mean "through this," namely, through this day of prayer God forgives Israel.

The passage is an alphabetical acrostic, each stanza commencing with a succeeding letter of the *alef bet*. The composition does, in fact, proceed all the way through the alphabet in this way, though the Polish rite, which we follow, has omitted all the eleven stanzas commencing with the letters between *kaf* and *shin*. The stanza commencing with the letter *tav* (*takif*) is inserted, however, to constitute a logical conclusion.

וּבְכֵן גְּדוֹלִים מַעֲשֵׂי אֱלֹהֵינוּ·

And Thus, Great Is the Work of Our God (see pp. 180–182)

וּבְכֵן לְנוֹרָא עֲלֵיהֶם בְּאֵימָה יַעֲרִיצוּ·

Therefore in Fear They Express Reverence to the Revered One

The authorship of this double-acrostic poem has not been ascertained with certainty, though it is attributed to Yannai,[3] one of our earliest liturgical poets and principal representative of the old Palestinian school of writers of sacred poetry.[4]

The poet's theme, of the supreme and omnipotent God enthroned upon the adoration of the angels yet still desiring the praise of worthless man, was taken up by later *paytanim* to become a recurring theme in their High Holy Day compositions. In this poem the refrains themselves are intended to provide a justification for the greater pleasure God takes in the praise of humans than in that of the angels. Man has been granted freedom of choice. When he exercises this in favor of his Maker's will, that constitutes true praise—*vehiy tehillatekha* ("In truth this is your praise"). The praise uttered by the angels is, on the other hand, simply a concomitant of the fact that—*umorakha aleihem*—"your awe is imposed upon them."

This poem belongs to the genre of numinous hymns that we have described above,[5] wherein there is no development or progression of idea and no expression of religious doctrine. It nevertheless pulsates with a mesmeric rhythm, created by the unbroken regularity of the two stresses in each short line, as well as in the alternating opening and closing refrains. When chanted against a background of drums and to the accompaniment of ritual dancing, this was the type of song that would have been employed in biblical times by members of the prophetic guilds in order to engender a trance to aid their emotional climb toward a mystical experience.[6] It is not dissimilar to genres of songs sung by primitive tribes as an accompaniment to their rhythmic dances, which were all impelled by a desire to communicate with the supernatural forces. The numinous poems were transfused with adoration of God and were chanted by *Merkavah* mystics as a stimulant to their esoteric exercises.

The greater the poet, the more confidently he experimented with the classical biblical vocabulary, molding and adjusting it to his poetic structure. In this poem a number of new Hebrew forms make their appearance. Thus, in the opening stanza we are offered a noun *kedach*, in the sense of "light" or "flame." It was employed in order to rhyme with *kerach* ("ice"), and is derived from the verb *kadach*, "to kindle a fire."[7]

In the third stanza, the poet stretches the normal meaning of the biblical root *yakhach* ("to decide," "prove," "argue") to create a noun *vekhach* in the sense of "assembly,"[8] parallel to *vaad* ("council").

In the sixth stanza we also have the phrase *milunei mar,* "from (man) steeped in bitterness." This less impressive coinage (*le-unei*) was derived from the biblical word *laanah,* "wormwood."[9]

The economy of words that the meter forced upon the poet meant that he was constrained to select phraseology that was pithy and pregnant with meaning. He certainly succeeded most impressively in this poem, and demonstrated thereby his total mastery of biblical usage, and his ability to cull the most apposite imagery from the most obscure and least-known passages of the Holy Scriptures, particularly in the books of Job and Isaiah.

וּנְתַנֶּה תֹּקֶף
We Will Celebrate the Mighty Holiness (see pp. 72–83)

קְדוּשָּׁה
Kedushah (see pp. 184–185)

וְכֹל מַאֲמִינִים
And All Believe (see pp. 84–85)

וּבְכֵן תֵּן פַּחְדְּךָ
Now Therefore, Impose Your Awe (see pp. 39–40)

וְיֶאֱתָיוּ כֹּל לְעָבְדֶךָ
All Shall Come to Serve You (see pp. 85–86)

אַתָּה בְחַרְתָּנוּ
You Have Chosen Us (see pp. 44–45)

וּמִפְּנֵי חֲטָאֵינוּ
But Because of Our Sins (see pp. 86–88)

עָלֵינוּ
It is Our Duty (see pp. 88–92)

אֱוֵ"אֱ הֱיֵה עִם פִּיפִיּוֹת
Our God . . . Inspire the Lips (see p. 93)

אוֹחִילָה לָאֵל
I will Hope in God (see p. 94)

אַמִּיץ כֹּחַ
The *Avodah*—Order of the Service of the High Priest in Temple Times

Introduction: The Temple

The need to "locate" God, and concentrate His presence in a confined space, which can be conceived of, visited, and revered by man, has always been natural and urgent to those who seek Him out in faith and love. The gulf that separates that mental and spiritual convenience from the true reality is alluded to by King Solomon in his address at the dedication of his Temple: "But can God indeed dwell on earth? Heaven itself, the highest heaven, cannot contain thee; how much less this house that I have built!" (1 Kings 8:27).

Nevertheless, however irrational, the enterprise proceeded because the belief always existed that while no sanctuary (and there had been a succession of these from the period of the Judges until Solomon's time) could "contain" God, He could nevertheless arrange for His Spirit to be especially manifested in a particular location, just as He could, and did, fill some of His chosen leaders, kings, and prophets with His special spirit or glory. As the popular image expresses it, one can kindle innumerable lights from one flame, without in any way diminishing the original source. Thus, God can arrange for His glory to be more potently sensed in one or another location, without it in any way impairing the concept or reality of a God "whose glory fills the entirety of the Universe." Indeed, this is precisely the implication of the paradoxical juxtaposition, in the *Musaf Kedushah,* of two sentiments: "The entire world is filled with His glory" (Isaiah 6:3) and "His ministering angels ask each other, 'Where is the place of His glory?'"

The notion of God's presence being concentrated in particular locations is well known from the Genesis account of the lives of the Patriarchs. Abraham built altars in the places where God appeared to him as he traveled through Canaan. He made a point of returning to those "holy sites" in order to invoke the name of God (Genesis 12:8; 13:3). Even Hagar felt disposed to mark the place where God appeared to her, to give her encouragement to return to the home of Sarai her mistress. She called the well *Be'er la-chai ro'iy,* "the well of the Living One who sees me."

When God appeared to Isaac by night, to give him similar encouragement amid his controversy with the Philistines over ownership rights of wells that he had dug, Isaac felt impelled to build an altar on that spot, to concretize the divine presence that was manifested to him there (Genesis 26:25). And when Jacob awakes from his graphic vision of the "gate of heaven," he designates the place as *Bet El,* "the house of God," and erects there a sacred foundation stone for that future house of God, in the form of a pillar, which he proceeds to consecrate with oil (Genesis 28:18).

Jacob's offspring were to suffer many agonies of exile and oppression in Egypt, and many challenges and struggles before they were able to conquer the promised land and fulfill their father Jacob's vow to build the Temple on the site he had consecrated. But already the Jewish people possessed that quality of patience and that sense of history and destiny that have always—until our own day—enabled us to keep our sights fixed upon heaven, and affirm, to paraphrase Maimonides, that even though salvation may tarry, we will nonetheless wait upon it until the day it comes.

Three names were applied to the Temple. Its first name, applied to it by its builder, King Solomon (circa 950 B.C.E.), was simply *Ha-Bayit*: "*The* house." It is this term that is constantly employed throughout the description of its design, erection, and consecration (1 Kings 5:16–8:64), though interspersed in that account is the name *Bet Ha-Shem*, "House of God," reminiscent of the term *Bet Elokim*, coined by Jacob, who first dreamt it into existence.

The second name is *Bet Ha-Bechirah*, "The house of [God's] choice," a term based on the recurring Deuteronomic reference to "the place that God *will choose* [*yivchar*], to make His name to dwell there" (12:5,11,21; 14:23; 16:2,6,11; et al.). This is also a term found in rabbinic literature, and known from the Passover *Haggadah*. It was also the term favored by Maimonides as the heading of the section of his code of law dealing with the Temple and the sacrificial system—*Hilkhot Bet Ha-Bechirah*.

The most popular term is, of course, *Bet Ha-Mikdash*, "House of [indwelling] Holiness," based upon the divine instruction, *Ve-asu liy mikdash*, "And they shall make for me a sanctuary, and I shall dwell in their midst" (Exodus 25:8). After the recitation, at the commencement of our daily Morning Service, of the passages dealing with the Temple sacrifices, we utter the plea, *She-yibaneh bet ha-mikdash bi-mheirah ve-yameinu*, "that the Temple may be rebuilt speedily in our days." And the identical sentiment is repeated at the conclusion of the *Amidah*, in a brief passage (*Yehiy ratzon*) embodying the verse from Malachi that looks forward to the day when the Temple service will be restored, so that "the offerings of Judah and Jerusalem shall be pleasing to the Lord, as they were in days of old, in years long past" (3:4).

The noun *temple* is from the Greek *temenos*, which is derived from a verb meaning "to cut off, sever." This was the term applied to a sacred enclosure or precinct adjacent to a temple. Bearing in mind the word's idolatrous association, and especially in the light of the acts of desecration perpetrated by the Greeks against the second Temple, it is perhaps surprising that that term was so popularly employed in the literature of English Judaica, or indeed as a designation of a house of prayer! In traditional Hebrew writings, the terms *bayit rishon* (lit. "the first house") and *bayit sheni* ("the second house") are exclusively employed.

The place of the Temple in Jewish religious life can be measured by the fact that laws relating to its administration, sanctity, vessels and components, and rituals and practices account for over half of the entire list of Judaism's 613 biblically mandated laws, as enumerated by Maimonides in his *Book of the Mitzvot*. The destruction of the Temple thus, in one fell swoop, neutralized half the entire format of Jewish religious expression. It caused the majority sections of three out of the six Orders of the Mishnah to become relegated to the realm of theory, topics preserved merely for nostalgic recollection and study, but with no practical application. These are the Orders of *Zera'im* (agricultural law), *Kodashim* (sacrificial system), and *Taharot* (purification rituals).

Adin Steinsaltz has succinctly expressed the implications of the loss of the Temple:

> The destruction of the Temple, therefore, deprived the Jewish people of the central axis about which the life of the people revolved and toward which all other life expressions were directed. Since that time, the Jewish people lack that central axis needed to direct the religious life, the national life, and the very existence of the people as a national body. Thus the destruction of the Temple was not only metaphysically but also historically and actually "the removal of the *Shekhinah* [the Divine Presence] from Israel." As long as the Temple exists, there is direction and significance to the flow of life. Whatever the number of Jews in the diaspora, and whatever the political and material position of the Jews in Israel, as long as the Temple exists, the entire nation knows that "the Lord dwells in Zion," and for the life of the nation there is not only a center but also a direction: there is a beginning and an end in the structure of life.[10]

The loss of the Temple occasioned the introduction into the religious calendar of the observance of three historical fast days: *Asarah Be-Tevet* (10th of *Tevet*), *Shivah Asar Be-Tammuz* (17th of *Tammuz*), and *Tishah B'Av* (9th of *Av*), each of which recalls a successive stage of the invasion and assault on Jerusalem and the Temple, culminating in its final destruction by the Romans in the year 70 C.E.

In this way and in many others—notably through the institution of the synagogue that is modeled upon it—the Temple has continued to live on as an inspirational, unifying, and sacred symbol. It is not surprising, therefore, that later generations should have sought to recapture the spirit of Yom Kippur past, in Temple times, when the varied rituals of that occasion, all directed toward securing atonement for the entire nation, generated an unprecedented level of rich, vibrant, and awesome spirituality, encompassing both those who participated in and those who witnessed the events of the day. The inclusion into our prayers of the *Avodah*, the description of the Yom Kippur ceremonial in Temple times—however pale a reflection of the authentic experience—is the way we attempt to link up, emotionally, historically and spiritually, with the way our ancestors celebrated the awesome holiness of this day in the place of supreme holiness, the Temple at Jerusalem.

The Sacrifices

While sin and sacrificial atonement occupy a most prominent position in the Torah's religious system, with a high proportion of its positive regulations being concerned with the various categories of sacrifice and its varied and rich rituals, perhaps surprisingly the Torah not only offers no rationale for it, but the initial reference to it, in the form of an instruction to Israel to build an altar, appears almost as an afterthought, at the very end of the Sidrah *Yitro*, as a postscript to the description of the Sinaitic Revelation and the giving of the Ten Commandments (Exodus, chapter 20).

Immediately after the enumeration of the commandments we are told that the people could not tolerate the sound of God's voice booming out the commandments. They fled from the mountain, and pleaded with Moses to be the intermediary, to relay to them the law of God: "Let not God speak with us, lest we die" (v. 16). According to tradition this flight from the mountain occurred after the second commandment was revealed, and hence only the first two commandments are couched in direct speech, in the first person, with God as speaker, while the rest of the commandments refer to God in the third person, being clearly spoken to Moses.

Immediately following the account of this particular incident, God gives Moses the first instruction to build an altar to enable Israel to offer sacrifices:

> And the Lord said unto Moses: Thus thou shalt say unto the children of Israel: Ye yourselves have seen that I have talked with you from heaven. Ye shall not make [ought] with Me; gods of silver or gods of gold ye shall not make unto you. An altar of earth thou shalt make unto Me, and shalt sacrifice thereon thy burnt-offerings, and thy peace-offerings, thy sheep and thine oxen. (Exodus 20:19–21)

Two facets of this passage are worthy of note, both of which have suggested to ancient sages and modern thinkers a rationale of the institution of sacrifices. First, its juxtaposition to the Revelation, and specifically to Israel's inability to enter into direct dialogue with God except through an intermediary and at a distance. Second, the instruction to make that altar follows immediately after a warning against making any idolatrous representations of the deity.

The inference we may draw from the above is that the purposes of the sacrifices are twofold. First, they are to serve as a substitute mode of supplication and adoration for any attempt to "call upon one's God" (1 Kings 18:24) directly, like the patriarchs and Moses and the prophets were able to do, and to expect a responsive heavenly voice. The people had just demonstrated that they were, in fact, unable to tolerate such a response. Second, that they were intended as a concessional substitute for the type of direct and tangible contact and relationship with the deity that idolatry offered. Hence, the verse prohibits the making of idols before proceeding to reveal the sacrificial laws.

We can now understand why, according to the school of Rabbi Ishmael, although the Torah records the instruction to build the Sanctuary (Exodus 25:8) before the episode of the Golden Calf (Exodus, chapter 32), in reality it followed it chronologically,[11] a conclusion with which Rashi concurs.[12] That school explained that the heathen nations, when they heard of the episode of the Golden Calf, condemned Israel as religious renegades who could never expect any further grace from their God. The instruction to erect the Sanctuary, to enable God to dwell in Israel's midst, was, accordingly, intended as a token of love and reconciliation, as well as a gesture to enable Israel to refute that spurious imputation. It is in the light of this that Rabbi Ishmael explained the term *Mishkan He-eidut*, "Sanctuary of testimony" (Exodus 38:21; Numbers 1:50,53, 10:11) not in the literal sense of "*containing*" the testimony (the two Tablets of the Law),[13] but in the sense of "the Sanctuary that *constitutes* a testimony," to the unimpaired God–Israel relationship.[14]

For Isaac Abarbanel, the association made by the Rabbis between the sin of the Golden Calf and the building of the Sanctuary (and the clear biblical association of the two, as referred to above), suggests a rationale for the latter as an antidote to the former, and, in the broader sense, the entire sacrificial system as a means of weaning Israel away from idolatry.[15] This could not be spelled out more clearly, in fact, than in the Torah itself:

> The purpose is that the Israelites should bring to the Lord the animals that they are now slaughtering in the open country; they shall bring them to the Lord at the entrance to the Tent of the Presence. . . . And they shall no longer sacrifice their slaughtered beasts to the satyrs whom they wantonly follow (Leviticus 17:5, 7).[16]

The identical explanation is offered for the taking of the Paschal lamb four days before the Exodus. Because Israel was steeped in idolatry while in Egypt, God gave them a similar type of offering in order to wean them away from idolatry to embrace His worship.[17]

This was clearly the approach of the great Maimonides, in his *Guide for the Perplexed*:

> By this Divine plan it was effected that the traces of idolatry were blotted out, and the truly great principle of our faith, the existence and Unity of God, was firmly established. This result was thus obtained without deterring or confusing the minds of the people by the abolition of the service to which they were accustomed and which alone was familiar to them. . . .
>
> All the sacrificial laws and restrictions served to limit this kind of (idolatrous) worship, and keep it within those bounds within which God did not think it necessary to abolish sacrificial service altogether.[18]

The Symbolism of the Sacrificial Act

We referred above, in our commentary to the Yom Kippur Torah Reading, to two particular aspects of the Temple sacrificial *Avodah* rituals: the *semikhah*, or placing of the hands upon the head of the animal, and the fact that food and drink were made available at ten service stations for the courier who guided the *Azazel* goat to its destination in the desert, even though biblical law forbids the taking of refreshment on this holy day of fasting. An examination of the symbolism of the sacrificial ritual will perhaps help to shed light on both of these.

Martin Buber expresses this most succinctly. He draws attention to two fundamental objectives of animal sacrifice. The first is the consecration of natural life. The subsequent eating of that sacrifice becomes a hallowed act. The second fundamental objective is "the sacramentalization of the complete surrender of life." Buber sees special significance in this context in the act of placing the hands upon the animal, in order to identify with it, and to share its fate. The one who brings the sacrifice symbolically asserts that he is, at the same time, offering *himself* in the person of the sacrifice:

> When the purified and sanctified man, in purity and holiness, takes food into himself, eating becomes a sacrifice, the table an altar, and man consecrates himself to the Deity. At that point, there is no longer a gulf between the natural and the sacral; at that point, there is no longer the need for a substitute; at that point, the natural event itself becomes a sacrament.[19]

We learn from Buber the precise objective of the laying of the hands, which, especially in the context of the sin-laden *Azazel*, becomes a meaningful symbolic assertion by the High Priest, of the psychological surrender by the nation of its title to life. If, as has been suggested, the sacrifices were initiated in relation to the sin of the Golden Calf, then divine sentence is brought into very sharp focus: "Now, therefore, leave Me alone, that My wrath may wax hot against them, and that I may consume them and make of you a great nation" (Exodus 32:10). The continued existence of Israel thus becomes a divine concession and act of special grace. She should, justly, have shared the fate of an *Azazel*. And the High Priest, representatively laying all Israel's hands on that animal, highlights that fact most forcefully, and effects that "sacramentalization of the complete surrender of life."

We may now explain why it is that the courier, who transports that animal to its doom, is enabled, should the need exist, to eat and drink on the holy day. Quite apart from the personal dangers of walking ten miles under the hot sun, there is also the consideration that, in the context of his awesome role in the expiation rite, an individual so pious as to be given this coveted holy duty would be best placed to convert the mundane act of taking refreshment into a veritable ritual of "the consecration of natural life" and a hallowed act of eating, rather than it remaining a mere satisfaction of a bodily appetite.

Are Temple References Still Relevant?

The issue of whether there is any point in including in our liturgy references to the Temple sacrificial ritual, which was suspended some two thousand years ago, is of consequence not only to Reform Jews, who already in the nineteenth century had those references expunged from the prayer books they published in Germany, but also to many Orthodox Jews, who find that they cannot muster quite the same *kavvanah* (religious concentration and enthusiasm) over, say, the *Shabbat Musaf* service, with its plea for the restitution of the regular offerings, and its catalogue of the various he-lambs and the ingredients of the oily gift-offerings as brought in the Temple. The same applies, of course, to this *Avodah* section of the Yom Kippur liturgy.

One approach is to regard these sections not as "prayers," in the sense of immediate, relevant, and dialogistic matters that we wish to bring to the notice of God, but as historical reminiscences of that bygone era when the Temple stood in all its glory as the nationalistic and spiritual focus, and unifying force, for the Jewish world.

Jewish prayer is very broad in its compass, and the recitation of study passages from talmudic literature, especially those pertaining to ancient sacrificial and agricultural-tithe law, is a common feature. If to recite prayers and petitions that our Sages have composed at various times is a good thing, then how much more meaningful it is to recount the laws of ancient Israel that were originally enunciated by God Himself!

Thus, at one level, those references to ancient sacrifices and meal-offerings were clearly intended to serve the purpose of putting us into a mood of nostalgic recollection, with the objective of stimulating us toward collective action in the cause of religious Zionist endeavor. Our miraculous return to Zion, after suffering the absence of its sovereignty for nearly two thousand years, must be attributed in some significant measure to the fact that our liturgy preserved a regular and graphic evocation of that glorious experience that once was, and must again become, ours.

It was not merely a physical return that was being promoted, but, through the medium of those Temple references, successive generations of Jews were given a powerful reminder of the spiritual dimension of the Jewish national cause, without which no full or heaven-blessed return is possible.

The manner in which even secular Jews can be moved by a visit to a holy site in Jerusalem suggests that we all bear within us a deep-seated emotional link to the historic roots of our national identity. The liturgical reminiscences that we dutifully preserve and lovingly utter in our services also serve the purpose of verbalizing and intensifying those emotional feelings.

אַמִּיץ כֹּחַ
You Are Great in Strength

In most older editions of the *machzor* it is not easily recognizable that this *Avodah* section—describing the Yom Kippur ritual in Temple times—is, in fact, one extremely long alphabetical poem, interrupted three times for prostrations and confession. The Birnbaum edition does, at least, commence each succeeding letter of the *alef bet* with a separate paragraph, and the ArtScroll, as expected, highlights the letters of the alphabet clearly, allocating a new line to each successive letter.

The author varies his alphabetical structure. Until the letter *samekh* he utilizes quatrains—four-line stanzas—each line commencing with the same letter of the *alef bet*. For the letters *samekh* and *ayin* he provides stanzas of eight lines; from *pay* to *shin* he increases this to twelve-line stanzas and for *tav* he provides no less than twenty-four lines.

The number of words per line is also varied, commencing with lines of five words, and, in a most unexpected place, near the very end of the poem and in the middle of his concluding name-acrostic, he changes to lines of four words. The author is the tenth- to eleventh-century poet Meshullam ben Kalonymos, generally regarded as having been an Italian scholar, though his tombstone was discovered in Mainz, Germany, his familial country of origin. His name is interwoven to form the acrostic of the final twenty lines of the poem, which reads *Meshullam Biribbi Kalonymos Chazak*.

His poem commences with a survey of biblical history, beginning with the order of Creation, the sin of Adam and Eve and their punishment, the slaying of Abel, the spread of idolatry, the flood, and the Tower of Babel. He refers to Abraham "the friend of God, who made known His name in the world," and who was the founding father of "a worthy and beautiful race." From this people God chose Levi to perform His service, separating one particular branch of that tribe "to minister in the Holy of Holies" as High Priest and to function as representative of Israel on the holiest day of the year.

This leads the poet into a description of the detailed sacrificial ritual, the immersions, order of robing, and the formulae of confession, all as described in the talmudic tractate *Yoma*.

נִלְוִים אֵלָיו נְבוֹנִים
The Elders of the Gate Gathered around Him

This section begins at the letter *nun* of our long alphabetical *Avodah* poem. It is based upon *Mishnah Yoma* (1:3 ff.), and describes the seven days of preparation that the High Priest had to undergo in order to be fully acquainted with all the procedures required in order to be able to discharge his awesome tasks faithfully on the great day.

The elders, who were chosen from among the members of the Sanhedrin, the supreme court of seventy-one judges that sat in the *Lishkat Ha-Gazit*, the Hall of Hewn Stones adjoining the Temple courtyard, were charged with reading to the High Priest the biblical portions dealing with the rituals of the day, and elaborating on all the laws and practices that oral tradition had evolved and transmitted. The elders insisted, however, that he did not rely exclusively upon listening to their expositions, but that he read aloud for himself the relevant scriptural portions in order to reinforce them in his memory. Jewish teachers, even at such an early period, were clearly aware of the most effective pedagogical principles and methods. They were committed to the principle of *Eino domeh shemiah liriyah*, "one cannot compare [merely] hearing something to actually seeing it [in print]." They were also aware that reciting things aloud helped to imprint them upon the memory.

Our necessarily concise poem does not go into all the details found in the Mishnah, but one facet of that instruction, given by the elders to the High Priest, provides an interesting insight into the nature of the High Priestly office during the period of the Second Commonwealth.

> They said to him: "My lord High Priest, read with your own mouth, since you may well have forgotten [the laws] or perhaps have never learnt them."[20]

The Talmud[21] not unsurprisingly, queries how anyone so ignorant could have been appointed in the first instance to such a religiously elevated position, for which Torah knowledge was a prerequisite! The answer of the Talmud is that this reflects the situation that obtained during the period of the decline in the quality of the Temple religious administration, especially following the Hasmonean period (second to first centuries B.C.E.), when the office of High Priest was sold to the highest bidder. This was certainly the situation during the last century of the Temple's existence, from the period of Herod onward, when Judea was under Roman occupation, and the appointment was used as a means of political leverage. High Priests were appointed, and then removed from office according to the whim of the Roman governors. Some, like Joseph Caiaphas remained in office for as long as eighteen years, while others survived only a few months. Inevitably, therefore, many High Priests were appointed who were totally ignorant of Jewish law and ritual procedure, but who had coveted the office purely as a vehicle of self-aggrandizement.

This situation is lamented by the Talmud, which preserves a doggerel reflective of the great gulf that separated the Sadducean High Priesthood from the masses of lower-class Judeans. The latter were frequently terrorized by the thugs employed as High Priestly bodyguards, and who carried out with great cruelty the extortion practiced by their masters.

Abba Shaul ben Botnit quoted from Abba Joseph ben Chanin:

> Woe is me because of the House of Boethos; woe is me because of their curses. Woe is me because of the House of Hanin; woe is me because of their slander. Woe is me because of the House of Kathros; woe is me because of their false documents. Woe is me because of the House of Ishmael ben Phiakhi; woe is me because of their fists. For they are High Priests, their sons are treasurers, their sons-in-law are overseers, and their servants come and beat the people with staves.[22]

The verses commencing with the letter *samekh* allude to a solemn instruction given to all High Priests (the elders obviously could not be seen to distinguish between educated and ignorant occupants of the office, and had, therefore, to follow the same procedure in the case of all incumbents) to be sure to follow the Pharisaic—rather than the Sadducean—tradition, and to create the incense smoke screen only after entering the Holy of Holies, and not beforehand. We are told that "the flesh of the High Priest trembled and he shed tears that they should suspect him [of being a Sadducean adherent], and they likewise would turn aside and weep at having to cast such aspersions on the man who occupied the most exalted spiritual office."

It is in the light of the religious differences between the Pharisees and the Sadducees that we may also explain the reference to High Priests who "perhaps have never learned" the laws and procedures. Since the Sadducees only studied and owed allegiance to the Written Law, and rejected the oral traditions as developed by the Pharisees, it would not be unusual, in the political climate we have described, to find an influential priestly family, reared in Sadduceanism, providing from among their ranks a High Priest who was totally ignorant of the way the Pharisees expected the Yom Kippur rituals to be performed.

The Mishnah and Talmud add numerous details of the *Avodah* preparations and rituals that are not alluded to in our concise *Avodah* poem. We are told that the High Priest had to be kept awake the whole night. It was feared that if he went to sleep he might have a seminal emission that would disqualify him from performing the day's rituals.

If the High Priest was a scholar of the Torah and of Pharisaic oral traditions, he kept himself awake by delivering to the accompanying elders a discourse on a matter of law. If he was not learned, the elders would lecture to him. If he was accustomed to read in the Bible, he would read for himself when he had finished his discourse; if he was not accustomed to read the Bible, the elders would read for him portions from the Books of Job, Ezra, and Chronicles, or other sections, which are particularly interesting and which would prevent him from falling asleep. If he did start to doze, young priests, standing by for that purpose, would snap their fingers to make a loud noise. They would then respectfully suggest that he stand up and dispel his drowsiness by taking a walk with his bare feet upon the cold stone floor. Toward dawn, they would recite before him from the Book of Psalms; according to some authorities they particularly chose the *Shir Ha-Maalot* psalms (120–134).

וְהַכֹּהֲנִים וְהָעָם

And when the priests and the people that stood in the court heard the glorious and awesome Name pronounced out of the mouth of the High Priest, in holiness and purity, they knelt and prostrated themselves and gave thanks, falling upon their faces and saying: "Blessed is the Name of His glorious kingdom for all eternity."

The people thronging the Temple court were, in the main, passive observers. Unlike present day congregations that are meant to recite as much of the prayers as are prescribed for the *chazan*, the Temple service was almost the exclusive preserve of the priests and Levites, with the visitors expected to observe a sacramental silence. There was, therefore, no congregational singing, and the participation of visitors to the Temple court was limited to making full prostrations during key parts of the service and to uttering the response to blessings, in the form of the verse *Barukh shem kevod malkhuto leolam va-ed,* rather than by employing our *Amen* response.

There was actually a regulation prohibiting the recitation of the *Amen* response in the second Temple,[23] even though it is already a well-established response in the biblical books dating from the Persian period.[24] Some rabbinic commentators believe that this prohibition was already operative in the first Temple.[25]

Precisely what the Temple authorities' objection to *Amen* was, is by no means clear, especially as the later synagogue pioneers clearly had no such objections, and the *Amen* response became a predominant feature of synagogue communal prayer. One suggestion is that *Amen* has an uncomfortable biblical association with the catalogue of curses mentioned in Deuteronomy, chapter 27, whereas the Temple was promoted as an exclusive source of blessing, and a vehicle of atonement.

Another suggestion takes account of the Sadducean influence on the priesthood that we have referred to above, and particularly the suspicions of Sadduceanism that were even directed toward the High Priest by the elders preparing him for the Yom Kippur ceremonies. S. T. Lachs suggests that the comprehensive term *Amen* represents an absolute affirmation of total identification with both the word and the intent of the one uttering the blessings and prayers to which the responses were made. Since the Sadducees rejected some basic and cherished Pharisaic theological principles, such as the beliefs in resurrection and in divine providence being extended not only to the people as a whole, but also personally, at the individualistic level, it was impossible, therefore, for those committed to Pharisaism to affirm, with a blanket *Amen,* total identification with the theological intent of a Sadducean priest or High Priest. Hence, it is suggested, it was the Pharisaic leaders who insisted that, instead, the response should take the form of a clear and independent statement: *Barukh shem kevod malkhuto leolam va-ed* ("Blessed is the Name of His glorious kingdom for all eternity").[26]

אָנָּה הַשֵּׁם
O God

Full prostrations were made by all present in the Temple on Yom Kippur whenever they heard the High Priest utter "the glorious and awesome Name." During the period of the first Temple the High Priests employed a twelve-letter Name of God, which was supposed to have been the authentic and divinely preferred name, a name invested with a mystical potency that could be released for the performance of supernatural deeds. This name was employed daily by the High Priest during the course of the blessing of the people (*Birkat Kohanim*).[27] However, since some unscrupulous people overheard it and utilized that name themselves for personal ends, with disastrous consequences, its use by anyone other than the High Priest was declared anathema. Since it would then have been regarded as unseemly, even for descendants of the High Priestly fraternity, to utter that special name outside the holy land—if not outside the precincts of the Temple—it was consequently not expressed or transmitted during the exile in Babylon, with the result that knowledge of it became lost.

For the early (Persian) period of the restored Temple, the priests employed the four letter (*Tetragrammaton*) name: *Yod-Hey-Vav-Hey*, accompanied by the authentic vowels that go with those consonants. Those vowels were subsequently forgotten due to the establishment of a rival Jewish Temple, with a rival priesthood, at Leontopolis in Egypt, a temple that set out to be a carbon copy of the Jerusalem Temple. The authorities of Jerusalem, alarmed at the employment of the divine Name by those renegade priests, reacted by insisting that it be withdrawn entirely from daily use in the Temple, and reserved for utterance once a year, by the High Priest alone, on the Day of Atonement. Even then, it was prescribed that he utter the *Tetragrammaton* inaudibly, so that it was muffled by the highly raised voices of the ordinary priests who employed the form of the divine name with which we are familiar, *Adonai*, which is in reality more of a title (Master, Lord), than a name. The priests of Leontopolis, as expected, followed suit; and with the destruction of both of those Temples, the tradition regarding the precise vowels of the divine Name has been entirely lost, and awaits revelation in the messianic era.[28] It goes without saying, therefore, that the vowels that accompany the occurrence of the divine Name in our Hebrew Bible are only arbitrary. They are actually the vowels extracted from the term *Adonai* (Lord). The Christians have followed this arbitrary arrangement to popularize the name *Jehovah*.

Prostrations

In the Temple, a prostration was made by the officiating priests at the conclusion of each and every ritual, from the offering of incense upon the altar to the clearing out of the ashes. The prostration was the symbolic act denoting completion and a request for permission to withdraw, like a courtier from the presence of his monarch. There were also prostrations, first by the High Priest and afterward by the ordinary officiating priests, during their processions into and out of the main court of the Temple when performing their rituals.

Prostrations were also prescribed for Israelites presenting their baskets of first fruits on Pentecost. They would lay them down at the side of the altar and make a prostration before withdrawing.[29] The Israelites in the outer court were also expected to make a prostration when they heard the shofar sounded at interludes during the Levitical singing that accompanied the libations of the two main *tamid* ("continual") daily offerings.[30]

One of the ten miracles that, according to the Mishnah, characterized the Temple experience was that, during the pilgrim festivals, when people crammed into the Temple court, there was, remarkably, sufficient space, when it came to making the full prostration, for everyone to do so.[31]

The precise form of Temple prostration is a matter of uncertainty. Some authorities believe that it involved bending the knees, followed by *pishut yadayim ve-raglayim,* the stretching out of the hands and legs, as a token of absolute submission, while others are of the view that it was a more simple bending of the knees and bowing, rather than a full prostration.[32] Certainly on Yom Kippur the communal prostration that accompanied the High Priest's confession involved "bending the knee, prostrating oneself, and falling upon one's face," with hands and legs fully outstretched.[33]

Outside the Temple, in the houses of prayer, prostrations were practiced in the daily prayers, and were an especially prominent feature of the fast day services. At first there was no regulation governing the number of prostrations or the particular prayers for which they were required. Hence Rabbi Akivah was famous for the numerous prostrations he made, especially when praying privately.[34]

As the *Amidah* became popularized as a statutory prayer, toward the latter decades of the Second Commonwealth (50–70 C.E.), the number of prostrations made was regarded as indicative of a certain level of piety. It was regarded as inappropriate for those below such levels to prostrate themselves with any degree of frequency. Thus, the High Priest was permitted to bow at the end of each blessing of the *Amidah,* the king at the beginning and at the end of each blessing (perhaps to publicly demonstrate his submission to the authority of the King of Kings), and the ordinary folk at the beginning and end of just two blessings (the first, *Avot,* blessing and the *Modim* blessing).[35]

As one enters the synagogue one should bow toward the Ark, and recite the verse, "And as for me, by Your abundant love, I will enter Your house; I will *bow down* toward Your holy Temple in reverence of You" (Psalm 5:8). Because kneelings and prostrations became such a prominent feature of Christian worship, the rabbinic authorities recoiled from it, and hence only token bowing is permitted, other than on the High Holy Days.

And Thus He Would Count: *Achat, Achat Ve-Achat*

An important element of the Yom Kippur *Avodah,* in Temple times, was the sprinkling by the High Priest of the blood of an ox within the Holy of Holies, and of a he-goat's blood in the outer enclosure. The sprinkling was based upon the biblical verse: And he shall take of the blood of the ox and sprinkle with his finger upon the Ark cover to the east (viz. with an upward movement), *and before the Ark cover shall he sprinkle seven times* (downward) *with his finger* (Leviticus 16:14). The High Priest would count aloud in order to be sure to sprinkle the correct number of times. He would call out *achat* ("once") each time he sprinkled with an upward motion, followed by *ve-achat* ("plus once") when he sprinkled downward. This was to prevent him calling *shtayim* ("two") as he made the first downward sprinkle, with the result that he would stop at the number seven, thinking he had completed seven downward motions, instead of only six (plus one upward).

וְיוֹם טוֹב הָיָה עוֹשֶׂה
The High Priest Declared a Holiday

The entry of the High Priest into the Holy of Holies was considered an act fraught with considerable personal danger, and it was, therefore, a moment of great relief—not only to himself but also to the Temple worshipers who regarded it as an auspicious sign—when he emerged safely after having made the great national confession.

Summoning courage from his successful mission, he would offer a prayer for national prosperity, security, and blessing.

The version of the High Priest's prayer found in our *machzorim* is a poetic expansion of the versions found in the Palestinian and Babylonian Talmud.[36] Here it is cast into an alphabetical acrostic, and it may be more than coincidental that the word *shanah* ("year") occurs twenty-four times—a multiple of the number of months in the year. The number twenty-four may reflect the fact that the High Priest was praying for twelve months of happiness both for his own family and, in addition, for the whole community.

Our liturgical version of this ancient prayer, uttered by the High Priest when he emerged safely from petitioning the Almighty within the Holy of Holies, is a variant and expanded version of the original. The prayer has come down to us in a number of variant forms, and because, throughout the talmudic period, prayers (and any other orally transmitted traditions) were not permitted to be written down, it was inevitable that errors would creep into the original version in the course of its oral transmission down the ages. When permission was ultimately granted to write prayers down, the errors were perpetuated in manuscripts—and generally compounded by the carelessness or ingenuity of scribes, who often thought nothing of making up a new word if they could not decipher or comprehend the original phraseology. When the age of printing arrived (fifteenth century), the particular manuscript of a work chosen for publication would, of necessity, therefore, also have contained errors, which were then perpetuated in printed form. Because the laity rests more comfortably in the belief that the version in "their" *siddur* or *machzor* is perfectly correct, it is generally only scholars who take for granted the existence of *shinnuyei nuschaot*, variant readings.

It is the employment of an unknown word, or a phrase that does not give a readily comprehensible meaning, that first alerts us to the possibility of some faulty reading. If, however, we have some parallel quotations from the same source in other works, then we can judge the relative merits of the respective readings, and decide which is the authentic version. This is not always possible, however.

One example of a word that does not suit its context, and that is clearly a scribal error, is the word *ha-kedoshah* in the phrase *kiy im le-yadekha ha-melei'ah ha-petuchah HA-KEDOSHAH ve-harchavah* ("but only of Your helping hand, which is full, open, *holy*, and ample"), in the Grace After Meals.

This was noted by the great rabbinic scholar Barukh Halevi Epstein, who points out, in his work, *Barukh She-amar*,

> the anomaly that in this phrase all the epithets (describing God's hand) are physical, whereas the middle one (*ha-kedoshah*) is spiritual. If it was intended to introduce a single spiritual element, the requirement of liturgical style would necessitate it being listed either at the beginning or the end of the list of epithets. Quite apart from this consideration, the reference to God's hand as "holy" is without precedent, and certainly when what is being emphasized is the need for its *abundance* to be vouchsafed.
>
> The problem may be solved, however, with reference to the well-known linguistic principle that letters belonging to the same group tend to interchange. Now the letters *Gimmel* and *Kof* are both palatals (sounds formed by compressing the tongue and the hard palate), so it is most likely that the original reading was not *ha-kedoshah* ("holy"), but *ha-gedushah* ("overflowing"). Indeed, the adjectives *malei* and *gadush* form a common couplet (*malei ve-gadush*), "full to overflowing" in Rabbinic Hebrew. Thus it would be most appropriate to find God's hand described as both *ha-melei'ah* and *ha-gedushah*.[37]

In the High Priest's prayer, we have another such problematic reading, occasioned by the use of the word *shechunah,* which means "parched" or "great heat."

The version of the prayer before the talmudic sages[38] had, simply, *shanah geshumah u-shechunah,* "a year of rain and drought." The talmudists were puzzled by such a reading, and immediately asked whether drought was a benefit that the High Priest should be praying for! Their answer was that the phrase should be explained in the sense of a plea that *im shechunah tehei geshumah*—"*if* there is drought, let the rains come." The version in our prayer book, *shanah telulah u-geshumah im schechunah,* "a year of dew and rain, *if parched,*" is a later, edited version, reflecting that talmudic clarification.

There are problems, however, with both the talmudic version as well as with that of our prayer book. In the former case, the very reference to *drought* at all may be questioned. Why not simply request "a year of rain"? After all, if that is forthcoming, then there won't be any drought! The version in our *machzor* is similarly problematic, for if the object of the prayer is to compensate for drought, then it is *rain* that is required, not *dew*!

The riddle is solved, however, by reference to the *Midrash Tanchuma,* which has the variant reading *shanah DESHUNAH geshumah u-telulah,* "that this may be a year of *fruitfulness,* with rain and dew [in their respective seasons]." This gives a most appropriate reading, since rain is required in winter to prepare the ground for the grain's development, and the nightly dew is needed in summer, to nurture the fruits of the fields. We may assume, therefore, that this straightforward reading was the original one, and that, in the course of transmission, the word *deshunah* became corrupted into *shechunah*!

The High Priestly reference to *shenat massa u-matan,* "a year of trading and merchandise," owes its origin, according to B. Z. Luria,[39] to the period following the Hasmonean rulers, John Hyrcanus and Alexander Yannai (second to first centuries B.C.E.), when Judea attained a place of major international mercantile importance, exploiting to the full the strategic control of the major trade routes that its position along the western flank of the fertile crescent afforded it, as well as its ability to levy taxes on, and sell import and export licenses to, all those utilizing the major ports along the coast of the Mediterranean. Many Judeans became involved in, and enriched by, the new trading opportunities and service industries that this endeavor opened up. Since prayer both reflects and responds to the needs and crises of life, a prayer for this prosperity to continue was as much in the interest of the High Priest and his cohorts—dependent as they were for their livelihood upon the largess of the community—as it was for the trading community itself.

The talmudic version of the High Priest's prayer[40] adds a strange plea that was not incorporated into the later liturgy: *Shanah shelo yaadi avid shultan midebet yehudah*—"a year wherein the wielder of supreme authority shall not be removed from the house of Judah." It has been plausibly suggested[41] that it was the early Pharisaic Rabbis who put this disclaimer into the mouth of the High Priest. It had been the unpardonable sin of the Hasmonean High Priestly dynasty that they usurped the prerogative of the tribe of Judah (and the lineage of King David in particular), by declaring themselves as kings. Hence, the later Pharisaic Rabbis, within whose theology the future (messianic) restoration of the House of David occupied an important position, imposed this disclaimer upon the High Priest on this most sacred day of the year. In the full flush of his spiritual glory, having just emerged safely from the closest proximity to the deity permitted to any man, he was brought down to earth by this formula, which made him acknowledge publicly the limitations of his authority and that of his priestly tribe.

Bearing in mind the period to which we have attributed some early elements of this prayer—that of the second to first centuries B.C.E.—we may well look to the period of Simeon ben Shatach's leadership of the (Pharisaic) Sanhedrin for the origin of this particular plea.

During the reigns of John Hyrcanus and Alexander Yannai the majority of the Sanhedrin members belonged to the Sadducean party. This was the party of the wealthy, patrician classes, to which the priestly and High Priestly fraternity was affiliated. Their influence in the country at that time was paramount,[42] and a purge of Pharisaic leaders and teachers ensued, when many were executed. Those who could, fled into exile, with the result that Torah learning and religious practice reached their lowest ebb—a situation that "made the world desolate," in the words of the Talmud.[43]

It was Simeon ben Shatach's towering personal authority that succeeded in reversing this situation. Under his patriarchate a reconciliation with the Hasmonean King Alexander Yannai was achieved, the Pharisaic scholars returned, their influence in the Sanhedrin grew rapidly, and "the crown of the Torah was restored to its former glory."[44]

It was clearly at that period, when the Pharisaic Sanhedrin was able to sweep away its Sadducean counterpart, and control endemic Sadducean tendencies within the influential priestly and High Priestly families, that such a public disclaimer was imposed by Simeon. By this disclaimer, the High Priest was affirming that his role was purely that of minister to God, relaying the prayers and administering the sacrifices of Israel to their Father in Heaven, and not that of *avid shultan* (wielder of temporal leadership), as the talmudic version of the prayer calls it.

Although it had been the heroic exploits of the early Hasmonean High Priests that had won back for the Judeans their independence, they had no right to flout the biblical propriety, that "the ruler's staff shall not depart from Judah" (Genesis 49:10). Each year, therefore, from the days of Simeon ben Shatach onward, the most illustrious representative of the priesthood was made to promise never to repeat that situation, but to affirm loyalty to the tribe of Judah, and, implicitly, to the royal house of David.

The Midrash preserves a much weaker version of this prayer: "And let not Israel impose authority, one upon the other."[45] This may well have been regarded as a more appropriate formulation in the period following the Roman invasion of Judea (63 B.C.E.), since it would surely have been regarded by Rome as a seditious sentiment to publicly acclaim the "supreme authority of the house of Judah."

Omitted in our liturgical formulation of the High Priest's prayer, but included in the versions of both the Babylonian and Palestinian *Talmudim*, as well as in the midrashic version, is a plea: *velo tikanes lefanekha tefillat ovrei derakhim*[46]—"And pay no attention to the prayer of travelers!" The latter naturally pray for the rains to cease so that they can travel unimpeded. This is a selfish plea, obviously uttered only during the rainy period, and there would be absolutely no need for such a prayer in the Middle East outside the rainy period! "Rain in its season" is, of course, a divine blessing and a precious commodity. Understandably, the High Priest had no compunction about asking God to disregard those who would put their own convenience before the common good.

The final plea, for the safety of people inhabiting the Sharon Plain—"that their houses may not become their graves"—is popularly explained as having been necessitated by the fact that the heavy rains made the clay soil in that area unsuitable for building upon.[47] The water would collect upon the roofs of the houses, and eventually seep through the walls, rotting them and causing the roofs to collapse inward upon the heads of the inhabitants.

An alternative theory has been propounded, however,[48] that discounts the problem of heavy rains. These were, after all, something to be desired, blessings that were even included in the High Priest's prayer! In any case, if the rains did affect housing, there was no reason why this could not be regularly monitored and inspected, providing ample opportunity for appropriate preventive action to be taken, such as the regular sweeping away of the water collection on the roof, and the replacement or strengthening of any rotting timbers! There was certainly no reason for people to be caught unawares, to the extent that they required the problem to be raised by the High Priest in his special personal prayer on this holiest of days.

The problem, it is suggested, was rather that of sudden and devastating earthquakes, which were not unknown in that Sharon area. Josephus[49] records a quake, unprecedented in its violence, as having occurred in 31 B.C.E., during which 3,000 people were buried under the debris of their homes. Another such quake was recorded in the area of Lydda and Emmaus, around the year 130 C.E.[50] Such a peremptory and violent visitation would seem to accord more with the sentiment of the prayer: "that their homes do not become their graves."

סְלִיחוֹת
Penitential Prayers

Although, as early as the ninth century, the distinguished leader of Babylonian Jewry and pioneering authority on our liturgy, Rav Amram Gaon, declared the *selichot* to be an obligatory part of the Day of Atonement service, they have somehow failed to retain their status in the popular imagination, and, during the past century, have even suffered omission in a number of Ashkenazi communities. This has been blamed either upon *chazanim* drawing out the service in such a way as to leave no time for recitation of *selichot* or on printers who, because of varying customs governing their recitation, omitted them from their editions, apart from a reference to the fact that "*selichot* are recited here according to the custom of the particular community."[51]

Selichot are prayers for forgiveness recited in the *Amidah* as a prelude to the *Vidduy* (confession). They are woven around the "Thirteen Attributes"[52] of divine mercy, on the basis of a talmudic tradition that "there is a divine promise that no prayer in which these Thirteen Attributes are invoked will fall on deaf ears."[53]

Originally the *selichot* comprised only biblical verses on the theme of forgiveness, which were said by the *chazan* before the congregational recitation of the Thirteen Attributes. From the tenth century a special genre of *piyyut* grew up, with compositions especially made for insertion into this section of the service. Three distinct types of *selichot* were established: *Tokheichah* ("Rebuke")—drawing attention to our guilt, worthlessness, sorry plight, and desperate need for mercy and redemption; *Akeidah* ("Binding")—describing the binding of Isaac, and imploring God to grant forgiveness on the merit of that unique act of faith, love, and obedience; and *Gezeirah* ("Decree")—recalling the tragic historical circumstances accompanying the various decrees of persecution inflicted upon our distinguished sages and communities.

Of the hundreds of *selichot* written under these three categories, it was inevitable that different communities developed a preference for particular compositions. Some communities were even known to vary their choice each year, until, in the course of time, certain compositions became favorites and won a permanent place. Our Polish, Ashkenazi selection comprises two *Tokheichot* (*Eyn Peh Lehashiv* and *Aniy Hu Ha-shoeil*), one *Akeidah* (*Et Ha-brit Ve-et Ha-Chesed*), and one *Gezeirah* (*Eileh Ezkerah*).

The second *Tokheichah* serves also as a personal devotional plea for the *chazan*—a common introductory feature for separate major components within a service.[54] This should logically have been placed first, however, in the order of *selichot*. The *Akeidah* is alphabetically constructed according to four-line rhyming stanzas, with five words in each line. The alphabetic arrangement is interesting; the first phrases follow the normal alphabetical progression from *alef*, whereas the second phrases, which complete each couplet, commence with *lammed* and progress alphabetically from that letter. To mark the concluding stanza, the letters *kaf* and *tav* are employed twice, after which the author weaves his name—*Meir bar Yitzchak Meir*—into the acrostic.

אֵלֶּה אֶזְכְּרָה
These Things I Do Remember

This is one of the most poignant *selichot* of the *Gezeirah* type, describing the frightful persecution inflicted upon the Jewish community of Palestine and its rabbinic luminaries by the Roman emperor, Hadrian. Having crushed the Bar Kochba revolt (132–135 C.E.), Hadrian imposed unacceptable edicts outlawing the study of Torah, the practice of circumcision, and other basic observances, on pain of death. Many great rabbis and teachers suffered martyrdom as a result of their heroic defiance of the edicts, though no talmudic source records the fact of these particular leaders being tried and executed at *one and the same time*, nor is the term *Ten Martyrs* found anywhere in the talmudic literature. In a minor work of the talmudic period, the *Midrash of Lamentations*, a list of martyrs of the period is given, which happens to include ten; but the term "Ten Martyrs" is not highlighted. It is only in the little known Midrash, *Eileh Ezkerah*, that the term is used together with the rationale of their plight, namely by reason of its association with the need to expiate the crime of the selling of Joseph.

Graphic descriptions of the torture of Rabbis Akivah, Hananiah ben Teradyon, and Judah ben Bava are given in the Talmud, but nowhere are they associated with any ten martyrs who perished at one and the same time! If any of the other scholars referred to had truly met a martyr's death it would certainly have been chronicled, and if such an unprecedented demonstration of martyrdom of the greatest sages of the age had occurred on one day it would have been inconceivable for the Talmud to have omitted reference to it. The Talmud never misses an opportunity to draw attention to days of particular significance in the religious life of Palestinian Jewry, such as the events that occurred on "the day" when they deposed Rabban Gamliel, or on "that day" when the Shammaites gained a majority in the Sanhedrin and pushed through some eighteen extreme measures calculated to sour and sever relations between Jews and Gentiles. The martyrdom of ten sages in one day would undoubtedly have called for a full talmudic description of such a multiple tragedy, with some attempt to make theological sense of its implications. For it to have been completely ignored in the Talmud, only to surface in a minor midrash, casts the greatest doubt on its historicity.

There are also other conflicting traditions regarding the names of some of those martyrs and the circumstances of their deaths. Rabban Shimon ben Gamliel, for example, lived before the destruction of the Temple in the year 70 C.E. He can hardly have been associated, therefore, with the other martyrs of that group who perished during the Hadrianic persecutions of 135 C.E.! All this leads to the inevitable conclusion that it is legend that is responsible for having created this particular dramatic situation, rather than historical fact.

This period of heroic resistance to the Roman conquerors inspired the creation of several midrashic legends and liturgical poems. The well-known lament *Arzei Ha-Levanon*, recited on the Fast of *Av*, is based upon the same theme, and our *Eileh Ezkerah* is actually prescribed in the Sephardic liturgy for recitation on that fast day!

Ever since the first great rebellion, which culminated in the siege of Jerusalem and the destruction of the Temple (70 C.E.), the Jews made several desperate attempts to throw off the Roman yoke. With each successive failure the Romans reserved their most intense vengeance for the great leaders of Jewry.

Our author, in order to heighten the dramatic effect, has merely condensed martyrological traditions associated with the great rebellion, the uprising against Trajan (117 C.E.), and those surrounding the Hadrianic persecutions, into one climactic event concerning ten martyrs.

It has been suggested that the inspiration for the idea of the number ten came from a circle of mystics of the talmudic period who, in their attempt to link cause and effect, sin and its expiation, depicted the martyrdom of the ten great sages as an effect of the sin of Jacob's ten sons in selling their brother Joseph into slavery, which episode is referred to in the opening section of the composition.

The poet depicts the Roman tyrant as adducing an incontrovertible argument against the sages of his day to support his contention that they should stand trial for the crime of Joseph's brothers in selling them "for the price of a pair of shoes."[55] The irony underlying this charge is self-evident: in the absence of any valid and contemporary justification for oppression of the Jew, the anti-Semite has no compunction in fabricating a charge, even if it requires him to go back nearly two thousand years for some evidence of guilt! The implication of this polemical "midrash" on Jewish guilt for the crucifixion would not have been lost on medieval Jewry.

Given that we have no hard evidence to support the historicity of the martyrdom of ten talmudic sages, we are faced with having to seek some explanation of the germ of such an idea. Solomon Zeitlin[56] traces its origin to the extra-Canonical Book of Jubilees, written around 150 B.C.E., a book that exercised a great influence on some Pharisaic brotherhoods immersed in messianic preoccupations and apocalyptic expectations. It was the theology of this sect that, in turn, helped to foster the rise of Christianity, although it also left traces on Jewish thought, as was the case with this legend of the ten martyrs.

The author of the Book of Jubilees writes that the Day of Atonement was fixed on the tenth day of the seventh month because that was the date when the children of Jacob dipped their brother Joseph's coat into the blood of the kid they had slaughtered. That sin was never forgiven, for which reason,

> it was ordained that their offspring, the Children of Israel, should afflict themselves on that day that their ancestors brought to their father Jacob the news that made him grieve. Therefore must they atone for themselves with a young goat on the tenth day of the seventh month, once a year for their sin . . . and for all their transgressions and errors.

It is now easy to see how this interpretation of the significance of the Day of Atonement gave birth to the legend of the death of *ten* martyrs, in expiation for the sin of the ten brothers of Joseph, and how our *Eileh Ezkerah* elegy came to be written under the influence of that book and its ideas. Zeitlin rightly stresses that the concept of each generation having to expiate for the sin of a previous generation was at sharp variance with mainstream Pharisaic-talmudic theology, which stressed that every person was responsible for his own sins and that children could not suffer for the sins of their ancestors.

But that is not the only sin that the apocalyptic literature required to be expiated in every generation. Adam's "Original Sin" was another, and another work of that genre, the second Book of Baruch, asserts that the Original Sin can only be wiped away by the blood of a sinless person who shall die for the salvation of the ungodly. Thus, we see clearly precisely from where Christianity drew its theology. And we also see the origin of the motif, in our *Eileh Ezkerah* elegy, of ten sinless people, the greatest sages of Jewish history, having to die together in order to expiate the sin of the children of Jacob. No wonder the talmudic sages rejected such a legend. Not only were they aware of its historical inaccuracy, but they were also totally opposed to allowing it to stand even as a midrashic or legendary tradition. Its entire theology was totally anathema to the concept of reward and punishment, sin and personal atonement, which the talmudic sages had inherited.

Nevertheless, the Holy Land was a small country, and the ideas of the books of Jubilees and Baruch did infiltrate mainstream rabbinic circles, ultimately encroaching into midrashic traditions and even the poetry of the synagogue and the liturgy of the holiest day of the year!

Asarah Harugei Malkhut—The Ten Martyrs

The ten sages whose deaths are chronicled in this elegy were all giants of the talmudic period who made unique contributions not only to the evolution of Jewish law, but also to the fostering of a resolute and heroic defense of the freedom of worship and the human rights that the modern-day free world so takes for granted. In challenging the oppressive regime of Rome, these leading sages were following in the footsteps of the Maccabees who, some two and a half centuries earlier, had taken on the might of Greece in order to resist the pagan onslaught of Hellenism and to secure the religious independence of the Jewish people.

It is not surprising therefore, that, inspired by such a heroic tradition, Jews down the ages have succeeded in maintaining their religious integrity in the face of the determined efforts—of the daughter religions in particular—to compromise it, and to remove every vestige of Judaism, its religious practitioners, and, in the Nazi era, each and every one of its adherents.

Entire books have been written on almost every one of the ten martyrs. We must content ourselves with highlighting just a few biographical details pertaining to the personality and unique contribution of each one.

Rabbi Ishmael, the High Priest

Rabbi Ishmael is described here as a High Priest. However, we have no evidence of any High Priest bearing the name Ishmael in the final decade of the Temple's existence (circa 60–70 C.E.). Furthermore, for him to have suffered martyrdom around 135 C.E., he would have had to have been an exceedingly young man to have reached that position, and yet to have lived on a further sixty-five years!

Indeed, one talmudic tradition describes him as a child, taken captive to Rome, at the time of the destruction of the Temple. It is related that Rabbi Joshua, on a mission to ransom Jewish captives after the great rebellion, was told that there was to be found in the central jail a little boy with beautiful eyes, curly hair, and very good looks. The rabbi went and stood outside the gate of the jail, lamenting the desperate situation of the numerous captives. He cried out, with a verse from Isaiah 42:24, *Who has given Jacob over to plunderers, and Israel to robbers?* Thereupon, that child, Ishmael, called out to him, by way of response, the continuation of the Isaiah verse: *It was the Lord, because we sinned against Him, and would not walk in His ways nor be obedient to His law.* Rabbi Joshua immediately proclaimed his conviction that, "this child is destined to be a great teacher in Israel. I shall not depart before redeeming him at whatever the price![57] He did so, and nurtured his young protégé to become the pioneer of a new approach to the hermeneutical interpretation of the Torah text.

Ishmael was a close colleague of Rabbi Akivah, and yet adopted principles of biblical interpretation that were at variance with Akivah's. They both founded *yeshivot*, to promote their differing approaches, and a number of our standard midrashim emanate from their respective academies. He expanded Hillel's seven rules of biblical interpretation, to a comprehensive system of "thirteen principles" (*Shelosh esrei middot*), as an indispensable guide to the halakhic process of interpreting, applying, and developing the law. So fundamental and well known were these principles that they made their way into the daily prayers as the natural choice for a study passage that people knew by heart and could recite in order to fulfill the *mitzvah* of learning as a prelude to prayer.

Ishmael felt deeply the loss of the Temple, and he once commented that, "in commemoration of that tragedy, we should really abstain forthwith from eating meat or drinking wine; however, we do not impose upon the community any stringencies that the majority cannot bear."[58] That sympathetic principle, combined with a second one, mentioned in the same context—"Do not forever reprove Israel for her transgressions; better she should sin in ignorance than consciously"—contributed greatly to the humanity of Jewish law, and its consistent rejection of bigotry and smug self-righteousness.

Rabban Shimon ben Gamliel

Shimon ben Gamliel was brought out to be executed together with Rabbi Ishmael. The latter begged the executioner to take his life first, so that he would be spared the anguish of witnessing the death of "one who ministered to Him that dwells above." Lots were drawn, and, indeed, his wish was fulfilled.

Shimon was the *Nasi* (Patriarch), head of the Sanhedrin, the supreme Jewish legislature, as well as political leader of Judea in that most stressful period that witnessed the destruction of the Temple. He was the fourth patriarch after Hillel, a leader of the Bet Hillel, the school of thought that adopted a more lenient approach to Jewish law, and, following Hillel's political philosophy, he was known as a moderate, favoring diplomacy in dealing with Rome, rather than confrontation. Indeed, one tradition—obviously discounted by our author—has it that he was assassinated by members of the Jewish zealot group who were agitating and preparing at that time for armed resistance.

The greatest compliments are those grudgingly proffered by one's enemies, rather than the gushing tributes of one's friends. It is highly significant, therefore, that Josephus, the renegade historian, and bitter opponent of Shimon, nevertheless referred to him as "a man endowed with the greatest intelligence and judgment, who, by his genius, could singlehandedly resolve a diplomatic impasse."[59]

Notwithstanding his towering authority, he was the most humble of men, and never gave a thought to his dignity when, at the annual *Simchat Bet Ha-Sho'evah* celebrations at the Temple on the festival of *Sukkot*, he would launch himself into the spirit of the occasion by entertaining all and sundry. His agility in balancing eight lit torches, without a single one falling from his hand, while he danced around the Temple courts, as well as his unmatched ability to perform *kidah* (a form of full-stretch bodily prostration, leaning on thumbs, followed by a backward lunge to bring oneself into an upright, standing position) is hailed and recorded for posterity in the *Tosefta*.[60]

For all that, when the dignity and traditional authority of the office of Patriarch was at stake, he did not flinch from bending colleagues and community to it. To that end, he introduced a measure that was singularly unpopular with the senior echelons of his colleagues. Hitherto, when any of the three senior judges of the Sanhedrin—himself, Rabbi Meir, and Rabbi Natan—entered, all stood up and greeted them in the same manner. Gamliel, to boost the status of his office at a difficult period when it was necessary to vest clear authority in the office of *Nasi*, took advantage one day of the absence of his two colleagues from the academy to institute a clear distinction in the deference to be shown to his office. This so upset Rabbi Meir and Rabbi Natan that they conspired to have Rabban Shimon deposed from office.

They were frustrated in their plan, however, and the halakhic authority of the *Nasi* was not impaired. Quite the contrary. The Talmud establishes the principle that, "wherever Shimon ben Gamliel gives a ruling in the Mishnah, the *halakhah* follows his view."[61]

Rabbi Akivah

Akivah is among the most well known and revered names in rabbinic literature, and regarded as the greatest sage ever to arise in Israel. His meteoric rise to scholarship and greatness is one of the most romantic of the talmudic biographies.

Akivah grew up as an illiterate shepherd on the estate of one of the wealthiest landowners, Kalba Savua. He was about forty years of age when his master's daughter, Rachel, fell in love with him. However, since she admired learning, her acceptance of his marriage proposal was conditional upon his promising to go away and study at a *yeshivah*. They betrothed secretly, and when Kalba Savua heard of it, he disinherited his daughter. They subsequently married and lived in great poverty.

Rachel still insisted that Akivah go off to study, and he remained away for twelve years, studying under the leading sages of the day, Rabbis Eliezer and Joshua. On returning home an ordained teacher, he overheard someone telling his wife that her faithfulness to her long-absent husband went beyond what was expected. Rachel replied, "If he consulted me, I would recommend that he stay at college a further twelve years!" Akivah took her at her word; returned for a further period, and became the most distinguished sage of his day.

On his return to his hometown, accompanied by twenty-four thousand disciples, Rachel went out to join the throng that had come out to greet him. As she made to approach Akivah, some of his disciples barred her way. Akivah immediately called out to them, "Leave her alone, mine [i.e., my acquisition of Torah] and yours is hers!" Needless to say, his father-in-law deeply regretted his early act of hastiness, and he made over to Akivah a half of his wealth![62]

It is, perhaps, in the light of his own experience, of romance being a most powerful stimulus to learning and spirituality, that we can explain why it is that, although most of his colleagues were uneasy about accepting the erotic sentiments of the book of *Shir Ha-Shirim* (Song of Songs) into the canon of sacred literature, Akivah declared vehemently that "if all the other biblical books are holy, *Shir Ha-Shirim* is the zenith of holiness."

Akivah's originality in applying his principles in order to expand and develop the *halakhah* is graphically described in a quaint midrash. This depicts the arrival of Moses in paradise where he found God designing the artistic flourishes, or "crowns" (*taggin*), that are placed above seven particular letters of the Torah wherever they occur. Moses asked God what the object of those flourishes was, to which God replied that at some time in the future a great man would arise in Israel, by the name of Akivah ben Joseph, and he would construct mountains of new interpretation and legislation out of each and every new flourish! Moses begged to be given a glimpse of that giant of Torah, and God transported him into the future, and into Akivah's academy.

Moses sat and listened to Akivah expounding, and soon realized that he could not understand any of the principles and terms with which the sages were operating, so dramatically had the Torah been developed and applied since Moses' day. Moses became depressed at his own inability to comprehend, when suddenly he pricked up his ears. A student was pressing Rabbi Akivah to reveal the precise origin of a particular concept. Akivah answered: "Indeed, this is not something we are able to explain, but we must accept it as *a law from our teacher, Moses, from Sinai*." Immediately, says the Talmud, Moses' spirit lifted!

The passage continues that Moses begged God, that, having shown him Akivah's Torah, he should also show him that sage's reward. God thereupon showed Moses a vision of Roman soldiers tearing Akivah's flesh with iron combs. Said Moses: *Zo Torah ve-zo sekharah?*—"Is this the reward offered to those who master the Torah?" God curtly replied: "Moses, be silent. This is my considered plan!"[63]

The savagery of the Roman repressions was so great, around the year 134 C.E., particularly the decree forbidding both the study and practice of Judaism, that, at the age of ninety-five, Akivah displayed unique moral courage and defied the imperial decree by continuing to teach his disciples in public, knowing full well that he was condemning himself to death.

While suffering a lingering death, he noticed the dawn breaking, and commenced the recitation of the *Shema*. A look of joyful serenity came over his face. When asked to explain how he could smile in such circumstances, he answered:

> because something that has troubled me all my life has just become clear. In the *Shema* I have just uttered we say that we must love the Lord our God with all our heart, all our soul, and all our might. I understand the idea of loving God with all our heart. I also understand the meaning of loving Him with all our might, that is with our wealth, that gives us might, power, and authority. But I never understood the meaning or application of loving Him with all our soul. Now, at this fateful moment, I understand its import for the first time. It means, even when He is taking away our soul, when we are forfeiting our life!

And he died as he reached the words, *Ha-Shem echad*—"The Lord is One."[64]

Rabbi Hananiah ben Teradyon

Rabbi Hananiah headed a *yeshivah* in Sikhnin in lower Galilee, and served as the head of the *Bet Din* in that town. He was especially active in raising funds for charity, to the extent that he was identified as the ideal type of custodian. Hence the talmudic maxim, "A person should not put money into a charity box unless it is under the supervision of someone like Rabbi Hananiah ben Teradyon."

While he was undoubtedly a great talmudist, only a few of his halakhic decisions and his midrashic interpretations have been preserved in the Talmud. One famous quotation of his, that has been preserved, is his statement in *Pirkei Avot* that whenever two or more people sit together, they are obliged to discuss Torah, and that if they do not do so, it is a *moshav leitzim*, "a gathering of scoffers." Conversely, "when two sit together and do discuss Torah, the divine presence dwells among them."[65]

It was that total immersion in Torah that, as in the case of Rabbi Akivah, was to cost him his life, for, in spite of the warnings of some of his colleagues, he did not heed the decree to desist from teaching Torah, but went out of his way to gather people together as a token of defiance, and to preach publicly to them.

In the terrible reprisals that followed the abortive Bar Kochba revolt (135 C.E.), he was sentenced to be burned at the stake, his wife to be executed, and his daughter to be sold into a brothel. "His execution is described in ghastly detail in the Talmud, but, as in all great martyrdoms, the spiritual triumphs over the material, and the nobility of the man shines out through the horror of his death."[66]

He was apprehended while teaching from a *Sefer Torah*. The soldiers wrapped the scroll around his body and tied him to the stake. They then brought tufts of wool soaked in water and bound them to his heart so that his death would be prolonged. His daughter was made to witness his agony. She cried out, "Father, how can I see you in this situation?" Hananiah replied, "If I was being burned to death alone, indeed, I could not bear it. But now that the *Sefer Torah* accompanies me, I am comforted by the thought that the One who will exact His vengeance for the fate of the Torah will exact vengeance for me also." When his disciples asked him, as his soul was about to depart, what he could see, he replied, "I see the parchment being burnt, but the holy letters flying heavenward."[67]

His Roman executioner was so overwhelmed by Rabbi Hananiah's faith and courage that he asked the sage what he could do for his own soul if he removed the damp tufts so that he would die quickly. Rabbi Hananiah promised him a heavenly reward, and he agreed. When Hananiah expired, a heavenly voice proclaimed, "Hananiah and his executioner have both been assigned a place in heaven."[68]

Rabbi Chutzpit Ha-Meturgeman

The title *meturgeman* means "mouthpiece," "interpreter," or "translator," connected to the noun *Targum,* which is the name given to the Aramaic *translation* of the Bible.

The office of *meturgeman* evolved in the context of the early synagogue. While the Torah was being read, this official would translate each verse into the Aramaic vernacular for the sake of the uneducated masses who could not understand the pure biblical style of Hebrew. In the course of time, those who served as *meturgeman* began to see their role more as interpreters than mere literal translators, and they embellished their presentations with midrashic comments, illustrations from history, and contemporary applications of the text. Indeed, the origin of the synagogue sermon and the midrashic exegesis can be traced to those early expositions.

But while the latter situation obtained in Palestine, there was a development of that office of *meturgeman* in Babylonia. There, some of the heads of the advanced academies of talmudic learning and legislation availed themselves of a similar kind of "interpreter"—which they dubbed an *Amora*—to help lighten the burden of their lecturing, and leave them more time for private study and research.

The head of the academy, while seated, would transmit to the *meturgeman* in a low voice the basic outline of his lecture, and the principles he was employing in reaching his particular interpretation or decision. The *meturgeman* would then proceed to deliver, in a loud voice, a full-blown discourse, clarifying all aspects of the presentation at a simple and popular level, so that all the students would understand it.

The Chutzpit referred to in our elegy was the *meturgeman* of the *nasi,* the patriarch of Palestine, Rabban Shimon ben Gamliel, whose fate he shared. On account of his total recall of all his mentor's teachings and interpretations, which he was forever quoting, he is referred to in the Talmud as, "the mouth that utters pearls." But he was clearly not merely an accomplished lecturer and mouthpiece of others, but also a noted halakhist in his own right, for we do find him quoted in the Mishnah (albeit only in one passage[69]) as the author of a halakhic opinion.

He was blessed with longevity, and it was at the age of one hundred and thirty that his life was brought to a cruel end. It is related that, after his execution, permission for burial was withheld, and his body was left exposed in the market place to suffer defilement and to be devoured by ravenous dogs. There is a tradition that it was the traumatic effect of witnessing that end to a saintly and scholarly teacher that caused Rabbi Elisha ben Avuya, one of the leading sages of the period, to become an apostate.[70]

Rabbi Eleazar ben Shamua

Rabbi Eleazar was one of the last generations of Rabbi Akivah's disciples and a transmitter of the traditions of his teacher. Because of the turbulent times, he was unable to obtain his *semikhah* (ordination) from Akivah and had to obtain it at a secret and hurried ceremony at the hands of the venerable sage, Rabbi Judah ben Bava (see below).

After the Hadrianic persecutions were over he seemed to have decided to leave the holy land, for we do not find his name mentioned among the group of scholars who set up a center of Jewish learning at Usha and introduced measures to revive Jewish life and religious practice. One tradition has it that he was on the point of leaving Israel, to join the academy of Rabbi Judah ben Betera at Netzivim, in Babylon, but that, when he reached Zidon, he balked at the thought of leaving Israel, and decided to return. "Residing in Israel," Rabbi Eleazar concluded, "is equivalent to the performance of all the other *mitzvot* of the Torah."[71]

We have no tradition regarding where he took up residence after that. He does appear, however, as a disputant with several colleagues, and we may conjecture, therefore, that he simply became a peripatetic teacher. This would accord with a talmudic statement in the name of Rabbi Judah (Ha-Nasi) that, "when we learned Torah before Rabbi Eleazar ben Shamua, we were so crowded together that there were six of us to every cubit."[72] He was held in the highest esteem and affection by his disciples. This is not surprising when we consider that he was the author of the statement, "Let the honor of your disciples be as dear to you as your own."[73]

Rabbi Chaninah ben Chakhinai

Chaninah was one of Rabbi Akivah's first generation of disciples, studying under him for twelve years at Bnei Brak, where Akivah initiated him into the secret doctrines of mysticism.

Studying away from his wife and family, he never once took a moment off from his Torah studies throughout all those years to return home. It is related that, when he eventually received a message from his wife that his daughter was now of marriageable age and that he should return to arrange matters, he arrived at his hometown, but did not recognize the streets, which had been developed during the years of his absence. He walked to the banks of the river of the town, and sat down. After a while he heard some girls calling to one of their friends, "daughter of Chakhinai, fill your pitcher, and let's be on our way." Only then did he realize that that was his daughter. He followed her to her home, and, when he entered unannounced, it was such a shock for his wife that she collapsed, and Chaninah had to pray to God to revive her![74] Indeed, she is mentioned in the Talmud as the model wife who enables her husband to fulfill himself. On the verse *I shall make for him* [Adam] *a helpmeet to be by him* (Genesis 2:18), the Rabbis say, "If man has real merit, he is provided with a help meet like the wife of Chaninah ben Chakhinai."[75]

The Hadrianic persecutions had such a traumatic effect upon him that from that time onward—he was then twelve years of age—until the day of his death, at the age of ninety-five, he fasted every single day from sunrise to sunset.

Rabbi Yeshevav the Scribe

Though referred to as a scribe, this was by no means his only claim to fame. In fact he was a distinguished colleague of Rabbi Akivah, with whom he disputed—sometimes quite vehemently—on many occasions. He was possessed of a unique depth of feeling and sympathy for the poor, with whom he would share everything he had. Rabbi Akivah was moved to caution him, when on one occasion he was about to disburse a high proportion of his property to the poor. Akivah reminded him that he had a duty to observe the halakhic principle that one could not give away to charity more than a fifth of one's possessions.[76]

During the Hadrianic persecutions he went into hiding at Sephoris with a group of colleagues among whom was Chutzpit the *meturgeman*, but, like the latter, he was apprehended and made to suffer martyrdom. His dying words were a call to his pupils: "Support each other, and love peace and justice."[77]

Rabbi Judah ben Dama

His name is mentioned in later midrashim as one of the ten martyrs, as well as in our elegy. However, most surprisingly, he does not appear—among the several Judahs of the talmudic period—as one of its scholars! There is an *Eleazar* ben Damah who lived at that same period, and who is likewise described as having suffered martyrdom, and it is conjectured that the names have become confused, and that in our text *Judah* has been written instead of *Eleazar*.

Eleazar ben Dama was a distinguished master of Torah, and on that basis he consulted his colleagues on the appropriateness of his branching out into the study of Greek philosophy. By way of reply, his colleagues quoted to him the verse, *This Torah shall not depart from your lips, but you shall meditate therein by day and by night* (Joshua 1:8). They advised him that at that point when it is neither day nor night—if it can be identified—one may study anything extraneous to Torah!

Rabbi Judah ben Bava

Rabbi Judah was regarded as one of the most pious men in the entire talmudic period. The only transgression his colleagues credited him with was his violation of the prohibition against rearing small cattle in the land of Israel, because of the damage to plants that those omnivorous animals did. Judah of necessity disregarded this by keeping a goat in his home, because he was an ailing man, probably tubercular, and his doctors had prescribed warm goat's milk for him. All his actions were for the sake of heaven, and tradition has it that whenever the Talmud refers to "a certain *chasid* [pious man]" performing some special act of piety, the reference is to Judah ben Bava.

After the martyrdom of Rabbi Akivah, Judah was especially concerned that the *semikhah*, the uninterrupted chain of rabbinic ordination, should not be brought to an end with the wholesale slaughter of scholars that he rightly feared was imminent. He thereupon set about ordaining some of the most erudite and senior students of the academy. The Talmud gives a graphic account of the dangers attendant upon such an act, and the measures Judah adopted to try to circumvent those dangers:

> May this man be remembered for blessing—Judah ben Bava is his name. When the wicked government decreed that whoever performed ordination and whoever received it should be put to death, and the town wherein it took place should be demolished, what did he do? He went and sat between two great mountains that lay between the two large cities of Usha and Shefaram. There (in that no-man's land) he ordained five scholars. As soon as the Roman scouts spotted them, Judah urged the scholars to flee as fast as they could. "But what about you, master?" they said. "I am as inconsequential to them as a stone that no one even bothers to overturn," he replied. However, the Romans did not leave the place until they had driven three hundred iron spearheads into his body, so that it resembled a sieve.[78]

Rabbi Judah, the last of the ten martyrs, was one of the oldest members of the Yavneh academy, which was *the* spiritual center, and seat of the *Nasi* and the Sanhedrin, during the period following the destruction of the Temple and up to the Hadrianic persecutions (132 C.E.), and at which most of the above sages had studied and taught at some time. The scholars of Yavneh have been described as

> the most brilliant and illustrious governing body the Jewish people ever possessed. Never before or since, have so much erudition and acumen, such a mixture of statesmanship and scholarship, been found in a single group. The assembly of scholars had become a Jewish senate, a far more spiritual replica of the mighty Roman legislature. Judaism . . . had reached the form it was to keep for a thousand years, a sophocracy or government by sages.[79]

Notwithstanding the horrendous persecution meted out to that unique spiritual and legislative fraternity, their executioners failed miserably to quench the eternal flame that those scholars and leaders lit at that period. It was a flame from which innumerable other flames have been lit down the ages, in the form of *yeshivot* and academies of learning wherein their immortal words and inspirational ideas have excited the hearts, challenged the minds, and dug new channels of Torah creativity. They were certainly martyrs in the physical sense. But in another sense they never died. For they live on to the present day and continue to speak to our generation, and to inspire it, as forcefully as they ever did their own.

On Martyrdom

Jewish history is indistinguishable from Jewish martyrology. But there are two distinctly opposite ways of looking at the act of martyrdom, of giving up one's life for a principle. Either one views it as *the* pinnacle of heroism, surrendering oneself for a moral or spiritual cause, impressing, and at the same time shocking, the world, in order to leave behind an ennobling and purifying legacy, or one views it as an act of supreme folly, and argues that absolutely nothing in life can justify the needless surrender of life.

Judaism's legacy of martyrdom ought to convince us that the former argument has wielded far greater influence on the religious psyche of our people. Surely, the doctrine of *Kiddush Ha-Shem*, of sanctifying the name of God, especially in public, in order to demonstrate our unswerving loyalty to God, and our dogged determination to carry out His will in the face of those who are attempting to snuff out any trace of it, should persuade us that, under all circumstances martyrdom is mandated, rather than abject submission.

The truth is, however, that although there is a biblical basis for martyrdom, especially when one is challenged in *public* (that is, in the presence of ten Jews or more)[80] to perform an act of apostasy or defiance of the Torah's cardinal principles—as implied in the verse "And I shall be sanctified among the children of Israel" (Leviticus 22:32)—yet, according to no less an authority than Maimonides, martyrdom is not something that can be expected of everyone. The Torah does not impose punishment upon those who, under duress, find themselves unable to summon that kind of courage, and, instead, perpetrate even the most heinous of crimes in order to save their skins.

Maimonides codifies his view as follows:

> Where one is enjoined to suffer death, rather than transgress,[81] and he commits the transgression, rather than suffer the consequences, he has profaned the divine name. . . . However, since the transgression was committed under duress, he is not punished with lashes, nor, it goes without saying, is he put to death by the court even if, under duress, he committed murder.[82]

Maimonides employed this distinction, between committing an act under duress and committing it willingly, in his famous *Iggeret Ha-Shemad* (Epistle on Martyrdom) that he addressed to the confused community of Fez in the year 1165. A fanatical Islamic sect, the Almohads, seized power, and demanded of the Jews conversion by force. Some Jews refused, and suffered martyrdom. One of those who succumbed to forced conversion asked a rabbinic authority (Maimonides, in his letter, conducts an absolutely devastating *ad hominem* critique of his rabbinic competence, yet he studiously avoids naming him) what his position and Jewish status was now that he had made the required public affirmation of Mohammed as prophet of God. He particularly wanted to know whether he would gain pardon and merit by continuing in secret to perform the *mitzvot* of Judaism. The authority replied that not only was there no merit in such deeds, but, quite the contrary, each and every *mitzvah* he performed would be regarded as an additional sin!

When Maimonides heard of that ruling, and the misery it caused, he immediately set about writing his public letter to the community, demonstrating how that "authority" had criminally erred in the advice he gave, particularly in not taking account of the fact that the many who had converted did so under duress. He concludes his letter with the prayer that the prediction of Jeremiah should be realized when, "In those days and at that time—declares the Lord—the iniquity of Israel shall be sought, and there shall be none; the sins of Judah, and none shall be found; for I shall pardon those that I enabled to survive" (Jeremiah 50:20).[83]

The situation facing the ten martyrs in our composition was clearly one where they felt that they had no such option. It was a situation of *gezerat shemad*,[84] when the Roman government set out to ban the teaching and observance of Judaism altogether. Had the Rabbis not made a courageous last stand, by continuing to teach Torah publicly, and bringing martyrdom upon themselves thereby, the Romans would have been emboldened to take advantage in the future of a simple ruse, namely that of threatening the religious leaders with death in order to get the Jews to comply and abandon their sacred mission. It was only by heroic means that the sages could inspire and encourage their communities to resist, to fight, and to defend their right to practice their religion against all odds. (For commentary on the rest of the *Musaf Amidah*, see pp. 154–163, 100–102.)

10

The Afternoon Service

It is customary on Sabbaths and festivals to commence the *Minchah* service with *Ashrei* and *U-va le-tziyyon goel*. On Yom Kippur these prayers are moved from their usual position to serve as an introduction to the *Neilah* service. The purpose of this is in order that the two *Amidahs* of *Minchah* and *Neilah* should be separated from each other, so as to emphasize the fact that the latter is an independent service.

Reading of the Law and *Haftarah*

Parashat Arayot

Amid the abundance of ritual that characterizes Yom Kippur one can easily lose sight of the fact that it can often be far more difficult to arrive at an appropriate relationship with our fellow man—particularly with members of the opposite sex—than with God. In our relationship with God one ought to be totally uninhibited; in our pursuit of appropriate moral conduct, however, self-control is necessary.

Hence, even on the holiest day of the year man is not allowed to ignore the area where his weak nature is generally most vulnerable, and for this reason the list of forbidden incestuous and adulterous relationships (Leviticus, chapter 18) is read from the Torah.

Another, historical, reason has been offered for the choice of this subject for reading on Yom Kippur. Tradition has it that during the period of the first commonwealth Yom Kippur was a day when a romantic matchmaking ritual was enacted. The young women of marriageable age would dress up in white and dance in the vineyards, inviting the young men to select their life's partner.[1] A portion of the law that draws attention to the prohibited categories of marriage partners (*arayot*) was therefore most appropriate.

While several such pseudohistorical, homiletical, and exegetical theories have been adduced to account for the selection of the *Parashat Arayot* as the Reading of the Law for Yom Kippur afternoon,[2] as well as the selection of Jonah as *Haftarah*, nevertheless the identical rationale may well underlie the choice of both, namely, to draw attention to the moral and spiritual exclusiveness of Israel and the dangers attendant upon her fraternization with the *goyim*. On Yom Kippur the special relationship and historic covenant that exists between God and Israel is a central argument in our plea for mercy. The need to stress our superior moral stature over the nations would certainly have been felt in that context.

What better portion to read, therefore, than *Parashat Arayot*, which highlights in several verses the importance of Israel remaining morally exclusive and adopting a posture of spiritual and social detachment:

> After the doings of the land of Egypt wherein ye dwelt, shall ye not do, and after the doings of the land of Canaan, whither I bring you, shall ye not do; *neither shall ye walk in their statutes*. (Leviticus 18:3)

> Defile not ye yourselves in any of these things: for in all these things *the nations are defiled* which I cast out from before you. (v. 24)

> For all these abominations have the men of the land done that were before you. (v. 27)

> Therefore shall ye keep My charge, that ye do not any of these abominable customs which were done before you. (v. 30)

The inappropriateness of the *Arayot* section as a reading for Yom Kippur afternoon, when forbidden sexual liaisons are furthest from most people's minds, is frequently pointed out. But the message of this Torah Reading is, in fact, identical with that of Jonah. In a word, it is the doctrine of *exclusivism*. Jonah was uncompromising in his efforts to leave the heathens to their own devices and their own fate. His philosophy was that Israel has no interest at all in their spiritual welfare. She has to keep aloof, and to regard them as a historic and contemporary source of defilement.

Jonah is the most passionate proponent of such a blunt, literal exegesis of *Parashat Arayot*. The Rabbis who not only included Jonah in the canon, but also prescribed it for the holiest day of the year as the *Haftarah* accompanying *Parashat Arayot*, clearly viewed them together as a most potent and useful polemical and political demonstration of the principle of religious and national exclusivism. (See below.)

The pathetic attempt of Jonah to flee from his spiritual mission is but a reflection of what most of us do before the memory of Yom Kippur has had time to fade from our minds. Like Jonah, most of us are more interested in our own comfort than in what is happening to our less fortunate fellow human beings. Like Jonah, in times of crisis—as when he was swallowed by the great fish—we plead, pray, and make firm resolve. When deliverance comes, however, we conveniently forget God—at least until the next Yom Kippur!

Jonah's Race to Nineveh

The book of Jonah poses so many problems that it is quite amazing that it earned a place at all in the collection of sacred histories, chronicles, and prophetic orations that gained the *imprimatur* of the Rabbis of the first century to be included in the *Kitvei Ha-Kodesh*, the Holy Scriptures.

None of his other prophetic exhortations has been preserved, other than his prosaic sentence of doom: *In forty days time, Nineveh will be overthrown* (Jonah 3:4), a statement that itself was contradicted by subsequent events.

The one other reference to him occurs in 2 Kings 14:25, in the context of a reference to the King of Israel at that period, Jeroboam II (783–643 B.C.E.): *He restored (Hu heishiv) the borders of Israel, from the approach to Hamath to the sea of the Arabah, according to the word of the Lord, God of Israel, which he spoke by the hand of His servant Jonah, son of Amittai, the prophet, who was from Gath-Hepher*.

The *Midrash Yonah*,[3] in a conscious attempt to link this solitary reference to Jonah with the events of the prophetic book that bears his name, unconvincingly interprets the phrase "he restored" as a reference not to the King but to the prophet! *Hu heishiv*, in the eyes of the Midrash, means "he brought to repentance (*teshuvah*)." This has the benefit of enabling the Midrash to provide an explanation of why Jonah chose, at the outset, to run away from his mission:

> Why did Jonah flee? Since on a previous occasion, when God sent him "to restore Israel's [spiritual] boundaries," his words had a positive effect [as it is written: "He restored the boundaries of Israel . . ."]. When God sent him

> on a subsequent occasion to announce the destruction of Jerusalem, the people repented, so the Holy One, blessed be He, in His abundant mercy, retracted His harsh sentence and did not destroy it; as a result of which the Jews called Jonah a false prophet!

This midrash certainly explains Jonah's unwillingness to assume, for a third time, the mantle of prophet. On the previous two occasions his divinely communicated sentence of destruction had been reversed, as a result of which he himself had become discredited as a prophet of doom. No wonder he was not eager to try again!

But this midrash also accounts for why no record has been preserved of the powerfully impressive prophetic utterances that Jonah must have given, in order to have succeeded in moving Israel to repentance on those two occasions referred to, the second of which even secured the continued existence of Jerusalem and the Temple itself. The averting of such a crisis surely justified full publicity, not total silence!

Even if we are disinclined to accept the authority and authenticity of this late midrashic tradition, the basic problem remains: How was it that a rebellious spirit like Jonah could have been chosen by God in the first place? The inevitable assumption that God must have required an established, experienced, and eloquent prophet, with a proven track record, in order to undertake such a hazardous mission of entering a heathen city and converting it to repentance, in turn provokes the question, Why then do we have no record, in our biblical tradition, of the earlier prophecies and speeches of that necessarily impressive preacher?

The above midrash may well have preserved a tradition that provides an answer to this question, namely, that Jonah was indeed dubbed a "false prophet" by the people of his day. It might have been for a reason similar to the one suggested by the midrash, namely, that some details of his prophetic statements—possibly those containing his own personal and overzealous embellishments of the awesome penalties in store for the wicked—were not subsequently fulfilled, giving an excuse therefore for his enemies (and *which* prophet did not have them?) to brand him in that way. These, and other personal, shortcomings—to which we will presently allude—might account for his unpopularity and why his speeches were not preserved.

Jonah is not presented as a particularly engaging, sociable, or sympathetic personality. It is true that at times of personal crisis he is quite capable of great passion, sensitivity, and grace of language, as is clear from his majestic plea to God from the belly of the fish (chapter 2), but he generally disregards sentiment and speaks in a brusque, concise, and inelegant style. This comes over in his dealings with the sailors (1:9) and when expressing his frustrations to God (4:2–3,8,9). Significantly, he totally ignores God's question, *Do you do well to be so angry?* (4:4), and when a similar question is asked later, *Do you do well to be so angry over the gourd?* (4:9), Jonah does not feel that he owes God the courtesy of an explanation. Instead, he gives vent to a self-vindicatory outburst: *I do well to be angry, even to death.* Viewed in this light, the fact that Jonah does not even see the need to offer any thanksgiving to God for his miraculous rescue from the fish (though he had solemnly promised to offer such sacrifices if delivered: see 2:10) takes on an added significance.

Indeed, the abrupt ending of the book may also be accounted for, given the short-tempered, introversive nature of Jonah. It ends with God asking Jonah a question that is rhetorical to the extent that it is God's final and incontrovertible argument for saving the Ninevites. Yet, in this situation—where Jonah, as much as the Ninevites, is on trial—even God's rhetorical questions call for a *response.* Would we not have expected Jonah at this point to acknowledge that he has been in the wrong all along, and that man must always pursue mercy in the same way as does God? That, surely, is the expected denouement of a story that began with the prophet scorning a mission of mercy, and should have ended with his having embraced it! The abrupt end suggests, however, that Jonah, true to form, simply did not have the grace to acknowledge the error of his ways, or, alternately, he *did* answer God, but his answer was totally inappropriate and too offensive to be recorded!

The abruptness of Jonah's speech is nowhere more in evidence than in the formula of the prophecy announced to Nineveh: *In another forty days, Nineveh will be overthrown* (3:4). This phraseology—a mere five words in the Hebrew—smacks rather of Jonah's authorship than of God's! An examination of all the passages in the Torah where God warns of the consequences of evil, and in the later books when He speaks his warning through prophetic intermediaries, will demonstrate that He never employs such an unqualified, peremptory sentence of doom. The rewards for obedience or repentance are always included (or implied), together with the consequences of continued waywardness. In the very first warning given to Pharaoh it is made clear that, "*if you refuse to let Israel* (my firstborn) *go, then* (viz. only then) *will I slay your firstborn*" (Exodus 4:23)—a form of warning that was repeated in the case of the majority of the ten plagues (see Exodus 7:27; 9:2,17; 10:4), and understood by Pharaoh, by inference, with regard to the rest. The second paragraph of the *Shema,* with its promise of reward for obedience and punishment for disobedience (Deuteronomy 11:13,16), may be regarded as God's favored formulation, indeed as the paradigm.

An assumption that the five-word prophecy of doom was Jonah's, not God's formulation, explains why, although God told Jonah (3:2) to "go to Nineveh and make the proclamation *which I shall give you*," yet nowhere is it stated that God actually gave Jonah a formula of proclamation! Only his journey to Nineveh was "according to the word of the Lord" (v. 3), *not* the message he gave!

Jonah's Subterfuge

Chapter 3, verses 3 and 4, are traditionally translated:

Now Nineveh was an exceeding great city, of three days journey [*mahalakh sheloshah yamim*]. *And Jonah began to enter into the city a day's journey* [*mahalakh yom echad*] *and he proclaimed and said, "Yet forty days and Nineveh will be overthrown."*

This rendering is based on the assumption that the measurements of distance refer to the actual dimensions of the city of Nineveh, namely, that it was such a great city that it took a full three days to walk from one end of it to the other. This leaves unexplained why Jonah uttered his proclamation after having traversed a single day's journey, that is but one-third of the way into the city!

Better sense is made if we assume that the term *mahalakh* ("journey") refers, not to the diameter or length of Nineveh, but to the distance from the point where the prophet stood (after having been spewed out of the fish; 2:11) *in order to reach* Nineveh.

We are told in these verses that it was a full three days journey, thus providing God with plenty of time in which to communicate to Jonah a carefully worded message of impending doom *unless the Ninevites change their ways*. (A parallel to this divine approach of delaying a disclosure for three days is provided by the *Akeidah*, when Abraham was not told the precise mountain that was to be his destination until he actually came across it on the third day.[4]

Jonah, in his typical hasty manner, conjures up another subtle plan to preempt God, in order to avoid having to give a message with a built-in promise of mercy for repentance. Jonah decides to cover that three-day journey in one day, and to arrive there even before God has a chance to transmit His proclamation to the prophet. This, we suggest, is the meaning of verse 4, which we render, "And Jonah began to enter the city *after* but a single day's journey." He had raced pell-mell, and, by having achieved this objective, he was able to utter *his own* prophecy of doom without any built-in conditions.

Only by rendering the verse in this way can we make sense of the opening verb *va-yachel,* "And Jonah *began* to enter the city. . . ." If he had *already penetrated* the city, a distance of a day's journey, the expression "*began to enter*" is hardly appropriate!

If our reconstruction of events is correct, this would explain quite clearly why Jonah was dubbed (on the evidence of the Midrash) a false prophet. He was false because he gave his *own* uncompromising prophecy, hoping thereby that the Ninevites would regard it as a *fait accompli* and be petrified into inaction.

To Jonah's great surprise, God could still achieve His purpose, with the result that Jonah's five words, rather than create mere panic, generated a unique demonstration of penitence.

The episode of the gourd may now be viewed as reflecting God's well-attested method of dealing tit for tat with those who challenge Him. Just as Jonah thought to frustrate God's Will by accelerating the natural, and covering a three-day journey in one day, so did God adopt the identical approach—though with a much more impressive and dramatic employment of the supernatural—by accelerating the growth and decay of that tree, likewise, in the course of a single day!

Jonah's way of responding—or ignoring—God was inexcusable; and his way of communicating with men would have clearly won him few friends. It is not surprising, therefore, that the Midrash should have left us with a tradition that Jonah was called a false prophet. This is possibly a late justification for the fact that none of his earlier speeches have been preserved. And the main reason why this should have happened was nothing more than as a result of the unpopularity of a man who simply could not communicate with others, and was so tightly wrapped up in his own zeal and piety that it nearly strangled him.

Jonah—Exponent of Jewish Exclusivism

In the light of the above, we may well pose the question why, indeed, was the book of Jonah included in the canon of *Kitvei Ha-Kodesh,* sacred literature? To answer this question we have to take account of the prime mover behind the very act of canonization, and the circumstances that motivated its introduction.

It is beyond doubt that Rabban Gamliel of Jabneh played a key role in fixing the canon (circa 90 C.E.), and his purpose thereby was to prevent the infiltration of sectarian, particularly Christian, writings into the Jewish fold. Gamliel's period coincided with the greatest expansion of Christian ideas and the dissemination of the Gospels far and wide. It was such a consideration that prompted Gamliel to introduce a prayer against (sectarian) heretics into the *Amidah,* in order to ensure that the latter could no longer fraternize with the Orthodox faithful in their synagogues, and it was probably the same fear that actually prompted that sage to standardize Jewish liturgy by making the thrice-daily *Amidah* obligatory.

It is not stretching the imagination too far, therefore, to suggest that it was for precisely the same reason that Gamliel, when fixing the Hebrew canon, determined to include the story of Jonah. No more convenient literary tradition could be employed to further the cause of separation between Jew and Gentile than this story, which tells of the lengths to which a prophet went to avoid bringing the Gentile city of Nineveh into proximity with the word of God.

While it is true that Jonah is not shown in a good light in the book itself, it is more than likely that Gamliel's sympathies lay squarely with the prophet. Had Jonah lived in Gamliel's period, when Judaism was sorely threatened by Romans and early Christian sectarians, his legacy of prophetic writings would certainly have been preserved and treasured, and his place in Jewish history, as *the* exponent of Jewish exclusivism would have been definitely assured.

אֵיתָן הִכִּיר אֱמוּנָתֶךָ
The Steadfast Patriarch Discerned Your Truth

This is an alphabetic composition in praise of the patriarchs Abraham and Isaac, the former who discovered God and disseminated faith, and the latter who demonstrated, by the *Akeidah,* the extent to which faith must be exhibited.

The poem is divided into two parts: the first half—until the letter *lammed*—is employed as a poetic accompaniment to the first (*Avot*) blessing of the *Amidah;* the second half of the poem is assigned to the second (*Gevurot*) blessing. As the second section of the poem deals with the theme of life and death, which, at the *Akeidah,* hung in the balance, it is most appropriately related to the subject matter of the second blessing of the *Amidah.*

The line commencing with the letter *tet* states: "He sustained the wayfarers (*ovriym*) with Your own food; he made known to passersby (*shaviym*) that there is none like You." This is an allusion to the midrashic tradition that Abraham would invite passersby into his home, and, after having fed them, he would call upon them to thank the one who provided the food. After their initial surprise that a host should presume to ask his guests for thanks, Abraham would explain that there was a God in heaven who was the true provider. He then proceeded to teach his guests how to recite Grace After Meals.[5]

The phrase *ovriym ve-shaviym* actually means "a wayfarer," "traveler" (lit. "those who pass one way, and who return home"), and it is indisputably in this sense that our poet is applying it. However, when used independently, the words may also mean "transgressors" and "penitents," respectively. The Routledge and Birnbaum translations have mixed the two meanings to give an incorrect rendering of the second phrase.

מְאֻהָב וְיָחִיד לְאִמּוֹ
The Only Child, Beloved of His Mother

This section of the above poem attributes the deliverance of Isaac from the *Akeidah* to the merciful initiative of the angels rather than to the original divine plan. This idea was inspired by the actual biblical account which speaks of "an angel of God from the heavens" calling out to Abraham to stay his hand.[6]

This poetic idea might easily be refuted by reference to the Ethics of the Fathers, which enumerates "the ram selected by Abraham (in place of his son)" as one of ten things that were created on the eve of the very first Sabbath of Creation.[7] According to this tradition the deliverance of Isaac was uppermost in God's mind at the very dawn of Creation.

Such a conflict of ideas will not perplex those familiar with the rich and variegated tapestry of midrashic folklore. Midrash is more a patchwork quilt than an integrated and uniform mosaic. It reflects the highly personal and vivid imagination of the talmudic sages as they dreamed their way back into biblical time to supplement whatever domestic, romantic, social, and spiritual details the biblical chronicle had left to the imagination.

The literal meaning of the line *richafo rachum limromo* is "the Merciful One spirited him [Isaac] away to his heavenly place," an allusion to the midrashic view of Rabbi Judah that Isaac actually died of fright as his father's sword approached his neck. However, when his soul heard the angel's command to Abraham not to touch his son, the soul reentered Isaac's body, and he revived.[8]

The motive underlying this fantastic piece of folklore is to establish the personality of Isaac as an expiatory symbol, an idea reflected in the final line of this poem: "Regard him as if offered in the Temple this day."

אֶרְאֶלִּים בְּשֵׁם תָּם מַמְלִיכִים
Heavenly Beings Acclaim God in the Name of the Perfect Man

Having sung the praises of Abraham and Isaac in the previous composition, this poem completes the picture by highlighting the merit of the third patriarch, Jacob, described in the Torah as "a perfect man [*Tam*] who stayed in the tent."[9]

According to the Midrash, the image of Jacob is engraved on the divine throne.[10] The second line of the poem alludes to this idea, and depicts the angels as flocking to the throne solely to view the beauty of that patriarch's countenance.

"His children are standing like angels this day." According to our Rabbis, on the Day of Atonement Israel stands like angels: free of sin, divorced from any preoccupation with their physical needs, and totally absorbed in the praise of God. The practice of wearing white garments on Yom Kippur is also in order to present ourselves in the guise of angels, to win divine mercy.

The poem embodies an acrostic on the author's name: *Eliyyah biribiy Mordekhay*, Elijah son of Rabbi Mordechai.

אֱמוּנַת אוֹם נוֹטֶרֶת
A People that Preserves Its Faith
יְכַפֵּר וְיִסְלַח
He Will Atone and Forgive
תְּפִלָּתֵנוּ מִמְּעוֹנוֹת
From Your Habitation Accept Our Prayer

These three lines, as printed in our *machzor* editions, appear as brief, independent petitions, with no relation to any poetic compositions. In fact, they each represent the refrain lines of compositions that have been omitted from our editions. A glance at the first line will actually reveal the name acrostic *Elazar* (Kallir): *Ēmunat . . . l̄emaankha āzor . . . z̄aakah r̄etzey*.

מִיכָאֵל מִיָּמִין מְהַלֵּל וְגַבְרִיאֵל
Michael Praises on the Right Hand and Gabriel

This line constitutes the refrain verse of the following composition, *Erelley hod potzchim*, which Routledge and De Sola include, but which Birnbaum has omitted and which ArtScroll has relegated to an appendix at the end of the *machzor*. The refrain was intended to be recited after every fourth line (taken from the angelic vision of Isaiah 6:2–3), which constitutes the end of each stanza. To avoid monotony these were omitted, apart from in the opening and closing stanzas.

Because the Isaiah passage refers to "One angel calling to another" (*ve-kara zeh el zeh*), the poet mentions only two representatives of the angelic hierarchy, Michael and Gabriel. In rabbinic lore there are actually four main categories of angels singing God's praises, the other two being Uriel and Raphael. In the prayers prescribed for recitation before retiring to sleep at night all these categories are petitioned to keep watch over the individual: "In the name of the Lord, the God of Israel, may Michael be at my right hand; Gabriel at my left; before me, Uriel; behind me, Raphael; and above my head the divine presence of God."[11]

כִּי רְכוּבוֹ בָּעֲרָבוֹת
For His Throne Is in the Heavens

This poem is by one of our earliest Palestinian poets, Yannai,[12] and was written as a prelude to the *Kedushah* prayer, which is based upon Isaiah's vision of the heavenly throne. This poem sets out to enlarge Isaiah's rather narrow conception of a heavenly court wherein God's praise is confined. It achieves this through its references to the many celestial realms—all of which are referred to in the Bible—where God's attributes are equally manifested: *aravot* (heavens), *shechakim* (skies), *meonah* (dwelling), *zevul* (habitation), *arafel* (dark regions), *Shemey Shamayim* (highest regions), *Shamayim* (firmament).

In the second part of the *Kedushah* there is a shift of direction from the angelic arena to the earthly domain, wherein man praises and God responds mercifully. To correspond with this in our composition, the poet moves to describe the adoration of God that is expressed here on earth not only by man, but by every element of nature: the waters, soil, trees, mountains, and hills.

11

The *Neilah* Service

On Sabbaths and festivals we recite four services: *Maariv, Shacharit, Musaf,* and *Minchah*. Yom Kippur is the only festival when a fifth service, *Neilah,* is added. In Temple times, however, *Neilah* was recited on certain other occasions, notably on the special fast days instituted by the authorities during periods of drought in order to pray for rain. It also formed part of the order of service recited by the *Maamadot,* the lay fraternities that corresponded to the priestly duty-rotas in the Temple. While the latter were officiating, twice a year for a week at a time, in Jerusalem, the *Maamadot* assembled to conduct a prayer vigil. This included four fast days, on which *Neilah* was added.[1] The Muslim practice of reciting five daily services was almost certainly borrowed from that old Jewish tradition.

Neilah is an abbreviated name. The full name of this service, as mentioned in the *Mishnah,*[2] is *Neilat She'arim,* "closing of the gates," though the precise sense of this term was a matter of dispute in talmudic times. Rav understood it temporally, namely, "the service recited (at sundown) at the time of the closing of the *heavenly* gates. R. Jochanan applied it, in its literal sense, to the service recited at the time of the closing of the gates of the *Temple.*"[3] Maimonides favored Rav's explanation of the term.[4]

The honor of performing the *mitzvah* of opening the Ark (*Petichat Neilah*) is one of the most prized of the whole year. In many communities it was put up for auction, and the highest bidder would frequently present the honor to a worthy elder.

The Spirit of the Hour

The Ark is opened for the repetition of the *Amidah*, and it remains open for the duration of the entire service. The open Ark ensures that the congregation remains standing—an appropriate posture for that most solemn moment when the divine judge is passing His final sentence upon us, and our spiritual exertions reach their zenith. Having spent over ten hours in fasting, it is surprisingly easy to muster the extra strength required to bring Yom Kippur to its climax in this way.

We might have expected the religious and emotional tension of the day to ebb, and the congregational fervor, concentration, and participation to become dissipated, as the final hours of this marathon vigil are played out. But the opposite is very much the case: this final period is the most awe-inspiring of the entire day. As the shadows of dusk deepen into the dark of nightfall, the cumulative effect of the day's spiritual exertion creates a spontaneously rising emotion. Absorption in prayer brings the Jew who has surrendered himself to the spirit of the day to the brink of a mystical union with God. At that point he penetrates the outer forms and structures of the prayers to mold them to his own purpose, and to construct out of them a veritable ladder with which to bridge the gulf between heaven and earth.

The tone of the *Neilah* liturgy admirably suits this mood, for the pivot of the service is an acknowledgment of the acute insignificance of human achievement when contrasted with the glory and unique creative genius of God:

> What are we? What is our life, our piety, our righteousness? What is our salvation, our strength, our might? What shall we say before You, O Lord our God and God of our fathers? Are not all the mighty men as nought before You, men of renown as if they had never lived, wise men as if bereft of knowledge, and men of understanding as if devoid of discretion? For most of their achievements are valueless, and the days of their life vanity in Your sight. Truly, the preeminence of man over the beast is a mere illusion, for all is vanity.

This eclipse of the human ego paves the way, toward the end of *Neilah*, for a crescendo of spiritual effusion, in which cantor and congregation cry out, at the top of their voices, a sevenfold repetition of the affirmation, *Ha-Shem Hu Ha-Elokim* ("The Lord, He is God"). This is no trite attempt at definition. It encapsulates the belief that there is no reality outside of God, and no power or will that He does not control. It is also demonstrative of the highest and deepest recognition that the "I" is not only of no consequence, but that it has been swept away by the flood of "Thou," which has coursed through the individual and collective body of spiritual Israel under the influence and spell of this unique day. It expresses the belief that the curious interplay of agonies and ecstasies that constitute the vagaries of our fate at the hands of divine providence are not arbitrary, that the *Ha Shem* (God as dispenser of mercy) and the *Elokim* (God who exacts justice) are never in conflict, but rather are expressive of a just and perfectly constructed symbiosis, personally created for the benefit and just deserts of each and every one of God's creatures.

מִסּוֹד חֲכָמִים וּנְבוֹנִים
From the Counsel of the Wise and Understanding (see pp. 31–32)

Repetition of the *Amidah* by the *Chazan*
אָב יְדָעֲךָ מִנֹּעַר
The Patriarch Who Knew You from Childhood

This alphabetical acrostic poem, by Eleazar Kallir, is employed here in a rather piecemeal manner, and only as far as the letter *lammed*. In certain Ashkenazi communities of Germany, however, the whole poem was recited. Our tradition has divided up (the first half of) the poem so that its first four lines (until the letter *dalet* in the phrase *degalav lavo*) are employed in the first blessing of the *Amidah*, its second group of four lines (until the letter *chet* in the phrase *chusan berakhah*) supplement the second blessing, and its subsequent four lines (*teva ziv* . . . until *le-eit katz chaz va-yira*) are included in the third blessing.

The poem is a tribute to the faith of the patriarchs, by whose merit Israel now petitions for mercy. According to the poet, Abraham's discovery of God's existence came in his early childhood, a statement derived from the talmudic view[5] that he was then a mere three-year-old. This is based upon the verse "Because [*eikev*] Abraham listened to My voice and kept My commandments" (Genesis 26:5). The numerical value of *eikev* is one hundred and seventy-two, and the verse may therefore be understood as implying that for that period out of the one hundred and seventy-five years of his life[6] he kept God's commandments. Thus, at the age of three he must have already known God, and even at such a tender age he entreated God "to let his descendants enter through this gate (of mercy)."

In the insertion into the second *Amidah* blessing, Isaac is described as "the one called seed of his father" (*ha-nikra la-av zera*), a reference to Genesis 21:12 where God consoles Abraham, at his having to banish his son

Ishmael, by informing him that "through Isaac shall your posterity be proclaimed." The continuation of the line (*ve-nifneh lasur mi-mokshei ra*), "And he turned aside from every evil snare," has been variously explained as referring either to the evil influence of Ishmael[7] or that of the daughters of the Canaanites,[8] or to the episode of King Abimelech, who was planning to abduct his wife Rebecca.[9] The final line of that quatrain (*chusan berakhah baasher zara*), "he was enriched by the blessing on his crops," would seem to support the last interpretation, as, immediately after the restoration of his wife by Abimelech, the Torah states, "And Isaac sowed (*vayizra*) in that land, and found in the same year a hundredfold; and the Lord blessed him" (Genesis 26:12).

שַׁעֲרֵי אַרְמוֹן
Gates of the Temple

This alphabetical poem calls upon God to open the gates speedily to Israel, although it is unclear which particular gates he has in mind: those of heaven, those of the Temple, or both. Again, we recite only the first half of this poem, until the letter *lammed* (*lelo alman*).

קְדוּשָּׁה
Sanctification (see pp. 184–185)
וּבְכֵן תֵּן פַּחְדְּךָ.... אַתָּה בְחַרְתָּנוּ
And Now Impose Your Awe (see pp. 39–40)
וּמִי יַעֲמוֹד חֵטְא.... מְרוּבִּים צָרְכֵי עַמְּךָ
Who Could Stand If You Recorded Sin—Your People's Needs are Many

A glance at the initial letters of each line will reveal that we have represented here only the concluding section of a poem that is constructed out of a reverse alphabetical acrostic pattern. Our composition commences with the letter *vav* and works backward to the letter *alef* (*Az yaalu veyiru be-ruach nedivah*), employing each letter twice for consecutive lines. Following on from the letter *shin* (*Shilum parim sefateinu*) the poet weaves an acrostic on his name, *Shelomoh Ha-Katan,* that is Rabbi Solomon ben Judah Ha-Bavli (tenth century). Solomon hailed from Babylon and appears to have lived for a time in northern Italy before moving to Germany where he fostered poetic activity and founded the great Ashkenazi payetanic tradition.

His poem is a tender plea for acquittal to a God who—in the words of Ezekiel, to which the poem alludes—"does not desire the death of a person but that he returns from his evil ways and lives."[10] It pleads also for an end to the sufferings of Israel and calls for the bestowal of the divine gift of intellectual enlightenment in order to understand the Torah better, and, consequently, to appreciate more fully the ways of God and the mystery of Jewish existence.

The stanzas commencing with the letter *mem* (*Merubim tzorkhei amkha*), until the end of the poem, appear to run on as an essential part of the main composition. In fact they are the second half of a separate poem by Joseph (Bekhor Shor) ben Isaac of Orleans, a twelfth-century northern French Bible commentator, Tosafist, and poet. These stanzas have been tacked on to the previous poem upon which they seem to have been modeled. The differing acrostic pattern of this section is clearly apparent. It is a forward alphabetical acrostic, beginning with two *mem* lines followed by one *nun* line, and maintaining this pattern for alternate letters throughout the poem.

The beginning of this section—*Merubim tzorkhei amkha*—is a quotation from the Talmud,[11] where it appears as the formula of a plea to be recited when in danger of one's life, at the approach of either wild beasts or bandits:

> Master of the Universe,[12] the needs of Your people, Israel, are many and their knowledge slender. May it be Your will to provide for each and every one sufficient for his livelihood . . . and to every individual whatever he is in need of.

It is difficult to understand the precise relevance of this formula to the emergency in question, for it appears more suited to be recited as a prayer for livelihood when in financial straits. Perhaps it was on account of its wider applicability that our poet employed it here as a petition for sustenance in the coming year.

The poet proceeds to lament the fact that the age of the great composers of prayer has long since passed, and, lacking inspiring and eloquent *chazanim* to lead the congregation, we have no means of achieving salvation from our troubles through the medium of fervent prayer.

From the stanza commencing *Kadosh re-eih* to the end of the poem, the author speaks in the first person, clearly adopting the role of a *chazan* offering prayers on behalf of his congregation. It is written in the style of the usual Reader's *reshut* recited at the beginning of the repetition of an *Amidah*. As *Neilah* does not have such a *reshut*, it is conceivable that this section was originally intended to serve that particular purpose.

It will be observed that the Birnbaum and ArtScroll editions intersperse the stanzas of this long composite poem with the *selichot* enumeration of the Thirteen Attributes (*Eil melekh*).

This seems to have been the original practice, which was probably curtailed whenever time was short, since *Neilah* had to be concluded before nightfall. There are still a number of varying traditions regarding the frequency of the recitation of the Thirteen Attributes in this service.

אֶנְקַת מְסַלְדֶיךָ
Let the Cry of Those Who Praise You

This single stanza, of four short phrases, is, in fact, merely the opening verse of a poem, the rest of which was omitted probably in order not to prolong the service. The rest of the poem, which was included in the book of *selichot*, used in Lithuanian communities, bears the author's name-acrostic: *Siylano*. Siylano was the religious leader of the community of Venosa in southern Italy during the ninth century. He was also one of that country's first liturgical poets, disseminating there the traditions of the school of poetry in Palestine, and particularly that of Kallir whose style he clearly emulates.

There is an interesting, though tragic, episode in Siylano's life which is recorded in the famous Chronicle of Achima'az (1034), a fellow countryman and poet. A visiting emissary, from the Jerusalem talmudic academy, gave a sermon in Siylano's synagogue in Venosa. As the visitor could not speak Italian, he supplied Siylano with a copy of his address for him to translate. The emissary later discovered that Siylano had doctored his translation in order to incorporate a vitriolic condemnation of his community. When the former returned to Jerusalem and reported the matter, it was decided to excommunicate Siylano for bringing the Palestinian representatives into disrepute, a situation that could affect the financial support upon which Palestine depended from the Diaspora communities. The ban was later lifted as a mark of gratitude to Siylano for his vigorous support of the rabbinic authorities, through the medium of his poetry, in their struggle against the Karaite heresy.

יִשְׂרָאֵל נוֹשַׁע בַּיְיָ
Israel Has Been Saved by the Lord

Once again our *machzor* quotes here only the opening stanza of a poem written by Shephatyah ben Amittai, ninth-century spiritual leader of Oria in southern Italy.

The penultimate stanza of the poem contains a plea for the destruction of Christian Rome (*Kalei Seir*). This may be related to the anti-Jewish decrees imposed by the Byzantine emperor, Basil I (867–886). Shephatyah was sent to the royal court of Constantinople in order to plead for the decrees to be rescinded. While there, he successfully exorcised an evil spirit from one of the princesses, in appreciation of which a reprieve was granted to his own and four other Italian communities. It is conceivable that this poem, with its opening sentiments "Israel has been saved by the Lord"

(Isaiah 45:17), might have been composed to mark this particular deliverance.

יַחְבִּיאֵנוּ צֵל יָדוֹ
He Will Shelter Us in the Shadow of His Hand

Once again our *machzor* represents here only the opening stanza of a fairly lengthy poem written by Isaac ben Samuel of Dampierre in France, a prominent Tosafist and one of the leading rabbinic authorities in the second half of the twelfth century. He is popularly referred to as *Riy Ha-Zakein* (Rabbi Yitzchak the Elder), and was a disciple of the renowned Rabbi Jacob (*Rabbeinu*) Tam.

The Lithuanian tradition included the whole of his poem in the repetition of the *Musaf Amidah*, whereas our Polish rite borrowed only the opening stanza. This stanza contains an acrostic on his first name *Yitzchak* (*Yachbi'einu Tzeil . . . Chon . . . Kumah*).

יַשְׁמִיעֵנוּ סָלַחְתִּי
Let Us Hear "I Have Forgiven"

This stanza is, again, merely the opening verse of a poem bearing the name acrostic of its author, Solomon ben Samuel. In the late thirteenth century he taught in a *yeshivah* in Acre, which in that period had become a distinguished center of scholarship in Palestine, helped by the arrival of hundreds of rabbis who made their way there after their expulsion from England and France.

Solomon was involved in a bitter controversy with the grandson of Maimonides, David ben Abraham, who held the office of *Nagid*,[13] and who sought to have Solomon excommunicated because of his widely publicized opposition to the teachings of Maimonides.

Solomon probably shared the tragic fate of the Acre community, which suffered massacre in 1291 at the hands of the conquering Mamluks.

יְיָ יְיָ אֵל רַחוּם...
The Lord, the Lord, a God Full of Compassion. . . .
אֶזְכְּרָה אֱלֹהִים וְאֶהֱמָיָה
Lord I Remember, and Am Greatly Amazed

The Thirteen Attributes (*Adonai Adonai . . .*) that introduce the poem *Ezkerah Elohim ve-ehemayah* are intended to serve as a refrain, to be repeated after every four-line stanza. To avoid monotony, as well as to save time, the refrains were omitted other than at the beginning and end.

The initial letters of each stanza are arranged to form the name acrostic *Amitai*, a reference to the Italian poet Amittai ben Shephatyah (late ninth century). The Routledge edition has adopted a revised version of the second stanza, reading, instead of *Middat ha-rachamim aleinu hitgalgeliy*, the phrase *Rachamekha aleinu galgeil*. Other reasons apart for preferring the original text, the revised version impairs the name acrostic by supplanting the letter *mem*.

Amittai was the son of Shephatyah ben Amittai, author of the poem *Yisrael Nosha ba-adonai*.[14] Like his father, whom he succeeded as spiritual leader of Oria in Southern Italy, he wrote poetry to express his reaction to the persecution of his day, and, in particular, that imposed by the Byzantine emperor, Basil I. In this particular poem these feelings reach their apogee, as he laments the fact that "each town stands solid on its site, whereas God's own city is razed as low as the grave."

The final stanza expresses a prayer that God, who responds to the anguish of His people, "should place our tears in a flask that they may be preserved," to ensure that mercy is never withheld, particularly during periods of "cruel decrees."

רַחֵם נָא קְהַל עֲדַת יְשֻׁרוּן
Have Mercy upon the Whole Community of Yeshurun
שַׁעֲרֵי שָׁמַיִם פְּתַח
Open the Gates of Heaven

We have already demonstrated the interrelationship of the *selichot* and the *hoshanot* recited on the festival of Tabernacles.[15] The presence of these two lines among the *selichot* of the *Neilah* service is a further testimony to this; for these represent the opening and closing lines of a *hoshana* composition (*Az ke-eynei avadim el yad adonim*) recited on *Hoshana Rabbah*, the seventh day of Tabernacles. That entire *hoshana* composition was certainly at one time recited during *Neilah*.

אֱלֹהֵינוּ... כִּי אָנוּ עַמֶּךָ
For We Are Your People
אָשַׁמְנוּ
We Have Transgressed (see pp. 157–158)
אַתָּה נוֹתֵן יָד לְפוֹשְׁעִים
You Give the Hand to Transgressors

As early as geonic times it was regarded as inappropriate to recite the detailed confessional of *Al Cheit* in the *Neilah* service. The day has all but passed by now and it can safely be assumed that we have abased ourselves and acknowledged our misdeeds as fully as possible. In its place, therefore, the two compositions *Attah notein yad* and *Attah hivdalta enosh* were introduced, the first of which makes a specific reference to the act of confession: "You have taught us, O Lord our God, to make confession before you of all our iniquities." That *Attah notein yad* stands in place of the detailed confessional, *Al Cheit,* may also be seen from the verse that precedes the former: *halo kol ha-nistarot ve-ha-niglot attah yodeia* ("Do you not know all that is secret or revealed?"). An examination of all the other services wherein *Al Cheit* is recited will confirm that that confessional is always introduced by such a statement affirming God's knowledge of man's secret thoughts as well as his revealed actions.[16] Furthermore, the paragraph that introduces *Al Cheit* always commences with the phrase *Attah yodeia* ("You know"), and it is precisely this phrase that precedes our *Attah notein yad* composition.

From the talmudic description of the *Neilah Amidah*[17] we learn that, at that period, immediately after *Attah ve-chartanu*, the Reader continued with the passage *Mah anu meh chayyeinu,* which is the second half of the composition *Attah notein yad*. We may therefore regard the latter as having been composed as an introduction to the section *Mah anu*.

The phrase *Attah notein yad* is rendered in all our translations as "You reach out your hand," to convey the idea that God attempts to provide opportunity, help, and incentive for transgressors to repent. However, a medieval commentary[18] draws attention to the fact that *yad* may also mean "ability," "freedom of action,"[19] thus conveying the very opposite idea, that God actually enables transgressors to defect from the righteous path by not restricting their freedom of choice. This interpretation calls to mind the famous talmudic maxim: "Whosoever seeks to purify himself finds that heaven assists him; whoever seeks to defile himself finds that heaven opens the door for him to enter (the impure regions)."[20]

There is one statement in this composition—and repeated in the next paragraph—that appears problematic: "You have taught us . . . to make confession before You . . . so that we may cease to perpetrate robbery (*oshek*)." Why was just robbery singled out from all other sins? The answer is that the author was clearly influenced by the talmudic view that desire for money (*chemdat mamon*) is the most potent of all seductions. "The majority sin through theft (i.e., dishonest dealings)," say the Rabbis, "and the rest through sex."[21] The Rabbis further assert that, of all the sins perpetrated by the generation of the flood, "their final fate was only sealed because of the sin of theft."[22]

Since Yom Kippur only atones for sins committed against God, not for those against our fellowman,[23] this reference to theft or dishonesty is an implied call for us to determine to make restitution, or pay compensation, to those of whom we may have taken wrongful financial advantage.

אַתָּה הִבְדַּלְתָּ אֱנוֹשׁ מֵרֹאשׁ
You Set Man Apart from the Beginning

The previous composition ends with a rather deprecatory assessment of human worth: "For man is in no wise superior to the beast, for all is vanity." To ensure that that teaching is not distorted into a philosophy of nihilism, our composition hastens to point out that, for all man's shortcomings (as implied in the word *enosh*),[24] "God set him apart" from the beasts, and endowed him with an intellectual and moral spirit. This is the import of the word *vatakireihu*, "you give him perception."[25]

The second verse—"For who can say to You: 'What are You doing?' Even though man be righteous, what can he give You?"—is difficult to relate to its context, being, in any case, a combination of two totally independent biblical verses.[26] It is probable that, having acknowledged man's uniquely independent intellectual capacity, the author was seeking to ensure that this did not lead to a doctrine of human infallibility. Although God "set man apart (intellectually) from the beginning," man must realize the limitations of his intellect, and must not seek to ask critically of God, "What are You doing?" And just as man must not demand justification of God's actions, so must he realize that "even though man be righteous, what can he give You?" Human righteousness is not a reciprocated gift that man condescends to bestow upon God for His kindnesses to us. Righteousness, in addition to being a Divine and moral imperative, is also a gift to ourselves; it is an augmentation of the quality of living.

Having quoted the verse "What can he [man] give You" (Job 35:7), the author is moved to draw attention to all the gifts bestowed upon us by God. Hence the continuation, *vatitein lanu* ("And you have given to us . . ."), which refers specifically to the gift of Yom Kippur, and, with it, the incomparable benefit of atonement and salvation.

שְׁמַע יִשְׂרָאֵל
Hear, O Israel
בָּרוּךְ שֵׁם כְּבוֹד מַלְכוּתוֹ
Blessed Be the Name of His Glorious Kingdom
יְיָ הוּא הָאֱלֹהִים
The Lord Is God!

For all that we have spent a whole day reciting some very inspiring and interesting poetic compositions, we rightly climax our prayers with two of the most familiar and beloved lines known to the Jew: the first two lines of the *Shema*. Following the recitation of this affirmation of faith in God the Jew sets off each morning to pursue his daily tasks with a commitment to the dignity and sanctity of labor. It gives him a sense of God's presence in every human situation, with the ethical and moral responsibilities that this imposes. These *Shema* verses, when recited each night, also express the Jewish conviction that sleep is not oblivion, but rather the time when the soul experiences its spiritual refreshment: "To him I entrust my spirit, when I sleep and when I awake."[27] Thus, as Yom Kippur reaches its climax, this jubilant public proclamation of the *Shema* gives expression to our feelings of spiritual elation and our confidence that, our prayers having been accepted, God will watch over us by day and by night, and will bless all our activities with success throughout the coming year.

The *Shema* verse is recited but once. Our authorities were sensitive to any repetition of this affirmation of faith in the one God in case it was misconstrued as recognition of the heretical concepts of duality or trinity. The second verse of the *Shema*, which affirms the eternity of God's Kingdom, is repeated three times, corresponding to His sole sovereignty in the past, in the present and in the future.

The final verse—"The Lord is God"—was uttered by the Israelites gathered on Mount Carmel to witness Elijah's vindication of the power of God over the prophets of Baal.[28] The two names of God in this, our shortest, affirmation, represent His twofold manifestations: the first name signifying God's attribute of mercy, the second that of strict justice. We affirm, hereby, that whatever lies in store for us in the coming year—whether blessing or suffering—proceeds from a righteous God who has decided our fate through the most delicate equipoise of those two attributes.

The repetition of this verse seven times was viewed as a mystical farewell to the *Shekhinah* (divine presence) that had descended from the seventh, and highest, heaven in order to be most accessible to Israel. Just as the sevenfold repetition of Psalm 47 on Rosh Hashanah escorted the *Shekhinah* down to the throne of mercy,[29] so, in the same way, we now escort her on her return. In this spirit we sound the *shofar* to accompany the ascending divine presence, in fulfillment of the verse, "God ascends with trumpet sound, the Lord amid the sound of the *shofar*" (Psalm 47:6).

There are also other explanations of the blowing of the shofar at this point. The most popular explanation, rejected however by Maimonides, was that it is to recall the ancient biblical institution of the Jubilee (fiftieth) year, which was inaugurated by a trumpet fanfare at the conclusion of Yom Kippur of the forty-ninth year of the fifty-year agricultural cycle. In the course of time, the calculation of the Jubilee fell into desuetude, and because of the doubt as to which year was, in fact, the Jubilee, it became customary to sound the *shofar* every year.

This interpretation, which links the *shofar* blowing to an institution associated with our ancient homeland, has the benefit of providing, at the same time, an explanation of the final joyful shout, "Next year in Jerusalem"—*Le-shanah ha-baah birushalayim.*

In Retrospect

Throughout Yom Kippur we have sought God, and pursued Him through the liturgical highways and byways, and their spiritual rhythms and cadences. We have tried to see His reflection in the historical reminiscences of the Temple ritual. We have fallen on our knees, made many confessions, and beaten our breasts till they ached in order to prompt Him to clasp us to Himself. And, as the night drew in, and *Neilah* transported us into the celestial heights, we felt that we had succeeded in catching up with our Beloved and in celebrating a joyous and rapturous reunion.

Amid that reunion, we experience the true meaning of His Unity. All the alleged contradictions of human existence—all the conflicts between faith and reason, all the grudges we bear against Him for ambitions unfulfilled, and for the slings and arrows of outrageous personal, family, and national fortune—all fall away, leaving us with a profound sense of peace and tranquillity of spirit, of acceptance and faith. The seemingly contradictory facets of God's treatment of His creatures, as reflected in the respective names of *Ha-Shem* (God of mercy) and *Elokim* (God of strict justice), all coalesce and become indistinguishable. *Ha-Shem hu Ha-Elokim,* "The Lord, He is God." It is all one: justice and mercy, good and evil, wealth and poverty, sickness and health, life and death, reality, eternity.

But Yom Kippur is but a one-day occasion, and there is no further time now for a mystical session of pure contemplation. The piercing sound of the *shofar* has brusquely interrupted such thoughts, to announce to us the termination of the festival and a return to normality.

The day is over. But it leaves behind an imprint, a stir within the Jewish soul that, if it does not dramatically transform us into a community of saints, at least makes us aware of the spiritual challenges that are eternally ours to confront. Yom Kippur teaches us to face up squarely to our personal shortcomings and our responsibilities, and to take into the coming year the realization that we are far from invincible, indeed that we are exceptionally vulnerable. It should have induced us to seek to improve the quality of all our relationships, and to achieve a blessed *at-one-ment* with our Father in Heaven.

Have a sweet year!

Notes

Chapter 1
The Morning Service—First Day

1. On these various prayer rites, see Jeffrey M. Cohen, *Blessed Are You: A Comprehensive Guide to Jewish Prayer* (Northvale, NJ: Jason Aronson, 1993), pp. 59–67.
2. Ibid.
3. See *Sefer Hasidim* (Jerusalem: Mosad HaRav Kook, 1957), p. 136.
4. Ibid., p. 493.
5. On the Cairo *Genizah*, see Jeffrey M. Cohen, op. cit., pp. 72–74.
6. R. Shimon b. Zemach, Responsum no. 160; *Hagahot Maymuni*, Laws of the Sabbath, chap. 30.
7. Daniel 10:5–6; Enoch 87:2; Testament of Levi 8:1.
8. Quoted in Bezalel Naor, "Two types of prayer," *Tradition* 25:3 (Spring 1991): 27.
9. Ibid.
10. Quoted by B. Naor (see n. 8 above), p. 32 n. 6.
11. Joseph B. Soloveitchik, "Redemption, Prayer, Talmud Torah," *Tradition* 17:2 (Spring 1978): 70–71. See also David Hartman, *A Living Covenant* (New York and London: Free Press, 1985), chap. 5.
12. Quoted in Abraham Sperling, *Taamei Ha-Minhagim* (Jerusalem, 1957), p. 20.
13. For a full treatment of the subject of how demonology has influenced marriage customs, see Jacob Z. Lauterbach, "The Ceremony of Breaking a Glass at Weddings," *Hebrew Union College Annual* 1 (1924): 427–466.
14. See his Commentary to *Mishnah Sanhedrin* 10:1.
15. *Pirkei Avot* 2:1.
16. See Talmud, *Makkot* 23b–24a: "David came and reduced the Torah to eleven commandments (since that number are enumerated in Psalm 15). Then came Isaiah who reduced them to six (see Isaiah 33:15). Then came Micah, and reduced them to three (see Micah 6:8). Then came Isaiah once again, and reduced them to two. . . . Then came Habakkuk and reduced them to one, as it is said, "The righteous shall live by his faith" (2:4).
17. Talmud, *Shabbat* 31a.
18. See L. Jacobs, *Principles of the Jewish Faith* (London: Vallentine Mitchell, 1964), pp. 18–25.
19. David Ibn Abi Zimra, *responsum* no. 344, quoted in Jacobs, p. 24.
20. Julius Guttmann, *Philosophies of Judaism*, tr. David W. Silverman (Philadelphia:

Holt, Rinehart and Winston, 1964), p. 179. See Jakob J. Petuchowski, *Theology and Poetry* (London: Littman Library of Jewish Civilisation, RKP, 1978), chap. 2.

21. The full stress is termed a *yated,* while the subsidiary stress followed by a full stress is called a *tenuah.*

22. Bathja Bayer, *Encyclopaedia Judaica* 16:835.

23. See section commencing *Illu fiynu malei shirah* ("Though our mouths were full of song as the sea . . ."), Routledge, p. 79; Birnbaum, p. 16; De Sola p. 96.

24. Its philosophical ideas seem to have been influenced by Saadya Gaon's famous treatise, *Emunot Ve-deiot.*

25. *Midrash, Shochar Tov,* ad loc.; Talmud, *Berakhot* 7a.

26. David Hartman, *A Living Covenant,* pp. 147–148. I acknowledge my reliance upon chapter 6 of this work for its helpfully analytical presentation of Rav Soloveitchik's philosophy.

27. The Spanish and Portuguese (*Sephardic*) Jews pronounced this word as *Kerovotz,* as a result of which a popular interpretation was suggested, explaining it as an acrostic of the initial letters of the verse *K̄ol R̄inah V̄iyeshuah Be-ōholey T̄zaddikim,* "The sound of joyful singing and salvation in the tents of the righteous" (Psalm 118:15).

28. The *piyyutim* evolved in Palestine under the influence of the great literary works of Midrash (third–seventh century C.E.).

29. Composers of *piyyut.*

30. On Yannai, see pp. 26, 84, 204, 253.

31. The term *yotzer* is derived from the concluding formula of the first *Shema* blessing: *Yotzer Ha-meorot.*

32. See his comment on Ecclesiastes 5:1.

33. Maimonides is bitterly critical of the *chazanim* who "are extravagant in praise, fluent, and long-winded in the hymns they compose." See his *Guide for the Perplexed,* ed. M. Friedlander (London: Routledge and Kegan Paul), p. 86.

34. Maimonides, *Guide for the Perplexed,* ed. M. Friedlander, p. 218.

35. See Julius Guttmann, *Philosophies of Judaism,* pp. 172 ff., 351.

36. Talmud, *Rosh Hashanah* 10b.

37. Jer. *Taanit* 2:13 (66a).

38. Cf. *Shulchan Arukh, Orach Chayyim* 581:2.

39. Exodus 32:13.

40. *Bereishit Rabbah* 56:5.

41. Genesis 27:1.

42. See Rashi ad loc.

43. Ezekiel 1:5–7.

44. 1 Samuel 4:4, 2 Samuel 6:2, Isaiah 37:16, Psalm 80:2, et al.

45. Isaiah 6:2.

46. Talmud, *Ketubot* 104a.

47. See G. G. Scholem, *Major Trends in Jewish Mysticism* (London: Thames and Hudson, 1955), pp. 57ff.

48. Rudolph Otto, *The Idea of the Holy* (trans. of *Das Heilige*) (Oxford: Oxford University Press, 1928), chap. 6.

49. See *Mishnah Berakhot* 5:4; Maimonides, *Hilkhot Tefillah* 9:1.

50. Moses Maimonides, Joseph Karo, Jacob Emden, and the Vilna Gaon were all vehemently opposed to the intrusion of *piyyutim*.
51. Genesis 18:25.
52. *Midrash Vayikra Rabbah* 10:1.
53. *Midrash Bereishit Rabbah* 14:6.
54. Talmud, *Rosh Hashanah* 10b. Some commentators explain the final phrase of the poem—"*Tesher* on which she was visited"—as an allusion to the month *Tishri*. Others explain the word as "a gift," the equivalent of *teshurah* (1 Samuel 9:7).
55. Talmud, *Rosh Hashanah* 16a.
56. *Mishnah Berakhot* 9:3.
57. This is precisely how Rashi (Talmud *Sotah* 40a) interprets the obscure phrase *al she-anachnu modim lakh*, found near the end of the *Modim De-rabbanan* prayer, namely, "We give thanks unto you . . . *for having implanted within us the urge to give thanks*."
58. Talmud, *Berakhot* 29a.
59. F. Heiler, *Prayer—History and Psychology*, trans. S. McComb (New York: Galaxy Books, 1958), p. 355.
60. Austrian Jewish novelist (1883–1924), *Paradise, Parables*, 25.
61. It occurs as the conclusion of the blessing *Borei nefashot*, recited after eating various foods and drinks.
62. D. Goldschmidt, *Machzor Leyamim Noraim* (Jerusalem: Koren, 1970), I. 72n.8.
63. Isaiah 42:13.
64. *Midrash Bereishit Rabbah* 58:1.
65. Talmud, *Rosh Hashanah*, 10b.
66. Genesis 21:1.
67. *Midrash Bereishit Rabbah* 53:5.
68. Cf. Judges 13:18.
69. Talmud, *Rosh Hashanah* 8b.
70. Genesis 12:3.
71. Talmud, *Avodah Zarah* 4b.
72. *Mishnah Rosh Hashanah* 4:5.
73. Esther 4:16.
74. See Genesis 31:1.
75. Barukh Halevi Epstein, *Barukh Sheamar* (Tel Aviv: Am Olam, 1979), p. 350.
76. See Nachmanides' commentary to Leviticus 19:2.
77. Routledge, pp. 155–91, Birnbaum, pp. 806–63, De Sola, pp. 44–103.
78. Talmud, *Shabbat* 24a.
79. I. Elbogen, *Monatsschrift*, 55, p. 437.
80. Talmud, *Berakhot* 17a.
81. Talmud, *Berakhot* 39b; *Shabbat* 61a.
82. See L. Jacobs, *Hasidic Prayer* (Schocken, 1978), chap. 9.
83. Talmud, *Arakhin* 10b.
84. Maimonides, *Mishneh Torah*, *Hilkhot Chanukah* 3:6.
85. This phrase occurs in the *Ha-yom harat olam* prayer, recited three times during *Musaf* after the *shofar* blowings that accompany each of the three main sections of *Malkhuyot*, *Zikhronot*, and *Shofarot*.

86. Talmud, *Taanit* 25b.
87. See his *Siddur Avodat Yisrael* (1937) p. 109, and commentary.
88. This issue, of whether or not to recite *Avinu Malkeinu* on a Sabbath, is dealt with in a modern volume of responsa by former Chief Rabbi Ovadia Yoseph (*Yechaveh Daat* [Jerusalem, 1977], I, no. 54, 155–161). He quotes the *Orchot Chayyim*, who offers a historic-halakhic reason for prohibiting its recitation on a Sabbath, which takes into consideration the fact that this prayer was originally introduced by Rabbi Akivah for recitation on public fast days, "and no public fasting is permitted on the Sabbath." Leaving aside the question of the close textual association of *Avinu Malkeinu* with the weekday *Amidah*, Rabbi Yoseph views the matter in relation to the halakhic consideration that "we may not petition for personal needs on the Sabbath." The *Avinu Malkeinu* certainly does petition for personal needs, and it was for that reason that other authorities prohibited its recitation both when Rosh Hashanah occurred on the Sabbath and on the intermediate Sabbath of the Ten Days of Penitence. They permitted its recitation, however, on Sabbath Yom Kippur because of the urgency of making a final desperate plea ("If not now, when?") before judgment was finally sealed (*Sefer Ha-Ittim*).

A consensus of the most distinguished codifiers of the *halakhah* draws a distinction, however, between purely "personal petition" for our private wishes and petition such as that expressed throughout the *Avinu Malkeinu*, which is rather a "communal petition" wherein the needs of the individual are indistinguishable from those of the community. They categorize *Avinu Malkeinu* as a "communal petition," which is permitted to be made on the Sabbath.
89. Genesis 12:2.
90. Ibid., 12:7, 13:15.
91. Ibid., 15:18.
92. Ibid., 13:16.
93. Ibid., 15:5.
94. Ibid., 15:4.
95. Ibid., 15:13.
96. Ibid., 16:10.
97. Ibid., 16:12.
98. Ibid., 17:2.
99. Ibid., 17:16.
100. Ibid., 17:18.
101. Ibid., 17:20.
102. Ibid., 21:17.
103. Talmud, *Rosh Hashanah* 16b; see *Rashi* on Genesis 22:17.
104. Deuteronomy 21:18–21.
105. See Pinchas H. Peli, *On Repentance* (Jerusalem: Orot Press, 1980), pp. 211–212.
106. 1 Samuel, Chap. 1.
107. Talmud, *Rosh Hashanah* 10b–11a.
108. Genesis 21:1.
109. 1 Samuel 2:21.

110. Libretto, *Fiddler on the Roof*, based on book by Joseph Stein (London: Chappell, 1964), p. 6.
111. *Avot* 3:2.
112. S. D. Goitein, "Prayers from the Genizah for Fatimid Caliphs, the Head of the Jerusalem Yeshiva, the Jewish Community and the Local Congregation," in *Studies in Judaica, Karaitica and Islamica* (Ramat Gan: Bar-Ilan University Press, 1982), pp. 52–57.
113. *Ms. Heb. f. 31* (Bodleian Library, Oxford), quoted by Paul Fenton (Yenon) in "*Tefillah be'ad ha-rashut u-reshut be'ad ha-tefillah: zutot min ha-Genizah,*" in *Mi-mizrach U-mi-maarav*, vol. 4 (Ramat Gan: Bar-Ilan University, 1983), p. 15. We acknowledge permission to reprint, granted by Bodleian Library, Oxford.
114. Barry Schwartz, "*Hanotein Teshua*: The Origin of the Traditional Jewish Prayer for the Government," *Hebrew Union College Annual* 58 (1986): 116.
115. Judges 7:19.
116. See S. Braun, *She'arim Metzuyanim Be-halakhah*, published together with text of *Kitzur Shulchan Arukh* (New York and Jerusalem: Phillip Feldheim, 1978), vol. 3, sec. 129:15, p. 163 n. 16.
117. Ibid.
118. Exodus 18:19.
119. Zephaniah 1:14–16.
120. Isaiah 27:13.
121. See F. Brown, S. R. Driver, and C. A. Briggs, *A Hebrew and English Lexicon of the Old Testament* (Oxford: The Clarendon Press, 1957), p. 1051 (*sub shofar*).
122. See *Midrash Shochar Tov* on Psalm 81:4, ed. S. Buber (Jerusalem, 1966), sec. 5, p. 184.
123. Numbers, chap. 16.
124. Talmud, *Rosh Hashanah* 16b.
125. Ibid.

Chapter 2
The *Musaf* Service

1. The translation of this stirring plea is given here in the light of Routledge's total omission of the prayer and De Sola's omission of a translation.
2. This rendering follows the talmudic interpretation (*Taanit* 16a–b).
3. Zechariah 8:19.
4. See also *Magen Avraham* on *Shulchan Arukh* 582:4.
5. The version in the *machzor* of D. Goldschmidt (Jerusalem: Koren, 1970) actually has the identical word *naalah* for our *naaleh* (see vol. I, p. 158).
6. This seems to be the import of the difficult opening phrase, which we understand, literally, as "turn from your (highest) habitation to sit upon the (*kes*) throne (of mercy)."
7. Talmud, *Sukkah* 51a–b.
8. *Mishnah*, *Rosh Hashanah* 1:2.
9. Talmud, *Taanit* 24b.

10. Day of Atonement *Machzor*, Routledge, p. 166, Birnbaum, p. 825, De Sola, p. 61.
11. Jer. *Taanit* 2, 13(66a).
12. Talmud, *Rosh Hashanah* 11b.
13. De Sola ed. includes, before this, the poem *Ometz addirei kol chefetz*. It is omitted in the other editions.
14. 1 Kings 19:11–13.
15. *Mishnah Rosh Hashanah* 1:2.
16. *Jahrbücher für jüdische Geschichte und Literatur* 1 (1974): 187.
17. Jer. *Rosh Hashanah* 1:3.
18. The source of Bokser's illustration is not known. I first read it in Rabbi J. Riemer's column in the bulletin (March 1990) of the Beth David Synagogue in Miami and have adapted it from that source.
19. On the background of the Amnon legend, see *Encyclopaedia Judaica*, vol. 2 (Jerusalem: Keter Publishing House, 1971), p. 862.
20. "Reflections" was written by Rabbis Rabinowitz, Kanter, and Riemer, and is printed in the *Mahzor for Rosh Hashanah and Yom Kippur*, ed. Rabbi Jules Harlow. Published by The Rabbinical Assembly. Copyright © 1972 by The Rabbinical Assembly. Reprinted by permission.
21. *Midrash Shemot Rabbah* 30:1.
22. M. Zulay, *Yediyyot ha-makhon lecheker ha-mikra*, vol. 6 (Jerusalem, 1946), pp. 199–201.
23. See on Psalm 91:1—"He that made his presence (*Shekhinah*) to dwell in the secret celestial realms, will reside in the shadow of the Almighty's clouds of glory."
24. E. Urbach, *Chazal—Pirkei Emunot Vedeiot* (Jerusalem: Magnes Press, 1969), p. 39.
25. This approach concurs with the view of R. Joshua that "in the final redemption, even if Israel does not repent, her redemption is guaranteed" (*Sanhedrin* 97b). This view is contested in the Talmud by R. Eliezer.
26. *Ramban*, commentary to Genesis 1:1.
27. See Jakob J. Petuchowski, *Theology and Poetry: Studies in Medieval Piyyut* (London: Littman Library of Jewish Civilisation, Routledge and Kegan Paul, 1975), chap. 4.
28. Ibid., p. 50.
29. See comment of *Rashi* on Talmud, *Sukkah* 41a, *Rosh Hashanah* 30a.
30. Rashi maintains that this verse refers to the future Temple although the verb is couched in the past tense. The prophets, when they describe something they see vividly as taking place in the future, regularly use the past tense, for it is as if they have already witnessed it. This device is called by grammarians "the prophetic perfect."
31. *The Authorised Daily Prayer Book*, ed. S. Singer (London: Singer's Prayer Book Publication Committee, 1962), p. 105.
32. Maimonides, *Yad, Hilkhot, Melakhim*, 11:4.
33. Talmud, *Megillah* 16b. The blessings of the weekday *Amidah—Ve-liyrushalayim* and *Et tzemach*, followed by *Shema koleinu* and *Retzeih*, will be seen to conform to the talmudic sequence.
34. See, however, Z. H. Kalisher, *Derishat Tziyyon* (Warsaw: K. Dombrowski, 1862), a tract devoted to proving that animal sacrifices may—and should—be

reinstituted independently of the Temple, the merit of which would hasten the advent of the Messiah.

35. See, however, n. 45 below.

36. Support for the view that *Aleinu* was composed in the Persian period is based on the reference to God as "King of the King of Kings." "King of Kings" was an honorific title of Persian monarchs—hence the necessity, at that time, of such a cumbersome reference to God.

37. N. Wieder, "*Be-etyah shel Gematria anti-Notzrit ve-anti Islamit*," *Sinai* 76 (*Tishri* 1975): 1–14.

38. He is referred to throughout the Talmud as, simply, *Rav*, the Master. In addition to his unique contribution to talmudic law, he also had a formative influence on Jewish liturgy. Its ascription to him is based on the talmudic (Jer. *Rosh Hashanah* 57a) term for *Aleinu*: *tekiata debei Rav* ("*Shofar* composition of the school of Rav"), though it is unlikely that he, personally, composed this prayer.

J. Heinemann, in chap. 10 of *Ha-tefillah bitkufat ha-tannaim vehaamoraim* (Jerusalem: Magnes Press, 1964), suggests that the first paragraph (only) of *Aleinu* actually dates back to Temple times, to the recitations of the duty-rotas of Priests and laymen (*Anshei Maamad*) who ministered at the Temple twice a year for a week at a time. The latter used to read from the Torah chapters of the Creation three times daily, probably to emphasize that, although God is worshiped, primarily, in the Temple, we should not lose sight of His cosmic role. The *Aleinu*, which acclaims God as the "Lord of all things . . . who formed the world in the beginning," was composed as an appropriate closing prayer to those readings from the Torah on the subject of Creation.

39. N. Wieder, loc. cit.

40. This is another factor that is noted by the proponents of the theory that this prayer was composed at an early period while the Temple was still standing.

41. For comment on the second paragraph of *Aleinu*, see pp. 90–92, 94–95.

42. *Zohar Bereishit*, 41a.

43. On the doctrine of *Tikkun*, see Gershom G. Scholem, *Major Trends*, pp. 233–315.

44. On the *Reshut*, see pp. 32, 93.

45. See Yom Kippur *Machzor*, Routledge, p. 159; Birnbaum, pp. 807–809; De Sola, pp. 49–51.

46. P. Birnbaum, ed., *High Holyday Prayer Book* (New York: Hebrew Publishing, 1951), p. 380.

47. For this usage, see Isaiah 13:14 where *sheon* and *hamon* are synonymous.

48. Commentary to the *siddur Otzar Ha-tefillot* (New York: Hebraica Press, 1966), p. 450.

49. See *The Scientific Study of Jewish Liturgy* (New York: Ktav, 1970), pp. 106–108.

50. For further remarks on the practical distinction between the concepts of "son" and "servant," see pp. 49, 95–96.

51. Maimonides, *Yad*, *Hilkhot Yesodei HaTorah* 2:2.

52. The quotation here is taken from the version of *Maasei Elokeinu* as recited during the Morning Service on the Day of Atonement. The translation, by Elsie Davis, is contained in the Routledge and Kegan Paul edition, p. 67.

53. Talmud, *Rosh Hashanah* 32a.
54. *Tosafot*, ad loc.
55. This is the considered view of A. Buchler in his oft-quoted article "The Reading of the Law and Prophets in a Triennial Cycle," *Jewish Quarterly Review* (OS), 5(1873), reprinted in *Contributions to the Scientific Study of Jewish Liturgy*, ed. J. J. Petuchowski (New York: Ktav, 1970), pp. 181–302. For his comment on the dating of the *Haftarot* as a statutory part of the synagogue service, see pp. 230–231.
56. See above, p. 95.
57. This also explains why the concluding formula of the blessing of the *Amidah* is *Oseh ha-shalom* (the old Palestinian version), instead of our usual formula: *Ha-mevarekh et ammo yisrael ba-shalom*.
58. Leviticus 9:22; Talmud, *Sotah* 38b.
59. See E. Werner, "The doxology in Synagogue and Church," *Hebrew Union College Annual* 19 (1945/46): 275–351.

Chapter 3
Tashlikh

1. *Sefer Maharil, Hilkhot Rosh Hashanah*, p. 38. Cf. Isserles on Tur, *Orach Chayyim*, chap. 583.
2. Jacob Z. Lauterbach, "Tashlik, a study in Jewish ceremonies," *Hebrew Union College Annual* 11 (1936): 207–340.
3. See 1 Kings 1:33–34.
4. Talmud, *Horayot* 12a; *Keritot* 5b.
5. See Jacob Z. Lauterbach, op. cit., 313 ff.
6. *Remah* on *Shulchan Arukh, Orach Chayyim* 583:2.
7. See Barukh Halevi Epstein, *Barukh She-amar* (Tel Aviv: Am Olam Publications, 1979).
8. Joshua Trachtenberg, *Jewish Magic and Superstition* (New York: Behrman's Jewish Book House, 1939), p. 113.

Chapter 4
The Morning Service—Second Day

1. See pp. 94–99.
2. *Avot* 5:1.
3. The classical commentator Abraham Ibn Ezra points to this expression as a proof that Isaiah already knew that the earth was round, and that the term *four corners of the earth* was merely a metaphor of distance. See his comment on this verse.
4. Cf. Psalm 115:16.
5. Talmud, *Kiddushin* 36a.
6. For the promise of *Chesed le-Avraham*, see Micah 7:20.
7. For an explanation of this reference and for supplementary comments on this composition, see pp. 28–29.

8. On Simeon bar Isaac, see above, pp. 107–108, 110.
9. On the *reshut*, see pp. 31–32.
10. *Midrash Vayikra Rabbah* 34(10).
11. Maimonides, *Yad, Hilkhot Yesodei Ha-Torah*, Chap. 2.
12. Jeffrey M. Cohen, "Pearls of Prayer," *Jewish Chronicle* (London) 4 June 1982, p. 39.
13. Routledge, p. 30; Birnbaum, p. 67; De Sola, p. 35.
14. See pp. 28–29, 84.
15. Exodus 34:6.
16. Talmud, *Rosh Hashanah* 17a.
17. Talmud, *Baba Batra* 15a; see also *Targum* on Psalm 89:1.
18. See p. 110.
19. *Midrash Bereishit Rabbah* 56:3.
20. The judicial terms *kattegor* and *sannegor*, employed in this line, are commonly found in the Talmud, being direct borrowings from the Greek legal offices of *Kategoros*, "public prosecutor," and *sunegoros*, "defense attorney."
21. Talmud, *Rosh Hashanah* 16b.
22. These are known as *tekiyot dimeyushav*, "notes blown while permitted to sit."
23. These are known as *tekiyot dimeumad*, "notes blown while standing (for the *Amidah*)."
24. See Tosafot to Talmud, *Rosh Hashanah* 16b. He quotes this interpretation in the name of the *Arukh*.
25. Isaiah 25:8.
26. For commentary on *Taiyr vetaria*, see p. 36.
27. See pp. 37, 107–108, 110–112.
28. Genesis 22.
29. Talmud, *Rosh Hashanah* 16b.
30. Joseph B. Soloveitchik, "Redemption, Prayer, Talmud Torah," *Tradition* 17:2 (Spring 1978): 71.
31. Jeremiah 31:1–19.
32. Ibid., v. 9.
33. Ibid., v. 10.
34. Ibid., v. 15.
35. Ibid., vv. 18–19.
36. See pp. 197–199.
37. See p. 199.
38. Talmud, *Berakhot* 19a.
39. Leviticus 26:14–44; Deuteronomy 28:15–68. See Joshua Trachtenberg, *Jewish Magic and Superstition* (New York: Behrman's Jewish Book House, 1939), pp. 56–60.

Chapter 5
The Jewish Doctrine of Repentance

1. Jonah 3:7–8.
2. Deuteronomy 6:5.
3. Leviticus 26:40.

4. 2 Samuel 12:13.
5. Talmud, *Mo'ed Katan* 25a; *Hagigah* 22b; *Sanhedrin* 100a; *Baba Metzia* 33a.
6. Talmud, *Yoma* 86b.
7. Talmud, *Sanhedrin* 99a; *Berakhot* 34b.
8. *Mishnah Yoma* 8:9. The limitation of Yom Kippur's efficacy to religious transgressions was derived from the verse "From all your sins *before the Lord* shall you be cleansed" (Leviticus 16:30).
9. *Tosefta Baba Metzia* 8:26.
10. *Yoma* 87a; Maimonides, *Hilkhot Teshuvah* 2:9.
11. Maimonides, ibid., 2:11.
12. For a more detailed statement of their outlook see Gershom G. Scholem, *Major Trends*, pp. 80–118; also A. Rubin, "The concept of repentance among the Hasidei Ashkenaz," *Journal of Jewish Studies* 16:3–4 (1965): 161.
13. Isaiah 6:6–7.
14. Ezekiel 18:23.
15. *Midrash Shir Hashirim Rabbah* 5(3).
16. *Yoma* 85b.
17. Ibid., 86a.
18. Ibid. See Rashi's comment ad loc.
19. See p. 49.
20. Cf. *Mishnah Avot* 4:11, 4:17, Talmud, *Shabbat* 32a; *Yoma* 87a; *Nedarim* 32b; *Sanhedrin* 87b, etc.
21. Rabbi E. L. Dessler, *Mikhtav Me-Eliyahu*, ed. Salomon A. Halpern and Aryeh Carmel (London: Chaim Friedlander, 1955), p. 88.
22. *Yoma* 87a; Maimonides, *Hilkhot Teshuvah* 1:4.
23. *Yoma* 86a.
24. *Shulchan Arukh, Orach Chayyim* 605:1.
25. *Ramah*, ad loc.
26. Chaim David Halevi, *Asei Lekha Rav* (Tel Aviv: Committee for the Publications of Ha-Gaon Rabbi Chaim David Halevi, 1978), III:16.
27. On the *kittel*, see earlier, pp. 10, 59.

Chapter 6
The Evening Service

1. Leviticus 23:27.
2. *Mishnah Yoma* 8:1.
3. The same abstention applies to the Fast of the Ninth of *Av*.
4. Psalm 60:10.
5. Talmud, *Baba Batra* 53b.
6. Song of Songs 7:2.
7. This is based upon the scriptural reference "And you shall see it (sc. the fringes) and remember all the commandments of the Lord your God." The Rabbis inferred from this that the law applies only as long as you can "see" the *tzitzit*, i.e., in natural daylight.

8. See Talmud, *Rosh Hashanah* 17b.

9. *Sefer Raviah,* ed. V. Aptowitzer (Berlin: Mekitzei Nirdamim, 1913–1935), vol. 2, pp. 187–188.

10. Talmud, *Keritot* 6b.

11. J. S. Bloch, *Israel and the Nations* (Berlin: Harz, 1927), p. 278.

12. Bathja Bayes, *Encyclopaedia Judaica,* vol. 10 (Jerusalem: Keter, 1971), p. 1168.

13. See *Otzar kol minhagei Yeshurun,* ed. A. E. Hirshowitz (Lemberg, 1920), p. 71. It is of interest that Yemenite tradition does not attribute any particular significance to *Kol Nidrei.* In their *machzor* it is relegated to a minor position toward the end of the service, and is recited without any accompanying melody.

14. Numbers, chap. 30.

15. *Mishnah Hagigah* 1:8.

16. See L. Zunz, *Die Ritus* (Berlin: Julius Springer, 1859), p. 106; N. Wieder, *The Judaean Scrolls and Karaism* (London: East and West Library, 1962), chap. 5 and Appendix.

17. Pl. of *Gaon,* "Excellency." This was the title given to the heads of the great Babylonian academies of rabbinic learning, seventh–eleventh centuries C.E.

18. A. B. Ehrlich, *Mikra Kifeshuto* (New York: Ktav, 1969), p. 298.

19. *Mishnah Nedarim* 1:2.

20. Loc. cit. 1:1.

21. Maimonides, *Peyrush Ha-Mishnayot, Nedarim* 1:2.

22. Numbers 30:3.

23. *Siddur Rav Saadya Gaon,* ed. I. Davidson, S. Assaf, and B. Joel (Jerusalem: Reuben Mass, 1963), p. 261.

24. Leviticus 23:32.

25. D. Goldschmidt, op. cit., p. 11.

26. See S. Baron, *A Social and Religious History of the Jews,* vol. 7 (New York: Columbia University Press, 1958), pp. 90–93.

27. Y. Kaufmann, *The Religion of Israel* (London: George Allen & Unwin, 1961), p. 11.

28. Y. Kaufmann, op. cit., pp. 62–63.

29. Genesis 3:1; Amos 9:3.

30. Genesis 1:21.

31. Isaiah 51:9.

32. See pp. 146, 159.

33. Exodus 34:6.

34. Talmud, *Eruvin* 22a.

35. *Midrash Vayikra Rabbah* 29(24).

36. 2 Samuel 22:26.

37. Levi ben Gershom, 1288–1344. French Bible commentator and philosopher.

38. 2 Samuel, chaps. 11–12.

39. 1 Samuel 13:14.

40. Talmud, *Rosh Hashanah* 17a.

41. Loc. cit. 17b.

42. Exodus 34:6–7.

43. Ibid.
44. Talmud, *Megillah* 22a.
45. *Magen Avraham* on *Orach Chayyim*, sec. 282.
46. Daniel Goldschmidt, op. cit., vol. 2, p. 28.
47. See Judges 14:5, Amos 3:4, 8, Psalm 104:21, Isaiah 5:29, et al.
48. Job 9:2.
49. Job 4:17. For our view, that Job was here replying to this specific point, we follow N. H. Tur-Sinai, *The Book of Job* (Jerusalem: Kiryath Sepher, 1967), p. 154.
50. Cf. Genesis 8:21.
51. Joshua 2:1.
52. See Psalm 89:1. The Rabbis explain the heading *Eytan ha-ezrachiy* as referring to Abraham (Talmud, *Baba Batra* 15a).
53. M. Adler, *Jews of Medieval England* (London: Jewish Historical Society, 1939), p. 127.
54. Talmud, *Rosh Hashanah* 17b.
55. Genesis 8:21.
56. See A. Rosenfeld, *The Authorised Selichot for the Whole Year* (London: Judaica Press, 1979), p. 14 and passim.
57. *Midrash Shir Hashirim* 2:16.
58. Talmud, *Yoma* 87b.
59. *Mishnah Yoma* 4:2.
60. Talmud, *Yoma* 36b.
61. Ibid.
62. Routledge, p. 48; Birnbaum, p. 551; De Sola, p. 54.
63. Talmud, *Yoma* 87b.
64. The opening words, *Ribbon ha-olamim*, are there expanded into *Ribbon kol ha-olamim*.
65. Talmud, *Yoma* 87b.
66. Arthur Marmorstein, "The confession of sins for the Day of Atonement," in *Essays Presented to J. H. Hertz, Chief Rabbi* (London: Edward Goldston, 1942), p. 298.
67. On this prayer book, see David Kaufmann, "The prayer book according to the ritual of England before 1290," *Jewish Quarterly Review*, Old Series, vol. 4 (1892), and the edition of Chief Rabbi I. Brodie (3 vols, 1962–1967).
68. This confessional is introduced there by the phrase *Modeh aniy lefanekha*, which actually accounts for the presence of this phrase in our prayer book even though it is clearly a formula of confession, meaning "I *admit* before thee." Our rite has actually omitted the succeeding confession, and the translators were, therefore, constrained to overcome the hiatus by rendering it "I *give thanks* before thee." See D. Kaufmann, op. cit.
69. See Jeffrey M. Cohen, *Blessed Are You. A Comprehensive Guide to Jewish Prayer* (Northvale, NJ: Jason Aronson, 1993), pp. 55–56.
70. Talmud, *Yoma* 86b.
71. For the well-known rabbinic parable on the joint responsibility of body and soul, see *Midrash Leviticus Rabbah* (*vayyikra*) 4:5.
72. E. Munk, *The World of Prayer*, vol. 2 (New York: Feldheim, 1961), p. 248. For an explanation of the distinction between all the categories of sacrifice enumerated in this composition, see Munk (ibid.).

73. Many of the texts of these and other *selichot* and *hoshanot* are identical, except that the former occur with the response *aneinu*, the latter with *hoshana*.
74. J. Heinemann, op. cit., chap. 6.
75. Ibid., see English preface, p. vii.
76. *Mishnah Taanit* 2:4.
77. See 2 Samuel 21:1.
78. See 1 Kings 8:35–37.
79. "May he who answered . . . he will answer *you*" (instead of "he will answer *us*").

Chapter 7
The Morning Service

1. Talmud, *Yevamot* 49b.
2. On *Yotzerot*, see p. 26.
3. The great Saadia Gaon actually objected to the presence of the *Or chadash* verse on that account, and the Sephardi rites consequently omit it.
4. *Midrash Shir Hashirim Rabbah* 5:2.
5. Ibid., 4:12.
6. On the *Reshut*, see pp. 31–32, 93.
7. Jeremiah 18:22.
8. Jeremiah 30:17, 2 Chronicles 24:13.
9. 2 Samuel 22:12.
10. See Proverbs 16:18.
11. *Chulshah* is postbiblical. The form *cheishel* is coined from the single occurrence of the verb *chashal* in Deuteronomy 25:18.
12. Isaiah 21:4, Job 21:6.
13. This form does occur once in the Bible, in Psalm 150:3.
14. For the regular form of the 3rd pers. masc. perf. of the verb *attah*, "to come," see Deuteronomy 32:2.
15. The form *ahav* does not occur in the Bible, other than in the plural *ahavim*: Hosea 8:9; Proverbs 5:19.
16. Malachi 2:13.
17. *Shir Hashirim Rabbah* 4:4.
18. Herman Wouk, *This Is My God* (London: A Four Square Book, 1959), pp. 79–80.
19. *Midrash Shemot Rabbah, Vayakhel* 48:1.
20. Genesis 25:27.
21. *Midrash Bereishit Rabbah* 78:6.
22. Genesis 32:29.
23. Jer. *Berakhot* 1, 8.
24. Talmud, *Shabbat* 88b.
25. Ezekiel 1:27.
26. See *Encyclopaedia Judaica* 7:1377ff.
27. Talmud, *Hagigah* 13b.
28. The word *mal* is from the root *mll* "to speak," from which comes the word *millah*, "a word."
29. *Mishnah Avot* 5:5.

30. *Mishnah Yoma* 8:9.
31. L. Zunz, *Ritus*, p. 107.
32. A. H. Weiss, *Dor Dor Vedorshav*, vol. 4 (Tel Aviv: Ziv, undated [reprint of original edition, New York and Berlin: Platt & Minkus, 1924]), p. 277.
33. See J. D. Eisenstein, ed., *Encyclopedia Otzar Yisrael* (Berlin and Vienna: Hebräischer Verlag "Menorah," 1924) 1, p. 47.
34. See p. 176.
35. Deuteronomy 4:24.
36. *Ramban, Commentary on Pentateuch*, ibid.
37. Genesis 15:17.
38. Exodus 3:2.
39. Exodus 13:21.
40. Exodus 19:18. For the significance and use of fire in Samaritan tradition, see Jeffrey M. Cohen, *A Samaritan Chronicle* (Leiden: E. J. Brill, 1981), pp. 205–211.
41. *Mishnah Avot* 3:15.
42. In the *Musaf* version this is also the case. There it follows on from the phrase *maasei adonai*, "God's deeds," which refer specifically to His dealings with men, and in particular the men who oppress Israel.
43. Rudolph Otto, *The Idea of the Holy*, chap. 6.
44. Gershom G. Scholem, *Major Trends*, pp. 59–60.
45. Isaiah 6:3.
46. *Pesikta Rabbati* 21:10.
47. See, for example, J. M. Cohen, *Understanding the Synagogue Service* (1974); E. Munk, *The World of Prayer*, 2 vols. (1961); B. S. Jacobson, *Meditations on the Siddur* (1966); A. Kohn, *Prayer* (1971); J. H. Hertz, *The Authorised Daily Prayer Book With Commentary* (1947).
48. See Eric Werner, "The Doxology in Synagogue and Church," *Hebrew Union College Annual* 19 (1945/46): 275–351.
49. Jeffrey M. Cohen, op. cit. 92–93.
50. The High Priest did, in fact, wear his golden robes for a short while, at the beginning of the day, in order to offer up the daily *tamid* (continual offering), before starting on the Day of Atonement ritual (see *Mishnah Yoma* 3:4).
51. Talmud, *Yoma* 53a. See also Jacob Z. Lauterbach, "A Significant Controversy Between the Sadducees and the Pharisees," *Hebrew Union College Annual* 4 (1927): 173–205.
52. See Exodus 30:3.
53. Moses Maimonides, *Guide for the Perplexed*, ed. M. Friedlander (New York: Hebrew Publishing Co., 1881), pp. 232–234.
54. Ibid., p. 234.
55. J. H. Hertz, *The Pentateuch and Haftorahs*, 2nd ed. (London: 1981), p. 481.
56. *Mishnah Yoma* 6:1–2.
57. See J. Newman, *Semikhah* (Manchester, England: Manchester University Press, 1950), p. 6 n. ii.
58. See *Mishnah Yoma* 6:3.
59. Ibid., 6:5.
60. Ibid., 6:6.

61. Ibid., 8:1.
62. See Deuteronomy 27:7.
63. End of Jerusalem Talmud, *Kiddushin*.
64. A. J. Heschel, *Man Is Not Alone* (New York: Jewish Publication Society of America, 1951), p. 186.
65. See Barukh Halevi Epstein, *Tosefet Berakhah* (Tel Aviv: Moreshet, 1987), on Leviticus 16:31, p. 119.
66. See Ch. Zuckerman, ed., *Otzar Chayyim* (Tel Aviv, 1966), 3: 105.

Chapter 8
Memorial of the Departed

1. See *Tur, Orach Chayyim* 220.
2. The Sephardim refer to their memorial prayers by the name *Ashkavah*, "laying to rest," with the implied suggestion that their recitation brings reward of tranquil repose to the departed. These are recited also on the eve of Yom Kippur, before the *Maariv* service.
3. *Shulchan Arukh, Orach Chayyim* 621.

Chapter 9
The *Musaf* Service

1. Nathan A. Scott, Jr., *Mirrors of Man in Existentialism* (Cleveland: Collins, 1978), chap. 1.
2. Ibid., p. 14.
3. See M. Zulay, *Piyyutei Yannai* (Berlin, 1938), p. 332.
4. We only have knowledge of the name of one poet—Yose ben Yose—before the period of Yannai.
5. See pp. 30, 182–183.
6. See 1 Samuel 10:5, 19:20–24, et al.
7. See Deuteronomy 32:22, Jeremiah 15:14, 17:4, et al.
8. This coinage suggests that the poet understood the verb *venivvakhechah* (Isaiah 1:18) as "let us *assemble* for judgment." It is clearly that particular biblical occurrence that inspired his creation.
9. See Deuteronomy 29:17, Amos 5:7, 6:12, et al. The passive participle *le-unei mar*, as coined by the poet, would mean, literally, "poisoned" or "infected."
10. Adin Steinsaltz, *The Strife of the Spirit* (Northvale, NJ: Jason Aronson, 1988), p. 121.
11. This accords with the well-known principle *Ein mukdam u-meuchar ba-Torah*, "The Torah does not keep to a strict chronological order." See *Midrash Tanchuma, Terumah*, chap. 8; *Shemot Rabbah* 51:4.
12. See *Rashi* on Exodus 31:18.
13. See Exodus 25:16,22.
14. See *Midrash Tanchuma, Pekudei* 2:6; *Vayikra Rabbah* 27:5.

15. See Commentary of Abarbanel on Jeremiah 7:21.
16. Leviticus 17:5,7.
17. *Mechilta D'Rabbi Ishmael, Pascha*, chap. 5. See also the rendering of *Targum Yonatan* on Exodus 12:21.
18. Maimonides, *Guide for the Perplexed*, ed. M. Friedlander (New York: Hebrew Publishing Co., 1881), pt. 3, chap. 32, pp. 153–155. Maimonides' rationale of the sacrificial system was roundly condemned by Nachmanides as "vain words," but defended by Abarbanel, who describes them as "holy words." For a full discussion of the entire concept and the attendant dispute, see A. J. Heschel, *Torah min ha-Shamayim*, vol. 1 (London: Soncino, 1962), pp. 36–53.
19. Will Herberg, ed., *The Writings of Martin Buber* (Cleveland and New York: Meridian Books, World Publishing Co., 1956), p. 271.
20. *Mishnah Yoma* 1:3.
21. Talmud, *Yoma* 18a.
22. Talmud, *Pesachim* 57a.
23. Talmud, *Berakhot* 63a; *Sotah* 40b.
24. See Nehemiah 8:6; Psalm 106:48; 1 Chronicles 16:36.
25. See *Tosafot Yom Tov* and *Ritva* to *Yoma* 69b.
26. See S. T. Lachs, "Why was the *Amen* response interdicted in the Temple?" *Journal for the Study of Judaism in the Persian, Hellenistic and Roman Periods* 19:2 (1988): 230–240.
27. Talmud, *Kiddushin* 71a.
28. For a fuller treatment of the employment of the divine names in the Temple of Jerusalem, see Jeffrey M. Cohen, *Blessed Are You*, pp. 7–8.
29. *Mishnah Bikkurim* 3:6.
30. *Mishnah Tamid* 7:3.
31. *Mishnah Avot* 5:5.
32. See *Encyclopedia Talmudit*, vol. 11, p. 235.
33. *Mishnah Yoma* 6:2.
34. Talmud, *Berakhot* 31a.
35. Talmud, *Berakhot* 34a.
36. Talmud, *Yoma* 53b; *Taanit* 24b; Jer. *Yoma* 5:3.
37. Barukh Halevi Epstein, *Barukh She-amar*, p. 211.
38. Talmud, *Yoma* 53b.
39. B. Z. Luria, "Tefillat Kohen Ha-gadol Be-yom Ha-kippurim," *Sinai* 30 (1966): 203–208. This plea, for a year of trading and merchandise, does not appear in the version recorded in the Babylonian Talmud (*Yoma* 53b). It is taken from the version preserved in the Palestinian Talmud (*Yoma* 5:2).
40. See n. 38.
41. See S. Goren, *Torat Ha-Mo'adim* (Tel Aviv: Avraham Tzioni Publishing House, 1964), p. 156.
42. Talmud, *Berakhot* 29a.
43. Talmud, *Kiddushin* 66a.
44. Ibid.
45. *Midrash Leviticus Rabbah* 20:4.

46. Talmud, *Yoma* 53b. The Palestinian version has the reading, *litefillat yotzei derakhim*, "to the prayer of those about to go out on journeys."
47. Talmud, *Sotah* 44a.
48. B. Z. Luria, op. cit., p. 207.
49. Josephus, *Antiquities* (15), 121.
50. See B. Z. Luria, op. cit., p. 208, n. 16.
51. D. Goldschmidt, *Machzor*, vol. 2, Intro., p. 13.
52. Exodus 34:5–7.
53. Talmud, *Rosh Hashanah* 17b.
54. See above pp. 31–32.
55. This is a reference to Amos 2:6, "For they sold the righteous for the price of a pair of shoes."
56. "The Legend of the Ten Martyrs and its Apocalyptic Origins," *Jewish Quarterly Review* (N.S.) 36 (1945): 1–16.
57. Talmud, *Gittin* 58a.
58. Talmud, *Baba Batra* 60b.
59. Flavius Josephus, *Vita*, 191.
60. *Tosefta, Sukkah* 4:4.
61. Talmud, *Ketubot* 77a. The Talmud actually qualifies this by adding that there are three exceptions, when the *halakhah* did not accord with Rabban Shimon ben Gamliel's view.
62. Talmud, *Ketubot* 62b.
63. Talmud, *Menachot* 29b.
64. Talmud, *Berakhot* 61b.
65. *Mishnah Avot* 3:3.
66. R. Travers Herford, *Sayings of the Fathers* (New York: Schocken Books, 1962), p. 66.
67. Talmud, *Avodah Zarah* 8a.
68. Talmud, *Avodah Zarah* 17b–18a.
69. *Mishnah Sheviit* 10:6.
70. Talmud, *Chullin* 142a.
71. *Sifre Re'eh* sec. 80.
72. Talmud, *Eruvin* 53a.
73. *Avot* 4:12.
74. Talmud, *Ketubot* 62b.
75. *Midrash Bereishit Rabbah* 17:3.
76. Talmud, *Ketubot* 50a.
77. See A. Jellinek, *Bet Ha-Midrash* (1953–1978), vol. 2, p. 71.
78. Talmud, *Sanhedrin* 13b–14a.
79. L. Finkelstein, *Akiba: Scholar, Saint and Martyr* (Northvale, NJ: Jason Aronson, 1990), p. 74.
80. See Talmud, *Sanhedrin* 74b.
81. This demand applies, according to the Talmud, only in a situation where the tyrant demands that his Jewish victim transgresses, on pain of death, one of the three cardinal prohibitions: adultery, murder, or idolatry. Maimonides explains

that, in an emergency situation, however, where the enemy is attempting to outlaw all Jewish practice (*gezerat shemad*), then, if the act is to be perpetrated in front of at least ten Jews, one must demonstrate *Kiddush Ha-Shem*, and suffer martyrdom, even for the sake of avoiding the transgression of a lesser prohibition.

82. Maimonides, *Mishneh Torah, Hilkhot Yesodei Ha-Torah* 5:4.

83. For a critique of Maimonides' approach, see A. Halkin and D. Hartman, *Crisis and Leadership: Epistles of Maimonides* (Philadelphia: Jewish Publication Society of America, 1985), pp. 46–90.

84. See n. 81.

Chapter 10
The Afternoon Service

1. *Mishnah Taanit* 4:8.
2. See Chaim Abramowitz, "Maftir Jonah," *Dor le Dor* 14:1 (Fall 1985): 3–10.
3. See J. D. Eisenstein, *Ozar Midrashim* (New York: J. D. Eisenstein Publications, 1915), pp. 217–222.
4. See Genesis 22:2, *On one of the mountains*, and v. 4.
5. *Midrash Bereishit Rabbah* 56:6.
6. Genesis 22:4, 15–18.
7. *Mishnah Avot* 5:5.
8. *Midrash Pirkey d'Rabbi Eliezer*, chap. 31.
9. Genesis 25:27.
10. See chap. 7, n. 21.
11. *The Authorised Daily Prayer Book* (Singer), p. 395.
12. See M. Zulay, op. cit., p. 334.

Chapter 11
The *Neilah* Service

1. *Mishnah Taanit* 4:1, 3; Talmud, *Taanit*, 26b.
2. Ibid.
3. The idea seems to have been that the sun is enclosed within the heavens at night time. See comment of *Mareh Ha-panim* on Jer. *Berakhot* 4:1. Rav may also have understood it in a theological sense, namely, "the service recited at the time of the closing of the *gates of mercy*."
4. Maimonides, *Yad, Hilkhot Tefillah* 1:7.
5. Talmud, *Nedarim* 32a.
6. Genesis 25:7.
7. See Genesis 21:9.
8. The evil of the Canaanites prompted Abraham to seek out a wife for Isaac from among his own kinsmen in Mesopotamia (see Genesis 24:4). Isaac's later assessment of the Canaanites was the same, prompting him, likewise, to advise his son Jacob not to intermarry with them (Genesis 28:1,8).

9. Genesis 26:7–11.
10. Ezekiel 18:32.
11. Talmud, *Berakhot* 29b.
12. While the Talmud—and the quotation from it in our poem—does not include an introductory formula invoking God by name, the *Divrei Chamudot,* a commentary on the *Rosh* (ibid.), insists that it must have been included in the authorized version of this prayer, as it is inconceivable to address a plea to God without calling upon Him with the conventional mode of address.
13. *Nagid* was the title of the leader of the Jewish community in Moslem countries.
14. See pp. 260–261.
15. See pp. 163–164.
16. This may well have been inspired by the biblical juxtaposition of these two themes. See Deuteronomy 29:28 and Deuteronomy 30:1–3.
17. Talmud, *Yoma* 87b.
18. This unpublished commentary, written by a contemporary of Rashi (tenth–eleventh century), is referred to in *Otzar Ha-tefillot,* ed. S. Goldman (New York: Hebraica Press, 1966), p. 582.
19. For this nuance of the combination of the verb *natan* with the noun *yad,* cf. Deuteronomy 16:17, Ezekiel 46:5, 11, et al.
20. Talmud, *Yoma* 38b.
21. Talmud, *Baba Batra,* 165a.
22. Talmud, *Sanhedrin* 108a.
23. *Mishnah Yoma* 8:9.
24. The word *enosh,* from the verb meaning "to be weak," is used in the Bible, instead of the usual noun *ish,* to emphasize man's transience and frailty. It is from the same root, *anash,* that the noun *ishah,* "woman," is derived, suggesting something more "delicate" and physically weaker than her male counterpart.
25. Cf. the noun *hakarah,* "perception," "recognition."
26. Cf. Job 35:7 and Ecclesiastes 8:4.
27. Quotation from the familiar *Adon Olam* poem.
28. 1 Kings 18:39.
29. See p. 64.

Bibliography

This bibliography lists all the works cited in the text and the notes to the text. An asterisk after the title of the book denotes works of a more popular nature, suitable for the general reader.

Abramowitz, Ch. "*Maftir Yonah.*" *Dor leDor* 14:1 (Fall 1985): 3–10.

Adler, H., ed. *Service of the Synagogue,** 6 vols. London: Routledge and Kegan Paul, 1906.

Adler, M. *The Jews of Medieval England.** London: Jewish Historical Society, 1939.

Aptowitzer, V., ed. *Sefer Raviah,* 2 vols. Berlin: Mekitzei Nirdamim, 1913–1935.

Baer, S., ed. *Seder Avodat Yisrael.* Roedelheim: Israel Lehrberger, 1868.

Baron, S. *A Social and Religious History of the Jews.* New York: Columbia University Press, 1958.

Bayer, B. "Kol Nidrey (Musical Rendition)," in *Encyclopaedia Judaica,* vol. 10, pp. 1167–1169. Jerusalem: Keter, 1971.

Birnbaum, P., ed. *High Holy Day Prayer Book.** New York: Hebrew Publishing, 1951.

———. *Tefillot, Yisra'el U-musar Ha-yahadut.* New York: Shulsinger, 1971.

Bloch, J. S. *Israel and the Nations.** Berlin: Harz, 1927.

Braun, S. *Shearim Metzuyyanim Behalakhah* (Commentary on *Kitzur Shulchan Arukh*). New York: Feldheim, 1978.

Brodie, I., ed. *Etz Chayyim,* 3 vols. Jerusalem: Mosad Ha-rav Kook, 1962–1967.

Buchler, A. "The Reading of the Law and the Prophets in a Triennial Cycle." *Jewish Quarterly Review* (Old Series), 5 (1873); reprinted in *The Scientific Study of Jewish Liturgy.* New York: Ktav, 1970.

Chavell, C., ed. *Peirush Ha-Ramban al Ha-Torah.* Jerusalem: Mosad Ha-rav Kook, 1959.

Cohen, J. M. *Blessed Are You: A Comprehensive Guide to Jewish Prayer.* Northvale, NJ: Jason Aronson, 1993.

———. "Pearls of Prayer." *Jewish Chronicle* 4 (June 1982): 39.

———. *A Samaritan Chronicle.* Leiden: Brill, 1981.

———. *Understanding the Synagogue Service.** Glasgow: Gnesia Publications, 1974.

Davidson, I. *Machzor Yannai.* New York: Jewish Theological Seminary of America, 1919.

Davidson, I., Assaf, S. and Joel, B. *Siddur Rav Saadya Gaon.* Jerusalem: Reuben Mass, 1963.

Dessler, E. *Mikhtav Me-Eliyahu.* Ed. S. A. Halpern and A. Carmel. London: Chaim Friedlander Publ., 1955.

Ehrlich, A. B. *Mikra Kifeshuto.* New York: Ktav, 1969.
Eisenstein, J. D., ed. *Encyclopedia Otzar Yisrael,* 10 vols. Berlin and Vienna: Hebräisher Verlag "Menorah," 1924.
Elbogen, I. *Toledot Ha-tefillah Ve-ha-avodah Be-yisrael.* Jerusalem: Dvir, 1924. (Hebrew trans. of *Der Juedische Gottesdienst,* Frankfurt am Main: J. Kauffmann, 1924.)
*Encyclopaedia Judaica.** Jerusalem: Keter, 1972.
Epstein, Barukh Halevi. *Barukh She'amar.* Tel Aviv: Am Olam, 1979.
———. *Tosefet Berakhah.* Tel Aviv: Moreshet, 1987.
Fenton (Yenon), P. "*Tefillah be-ad ha-rashut u-reshut be-ad ha-tefillah: zutot min ha-Genizah,*" *Mi-mizrach U-mi-maarav,* vol. 4, p. 15. Ramat Gan: Bar Ilan University, 1983.
Finkelstein, L. *Akiba: Scholar, Saint and Martyr.* Northvale, NJ: Jason Aronson, 1990.
Friedlander, M., ed. *Guide for the Perplexed.* London: Routledge and Kegan Paul, 1904.
Goitein, S. D. "Prayers from the Genizah for Fatimid Caliphs, the Head of the Jerusalem Yeshiva, the Jewish Community and the Local Congregation," in *Studies in Judaica, Karaitica and Islamica,* pp. 52–57. Ramat Gan: Bar Ilan University Press, 1982.
Goldman, S., ed. *Otzar Ha-tefillot.* New York: Hebraica Press, 1966.
Goldschmidt, D., ed. *Machzor Leyamim Nora'im,* 3 vols. Jerusalem: Koren, 1970.
Goren, S. *Torat Ha-Moadim.* Tel Aviv: Tzioni, 1964.
Guttmann, J. *Philosophies of Judaism.* New York: Schocken Books, 1964.
Halevi, Ch. D. *Asei Lekha Rav.* Tel Aviv: Committee for the Publication of the Works of HaGaon, Rabbi Chaim David Halevi, 1978.
Halkin, A., and Hartman, D. *Crisis and Leadership: Epistles of Maimonides.* Philadelphia: Jewish Publication Society of America, 1985.
Hartman, D. *A Living Covenant.* New York: Free Press, 1985.
Heiler, F. *Prayer—History and Psychology.** New York: Galaxy Books, 1958.
Heinemann, J. *Ha-Tefillah Bi-tekufat Ha-Tannaim Ve-ha-Amoraim.* Jerusalem: Magnes Press, 1964.
Herberg, W. *The Writings of Martin Buber.* Cleveland and New York: Meridian Books, World Publishing Co., 1956.
Hertz, J. H., ed. *The Authorised Daily Prayer Book With Commentary.** London: Shapiro Vallentine, 1947.
———. *The Pentateuch and Haftorahs,** 2nd ed. London: Soncino Press, 1981.
Heschel, A. J. *Man is Not Alone.** New York: Jewish Publication Society of America, 1951.
———. *Torah min ha-Shamayim,* vol. 1. London: Soncino Press, 1962.
Idelsohn, A. Z. *Jewish Liturgy and its Development.** New York: Schocken Books, 1932.
Jacobs, L. *Hasidic Prayer.** London: Routledge and Kegan Paul, 1972.
———. *Principles of the Jewish Faith.** London: Vallentine, Mitchell, 1964.
Jacobson, B. S. *Meditations on the Siddur.** Tel Aviv: Sinai, 1966.
———. *Netiv Binah,* 5 vols. Tel Aviv: Sinai, 1976–1978.
Jellinek, A. *Bet Ha-Midrash.* Leipzig: Friedrich Nies, 1853.
Kalischer, Z. H. *Derishat, Tziyyon.* K. Dombrowski, 1866.
Kaufmann, D. "The Prayer Book According to the Ritual of England Before 1290." *Jewish Quarterly Review* (Old Series) 4 (1892): 20–63.

Kaufmann, Y. *The Religion of Israel*. London: George Allen & Unwin, 1961.

Kohn, A. *Prayer*.* London: Soncino, 1971.

Lachs, S. T. "Why was the *Amen* response interdicted in the Temple?" *Journal for the Study of Judaism in the Persian, Hellenistic and Roman Periods* 19:2 (1988): 230–240.

Lauterbach, J. Z. "The Ceremony of Breaking a Glass at a Wedding." *Hebrew Union College Annual* 1 (1924): 427–466.

———. "A Significant Controversy Between the Sadducees and the Pharisees." *Hebrew Union College Annual* 4 (1927): 173–205.

———. "*Tashlikh*, a Study in Jewish Ceremonies." *Hebrew Union College Annual* 11 (1936): 207–340.

Levy, E. *Yesodot Ha-tefillah*. Tel Aviv: Tzioni, 1963.

Luria, B. Z. "*Tefillat Kohen Ha-gadol Be-yom Ha-kippurim*." *Sinai* 30 (1966): 203–208.

Marmorstein, A. "The confession of sins for the Day of Atonement," in *Essays Presented to J. H. Hertz, Chief Rabbi*, pp. 293–305. London: Edward Goldston, 1942.

Munk, E. *The World of Prayer*,* 2 vols. New York: Feldheim, 1961.

Naor, B. "Two types of prayer." *Tradition* 25:3 (Spring 1991) 27.

Newman, J. *Semikhah*. Manchester, England: Manchester University Press, 1950.

Otto, R. *The Idea of the Holy*. Translation of *Das Heilige*. Oxford: Oxford University Press, 1928.

Peli, P. H. *On Atonement*. Jerusalem: Orot Press, 1980.

Petuchowski, J. J., ed. *Contributions to the Scientific Study of Jewish Liturgy*. New York: Ktav, 1970.

———. *Theology and Poetry*, Littman Library series. London: Routledge and Kegan Paul, 1978.

———. *Understanding Jewish Prayer*.* New York: Ktav, 1972.

Rabinowitz, S., Kanter, S., and Riemer, J. "*Reflections*," *Mahzor for Rosh Hashanah and Yom Kippur*.* Ed. Jules Harlow. New York: The Rabbinical Assembly, 1972.

Rosenfeld, A., ed. *The Authorised Selichot for the Whole Year*.* New York: Judaica Press, 1979.

Rosenthal, E. I. J., ed. *Saadya Studies*. London: Oxford University Press, 1943.

Rubin, A. "The Concept of Repentance Among the Hasidei Ashkenaz." *Journal of Jewish Studies* 16:3–42: 161–173.

Scherman, N., and Zlotowitz, M., eds. *The Complete ArtScroll Machzor*.* New York: Mesorah Publications, 1986.

Scholem, G. *Major Trends in Jewish Mysticism*. London: Thames & Hudson, 1955.

Schwartz, B. "*Hanotein Teshua*: The Origin of the Traditional Jewish Prayer for the Government." *Hebrew Union College Annual* 58 (1986): 116.

Scott, N. A., Jr. *Mirrors of Man in Existentialism*. Cleveland: Collins, 1978.

Singer, S. *The Authorised Daily Prayer Book*.* London: Singer's Prayer Book Publication Committee, 1962.

Sola, De, D. A., ed. *The Complete Festival Prayers*,* 5 vols. London: Shapiro Vallentine, 1948.

Soloveitchik, J. B. "Redemption, Prayer, Talmud Torah." *Tradition* 17:2 (Spring 1978): 71.

Sperling, A. *Taamei Ha-Minhagim*. Jerusalem: Eshkol Publishing Co., 1957.

Steinsaltz, A. *The Strife of the Spirit*. Northvale, NJ: Jason Aronson Inc., 1988.

Trachtenberg, J. *Jewish Magic and Superstition*. New York: Behrman's Jewish Book House, 1939.

Travers Herford, R. *Sayings of the Fathers*. New York: Schocken Books, 1962.

Tur-Sinai, N. H. *The Book of Job*. Jerusalem: Kiryath Sepher, 1967.

Urbach, E. *Chazal—Pirkey Emunot Vedeiot*. Jerusalem: Magnes Press, 1969.

Weiss, I. H. *Dor Dor Vedorshav*, 5 vols. Jerusalem/Tel Aviv: Ziv, undated (reprint of original edition, New York and Berlin: Platt & Minkus, 1924).

Werner, E. "The Doxology in Synagogue and Church." *Hebrew Union College Annual* 19 (1945–1946): 275–351.

Wieder, N. "*Be-etyah shel gematria anti-notzrit ve-anti-Islamit.*" *Sinai* 76 (Tishri, 1975): 1–14.

———. *The Judaean Scrolls and Karaism*. London: East & West Library, 1962.

Wouk, H. *This Is My God.** London: Four Square Book, 1959.

Yoseph, O. *Sefer Yechavveh Daat*, 3 vols. Jerusalem: Yeshivat Porath Yoseph, et al., 1977.

Zuckerman, Ch. *Otzar Chayyim*. Tel Aviv, 1966.

Zulay, M. *Piyyutei Yannai*. Berlin: M. Zulay, 1938.

Zunz, L. *Die Ritus des Synagogalen Gottesdienstes*. Berlin: Julius Springer, 1859.

———. *Die Synagogale Poesie des Mittelalters*. Berlin: Julius Springer, 1855.

Primary Rabbinic Sources

Eisenstein, J. D. *Ozar Midrashim*. New York: Bibliotheca Midraschica, 1915.

Gersonides (R. Levi b. Gershom), *Commentary on the Torah*, various editions.

Jacob ben Asher, *Tur*. Warsaw, 1882.

Karo, Joseph, *Bet Yosef*, commentary on the *Tur*.

Magen Avraham (R. Abraham Abeli Gombiner), commentary on the *Shulchan Arukh*, various editions.

Maharil, Sefer (R. Jacob Halevi Moellin), 1st ed., Sabionetta, 1556.

Maimonides, Moses, *Commentary on the Mishnah*, various editions.

———. *Guide to the Perplexed*, trans. M. Friedlander. London: Routledge and Kegan Paul, 1904.

———. *Yad Ha-Chazakah*, various editions.

Maimuni, Abraham, *Hagahot Maimuni*, ed. A. H. Freimann. Jerusalem, 1937.

Margulius, R, ed. *Sefer Chasidim*. Jerusalem: Mosad Ha-rav Kook, 1957.

Midrash, Pirkei de Rabbi Eliezer, Warsaw, 1852; trans. G. Friedlander. New York, 1965.

Midrash, Rabbah, Romm, Vilna, Jerusalem, various editions.

Midrash, Shochar Tov, ed. S. Buber. Romm, 1891; Jerusalem, 1966.

Mishnah, various editions; trans. H. Danby. Oxford: 1933; Commentaries: P. Blackman. Oxford: 1951–1956 (7 vols.); P. Kehati. Jerusalem: 1963 (12 vols.).

Nachmanides, *Peirush Ha-Ramban al Ha-Torah*. Jerusalem: Mosad Ha-rav Kook, 1960.

Rashi (R. Solomon ben Isaac), commentary on Bible and Talmud, various editions.

Sefer Ha-Ittim (Judah ben Barzillai), ed. R. J. Schorr, 1902.

Shulchan Arukh, see Karo, Joseph.
Siddur Rav Saadya Gaon, see Davidson, I.
Talmud, Babylonian, Romm, Vilna, Vienna, Jerusalem, various editions; English trans. ed. I. Epstein. London, 1948–1952.
Talmud, Palestinian, Krotoschin, 1886; *Talmud Yerushalmi Ha-Gadol,* 6 vols. Vilna, 1922.
Tashbatz (*Teshuvot Shimon b. Tzemach Duran*). Amsterdam: 1738–41.
Tosephta, ed. M. S. Zuckermandel. Jerusalem, 1963.
Tur, see Jacob ben Asher.
Zohar, First ed. Leipzig (1840). English ed., ed. H. Sperling and M. Simon, 5 vols. London, 1931–1934.

Index

About the Author

Rabbi Jeffrey M. Cohen has distinguished himself in the field of religious affairs as a broadcaster, lecturer, writer, and reviewer. A graduate of the Yeshivot of Manchester and Gateshead, Rabbi Cohen received a master's degree in philosophy from London University and a Ph.D. from Glasgow University. He is the author of several books, including *Understanding the Synagogue Service, Understanding the High Holyday Services, A Samaritan Chronicle, Horizons of Jewish Prayer, Moments of Insight,* and *Blessed Are You: A Comprehensive Guide to Jewish Prayer,* as well as over 200 articles. He is a member of the cabinet of the chief rabbi of Great Britain. He currently serves as the rabbi of Stanmore and Canons Park Synagogue—the largest Orthodox congregation in Great Britain. He and his wife, Gloria, reside in London. They have four children and three grandchildren.